D1171896

THE SCOPE OF STATE POWER IN CHINA

THE SCOPE
OF STATE POWER
IN CHINA

Edited by

S. R. Schram

*Professor of Politics with reference to China
in the University of London*

E·S
F

Published on behalf of the
European Science Foundation
by

SCHOOL OF ORIENTAL AND AFRICAN STUDIES
UNIVERSITY OF LONDON

THE CHINESE UNIVERSITY PRESS
THE CHINESE UNIVERSITY OF HONG KONG

ST. MARTIN'S PRESS

1985

11971304

$31.05

Published in Europe by the School of Oriental and African Studies, Malet Street, London WC1E 7HP; in the Far East by The Chinese University Press, The Chinese University of Hong Kong, Shatin, N. T., Hong Kong; and in North America by The Chinese University Press and St. Martin's Press, New York.

ISBNs
School of Oriental and African Studies   0-7286-0122-2
The Chinese University Press   962-201-328-7
St. Martin's Press   0-312-70338-4

Library of Congress Cataloging in Publication Data
Main entry under title:

The Scope of state power in China.

  "Published on behalf of the European Science Foundation."
  Includes bibliographical references and index.
    1. China—Politics and government—Addresses, essays, lectures.
I. Schram, Stuart R.
JQ1502.S36   1985   320.2'0951   85-8299
ISBN 0-312-70338-4 (St. Martin's Press)

Printed in Hong Kong by Caritas

EUROPEAN SCIENCE FOUNDATION

The European Science Foundation is an international non-governmental organisation with its seat in Strasbourg (France). Its members are academies and research councils with national responsibility for supporting scientific research, and which are funded largely from government sources. The term 'science' is used in its broadest sense to include the humanities, social sciences, biomedical sciences and the natural sciences with mathematics. The ESF currently has 48 members from 18 European countries.

The tasks of the ESF are:

- to assist its Member Organisations to co-ordinate their research programmes;
- to identify areas in need of stimulation, particularly those of an inter-disciplinary nature;
- to further cooperation between researchers by facilitating their movement between laboratories, holding workshops, managing support schemes approved by the Member Organisations, and arranging for the joint use of special equipment;
- to harmonise and assemble data needed by the Member Organisations;
- to foster the efficient dissemination of information;
- to respond to initiatives which are aimed at advancing European science;
- to maintain constructive relations with the European Communities and other relevant organisations.

The ESF is funded through a general budget to which all Member Organisations contribute (according to a scale assessed in relation to each country's net national income), and a series of special budgets covering Additional Activities, funded by those organisations which choose to participate. The programmes of the ESF are determined by the Assembly of all Member Organisations. Their implementation is supervised by an elected Executive Council, assisted by the office of the Foundation which consists of an international staff directed by the Secretary General.

Contents

Contents

Preface

Stuart R. Schram

The present volume contains a selection of papers presented at conferences organized by the Project "The State in China: Concepts and Realities." The project grew out of discussions on this theme which took place at the biennial gathering of the European Association for Chinese Studies in Paris in September 1976. Subsequently the European Science Foundation kindly agreed to sponsor this undertaking, and to provide generous financial support for the five-year period 1979-83, contributed by a number of its member organizations.* The project thus became one of three "Additional Activities" in Chinese studies adopted by the ESF Standing Committee for the Humanities. It has also remained, however, under the auspices of the European Association for Chinese Studies, and the members of the Association have taken an active interest in its work, in which many of them have participated.

Financial and administrative support having thus been secured, the project was formally launched in 1979, with a Steering Committee composed of Marianne Bastid-Bruguière, Karl Bünger, Piero Corradini, Jacques Gernet, Brian Hook, and Stuart Schram. Until 31 March 1980, the Chairman of the Steering Committee was Professor Piero Corradini, and the project secretariat was located at the Is.MEO in Rome. From 1 April 1980, I succeeded Professor Corradini as Chairman, and the secretariat was moved to the School of Oriental and African Studies in London.

I should like to express here my gratitude to the Assistant Secretary of the School, Mike Strange, who dealt so efficiently with the affairs of the project during the ensuing four years, and likewise my appreciation to the S.O.A.S. Publications Committee for its willingness to sponsor this book, and my thanks to the School's Publications Officer, Martin Daly, for his very

*These include the Statens Humanistiske Forskninsråd (Denmark), the Centre National de la Recherche Scientifique (France), the Deutsche Forschungsgemeinschaft (Federal Republic of Germany), the Consiglio Nazionale delle Ricerche (Italy), the Nederlandse Organisatie voor Zuiver-Wetenschappelijk Onderzoek (Netherlands), the Humanistisk-samhällvetenskapliga Forskningsrådet (Sweden), the Schweizer Nationalfonds zur Förderung der Wissenschaftlichen Forschung (Switzerland), and the British Academy (United Kingdom).

helpful assistance in editorial work on the volume.

From early times, the state in China has encompassed and penetrated the life of society to a remarkable degree, and the range of problems meriting study is therefore vast. While recognizing the limits on what could be achieved during the five years for which the project had been funded, the Committee was reluctant to concentrate too narrowly on one period or one dimension of the theme, for our purpose was not only to encourage research by scholars resident in Europe on various specialized topics relating to the state, but to promote a dialogue between historians of traditional China and social scientists concerned with contemporary developments.

We therefore defined the issues at the outset in very broad terms. On the one hand, we proposed to consider the structure of the state in China, and the originality of certain institutions, as well as the foundations and limits of state power. On the other hand, we wanted to examine the role of the state as the shaper of the moral and material world, i.e., the state as the source of moral values, and the power which fashions society and the economy.

These various aspects of the theme were distributed among the three conferences organized by the project: at Royaumont, near Paris, in March 1980; at Schloss Reisensburg, near Ulm, in September 1981; and at the Bellagio Study and Conference Center in May 1983. This book contains a selection of papers originally presented at the first two of these. It thus deals with the structure and historical development of certain state institutions, the role of the state in defining and imposing moral values, and the economic functions of the state. The theme of the foundations and limits of state power in China will be taken up in a second volume, drawn from papers written for the Bellagio conference, to be published subsequently.

The essays included here have all been very substantially rewritten, and (in the case of those dealing with contemporary problems) brought up to date. They are presented to the scholarly public, not as a comprehensive survey of the problem of the state in China, from the Qin dynasty to the present day, but as a collection of studies linked together by a significant degree of thematic continuity.

The Foreword, by Professor Karl Bünger, of the University of Bonn, deals with the problems posed to Western observers by the phenomenon of the state in China, by way of a prologue to the work of our project as a whole; the Introduction, by Professor Jacques Gernet of the Collège de France, takes up specifically the themes raised by the essays in this book. Between them, they have left me very little to say, but I shall none the less make two or three points of substance by way of conclusion.

First of all, the reader will soon discover that there is no systematic discussion of the definition of the state, and of whether or not this term can be applied to China at all prior to modern times, though both Bünger and Gernet raise the matter briefly, and several of the other authors touch on it. The reason for what some might see as a gap lies in the conviction, shared by most participants in our conferences, that, while the precise nature of the state has varied from one period to another, a political entity to which this term can meaningfully be applied has existed in China at least since the Qin. Bünger and Gernet argue this view, and Anthony Hulsewé, in his article on the role of the state in the economy, has provided powerful evidence in support of it. Some other contributors (Loewe and Grimm, in particular) have expressed doubts on the subject. This does not seem to us to be a matter for any particular regret, since the purpose of this volume is not to carry a theoretical debate on the definition of the state through to conclusion, but to provide illustrative materials to serve as the basis for further discussions.

My second and third points are closely linked, and serve to illustrate how difficult it is to disentangle the structure of the state from its nature and functions, though such distinctions are useful for purposes of analysis. On the organizational side, Vandermeersch, in his contribution on the nature of Chinese law, has stressed the importance of the fact that the state in China was the sole font of authority, with no rival such as the Church in the West, and Gernet has also developed this idea. It seems to me that there is a direct line of descent from this perspective to the concept of *yiyuanhua* 一元化, or "integrated" or "monistic" leadership of the whole polity, and indeed of the whole of society, by the Party, as discussed in von Senger's article and my own. But at the same time, the unique and unchallenged position of the state in China makes of it the source of doctrine and of moral values, and the continuity in this domain extends from the earliest times (discussed by Vandermeersch, and by Gernet) to current efforts to elaborate and inculcate a "socialist spiritual civilization" which will give content and meaning to the more concrete and prosaic aspects of the "Chinese road to socialism". (These very recent trends will be evoked in the second volume of this series, dealing with the foundations of state power). In a word, it seems plausible that, neither in the realm of organization nor in that of ideology and culture would Mao and his successors have striven so hard to promote uniformity if the unitary nature of state and society had not been accepted, on the whole, in the Chinese tradition, for the past two thousand years, as both natural and right.

Foreword

The Chinese State between Yesterday and Tomorrow

Karl Bünger

In the natural sciences, today's scholar is commonly asked to be aware of, if not accountable for, the choice and possible consequences of his research. Similar demands have also been made of historians. Such considerations are not usually evoked in the case of the studies with which we are concerned here, but some reflection on the general implications of our research and its possible results still seems appropriate.

Since the Opium War, China has been an object of world politics, rather than an actor on the world political scene. This situation changed considerably, indeed dramatically, after 1945. Not only did China emerge from the war free from the fetters of the so-called unequal treaties, and the economic, territorial, and political limitations which they had placed on her sovereignty, but, unexpectedly, she also found herself in the position of a major political power, through the privilege of holding one of the five permanent seats on the Security Council of the United Nations. Thus although she was not an industrialized country, and did not have the military might of the other four powers, China nevertheless gained the opportunity of taking a hand in the shaping of world politics. Arnold Toynbee recognized this change in 1966:[1]

> If Russia and America did relinquish to China their opportunity for putting the world in order, and if China did then choose to seize her chance, she would have better tools for doing the job than those that a Russo-American consortium could command. China would have unity, she would have numbers, and above all, she would have history.

Although Toynbee knew, and stated himself, that this was a fictitious, indeed an illusory chance, because it depended on the assumption that America and Russia would renounce their opportunity to put the world in order, his remark was greeted with some head-shaking by historians at the time. Yet his words are worthy of further consideration, since they were not lightly put forward.

As a result of China's changing role in the world, it has become more important than during previous centuries for the Western world to be informed

[1] Arnold Toynbee, *Change and Habit: The Challenge of Our Time* (London: Oxford University Press, 1966), p. 158.

about present-day conditions in China, the changes in her governmental structure, her political leaders, their methods of economic planning and their military doctrine, even their philosophical and ideological views. Much information on these topics is provided by diplomats, journalists, and businessmen. But there remains ample scope for the scholar trained in linguistic, comparative, historical, and social science fields. Less preoccupied with day-to-day tasks and current trends, he may contribute a long-term view and explain events within a larger context.

Given the changed conditions after 1945, it is not surprising that political developments in China should have aroused much more attention in the West than was accorded to "things Chinese" during the preceding hundred years, when the study of this domain was left mostly to a small circle of specialists and seekers of the exotic. More surprising, on the face of it, is the rising interest in the history of China's institutions in earlier periods. An increasing number of scholarly papers on this subject is published every year, providing us with more insight and documentary evidence than ever before.

This phenomenon, which accords well with Toynbee's remark about historical experience being an asset for political action today, will be one of the themes of my Foreword. A second topic will be our changing image of the Chinese state resulting not from changes in China herself, but from changes in the West. Here I shall show how fashions in Western thought have influenced our assessment of conditions in China.

THE SIGNIFICANCE OF THE HISTORICAL DIMENSION

We must ask ourselves how far it is useful or necessary to extend our investigations to the institutions and the political thought of the former Chinese empire. Did not the revolutions of 1911 and 1949 bring about such radical changes that elements from earlier times can be neglected? Apart from Toynbee's remarks, it is also a common observation that, a few years after a revolution, a great deal of what existed before turns out to have survived the political upheaval, including even political and social elements which the revolutionaries expressly set out to eliminate. Scholars such as Walter Ullmann have dealt with the medieval roots of our current political thinking, and others have demonstrated that basic principles dating from the period of absolutism still govern the "modern state" of today.

Such general conclusions drawn from the historical experiences of Europe need not be equally valid for China. It is, however, very probable that they do apply since, in China, the revolutionary change has meant the assimilation of political and social elements from an alien culture, a much more difficult process than that of revolutions in European countries. In any case, those students of contemporary China who believe that a total break with the past has taken place have yet to demonstrate this. And the necessary proof can be provided only by a comparison with the previous conditions, in other words by giving the study of the past a place in research on the present. In fact, we often find in the literature on contemporary China explicit references to traditional elements.

There are other and more basic reasons for scholars to study the history of the state in China, quite apart from the goal of understanding and appraising the present. Let us remember that the state is a historical concept. Its emergence and development does not follow the fixed laws of the natural sciences. It is man-made, and has many forms. This is especially obvious in the case of the "modern state." Jacob Burckhardt has called it a "work of art" (*Kunstwerk*). It developed in Europe in the period between the fifteenth and nineteenth centuries. In China, however, we find all the essential traits which the European historians attribute to the concept of the modern state developed at a much earlier time than in Europe.[2] This occurred in spite of the lack of some of the historical conditions which have been taken as essential for state-building in Europe, for example, the struggle between the political authorities and the Church, and the invention of the concept of sovereignty. It would widen our insights into European and world history if we could isolate those factors in Chinese history which led to the same institutional results as in Europe. Let us remember that the main governmental institutions of China were taken over by most of China's neighbouring countries, and endured in China even during those long periods when she was under the rule of alien conquerors.

If I say that we find already in traditional China the main institutions which characterize the "modern state" in Europe, I do not mean that this occurred in an identical sequence of phases, nor that there were not basic peculiarities of the Chinese state, just as there is a great variety of institutional forms among the European nations. As an example of a different relation between the phases of institutional development, we may refer to legislation. F. A. Hayek[3] described legislation as "among all inventions of man the one fraught with the gravest consequences, more far-reaching in its effects even than fire and gunpowder." In the continental European languages we have two distinct expressions, *ius* (*droit, diritto, Recht*) and *lex* (*loi, Gesetz*). It

[2] I argued this thesis at a symposium held at the University of Leiden, in a paper entitled "The Genesis of the Chinese State and Its Institutions in the Light of European History," which I hope to publish.

[3] F. A. Hayek, *Law, Legislation and Liberty*, Vol. 1 (London: Routledge & Kegan Paul, 1973), p. 72.

took a long time before legislation succeeded in replacing *droit*, which had been custom and customary law (*consuetudines et mores*), and which had dominated the minds of the people during the Middle Ages, until finally in the modern European states customary law was eliminated almost entirely, leaving the field to statute law. In China we see the positive law of the state from the very beginning of the process of state-building as the only kind of recognized law (*fa* 法), but leaving wide parts of what is called "private law," the rules of behaviour in the daily life of the people, to the customs and *mores* of the people.

There is another phenomenon pointing to the importance of the historical side of the Chinese state. During recent decades we have witnessed an increasing interest on the part of sociologists and anthropologists, as well as of historians devoted to the idea of a world history, in the development of the institutional history of China. Max Weber was the first who tried systematically to apply the sociological perspective to this field of study. Unfortunately, he did so on the basis of inadequate material which was all that was available to him at the time. Etienne Balazs was influenced by him in a general way, and Otto Franke also took over certain concepts and expressions from Weber, but otherwise sinologists paid little attention to his work. Only after Max Weber's writings had been translated into English did more basic sociological works drawing the historical Chinese state into their comparative reflections begin to appear. At the same time, historians of China, following a general trend in historiography, began to pay more attention to the social and economic institutions of the Chinese state.

The questions raised by sociologists about the history of the Chinese state are linked to general theories of state-building, and of economic and social development. They revolve in particular around problems such as "modernization," bureaucracy and feudalism. A favourite topic seems to be why Japan succeeded, and China did not, in quickly finding a way to integrate herself into the political and economic order dominated by the West. These debates have been reviewed by Frances Moulder.[4] The answers of authors to questions like this differ considerably, and their arguments are often contradictory, even within expositions by the same writer. Feudalism plays a favourite role in these discussions, and sometimes it is seen as a factor promoting "modernization," as in the case of Japan, sometimes as a hindrance, as in the case of China. It is, as has been pointed out,[5] a favourite argument in the English-language literature, because it relates to something familiar. The very vagueness

[4] F. V. Moulder, *Japan, China and the Modern World Economy* (Cambridge: Cambridge University Press, 1977).

[5] Conrad Totman, "English Language Studies of Medieval Japan," *Journal of Asian Studies*, Vol. 38, No. 3 (1979), pp. 541-51.

of the concept of feudalism, which is used to lump together quite different sorts of governmental systems, contributes to turning the debates into a *dialogue de sourds*. Similarly, bureaucratic organization is viewed as a decisive factor for "modernization" or Westernization, but sometimes negatively.

If we want to explain the peculiarities of the state in China and their causes, we cannot stop at describing the political institutions and modes of thinking, but have to take into consideration also the given external circumstances of the process of state-building. These conditions are often of a permanent nature. Comparisons with Europe will help us to ascertain the relative differences.

For the geographical setting, for instance, Fernand Braudel has given us, in the introductory section of his work on the Mediterranean world,[6] an impressive characterization of the influence exercised by the highly broken and indented coastline of the European continent on the political history of Europe and on the differing character of the European countries as regards both their organization and the style of their political behaviour. Anyone who reads G. S. Graham's book[7] on the foreign settlements in China will agree with Adshead[8] that there is here material for a "future Oriental Braudel." Other environmental factors have been pointed out by Marc Bloch in the first chapters of *La société féodale*.[9] He, too, demonstrates the influence of topographical conditions on the structure of the state, not only on its origins, but down to the present day. The sheer size of a country will manifest itself in the organization of the state, which will reflect also the facilities of transport and communication.[10] Similarly, population density is a factor in administrative organization, as is well recognized in the science of organization.

Finally, not the least important of the factors contributing to state-building is the political environment of the country. The English historian and political scientist, well known at the turn of the century, Sir John Robert Seeley, referred repeatedly, and with emphasis, to the dependence of the political structure of one country on that of its neighbours. Seeley's view has

[6] Fernand Braudel, *La Méditerranée et le monde méditerranéen à l'époque de Philippe II*, rev. ed. (Paris: Colin, 1966). English translation: *The Mediterranean and the Mediterranean World in the Age of Philip II*, Vol. I (New York: Harper & Row, 1972).

[7] G. S. Graham, *The China Station. War and Diplomacy 1838-1860* (Oxford: Oxford University Press, 1978).

[8] S.A.M. Adshead, review of Graham, *op. cit.*, in *Pacific Affairs*, Vol. 52, No. 3 (1979), p. 502.

[9] English translation: Marc Bloch, *Feudal Society*, Vol. 1 (London: Routledge & Kegan Paul, 1962).

[10] On this see, for example, Paul Claval, *Espace et pouvoir* (Paris: Presses Universitaires de France, 1978) who refers to Ibn Khaldun.

been adopted by Otto Hintze, whose principal essays on the comparative history of European state institutions have been translated into English.[11] Recently Quentin Skinner,[12] too, has given numerous examples of how external pressure or threats led to changes in the political character of a country. Frances Moulder, when comparing Japan with China, sees the different level of intensity of outside political influence as decisive for the different courses taken by the two countries in political and economic modernization.

SOURCES OF ERROR IN OUR UNDERSTANDING OF THE CHINESE STATE

We are all, no doubt, agreed that our knowledge of the state in China in its present as well as in its historical form suffers from gaps, and is in part distorted. This is not the place to deal with the gaps in our knowledge, nor to draw up a catalogue of investigations which ought to be undertaken in the future. I prefer to limit myself to pointing out some sources of misunderstanding, and some dangers, which have emerged in the past in the observation, description, and evaluation of the object of our studies.

A survey of this kind proceeds, naturally, from the (perhaps utopian) hope that we may be able to learn from these errors and avoid similar ones. That we will no doubt commit other errors, which will become apparent subsequently, should not deter us from the attempt. Nor do we regard ourselves as in some way cleverer than our predecessors; on the contrary, we must be mindful of Jacob Burckhardt's warning[13] against "the claim that we in this present moment have the right to judge everything that has gone on before, because we happen to have at this moment the chance to speak." "The present is as vain as a monkey," he said of his own time. We have only one advantage, that of coming later and thus being able to take advantage of the experience of those who have gone before. To do this is manifestly one of the tasks of scholarship.

We are interested here, mainly, in misunderstandings of which the causes lie in ourselves. Our first thought will be of the inadequacy of the range of terminological instruments which is available to us for the comparative

[11] *The Historical Essays of Otto Hintze*, edited with an introduction by Felix Gilbert (New York: Oxford University Press, 1975).

[12] Quentin Skinner, *The Foundations of Modern Political Thought* (Cambridge: Cambridge University Press, 1978).

[13] See Werner Kaegi, *Europaische Horizonte im Denken Jacob Burckhardts* (Basel: B. Schwabe Verlag, 1962), p. 174.

observation of the political institutions of foreign cultures. This fact is lamented, but nevertheless is inescapable. For even if we do not consciously and explicitly make comparisons with our own political institutions, but seek rather to limit ourselves to the description of "things Chinese," we nevertheless make comparisons when translating Chinese words into equivalent expressions of a European language and thus equating them with our own notions. Since things in China rarely correspond to those in European countries, the transmission of our observations can only be an approximation. Provided that we are aware of this problem, we can at least take special pains in the choice of our words and concepts. We can do this, for example, by avoiding deprecatory or simply disapproving words, such as despotism, which has been marked from the outset with a negative judgment. Instead we should use terms such as autocracy or monarchy which in our political language are less burdened with value judgments. Another such catch-word is "feudalism" which today has lost any exact meaning.

A detailed exposition of self-inflicted misunderstandings and errors would take too much space. A few examples may suffice. Already the reports of the first European emissaries to "the other world" in the thirteenth century, to the court of the Mongol khans, and later to Peking, display the marked dependence of their authors on the prevailing intellectual attitudes in their home countries. Heinrich Euler[14] has analysed these differences on the basis of the reports of Plano Carpini, sent out by Pope Innocent IV, and of William of Rubruk, an emissary of Louis IX, and of some later missionaries. Euler finds the cause for the shift in reporting, which can be noted within a space of only fifty years, in a change in the Western view of the world, taking place at precisely that period, namely in the relationship between faith and knowledge, and in the challenge to the primacy of the theological authorities. Under these conditions it is not surprising to read in a report of a missionary, the Bishop of Zayton, who obviously felt uncertain of the evaluation of his accounts by his confrères at home, that he would rather not describe all the things he saw, because they would sound unbelievable. That is what happened to Marco Polo who travelled at about the same time in China. For a century his report was considered a fabrication.

The Enlightenment shows Europe in a different intellectual climate, with a different image of China. Free from many of the former prejudices and preconceptions, it could be more impartial and objective because it was based upon much more factual information, supplied mainly by learned missionaries from the Jesuit order. European intellectuals turned their interest especially to Chinese governmental institutions, which were regarded as exemplary even

[14] Heinrich Euler, "Die Begegnung Europas mit den Mongolen im Spiegel abend-ländischer Reiseberichte," *Saeculum* 23 (1972), pp. 47-58.

by those who were otherwise critical of China. Certain of China's political institutions appear to have provided the impetus at that time for political innovations in some European countries. That did not, however, prevent the China enthusiasts of those days from encountering strong resistance and criticism, as is shown by examples such as the burning of books on China, among them that of Louis LeComte, on the order of the Theological Faculty in Paris in 1700, and the expulsion of Christian Wolff from the University of Halle in 1723, which gave rise to a flood of writings from the main intellectual centres of Europe. These measures, though prompted by theological disputes, were above all a reaction to implied criticism of the existing political system as a whole, in which the Church played a major role.

In the nineteenth century the situation changed entirely. The European observers now regarded the social and political system of China as inferior, if not contemptible, so that it would be better to do away with it and replace it with a European system. John Stuart Mill's[15] opinion may stand as an example for many others. He did not deny that China was a "nation of much talent, and, in some respects, even wisdom, owing to the rare good fortune of having been provided at an early period with a particularly good set of customs, the work, in some measure, of men to whom even the most enlightened European must accord, under certain limitations, the title of sages and philosophers." But starting from the notion of the "despotism of custom" he puts China as "a warning example" for the Europeans, because the Chinese "have become stationary—have remained so for thousands of years; and if they are ever to be farther improved, it must be by foreigners." Similar views have been expressed by Kant and Hegel, and they seem to represent the prevailing opinion in Europe in the second half of the century.

Many factors came together to contribute to this feeling of superiority towards China. The European supremacy in technical and natural sciences was undeniable. Equally obvious was the military inferiority of the Chinese, shown in the Opium War and subsequent wars, resulting in treaties by which the foreign countries gained for their nationals exemption from Chinese jurisdiction and territorial rights in port-colonies. In the eyes of politicians, merchants, and the ordinary man in Europe, these military realities constituted sufficient proof of the higher moral and intellectual standard, and the better social and governmental institutions in their home countries. But was it the test of military strength alone that convinced philosophers and historians like Mill that China should or could imitate European institutions? Obviously they did not share the scepticism of Montaigne, who like others before him had warned against such political transplants, and they differed

[15] J. S. Mill, *On Liberty*, Ch. III.

from the ideas of Leibnitz and some of his contemporaries who advocated cultural exchange for the good of both sides instead of a one-sided borrowing. The intellectual climate in nineteenth-century Europe was dominated by other ideas: the quasi-religious faith in progress, necessitating constant changes in social and political institutions; the belief that, since man had made his own social and political order, he could also change it at will at any time and without much regard for specific physical conditions, historical roots, and the psychological patterns of the country in question; the lessons of political and economic experience in England and in continental Europe, where great political and economic changes had occurred during the nineteenth century; finally, the birth of the concept of the nation-state, with its emphasis on military and aggressive thinking. This general trend of thought allowed the men of the nineteenth century to put away any doubts that had existed in earlier times about the feasibility and possibility of introducing European models into China by a stroke of legislation, this simple device of European statecraft. Since no changes had taken place within the Chinese governmental structure which could in any way compare with the great changes in Europe, the Chinese system appeared to be outdated. It was considered as representing an early step on the way to the more advanced European systems, just as Chinese philosophy was classified together with Greek philosophy as an early stage in a one-way evolution at the end of which stood the accomplishments of Europe.

This way of thinking prevailed until the twenties of our century, and its influence can be seen in some of today's writing. With the Chinese revolution of 1911, the interest of the European scholars in the institutions of imperial China lost any contemporary relevance which it may still have had after extraterritorial rights had been granted, and research on such matters was left to an esoteric circle of scholars.

After the foundation of the People's Republic of China and the beginning of the Cold War, we witness a new intellectual fashion, namely a one-sided outlook based on ideology, which took over to a certain extent the role, discussed above, which religious teachings had once played in the evaluation of foreign cultures. Such an approach determined foreign policy, and even made its influence felt in scholarly research on China. It found expression in the departmental organization of foreign ministries in some Western countries, and in the foundation of some scholarly research institutions.

The fashionable new ideological view, with its concepts and slogans, was not limited to the observation of contemporary China, but was now extended to the studies of her institutions and social and political order in earlier periods. This certainly is a legitimate goal for research, but it is also one which can easily lead to the danger of anachronistic and, if this neologism be allowed, anaculturistic misinterpretations.

To sum up, we may say that self-inflicted misunderstandings and errors in the evaluation of the Chinese state and its institutions were and are a constant feature of our observations. They are caused partly by the national political interests of the home country of the observer, but even more by the general intellectual climate which influences his evaluation, sometimes to the point of gross distortion. The general points of reference have changed considerably during the course of European history, and are still changing constantly. We observe a similar phenomenon in historiography generally, where the influence of theory on historical interpretation is well known, and even for the physical sciences Einstein stated "it is the theory which decides what we can observe." Still, in approaching the study of the state in China, it is good to be aware of the sources of misinterpretation and error.

THE PRESENT BETWEEN THE PAST AND THE FUTURE

China's search for a new state form, which has lasted for a century, is not yet concluded. One does not need to be a prophet to say that neither the present organization of the state, nor the political thinking which prevails today, represents more than a transitional stage. China still finds herself in an era of experiment.

China's leaders today stand in a quite different situation and are faced with quite different tasks from those which confronted their predecessors seventy or ninety years ago. In saying this, I leave out of consideration the factors of foreign policy, which have not basically changed since the order of the community of nations which the European states developed in the nineteenth century was extended throughout the world, and which harbours the idea of a rivalry for power and thus bears within itself the seeds of war.

Let us limit ourselves here to questions of the state structure, and of the social and economic order it establishes. A hundred years ago, the Chinese rulers faced (as the example of Japan also serves to show) three possibilities: (1) to reform the institutions which had grown up in the course of history; (2) to copy the Western model; or (3) to develop her own new institutions, drawing where appropriate on foreign examples. The first possibility no longer exists, since the old order has been eliminated. As for imitating foreign models, that is what China has sought to do during the greater part of the twentieth century. The third possibility, that of devising China's own new institutions, is long and difficult, even though in the end it may be the most promising. It is this way which China has in part pursued since 1949, to the extent that it has experimented with leaving open a permanent legal definition of its internal state organization, and has also in large measure left open the final goal.

Today many additional considerations weigh against the policy of imitating foreign models. Since 1911, China has undertaken an imposing series of attempts to import Western political institutions. The various constitutions of a Western type bear witness to this. Their obvious failure is based in large part on the initial failure to take account of China's real situation, and in the lack of understanding of the difference between the historical preconditions in Europe and in China.

The political institutions and theories which have been taken over from Europe owe their origin there to the peculiarities of the course of European history, which in China are in part completely absent and in part only approximately valid. Examples of this lie in the orientation, in the Middle Ages, towards life in the other world, which in many respects is reflected also in the political realm; the political role of the Church, which contributed so much to the genesis of the concept of sovereignty; the institution of hereditary nobility, which in China, to the extent it existed at certain times at all, had no such well-defined role as in Europe; vassalage and feudalism, which very early in China lost its basis of the combination of land ownership and political power; absolutism, combined with the concept of divine right; the state based on the various estates (*Ständestaat*) as the precondition for parliamentarianism; the repeated upsurges of extreme individualism; a view of law and justice which gave central importance to litigation rather than avoiding it.

The road of the European countries to "modern statehood" has been long. In retrospect it does not follow a straight line of development, but is studded with distractions from the goal and even with contradictory directions. Some historians call these absurdities of development. It is only when we take the European pattern of development as the only, or at least the normal way of development and consider every change of direction as "progress," i.e., an improvement on the existing situation, that we may look down on Chinese history as "constant stagnation." If, however, the European phenomena, from the view of world history, do not have universal significance, and if, as I believe, China developed all the essential institutions of a "modern state" in the sense in which this term is generally used by historians (industrialization not being an indispensable trait), then it appears absurd to imagine that China, as well as other countries, must to a certain extent first "complete" various phases in the history of Europe in order to reach the standard which the European countries have attained.

No doubt the Chinese state in the middle of the nineteenth century was in need of reform in many of its institutions and modes of thought. But one may ask today whether it was necessary or wise to eliminate many institutions

KARL BÜNGER

existing in China in so radical a fashion, and to re-introduce them in a European version, which was inferior to the traditional Chinese form, or to abolish other institutions precisely at the time when they were being introduced in Europe for the first time. Examples of such a way of proceeding are the regulations regarding the responsibility of the bearers of public authority, which, as can be seen today, are urgently in need of reform in many Western countries, and were implemented much more successfully in traditional China; or the competitive examinations for entry into the public service, which were abolished in China just as they were being introduced in Europe in order to do away with the system of patronage.

During the last 30 years the conditions for adopting European models for "modernizing" political and social institutions have changed considerably. Before the 1950s the foreign models had the privilege of undisputed success within their home countries. This is no longer the case. The countries which provided the models are in great structural and economic difficulties. The literature abounds in criticism of their own political institutions, and in plans for their reform. I am referring not to revolutionary views, but to the writings of quite conservative authors with titles such as "The crisis of the state" or "Ungovernability," and on topics such as the limits of law and legislation, and the state of the judiciary. The general feeling is that important institutions of European origin are in need of reform to meet the exigencies of world-wide changes. Obviously they have lost part of their former attractiveness for East Asian countries seeking a way to the future. The question now debated in international conferences is not only how these countries can keep their own "identity," but which of their own traditional institutions are better suited for the future than the European ones, with their nineteenth-century origins.

The example of Japan is relevant here. Until 1949 and after, it was common to include Japan in the group of countries with European law, after it had given itself a European-style constitution and, in vast and comprehensive works of codification, introduced European laws and European legal concepts. Today, we see that this is not the case; more and more people are saying that Japan should not be counted among the family of countries with European law, but displays rather both in practice and in her legal thinking peculiarities which are basically at variance with the European systems.

What is true of law is also true of other fields of public life and institutions. Ezra Vogel's recent book provocatively entitled *Japan as Number One*[16] deals

[16]Ezra Vogel, *Japan as Number One: Lessons for America* (Cambridge, Mass.: Harvard University Press, 1979). The book has provoked lively discussion. See, for example, *The Journal of Japanese Studies*, No. 6 (1980), pp. 416-39. Other publications

xxiv

with various Japanese institutions, including state institutions, which have demonstrated themselves today, under the changed conditions of the postwar period, to be superior to the comparable American systems, and recommends that the United States should copy them. Vogel explains Japanese superiority by the fact that the reception of Western models was by no means so complete as people used to think, but took place selectively and was accompanied by the retention of traditional Japanese practices and modes of thought, which now show themselves to be better adapted to the modern world.

He does not probe further into these traditional elements, but if we examine the matter more carefully, we find that precisely those elements are involved which are also to be found in Chinese history, and which might be regarded as part of the common East Asian cultural heritage, since they are also to be found in other countries of this region, such as Korea and Vietnam. It is striking to note that most of these traditional elements relate to institutions and modes of thought of which the counterparts in the West are today called into question, and of which the reform is currently being actively discussed by the governments of the Western countries.

Thus we come back to the view I expressed at the outset. Not only have foreign models failed to prove themselves successfully in China, but the Western system of government is not a very attractive model. Thus China's situation is very different from that of three generations ago, not least because, in the interval, Soviet models have also been tested and found to be of limited use.

on the topic followed, among them Endymion Wilkinson, *Japan versus Europe: A History of Misunderstanding* (Harmondsworth: Penguin, 1983).

Introduction

Jacques Gernet

Although it might have been feared that conferences such as those which gave rise to the present volume would never proceed beyond generalities, the results were, in the end, extremely encouraging. The most surprising aspect of the matter was, perhaps, that modernists and specialists in the study of earlier periods, who all too often pay no attention to one another's work, discovered that they spoke the same language, and that the problem of the state remained posed throughout the whole of Chinese history.

Before undertaking the difficult task of trying to formulate some observations which are not already implicit in what the authors themselves have written, I want to make one remark of a general character not directly linked to the contributions to this volume. This concerns the written word as an instrument of government. When we speak of bureaucracy—and the Chinese state, however far back we go, has always been a bureaucratic state—the term immediately conjures up an image of paperwork. Did not Sima Qian 司馬遷 tell us that the first Qin 秦 emperor had to deal daily with whole cartloads of wooden or bamboo slips? We also know that, beginning with the second century A.D., paper became the widespread and relatively cheap writing material in common use in China. This was altogether different from the costly parchments with which people had to manage in the West until the end of the Middle Ages, or even from the *ola* or specially treated palm-leaves used by the Indians.

It could be argued that this is a mere detail, but this apparently simple detail is perhaps of very great consequence. The written word has played a much greater role in China than in other civilizations. Think, for example of the pre-eminent role of the spoken word in Roman law, and in our own traditions as a whole. The written word, in contrast, has the advantages of leaving a trace, of maintaining a recollection, of serving as a proof. It is objective, impersonal, and it thereby favours abstract relations at the expense of direct personal relations. In sum, it is a factor of rationalization. The written word permits a greater degree of continuity in tradition, and the development of jurisprudence. In China, one does not discourse upon the law and legal principles; one consults the precedents. The question can at least be asked: Would the institutions of the state have developed to the same extent in China without paper?

It is also probable that the rapid and cheap reproduction of the written word beginning in the tenth century, thanks to the invention of printing, by multiplying the number of educated people and facilitating the dissemination of orders, and of news, was not without influence on the great expansion of the administrative machine during the Song 宋 dynasty. Similarly, is it an accident if the birth of the modern state in the West coincides with the development of printing on paper, and with the definitive abandonment of the use of parchment? These material circumstances deserve perhaps to be taken into account, just as today we may well ask ourselves what kind of society will result from the use of the computer.

Be that as it may, the functioning of China's institutions manifests a type of rational organization which was not achieved in the West until the modern era, in other words fairly recently.

Turning now to the substance of the articles contained in this volume, three basic themes can be distinguished. There are, first, problems of administrative organization, and in particular of the functioning of the central power, and the persistent question of the balance between centralization and decentralization, which is very much a live issue today. To what extent can information and stimuli make their way upwards in a centralized state, and affect the course of political action?

There is one observation which is assuredly valid regarding this whole range of problems: there is no such thing as an eternal Chinese state. The state is the product of history, and of a set of social, technical, economic, and intellectual conditions, and important changes have taken place. The administrative system has a history. It appears plain that the great turning-point was situated in Song times, when the very nature of the state was transformed, simultaneously with the transformation of Chinese society. Previously, the power of the emperor existed in solidarity with that of a certain number of great families which formed his clientele. Beginning with the Song, he relied rather on the much broader class of the literati, and on a mandarinate which could be described as more anonymous. The result was at once to isolate the emperor, and to strengthen his autocratic tendencies.

The second main theme evoked in this volume is that of the role of the state in the organization of society as a whole, and in shaping the customs and mentality of the members of society. Exemplary behaviour, rites, morality, and indoctrination have always been considered in China as means of government. There is here a very great difference from the West, where the distinction between law and morals was the rule, and where it was the Church which shaped public morality, pursuing in this its own aims, not always the same as those of the secular state. In China, on the other hand, the idea had long been established that men and their mental attitudes counted for more than brute force, wealth, technology, legal dispositions and so on—in a word, more than all those things which in the West have constituted the political domain.

This results, no doubt, from the separation we make between those things which belong to the domain of the individual conscience and those things which fall within the scope of our duty of obedience to the civil authorities, between what we owe to God and what we owe to Caesar. Such distinctions are unknown in China. In any case, in China psychology, customs, and patterns of thought are political variables, and have remained so until the present day. All the revolutionaries since the end of the Manchu dynasty have shared the same fundamental tenet: the only way for China to recover her power and dignity is to forge a new man, combative and patriotic. It is a *Leitmotiv* in the thinking of Sun Yatsen 孫逸仙, Lu Xun 魯迅, Mao Zedong 毛澤東, and many others. Mao Zedong identified education and revolution, and in the slogan "red and expert," it was assuredly the first of these terms which carried the greatest weight. Similarly, under the empire, the Confucian education of the mandarins counted for more than their capacities in technical domains.

Mark Elvin's paper on rewards for widowly virtue and filial piety was remarkably revealing regarding the objectives of the Manchu state.* The model was one of total subordination of the son to the father, the wife to the husband, and of the annihilation of the personality. Long ago Montesquieu showed, with reference to filial piety, how the reflexes thus acquired had both domestic and political functions. It would appear that this resolve to inculcate a spirit of submission was accentuated during the Qing 清, under a regime particularly concerned about the maintenance of public order. The reinforcement which very probably took place in repressive morality under the last dynasty poses questions of great interest.

Another means of action available to the state in its efforts to shape society is the classification of people by handing out titles, dignities, favours, wealth—and also by inflicting the negative equivalents of these, degradations, fines, punishments. These have been in China, as Han Feizi 韓非子 put it, "the two levers of power." The only chapter in the present volume which treats this theme systematically is that of Billeter, which analyses the system established since 1949 as a vast enterprise for the creation of social classes, by means of a classification imposed on the whole of society.

*Just as this volume was being prepared for publication, Dr. Elvin saw fit to withdraw his contribution and to publish it elsewhere. Consequently it does not appear below.

But can the organization of society be separated from the organization of territory? The state intervenes constantly in the spatial distribution of the population, and in the lives of those making up the population, and it does so from the very beginnings of the empire. Should we not take into account the transfers of populations, the deportations, the creation of military and agricultural colonies, and the organization of groups of families having collective responsibility for one another? All this has played a great role in the process of the shaping of society by the state which is one of the principal themes of this volume.

Some of the articles published here raise the question of differences in categories between China and the West, and show that the way in which distinctions are drawn does not correspond. Thus, Vandermeersch shows that there is nothing in China comparable to Montesquieu's three powers, legislative, executive, and judicial, but a different division into powers of decision, of execution, and control. In addition—or rather, as a corollary of this difference in the distribution of powers—there is a radical difference between Western law, which distributes rights and obligations between two parties, and Chinese conceptions of legal regulation. In China, law is either an administrative measure, or a cosmic and social model.

The third basic theme is that of the state and the economy. Marianne Bastid examines a question which was of crucial importance in the development of the monarchies of Europe: that of the growth of the financial resources of the state, which in the end came to dominate everything else. In the modern systems of the West, the Ministry of Finance (or its equivalent) is all powerful. In China, on the other hand, it appears that there is no such thing as a strictly financial domain, nor is there even an economic function as we understand it. There is no Ministry of Finance, but only different organs dealing with financial matters. The *hubu* 戶部 or Ministry of Populations, and various specialized imperial departments divided up the financial tasks of the state in accordance with a division of functions derived from history. On the other hand, the expansion of taxation in the aftermath of the war against the Taipings resulted, contrary to what happened in the West, in a weakening of the central power, and hence made it more difficult for the Manchu empire to adapt itself to the modern world. Thus, in different human and political contexts, the same causes do not produce the same effects. Moreover, the political categories are different.

This analysis of Marianne Bastid's raises a more general question: have the Chinese ever had a notion of the economy as a specific domain? The economy and the currency are managed; they are far more instruments in the service of the state than autonomous forces to which the state is exposed. As Marianne Bastid has put it, "finance is subordinate to politics and not the reverse."

Elsewhere, she states: "The principle of the Reform Movement is the adjustment of the relations between the sovereign and his subjects, the unity of hearts which permits peaceful regulation of society by the state, and in consequence of this the prosperity of the population and the power of the nation." Thus we come back to the theme of the primacy of man over technology and wealth. "To govern," she writes, "is to regulate, maintain harmony and equilibrium, not to command and compel." We are led to think of the opposition between the power of constraint (*kratos*) which defines political power in Greece, and the Chinese notion of government: *zhi* 治, to govern, signifies literally to regulate, especially to regulate the flow of water, to treat and to heal.

Our notion of the economy is linked to the development of commercial capitalism and of the modern state. It implies that money has become the measure of all things. This concept of the economy is, thus, relatively modern, and even more recent in the Far East than in the West. But at the same time it is a fact that the Chinese state, which had at its disposal vast sources of wealth, thanks to the taxes it collected in money and in kind, and also controlled an enormous labour force, did in reality play a role, during China's long history, which can properly be called economic, and which has no parallel anywhere in the world. The Chinese expression which served to translate the modern term of economy carries with it the memory of these ancient realities: *jingji* 經濟 , which is the abbreviation of *jingshi jimin* 經世濟民, signified literally "to order the world and succour the people." It evoked the social responsibilities of the state, its constant interventions to maintain the equilibrium between factors such as money and food supply, or surplus and penury, as well as the role of the state in shaping the environment (canals, roads, fortifications). *Oikonomia*, for the Greeks, was on the contrary the domestic arts taught to young women, or at the very most the art of managing one's patrimony. And when economic preoccupations did appear in the West, it was not the action of the state, which as yet had scarcely any real existence, that brought them forth, but the activities of the merchants. From this we see clearly how different have been the historical itineraries followed at the two extremities of the Eurasian continent. If "economic" thought appeared in China with the first manifestations of centralization in the realm of the state, it remained, of course, rather rudimentary. Not only that, but it was, in fact, the very intervention of the state which served to disguise and conceal the mechanisms of the economy. But the reflections of the Chinese in this domain nevertheless evoked, as can be seen from some of the contributions in this volume, questions which have become topical today in the West. And above all, they raise the fundamental question: "What part should the state play in controlling the economy?"

Already at the time of the Han dynasty, a confrontation can be observed between the partisans of *laissez-faire*, and those of a regulated economy.

One could say that in China, the state is all. History explains this. The state was not an organism which developed little by little and was obliged to make a place for itself among other powers, as was the case in the West, where the state had to impose itself on the independent powers of the Church, of feudalism and of the nobility, come to terms with the merchants, and seek the support of the financiers. In China, the state was an established reality from the beginning, or in any case from the time when the formula was worked out in the state of Qin, before it was extended to the whole of the Chinese realm. It was the great organizer of society and of territory. The administrative division into districts responsible to the central authorities came into existence in China in the third century B.C., whereas in Europe no equivalent appears prior to the French Revolution, which established departments and prefectures. The only problem for the Chinese state, in the course of its long history, was to prevent the development of powers other than its own, such as that of the merchants, the armies, the religious communities, and to prevent dangerous splits at the top. It is this which explains the constant effort to devise mechanisms and arrangements capable of preventing the development of parallel powers, not only outside the central state power, but also within it.

These very different paths of historical development gave rise to different conceptions. In China, the state never plays the role of arbiter between parties. Its laws do not have as their aim the distribution of rights or powers (legislative, executive, and judicial), nor do they seek to provide a framework for the settlement of litigation, although these are precisely the functions of law in the West. Criminal law and administrative regulations occupy the dominant place, but as a result of the operation of other mechanisms already evoked, even these types of legislation play only a subordinate role—far less important, in the last analysis, than penal or civil law in the West. We can understand, therefore, why the limitation of the rights of the sovereign, which was so fundamental an aspect of the system of constitutional monarchies in the Western perspective, was not understood in China at the time of the attempts at reform in 1905-1908. The imitation of Western institutions was inspired simply by the desire to copy those things which led to the success of the West. They were concerned with the means for "enriching the state and making it strong militarily" (*fuguo qiangbing* 富國強兵) or at the very most (in harmony with traditional concerns) with procedures for finding out more effectively about the state of mind of the population. In this context, Japan was regarded by the Chinese, at the end of the nineteenth and the beginning of the twentieth centuries, as the most exemplary model. If Japan had become a powerful state, this was because it had copied Western institutions, taken not as an end in themselves, but as the secret of success.

Finally, I would like to make some observations on a topic which is not dealt with in the essays published here, although in fact it is inseparable from the themes we have been discussing, namely the problem of the origin of political power, and of its foundations, both concrete and religious. The cosmic nature of the Chinese state is manifested in a whole series of terms and rituals. The emperor is the Son of Heaven, he rules on the strength of a Mandate of Heaven, he sacrifices to Heaven and to Earth, and he alone has the authority to do so; he is responsible for the natural and social order. China is not one nation among others; it *is* civilization, or at least regards itself as such. It is therefore necessary for the emperors to rely on literati who are specialists precisely in rites and precedents. Otherwise, the whole edifice would collapse. In the final analysis, it is such collective images and beliefs which constitute the most solid foundations of imperial power.

Nevertheless, one must also note that, if the role of armed force and of constraint is less important than in the West, it is decisive in the foundation of empires, and these empires could not maintain themselves without constraint. The state as power of repression, with its armies and its judicial system, must not be neglected.

Looking at the substance of this volume as a whole, I think there is one conclusion which must be drawn: we have our own patterns of thought and institutional frameworks which are the products of a particular historical experience. More often than not we are tempted to apply these patterns without thinking to a universe which has undergone a completely different type of development. Does not the chief interest of a study of the state in China lie precisely in revealing and making explicit these differences and this lack of correspondence between certain aspects of Chinese and Western experience? If, on the contrary, we uncritically apply our own categories and preconceptions to Chinese reality, we run the risk first of all of failing to understand the originality of the phenomena in question, and secondly of wrongly interpreting the facts regarding China in order to force them into our own intellectual framework. This remark applies to all research on China, both past and present.

One of our principal tasks is undoubtedly to make comparisons, in order to grasp the essential and significant differences. As Karl Bünger has emphasized in his Foreword, the comparative approach to political problems is particularly fruitful. The greater the differences between the civilizations under study, the more this is true. This should lead us to raise questions going beyond a simple description of institutions. For example, one ought to consider the problem of the relation between religion and politics. In the West, the Church and the secular authorities shared power over the people for a long period, because men were composed of two distinct realities: the body and the soul. In India, the Brahmins have always ranked above the Kshatriya, and religion was dominant over the profane powers. In China, it is the state which has controlled all manifestations of religious life and integrated them into its system, while seeking to suppress everything which remained outside this system. Morality, politics, religion, rites, and customs were thus intimately united. And from all this there result very different types of men. I think we must carry our reflection at least as far as this if we wish to avoid errors of judgment such as that which would lead us to argue that China lagged behind the West because it did not have the notion of the rights of the individual. To argue in this way is to forget that the individual, as we conceive him, is the product of our own history, with all of its peculiarities.

PART I

Patterns of Rule

1. An Enquiry into the Chinese Conception of the Law

Léon Vandermeersch

Most authors concerned with the nature of Chinese law have analysed it solely in terms of its content and its effects.[1] If, however, we wish to understand the ideas which, in a given society, underlie what makes up the law, the way in which law is conceived, and the nature which is attributed to it, we need rather to study its source. We need to look at the institutional origins of those provisions which are regarded as legal, and to consider what determines that the law is the law. What follows is an outline of some research along these lines, whose subject is imperial China. I recognize that my enterprise is a bold one, and that the field under survey—the institutions of Chinese society through a 2000-year period—is large enough to demand a much lengthier treatment, of which this article can be no more than a beginning.

I wish first of all simply to point out the difficulties which arise when one tries to apply the juridical category of law to those acts and instruments which proceed from the authority of the emperor—the only authority which can be formally considered as the source of legality, if indeed legality may be said to exist. I then suggest that these difficulties can be accounted for by the wide divergence between Chinese ritualism and juridical practice. Finally, through an examination of how codification developed, I draw attention to the true nature of the Chinese codes, which in my view have the character of administrative regulations, and not that of a corpus of legal provisions. I will say at the outset that this leads me to believe that it has never been possible to speak, in China, of *the law* in the sense which that term has when applied, in the Western juridical tradition, to actual positive laws.

Whatever played the part of positive law in imperial China could stem

N.B: In quoting and citing passages of the *Twenty-Four Histories* 二十四史 , I refer to the latest edition of this collection, published in Peking from 1959 to 1977. In the case of the *Shitong* 十通, references are to the Formosa republication (Taibei: Xin Xing shuju 新興書局, 1959-1960), which is photographic reproduction of the Commercial Press edition (Shanghai, 1937) whose pagination it retains.

[1] A notable exception is Thomas A. Metzger's fine work, *The Internal Organisation of Ch'ing Bureaucracy* (Cambridge, Mass.: Harvard University Press, 1973). This work is discussed below.

3

from only one source, the will of the emperor—as in Ulpian's adage, *quod principi placuit legis habet vigorem*. We shall consider just two of the many texts which bear witness to this situation, the first being taken from the beginning and the second from the end of the imperial age.

When Du Zhou 杜周, commandant of justice under the Emperor Wu of the first Han dynasty, was criticized for making his judgments conform with the wishes of the Emperor, he replied as follows:

> Where then do those texts come from which have the greatest authority (literally, 三尺安出哉 , which are recorded on documents three feet long)? What the rulers of old considered to be just is made clear in the form of statutes (*lü* 律); what has been regarded as just by the rulers who have succeeded them has been added in the commentaries in the form of instructions (*ling* 令).[2]

In other words, statutes and instructions (*lü* and *ling*, which are normally considered to constitute the legislation of the Han) have their sole source in the imperial will (and thus cannot be opposed to the actual wishes of the emperor).

Our second example is drawn from the *Siku tiyao* 四庫提要 towards the end of the note about the compilation of the rescripts of the Emperor Shizong 世宗 (Yongzheng 雍正):

> Here we may perceive the unfailing diligence of our sovereign, conscientiously set forth in seven volumes. [It is here that] there is the deep source from which comes the law of the [dynastic] house (*jiafa* 家法).[3]

The expression *jiafa* has no technical meaning, but is purely philosophical. It refers to the entire normative basis of the empire, which is united under the authority of the sovereigns of the dynasty just as a family is united under the father's authority. This basis of normality is categorically stated to proceed in its entirety from the imperial rescripts.

Chinese tradition, indeed, constantly gives expression to the idea that all absolute positive rules must have their source in the power of the emperor. But this idea lacks clarity, because the imperial function was never subjected to any institutional analysis. This was probably the effect of the respectful reserve which forbade discussion of matters germane to the sovereignty of the emperor, who was simply placed at the head of the state, above all its organs and institutions, and who was seen as the origin of all power. This is confirmed,

---

[2] *Hanshu* 漢書, 60.2659. This is cited by Wang Yü-ch'üan in his article "Outline of the Central Government of the Former Han Dynasty," in John L. Bishop (ed.), *Studies of Governmental Institutions in Chinese History* (Cambridge, Mass.: Harvard University Press, 1968), p. 10 ("Harvard-Yenching Institute Series XXIII").

[3] *Siku quanshu zongmu tiyao* 四庫全書總目提要 (Shanghai: Commercial Press, 1933), 45.10.1207.

as Cai Yong 蔡邕 notes, by the fact that he was referred to, in the language of administration, by a special pronoun, the pronoun *shang* 上, the one above. No distinction was drawn between the different aspects of his power.[4]

However, if Chinese tradition lacks any institutional theory of sovereignty, the organization of the state apparatus was, by contrast, systematically and elaborately developed from the *Zhouli* 周禮 onwards. Since that apparatus is supposed to put into action the initiative of the sovereign, its structures afford us our best chance of discovering the outline of a differentiation of powers. The interlocking of the different branches of the service is considerably complicated by the requirements of ritual: elements of cosmological rationalization are introduced, ranks are hierarchically stratified, titles are carefully conserved. It is none the less possible to establish a fairly clear demarcation between the organs of the imperial state, and to differentiate between advisory organs, executive organs, and organs of control. From the Six Dynasties to the Song, the first comprise the Imperial Chancellory (*menxiasheng* 門下省) and the Secretariat (*zhongshusheng* 中書省); the second, the services of the Department of State Affairs, literally of the Masters of Documents, (*shangshusheng* 尚書省) and of the local administration; the third, the services of the Board of Censors (*yushitai* 御史臺). It is well known that this triple structure was already beginning to form under the Han dynasty, and that it can be traced beyond the Song and Yuan dynasties, remaining visible in the different institutions which were set up under the Ming and the Qing. It was the role of the advisory organs to prepare decisions, of the executive organs to apply them, and of the organs of control to oversee the functioning of the apparatus as a whole. This allows us to describe the functions of power, in the Chinese institutional tradition, in terms of a threefold articulation between the power of decision, the power of application and the power of supervision. This takes the place of the traditional Western distinction between legislative, executive, and judicial powers. There are analogies between the two forms of organization, but they clearly do not correspond exactly. Thus the West has no specific conception of the power of supervision, which is dispersed between the executive and the judiciary. In China, conversely, it is the judicial power which is not specifically conceived, being indistinguishable from the power of application which is entrusted to the administration, and which is indeed the administration's most important aspect. But our problem is rather to examine the power of decision as it is found in Chinese institutions and to consider whether there exists, between that power and the legislative power of Western tradition, such a correspondence as would allow us to speak of law in the Chinese case.

---

[4] *Duduan* 獨斷 , Saoye shanfang 掃葉山房 ed. (no date or place), folio 2, recto.

We might at first expect, within the advisory organs themselves, whose role is to prepare imperial decisions, to locate certain services or branches entrusted with the drawing-up of decisions of more general scope, which we might wish to characterize as legislative instruments. No such distinction can in fact be drawn. If the Chancellory and the Secretariat have distinct roles, this is a matter above all of the control which the former enjoys over the latter, a control exercised through the procedure of the *fengbo* 封駁 , the referring back with criticism of instruments drawn up by the Secretariat. As for the Grand Secretariat (*neige* 內閣) and the Grand Council (*junjichu* 軍機處) of the Ming and the Qing, their powers were by and large the same, although the latter, once it had been established in the reign of Yongzheng, exercised those powers secretly, in the bosom of the emperor's confidence, and in a less formal and far more authoritative manner.

We must turn, then, to the imperial acts and instruments themselves, and try to discover in them such characteristics as would distinguish laws properly speaking.

One might have expected to find systematic collections of these acts, for each dynasty if not for each reign; they were, after all, meticulously and interminably filed in the different services through which they passed, whose officials strove to outdo each other in the labour of copying and recopying. Surprisingly, we shall not find them, for although collections of the sort we have in mind are indeed occasionally referred to in Chinese bibliographies, they are no more than occasional compilations, often prepared by scholars acting in a private and unofficial capacity; and they are invariably incomplete. It is in the bibliographical catalogue of the *Xin Tangshu*[5] that we find for the first time an entry devoted to collections of imperial acts, which are called by the generic name of *zhaoling* 詔令 (an expression which I translate, conventionally, as sovereign decisions). Under this heading are brought to-gether twenty-two titles concerned with collections of sovereign decisions made by certain emperors of the Jin, Southern Song and Tang dynasties, together with a number of more heterogeneous anthologies. Later on, this heading disappears from the bibliographies of the official histories, which no longer contain any trace of collections of sovereign decisions. The heading reappears in the *Siku tiyao*, where it is accompanied by the following interesting introduction:

> Whatever is propagated by the word of the monarch may be called sovereign decisions (*zhaoling*). This category is established for the first time in the history

---

[5] *Xin Tangshu* 新唐書 , 58.1472-73. Many of the titles listed here are already found in the bibliographical chapter of the *Jiu Tangshu* 舊唐書 (p. 1998), where however they are not given a separate heading.

section of the Tang bibliography. In his *Qianqing tang shumu* 千頃堂書目, Huang Yuji 黃虞稷 (1629-91) moved the heading concerned with Imperial edicts (*zhigao* 制誥) into the section of collections of texts, where he placed it below the heading for separate collections of texts (*bieji* 別集). And yet [it is said of sovereign decisions that they are] "promulgated just as sweat is sweated"[6] "in the palace which radiates light" [it is the *mingtang* 明堂 which is referred to]; and this means that they are never issued in vain. Social order or disorder, the success or failure [of a dynasty], the cause of these must be sought in these sovereign decisions. They are the pivot of government. We are, therefore, by no means dealing with a purely literary genre. To bring these texts down to the level of poetic genres is to denigrate them in respect of their reason. The manifestos and proclamations [of the ancient kings], of which an account is given in the *Book of Documents* (*Shangshu* 尚書), have a subtle meaning which the canonical text clearly illuminates. Here, then, we enter [the collections of sovereign decisions] in the section devoted to history, as was formerly done, and return to the thinking of the old [bibliographical classifications].

It is to be noted that the sovereign decisions are accorded an importance and a function exactly like those which we attribute to laws: what is in question is "the foundation of the social order," "the pivot of government." But it is also to be noted that they have often been treated as a genre of literature. This tradition goes back at least as far as the nineteenth chapter of the *Wenxin diaolong* 文心雕龍 . It is to be explained by the fact that the imperial acts were drawn up by men of letters who were called to this service by virtue of the quality of their style. They were expert in treatises drawn up in a formal style (*daiyan* 代言); and to indite these did indeed require all the skill and learning of the specialists of the Hanlin Academy, for they had a profoundly ritual character. The scope and functioning of the imperial acts is, moreover, dominated by this ritual character, to such an extent that their political role properly so called becomes altogether blurred, as is apparent the moment one tries to get a clear view of the variety of their forms and of the principles governing their employment. This enterprise, already extremely difficult, is further bedevilled by the terminological changes which always accompany, to some degree, changes of imperial dynasty. One instance of this is the decision made by Qin Shihuang 秦始皇 who, when he founded his empire, proclaimed that his mandates were to be referred to by the word *zhi* 制 instead of the word *ming* 命 , while his ordinances were to be known no longer as *ling* 令 , but as *zhao* 詔 .[7]

It is none the less possible to discern, among the various categories of sovereign decision, a broad division into two groups. On the one hand there

---

[6] This alludes to a clause in the *Yijing* 易經 which has to do with the fifth monogram of the fifty-ninth hexagram, where the decisions of the sovereign are likened to sweat because they are irrevocable, just as sweat, once transpired, can never be reabsorbed.

[7] *Shiji* 史記 , 6.236.

are those acts and instruments, to which I shall give the generic name of edicts, which spring from the initiative of the imperial authority itself; on the other, there are those issued by the imperial authority in response to documents entreating for a decision to be made. These latter I shall call rescripts. In the terminology of the Qing, which is the most modern, edicts are known as *yu* 諭 and rescripts as *zhi* 旨, as is clear from the opening lines of the chapter of the *Da Qing huidian*, which are devoted to the Grand Council, and from the commentary upon them:

> The grand councillors are responsible for the composition of edicts (*yu*) and of rescripts (*zhi*). Edicts and rescripts are promulgated [in the following manner]: once they have been drawn up, they are sent on to the Grand Secretariat.
>
> [From the commentary]: That which is specially promulgated is an edict, that which is promulgated in consequence of an entreaty addressed [to the sovereign authority] is a rescript.[8]

The next lines of the commentary show, however, that the terminology was not perfectly rigorous even where the point had been set out as clearly as this:

> Certain of these acts which respond to an entreaty, inasmuch as they are issued and published with reference to all the services of the court and of the state, are also edicts. Edicts of this form are referred to by the formula, imperial edicts received by the Grand Secretariat; rescripts, by the formula edicts received.

Leaving aside the question of form, the distinction between edicts and rescripts is in any case fairly illusory from a political point of view. For one thing, the emperor in fact generally issued edicts at the prompting of his high officials who might suggest them during the audiences which he held at the time of council meetings or who might incorporate them into the statutory memorials which made their way through the hierarchical network, and which could be made the object of rescripts. A case in point is provided by the edicts in which the Song Emperor, Renzong 仁宗, put into practice the reforms proposed by Wang Anshi 王安石. The entire substance of those reforms is already present in the famous *Memorial to the Throne in Ten Thousand Characters*, the *Wan yan shu* 萬言書, in which the celebrated statesman reports on his service as overseer of the judiciary of Jiangdong 江東.[9] For another thing, simple rescripts could have very far-reaching political scope, even where their form was reduced to a mere confirmation in red (*zhupi* 硃批) by which a single word of approval was inscribed, in the vermilion imperial ink, in the margin of a document appealing for this or that measure. Thus the reform of the land tax system proposed by Yang Yan 楊炎 at the end of the eighth century, which was to bring in its wake a

[8] *Da Qing huidian* 大清會典, 1899 ed., 2.4.
[9] Cf. *Songshi* 宋史, 327.10541-42.

8

profound transformation of the structure of medieval Chinese relations of production, was promulgated in two stages. In the first month of the year 780, the Emperor Dezong 德宗 took advantage of the edict of amnesty which accompanied the inauguration of the new era (the Jianzhong 建中 era) both to announce the changes in the tax system and at the same time to send out commissioners for promotions and demotions (*chuzhishi* 黜陟史) who were responsible for agreeing with the provincial authorities on the measures to be taken. But the ordering of the new regulations was definitively established by rescript on the subsequent report addressed to the emperor by Yang Yan in the eighth month.[10]

It remains clear that the most solemn imperial acts were the edicts; and it is therefore in the category of edictual acts that we may perhaps find some anticipation of or provision for enactments of a legislative kind. Let us see what we can learn about this category from the historical record.

Under the Han, there were four classes of edicts. Those in the first class were called *ceshu* 策書, diplomas.[11] They were used solely in the granting of the noble titles of marquis and king, and in the nomination of the three highest state dignitaries (the three dukes, *san gong* 三公). Those of the second class, known as *zhishu* 制書, mandates, were employed for matters involving imperial prerogative—orders of amnesty or of reprieve. In the third class, the *zhaoshu* 詔書, ordinances, we find instructions given to officials in general (and the same name, ordinances, was applied to both the main types of rescripts, those which involved and those which did not involve the intervention of the director of the Department of State Affairs (*shangshuling* 尚書令). The edicts, finally, of the fourth class, called *jieshu* 戒書, recommendations, were used more particularly in communicating with the high officials of the provinces and of the frontier marches.[12]

Under the Tang, there was a formal division of edicts into seven different classes. Those of the first class, the *ceshu* 冊書, diplomas, were reserved, as they had been under the Han, for investitures and for the nomination of the

---

[10] Cf. *Tang huiyao* 唐會要 (Shanghai: Commercial Press, 1935), Vol. III, 83.1535-37.

[11] It is well known that a difficult problem is posed by the translation of technical terms referring to Chinese national institutions which have no counterparts elsewhere. In translating terms such as *ceshu*, I have striven, not always successfully, to find expressions which retain some mutual coherence (by which I mean expressions possessing common elements wherever common elements are found in the Chinese). These translations, it is plain, are very artificial and must be taken as purely conventional. I make no pretence that they are definitive; they are temporary solutions, but it is to be hoped that we shall one day have the benefit of a terminological vocabulary commonly accepted among translators.

[12] Cai Yong, *Duduan*, folios 1-2.

highest dignitaries; they were used in connection with the conferring of titles which involved the ceremony known as the *linxian* 臨軒 , the coming down beneath the eaves, by which the Emperor, instead of proceeding to the rites in the throne-room, discomposed himself to the extent of going in person to meet the recipient. The second class of edicts, *zhishu*, mandates, were employed (as under the Han) for amnesties and pardons, for the granting of the highest rewards and the imposition of the most severe punishments, for nomination of high dignitaries, and for the abrogation of ancient institutions. Edicts of the third class, known as *weilaozhi* 慰勞制, mandates of encouragement, were used to congratulate and to exhort. Those of the fourth class called *fa(ri)chi* 發(日)敕, dated decrees, were employed to increase or reduce the staff of officials in this or that service, to abolish or create a Prefecture or Sub-prefecture, to send out an expeditionary force, to strip a dignitary of his dignity, to appoint officials of the sixth degree and below, to impose penalties of exile and above, and to authorise expenditure of amounts greater than five hundred rolls of silk, two hundred thousand cash, five thousand bushels of grain, twenty slaves, fifty horses, fifty oxen or five hundred sheep. Edicts of the fifth class, *chizhi* 敕旨 , decretal instructions, were used where an official had requested formal confirmation of instructions previously issued. The sixth class of edicts, known as *lunshi chishu* 論事敕書 , special decrees, were used when letters of compliment were addressed to high officials and when strict injunctions were addressed to officials of inferior degree. Edicts of the seventh class, finally, called *chidie* 敕牒 , decretal missives, were used for day-to-day business.[13]

Under the Song, there were still seven classes of edicts, of which the first two, the diplomas and the mandates, functioned much as they had done under the Tang. Edicts of the third class, called *gaoming* 誥命 , patents of mandate, were used for nominations, transfers, and the granting of all kinds of titles (except those which required an edict of the first class). The fourth class, known as *zhaoshu* 詔書 , ordinances, were employed to address the heads of the great metropolitan and provincial services; when those responsible for lesser services were to be addressed, edicts of the fifth class, called *chishu* 敕書 , decrees, were used. Those of the sixth class, known as *yuzha* 御札 , imperial briefs, were employed in connection with the promulgation of accessions to the throne, the carrying out of great sacrifices, the inauguration of new eras and other liturgical measures. Edicts of the seventh class, called *chibang* 敕牓 , decretal bills, were used where officials of all kinds were to be

[13]Cf. *Da Tang liudian* 大唐六典 (Taibei: Wenhai chubanshe 文海出版社, 1962), 9.194. See also R. des Rotours, *Traité des fonctionnaires et Traité de l'Armée* (Leyden: Brill, 1947), Vol. I, pp. 174-77; and *Xin Tangshu*, 47.1211.

rewarded or reprimanded, and when remonstrances were addressed to the civil population or to soldiers.[14]

The Ming had nine classes of edicts. The terminology employed, which is rather different from that found under the Song and the Tang, is given in the *Mingshi* 明史: there were ordinances (*zhao* 詔), patents (*gao* 誥), mandates (*zhi* 制), diplomas (*cewen* 冊文), edicts (in the strict sense) (*yu* 諭), letters (*shu* 書), credentials (*fu* 符), orders (*ling* 令), and dispatches (*xi* 檄).[15] No details as to the use of these different kinds of edict are to be found either in the *Mingshi*, or in the *Da Ming huidian* 大明會典, or in the *Shitong* 十通;[16] but the Ming tradition remained very largely in force under the Qing, who must have followed the practice of the previous dynasty, at any rate in respect of the most important kinds of edict (ordinances, patents, mandates, edicts in the strict sense).

Under the Qing, the different classes of edict were reduced to four, but several subdivisions existed within each class:

(1) mandates (*zhi* 制) were used when great solemnities were to be decreed to officials of all kinds;

(2) ordinances (*zhao* 詔) were used to proclaim great political decisions having constitutional force (*yixian* 彝憲) to all officials and to the people as a whole;

(3) patents (*gao* 誥) were employed, from the Jiaqing 嘉慶 era onwards, concurrently with ordinances when great political decisions were to be proclaimed; and, in the form of patents of mandate (*gaoming* 誥命), they were used to grant honorific distinctions to officials of the fifth degree and above, as well as to confer hereditary titles;

(4) decrees (*chi* 敕) were used in the form of decrees of mandate (*chiming* 敕命) to grant honorific distinctions to officials of the sixth degree and below and to confer non-hereditary titles; in the form of decretal edicts (*chiyu* 敕諭), they were used for sovereign declarations sent to foreign countries, as well as for the nomination of extra-metropolitan officials, which might be made by decrees of nomination (*zuomingchi* 坐名敕) or by communicated decrees (*chuanchi* 傳敕).[17]

This glance at the history of edictual forms,[18] rapid though it has been,

[14] Cf. *Songshi*, 161.3783.

[15] Cf. *Mingshi*, 72.1732.

[16] I have not yet found precise details as to the way in which these various kinds of edicts instituted under the Ming were used.

[17] Cf. *Da Qing huidian*, 2.4. (See the photographic republication, Taibei: Zhongwen shuju 中文書局 , 1963, p. 38c-d.)

[18] In this brief survey, I have left unconsidered not only data concerning the lesser dynasties, but also material relating to the Yuan dynasty. In this latter case, the inter-

does at least allow us to make the following observations. First of all, in no epoch does there exist a category of edicts reserved for the promulgation of measures of a legislative kind. One might initially be inclined to make an exception, in this respect, of the ordinances (and in part the patents) of the Qing, whose use was confined to affairs described as having constitutional force (as I have roughly translated *yixian*). But the expression *yixian* in no way denotes positive laws; it refers to the fundamental laws of nature insofar as these are models for the right conduct of government, as can be clearly seen throughout the first chapter of the *Wenxin diaolong* "Yuandao" 元道 ("On the Fundamental Dao"), from which the term is borrowed.

Obviously, none of this means that no decision whose scope was that of a legislative measure was ever promulgated by edict. We are simply saying that it is impossible to trace, in the rules governing edictual forms, any conception of positive law as a special category of sovereign decisions. What, then, does this formalism express? It expresses the idea of *rite*—that is, of the formal ordering of things—understood by way of a double hierarchy: both the hierarchy of the various activities organized by the different types of edict, a hierarchy conceived in terms of the liturgical importance of the actions involved; and the hierarchy of the people, in their various qualities, who fall within the edicts' scope, a hierarchy conceived in terms of the social rank of the individuals concerned. The sovereign decisions which require the most solemn forms, and which are regarded as the most important, are those which prescribe the carrying out of the greatest ceremonies of the cult (above all, the great sacrifices to Heaven or to the imperial ancestors) and those which concern the greatest personages of the state (above all, the empress, the crown prince, and the members of the imperial family). As we descend the scale, and approach the ordinary activities of life (so far as deeds and actions are concerned) and the mass of the populace (so far as persons are concerned), we find that the decisions involved require acts of less and less solemnity, and can in general be made by way of a mere rescript. It is quite true that imperial authority could nevertheless choose to stress the political importance of a decision by issuing it in an edict of more solemn form than the decision's content would ritually require. Such cases amount to a political manipulation of the ritual forms, whose character might be more or less disguised by the invocation of ritualistic motives. They do not in any event amount to the emergence of the category of law.

Such a category, which asserts the superiority, over all other instituted rules, of one instituted norm superior by virtue of its universality (*lex est*

---

mingling of Mongol and Chinese institutions raises great difficulties, which it seemed unnecessary to grapple with, given the object of the present study.

commune praeceptum), is bound up, in fact, with the juridical conception of the social order. The principle of the juridical order is that the rights of each person are guaranteed (*suum cuique tribuere*). Since individuals can be assured of their rights only insofar as those rights are not encroached upon by the rights of others (*alterum non laedere*), a norm is established which confines the exercise of each individual's rights within limits which make them compatible with the rights of others. The idea of law is fundamentally the idea of such a norm, which must of necessity be universal if some individuals are not to be favoured at the expense of others. Correlative ideas, essential to the juridical order, are those of the rights of the subject and of individual liberty.

The principle of the ritual order is altogether different. Social relations, in that order, are modelled upon forms—rites—which are the reasons (*li* 理) of things. Only in conformity with those reasons can the world function harmoniously. Once the rites have been respected, and harmony has thereby been introduced into society, each individual spontaneously behaves as is most fitting for all and for himself. Ritualism, which dispenses completely with any idea of rights or of liberty, accords, by contrast, the greatest importance to the idea of spontaneity (*ziran* 自然). The prescriptions of ritualism do not in principle involve any coercion: "punishments do not fall upon the aristocracy," the *Liji* 禮記 tells us, and the epoch in question is one where none but aristocrats were governed by the rites. When we read in the *Yijing* that sovereign edicts are like sweat, the idea is again involved that they act persuasively, by impregnation. Cheng Yi 程頤 writes that:

> The hearts of men must be bathed in the sovereign edicts, just as a man's members are bathed in the sweat of his body; and then men will subject themselves with confidence, and follow [the emperor in the right path]. Then the scattering abroad [of beings] in the universe may be brought into harmony.[19]

People are persuaded to subject themselves to the rites by the prestige and the imposing forms of the greatest ceremonies, and by the ascendancy, and the example, of the highest personages of the social hierarchy. This is why the most important edicts are those which concern great liturgical celebrations, and those which involve great dignitaries. The sovereign, being in possession of the Way, has only to determine, on each occasion, the conduct of those who are to give the example. This is decided on the basis of their place in the hierarchy, and the rest follows of itself. The Chinese, after all, have always upheld as their model the administrator who never intervenes

---

[19] Commentary on the fifth monogram of the fifty-ninth hexagram, in the *Yi Chuan Yi zhuan* 伊川易傳 (*Er Cheng quanshu* 二程全書, *Sibu beiyao* 四部備要 ed., Shanghai: Zhonghua shuju 中華書局, 1936), 12.45b.

13

in the affairs of those whom he administers, the latter acting, under the influence of his virtue, in spontaneous conformity with the norms of the social order.

This is the ideal image of the ritual régime. In fact, just as juridical practice always involves more or less pronounced elements of ritualism (as we can see in the formalism of the law), so too ritualism has always felt the need for mechanisms of a juridical type. Its rites, as purely formal norms of conduct, have always in other words been supplemented by a system of obligations imposing or proscribing certain deeds, a system enforced by the coercion of the state apparatus. This system was developed in ancient China by the Legalists who were the theoreticians of anti-ritualism; but it was developed in a way which completely distorted its meaning from a juridical point of view. The Legalists' pseudo-law, which had nothing to do with the idea of right, was formulated purely and simply as an instrument of government. Its real character was always that of a rule imposed upon its subjects by the state administration—a rule enforced by particularly severe sanctions. Thus the extraordinary penal apparatus built up in Qin was designed and operated to force all social activity into channels which served the ends chosen by those in power, by which the state was to increase its wealth and expand its empire.

The intolerable nature of such a regime was the principal reason why the Qin dynasty was overthrown. And the first act of the founder of the new Han dynasty, once his troops had entered the metropolitan zone, was to reduce to a minimum the hated penal code, which was cut back to three chapters (soon afterwards increased to nine by the Prime Minister Xiao He 蕭何) whose aim was to suppress malicious actions (*yujian* 禦姦).[20] What was swept away, in other words, was that entire part of the draconian Qin regulations which organized, under the constraint of penal sanctions, the life and activities of each individual—which insisted that the household should be no larger than the nuclear family, which imposed forced labour in the fields, which required active participation in military campaigns, etc. The apparatus built up by the Legalists was to be used henceforth solely for the repression of wrong-doing; and the principles of ritualism were to govern all other aspects of social organization. Thus the regulations of the Qin, as inherited by the Han, were to play no more than a minimal, supplementary, role; but their nature none the less remained unchanged, and they continued to constitute a pseudo-law. The way in which the functions of this pseudo-law were conceived was no more affected under the Han than it had been under the Qin by any notion of the rights of the subject. It continued as a purely administrative instrument, whose role was much rather to keep public order from the point of view of

[20] Cf. *Hanshu*, 23.1096.

the state than to protect the security of the person and of property from the point of view of individual citizens. The provisions of the pseudo-law are not so much addressed to private individuals (in the form of prohibitions against this or that reprehensible act) as to officials, whom they instruct as to the prescribed punishment to be inflicted on those guilty of various misdeeds. This is proved by the debate over the suppression of punishment by mutilation. This question, which dominates the whole history of penal justice under the Han, is posed, not in terms of respect for the human person, but in so to speak symmetrical terms of the abolition of abuses perpetrated by cruel officials (*kuli* 酷吏).[21]

It is true that the provisions we are considering are distinct from the general run of prescriptions issued by imperial edict; and their specificity is highlighted by the name given to them, *lü* 律, which properly denotes the laws of musical harmony. To what, then, is this specificity due? Not to the formal source from which they spring, for before they enter into force they too must be promulgated by edict. It is due to just two characteristics: they are traditional, and they are codified from the first. Traditional since they in fact comprise a selective restatement of the provisions in force under the previous dynasty; codified from the first, since at the time of their promulgation they already have the form of a complete and organized totality. Do these characteristics in any way affect their nature as administrative regulations? They arise from the particular importance of the domain governed by these provisions, the domain of public order, which must be maintained with no lapse in continuity (hence the tradition that rules remained the same from dynasty to dynasty) and with no area left uncovered (hence the need for an immediately comprehensive code). As for their name, this simply indicates that they are constants of the social order just as certain proportionalities of pitch are constants of the harmonic order. The metaphorical reference to the laws of nature has no relevance to positive law as this is conceived by juridism. It is for this reason that the term *lü* seems to me less well translated as penal law than as statutes—by which is meant the statutes of society in general from the point of view of the requirements of public order.

These statutes lasted more than two thousand years, during which period

---

[21] Sima Qian, as we know, had devoted a whole chapter of the *Shiji* (ch. 122) to cruel officials. In discussions as to whether punishment by mutilation should or should not be kept up (which are to be found scattered in the *Xingfa zhi* 刑法志 of the histories of the Han and the Six Dynasties) the question is invariably posed in these terms: Is it or is it not wise to have recourse to such methods for the preservation of the moral order? We never find the issue discussed from the point of view that the human person should be respected, no matter what crime had been committed. See, for instance, A.F.P. Hulsewé, *Remnants of Han Law* (Leyden: Brill, 1955), pp. 346f.

—especially from the Han to the Tang—they were progressively perfected without ever changing their nature. In character, they remained a set of administrative regulations in the field of public order, regulations transmitted from one dynasty to the next, which may have been revised from time to time (mainly when dynasties changed) but whose content, if not their systematic structure, continued virtually unaltered from the *Tanglü shuyi* 唐律疏議 of 737[22] until the end of the empire. Throughout, they retained the exclusively penal character inherited from their Qin prototype; for the Chinese never in fact established, following the overthrow of the Legalist regime, a truly juridical system, which would have been altogether foreign to their traditions. What they set up was a compromise between Legalism and ritualism, by which the repressive interventionism of the administration was kept to the indispensable minimum, and things were left apart from that to spontaneity educated by ritual. This is why the whole sphere of what we call contractual law, and all the procedures of commercial practice, remained in China entirely the affair of the partners involved, except where the administration was able to find a "public order" pretext for seizing hold of this or that sector, which then fell *ipso facto* into the penal domain. And this, reciprocally, is why the entire activity of district officials vis-à-vis those whom they administered (if we leave aside the extensive field of taxation and fiscal organization) was limited, roughly speaking, to the exercise of criminal justice.

The anti-Legalism of the dominant Confucian ideology expressed itself in a tendency towards the limitation and simplification of the statutes. The number of provisions, which is unknown for the Han period, rose under the dynasties of the South as high as 1,522 articles, leaving aside the Liang 梁 period, in which Confucianism could have little influence in a milieu permeated with Buddhism, and when there were as many as 2,522 articles. In the North, the number of articles under the Wei 魏 was no more than 832, a figure which rose to 1,537 under the Later Zhou 周, fell again to 949 under the Qi 齊, and remained steady at a mere 500 articles under the Sui 隋 and the Tang.[23] The statutes of the Tang were adopted wholesale by the Song, apart from the relatively unimportant addition of 44 articles to the introductory chapter of the *General Principles and Terminology* (*Mingli* 名例) in 964. The Ming at first increased the number of articles to 606, but by the year 1397 it had been reduced to 460. Under the Qing, the figure was eventually

---

[22] On the reasons as to why this dating should be preferred to the traditional dating of the work to the year 653, see Niida Noboru 仁井田陞, *Tō rei shūi* 唐令拾遺, second ed. (Tokyo: Tōkyō Daigaku Shuppankai 東京大學出版會, 1964), p. 15.

[23] See the synoptic table of medieval Chinese codes drawn up by Balazs at the end of his translation of the *Traité juridique du "Souei-chou"* (Leyden: Brill, 1954), p. 208.

to fall to 436 articles.[24]

And yet throughout these centuries the administration continued to grow more extensive and more complicated, and to develop a multitude of bonds which connected it with its subjects. These bonds arose from the needs of the fiscal system, of military service, of the ordering of the great public services, of the organization of education and of the official examinations, of the planning of liturgical celebrations, and so on. This led to another tendency, opposed to that which we have just discussed, by which a mass of new regulations sprang up alongside the fixed statutes of tradition. These new regulations thus supplemented and amended the statutes in the realm of public order itself; and their source, like that of the statutes, was to be found in sovereign decisions. This was true in a double sense. First of all, they had to be promulgated by edict before they could enter into force; and then, from the point of view of their content, they were simply the codification of previous particular decisions or of authorized administrative practices, practices (that it to say) in which the administration was conforming with directives it had received by way of edicts and rescripts. This whole great mass of material, which we can bring together under the name of codified regulations, can be the subject, here, only of a few brief remarks.

The first form of codified regulation appears at the beginning of the Han dynasty, under the name of *ling* 令 (codified) instructions. The term is used in the first place as a simple synonym for the usual technical term edicts (*zhao* 詔).[25] It is employed to denote edicts in general, more especially as these are found in the administrative records. But when from these records certain edicts were selected whose provisions had permanent force, and which remained applicable after the death of the emperor who had promulgated them, the term took on a technical meaning, and came to designate in particular collections of edicts of this kind classified in this way. It would seem clear that at the time the provisions in question were those which supplemented the provisions of the statutes, and which were in fact of the same kind. Under the Han, too, we find compilations of (jurisprudential) examples (*bi* 比), which illustrate how regulative provisions were extended to cover situations which the regulations themselves had not anticipated. When a systematic and codified selection of such examples was drawn together and promulgated, their force was no longer that of mere instances; they took on

[24] On the Song addition of 44 articles, cf. *Yuhai* 玉海 (Taibei: Dahua shuju 大化書局, 1977), 66.1309a. On the number of articles in the code under the Ming and the Qing, cf. D. Bodde and C. Morris, *Law in Imperial China* (Cambridge, Mass.: Harvard University Press, 1967), pp. 59-60.
[25] The term *zhao* having just been substituted for *ling* by Qin Shihuang (cf. n. 7 supra), the word *ling* had fallen back into the common usage, with the same meaning.

normative value, and were known as *ke* 科 , judicata. The officials of the Han also compiled, by way of inspiration, collections of historical precedents (*gushi* 故事), which were rather similar to the examples.[26]

As these codified regulations continued to proliferate, they developed along the following schematic lines. Provisions which were at first no more than subsidiary in character, but whose number none the less continued to grow, eventually came to constitute a special category of regulations; and to these new regulations, subsidiary provisions of a new type attached themselves in their turn. When the categories of regulations threatened to multiply beyond reasonable bounds, they were reunified, very often under a new name.

Thus in the period of the Six Dynasties, the instructions (*ling*) were no longer simply complementary to the statutes. In nature, they were no longer repressive, but merely prescriptive; and if their prescriptions were not carried out, the appropriate sanctions were laid down by a new provision of the statutes covering contravention of instructions (*weiling zhi zui* 違令之罪).[27] Under the Northern Wei, the judicata became transformed into types (*ge* 格), which were codified, and to which were added, when they were collected together, various fiats (*chi* 敕) by way of illustration.[28] Under the Tang, apart from the statutes, the body of codified regulations comprised the categories of instructions and types, as well as a fresh category, the models (*shi* 式), of which no example has come down to us. As for the category of fiats, this was homonymous with that category of edicts also known as *chi* 敕 (translated above, in its other usage, as decrees, in order to avoid ambiguity); and it thus tended to be dissolved away into the category of types.[29]

The codification and recodification of instructions, types, and models continued under the Song, who also renewed the separate codification of the fiats, which from the time of the Five Dynasties regained their old importance as regulations complementary to the statutes,[30] and indeed began gradually to usurp the function of the latter: the Emperor Shenzong 神宗 decided that judicial decisions must be based upon the articles of the codes of fiats, rather than upon the statutes, whose re-issue he suspended.[31]

[26] On the whole of this paragraph, see Nakada Kaoru 中田薫 , *Hōsei shi ronshū* 法制史論集 (Tokyo: Iwanami Shoten 岩波書店, 1964), pp. 189-210.

[27] *Op. cit.*, pp. 80-84.

[28] *Op. cit.*, pp. 230-36.

[29] Cf. Chen Guyuan 陳顧遠 , *Zhongguo fazhi shi gaiyao* 中國法制史概要 (Taibei, 1964), pp. 75-76.

[30] *Op. cit.*, pp. 76-77.

[31] This is how the belief arose that the *lü* disappeared during the Song epoch, the codes of that epoch, from the Yuanfeng 元豐 era onwards (1078-85), being made up of collections of *chi-ling-ge-shi* 敕令格式 in which the *chi* took the place of the *lü*. In reality, the

The promulgation of the last collection of instructions (*ling*) in Chinese history took place under the Ming, in 1367. After this, considerable progress took place, in that the entire body of codified regulations was unified. Those provisions of a penal character which were not part of the statutes were first of all brought together, under the name of *tiaoli* 條例, sub-statutes, in a collection entitled *Wenxing tiaoli* 問刑條例 (*Sub-statutes* [*by Way of Answer*] *to Judicial Questions*) which was promulgated in 1500 and re-issued in 1549; and in 1585 the sub-statutes were annexed to the statutes in comprehensive collections which were regularly revised.[32] Furthermore, all provisions concerning the structures of the state and the functioning of the administration were codified under the title of *Da Ming huidian* 大明會典 (*Constitutions of the Great Ming*) to 1502. This was promulgated in 1511, and then revised in 1550 and 1587.[33] Finally, from 1587 onwards the code of statutes and sub-statutes was integrated into the *Constitutions*.[34]

The Qing, following the practice of the Ming, promulgated on the one hand (after several editions of the statutes) the *Da Qing lüli* 大清律例 (*Statutes and Sub-statutes of the Great Qing*) in 1740;[35] and on the other hand a series of editions of *Constitutions of the Great Qing* (*Da Qing huidian* 大清會典) in 1690, 1733, 1763, 1818, and 1899.[36] To the *Constitutions* were regularly annexed, from 1763 onwards, sub-regulations (*zeli* 則例) (1763) or consecrated sub-regulations and precedents (*shili* 事例) (1818, 1899). These were regularly compiled, within the services, on the basis of solutions of cases (*cheng'an* 成案), which were themselves extracted from the totality of cases considered, by means of an ingenious procedure of continuously renewed assimilation. This procedure, well studied by Metzger,[37] undoubtedly represents the most sophisticated development of the administrative function to be found in the whole of world history before the contemporary period. But it is certainly the administrative function which was thus developed, and not, as Metzger tends to suggest, the legislative function—unless we are to

---

lü continued to exist, but in a purely theoretical manner. See, on Song codification, apart from the work cited above by Chen Guyuan, Niida Noboru 仁井田陞 , *Chūgoku hōsei shi* 中國法制史 , fourth ed. (Tokyo: Iwanami Shoten, 1957), pp. 66-67.

[32] Cf. Yang Honglie 楊鴻烈 , *Zhongguo falü fada shi* 中國法律發達史 (Shanghai, 1930), Vol. II, pp. 748, 758, and 775-76.

[33] Cf. Yang Honglie, *op. cit.*, pp. 757 and 759.

[34] The 1587 *Da Ming huidian*, which contains the statutes and sub-statutes, has been published in Taibei in a photographic reproduction by the Dongnan shubao she 東南書報社 (1973).

[35] Cf. Bodde and Morris, *op. cit.*, p. 57.

[36] Cf. Metzger, *op. cit.*, p. 217.

[37] See especially ch. 3 of Metzger, *op. cit.*, n. 1 (pp. 165-232).

deny any specific character to positive law, and make it indistinguishable from whatever else may have a peremptory character and emanate from an organ of the state.

What is in fact disclosed in the development of Chinese codified regulations is a history of progressive refinement, as relations were perfected between the emperor's power of decision and the administration's power of application. This process was especially aided by two essential components of the procedural machinery by which the apparatus functioned: first of all, the system of written proceedings, which applied from top to bottom of the administrative hierarchy, and which in China developed early on to an unparalleled extent; and secondly, the use of the rescript form for the making of sovereign decisions, a practice which was very general if we allow that edicts themselves were most often in reality disguised rescripts. These two perfectly interlocking components brought about an ever perfect system of state regulation—of regulation, and not of law. This explains certain fundamental aspects of Chinese state practice. First of all, there is no specialized judicial power: it is obvious that the existence of a distinct jurisdictional function is impossible where there is no distinct legislative function. Also, although the judge (that is to say, the administrator in his capacity as judge) was always strictly enjoined to base his judgment upon a text,[38] no principle ever evolved equivalent to the principle of *nulla poena sine lege*. On the contrary: existing provisions were as a rule extrapolated to cover cases not provided for in the regulations, and venial misdemeanours could always be punished on the basis of a "catch-all" article of the statutes, which condemned to a flogging "whoever had acted in a manner in which he should not have acted."[39] The fact is that, in the absence of law, the problem of the legal relation between the state and the subject did not arise. The only problem considered was that of the relation of power between the official and the emperor, and it was to prevent the latter's power of decision from being usurped by the former that officials were obliged to base their sentences on one of the categories of the codified regulations (from which the relevant article had to be cited) and even, in cases where they had proceeded by analogy, to seek ratification for their judgments, in most cases, through a memorial addressed to the emperor.[40] Then again, there is the fact that the various categories of

---

[38] In the *Tanglü shuyi*, this obligation is stipulated in the sixteenth article of the chapter *duanyu* 斷獄.

[39] *Tanglü shuyi*, ch. *zalü* 雜律, art. 62.

[40] On the question of the lack of any principle of *nulla poena sine lege* in China, and on the way in which the judges employed reasoning by analogy, see Dai Yanhui 戴炎輝, *Tanglü tonglun* 唐律通論, third ed. (Taibei: Guoli Bianyiguan 國立編譯館, 1977), pp. 8-9 and 14-15. The contrary point of view is argued by Fu-mei Chang Chen, "On Analogy in

provisions possessed an authority inversely proportional to their level of codification, so that we read that, under the Tang, "where there is a fiat (*chi* 敕), we do not refer to types (*ge* 格) or to models (*shi* 式), where there is a type or a model, we do not refer to instructions (*ling* 令) or to statutes (*lü* 律)."[41] Under the Qing, similarly, sub-statutes were of greater weight than statutes.[42] For indeed there was no question of referring to a law, to which all decisions would be subject; one referred to the most adequate decision, which always meant the most recent decision.

But what then can be the use of the codification, since no law emerges from it—since, on the contrary, those elements which are most highly codified (the statutes) have the least authority?

First of all, from a practical point of view, the codification obviates the need to require the sovereign power to repeat its decision on a particular case every time that a similar case arises. Secondly, and above all, the codification gives form from a theoretical point of view. It makes visible the broad lines of the state's structure and allows these to be made conformable, in terms of ritualist rationality, with the great norms of nature. Commenting on the definition given in the *Shiming* 釋名, by Liu Xi 劉熙, of the term *lü* 律 statute ("the bond: that which binds the heart of man by preventing it from slackening"), Shen Jiaben 沈家本 makes the following remarks:

> The *Shiji* declares that "in everything that he institutes or lays down as a law-model (*fa* 法), the sovereign acts in conformity with the six musical tubes (*lü* 律) [=statutes]."[43] In the "Monograph on the Calendar and the Musical Tubes" of

Ch'ing Law," *Harvard Journal of Asiatic Studies*, Vol. 30, 1970, pp. 212-24. But her argument resolves itself essentially into a discussion of the point: was or was not reasoning by analogy the sufficient basis of a judgment under the Qing? But this is no more than a question of fact; and even if the collections of trial records for the Qing epoch show almost no cases of judgments based upon analogy (this is the author's conclusion, a rather sweeping one in my view), this means at the most no more than that the Qing disposed of an exhaustively adequate repertory of statutes and sub-statutes. To prove that Chinese practice acknowledged the principle of *nulla poena sine lege*, we would have to give instances of judgments quashed on the grounds that they had made a wrong use of analogy—or we would at the least have to cite documents in which that principle was expressed (and this is not a matter merely of the judge's being obliged to base all his judgments on a text of the regulations).

[41] Cited by Chen Guyuan, *op. cit.*, p. 76.

[42] Metzger, *op. cit.*, p. 86.

[43] Shen Jiaben cites a passage from the beginning of ch. 25 of the *Shiji* (p. 1239). Once it is conceded that, as I believe, Chinese institutions had no understanding of the law as a precise juridical category, then the translation of the term *fa* 法 poses a difficult problem. In the ritualist tradition, *fa* is related to the great cosmological principles which govern the doings of the earth. More particularly, it denotes those principles under the aspect in which they must be imitated by the regulations which govern society; and thus

the *Hanshu*, we read that "once the [measurements of] the musical tubes [=statutes] have been deduced from the calendrical values, the instruments are fixed; circles are traced with the compass and squares with the set-square, weights are weighed in the scales, and true measure is taken with the water-level and the cord. When things of mystery have been studied and hidden things examined, when the depths have been sounded and the furthest reaches attained, we can but make use of our discoveries. [And then] he who measures length loses no fraction of an inch, he who calculates quantities loses not a pinch, he who weighs weights loses not a grain."[44] And again: "Now the musical tubes [=statutes] are *yin* 陰 and *yang* 陽, they are [multiples of] nine and six. This is the source of the symbols which are combined in the hexagrams. This is why the musical tube *huangzhong* 黃鐘 [the standard tube by the measure of nine] governs the primordial dynamism; and this is what we call the statute-standard (*lü* 律). This statute-standard is the law-model (*fa* 法). There is nothing which does not conform to it."[45] Thus the secret of the six musical tubes also gives us the exact measure of a fraction of an inch, a pinch, a single grain. This must be the nature of whatever is established as a law-model. This is why the statutes have been given the same name as the musical tubes. In the *Erya* 爾雅 [which Shen Jiaben has quoted two pages earlier] four glosses derive from that source the primitive meaning [of the term statutes]. The gloss of the *Shiming*, which explains it as "that which binds the heart," by no means offers a conclusive answer as to the proper meaning of the word statutes.[46]

The statutes were always divided into six, nine or twelve chapters: six in the primitive codification constituted by the *Fajing* 法經 of Li Kui 李悝, according to the *Jinshu* 晉書;[47] nine in the Han period; twelve under the Tang. These are the fundamental musical numbers governing the harmony of the universe: six is the number of the tubes (*lü* 律) in the strict sense (the *yang* tubes, known as *lü* 律 to distinguish them from the *yin* tubes, which were called *lü* 呂); nine is the number of the standard tube, *huangzhong*; twelve is the total number of the musical tubes (*lü* 律) in the broad sense

---

it comes about that those regulations too can be called *fa*. In the Legalist tradition, *fa* has to do with all those obligations which the sovereign power pronounces by edict. Finally, *fa* has a technical meaning, referring (for instance, in the specialized monographs of the official histories) to the entire corpus of what has been codified. These three senses of the term *fa* constantly overlap and impinge on each other; meanwhile, not one of them includes the essence of what Western tradition imputes to the *lex* of the Roman jurisconsults. I have rendered *fa*, in the text cited, as law-model, an expression which I have invented, in the absence of anything better, to indicate that what is in question is substantially, and in a very general sense, that to which one must conform.

[44] Shen Jiaben cites a passage from ch. 21A of the *Hanshu* (p. 956).

[45] This passage, too, comes from ch. 21A of the *Hanshu* (pp. 975-76).

[46] Shen Jiaben 沈家本, *Lüling jiujuan* 律令九卷, beginning of *juan* 1. (See *Shen Jiyi xiansheng yishu jiabian* 沈寄簃先生遺書甲編, Shanghai, 1929, second *tao*, ninth *ce*, folio 2, verso.)

[47] Cf. *Jinshu*, 30.922.

22

(the six *yang* tubes together with the six *yin* tubes). In this way the statutes of social harmony were established in conformity with cosmic harmony. Similary Six Ministries were organized under the constitutions, to reflect the departments ritually organized in the *Zhouli*, the departments of the Heavens, of the Earth, and of the four seasons. Similarly, too, the collections of consecrated sub-regulations and precedents (*shili* 事例) were revised, under the Qing, on a five-yearly pattern, for it was at five-yearly intervals that an embolismic correction was made to the calendar, in compensation for the deficit caused by following the lunar months.[48] Many more examples could be invoked to illustrate this quest for formal correspondences between the structures of society and the structures of the cosmos, a quest which is apparent in Chinese codification.

When, from the Ming onwards, all the codes were brought together into a unity, this too was in response to the needs of ritualist rationalism. The first outlines of unification are to be found in the *Sixfold Constitution of the Great Tang (Da Tang liu dian* 大唐六典), which was compiled between 722 and 739; a doctrinal reworking took place in the great unofficial compilations, the *huiyao* 會要 (from which the official Ming and Qing constitutions took their name: *huidian* 會典 is a crasis of *huiyao dianzhang* 典章).[49] This was the outcome of a continuing effort to integrate all the machinery of the state into a single structure whose movement would reflect, at the level of society, the dynamics of the universe. We may note in passing that this development culminated, at the beginning of the Ming period, in a redistribution of the twelve chapters of the statutes into six new chapters, each bearing the title of one of the great administrative departments. Thus it was eventually possible to insert the code of the statutes quite readily into the midst of the constitutions, which is surely one more proof that Chinese codified regulations were administrative by nature.

Once all the forms of regulation had been brought into a unity, the constitutions came to appear as the universal law of the state. But "law," here, must be taken in its ritualistic sense, to denote the *fa* 法 , law-model, which is recognized *a priori* to be the norm of all natural phenomena; the juridical meaning of the term has no pertinence. Whereas in the Western tradition the idea of scientific laws of nature is derived from the idea of positive laws of society and of the polity, the Chinese tradition conceives law first of all as cosmic law, which transcends society. It is the law of Heaven, and must be respected by the sovereign decisions which set in motion the entire apparatus of the state;

[48]Cf. Chen Yunian 陳與年 (trans.), *Qingguo xingzhengfa* 清國行政法 (Shanghai: Guangzhi shuju 廣智書局 , 1906), p. 27 (and p. 23 for the calendrical explanation). (Translated from the Japanese of Oda Yorozu 織田萬 .)
[49]Chen Yunian, *op. cit.*, p. 9.

and if it is not respected, immanent justice will mete out the penalty of *geming* 革命, alteration in the mandate of sovereignty, i.e., of revolution.

I should like to add two remarks in conclusion.

We might note, first, that although juridism, and hence the conception of law to which it gives rise, were foreign to Chinese thought, Chinese social relations have none the less always involved practices of a juridical kind. But this juridical practice was never reflected upon, it was never theorized; it was governed simply by manners and customs. This is why the notion of the rights of the subject, which is implicit (for instance) in contractual practice, was never developed into a general conception of rights. In the same way, although liberty was consciously recognized as a value, and although that consciousness is evident in everything which marks the status of a slave as different from that of a freeman (as we should say: the Chinese term is *liangren* 良人, literally individual of good disposition), no explicit formulation of the value of liberty was ever arrived at. Does this mean that the imperial régime was a régime of unrestrained oppression? Leaving aside horrific clichés on the subject of feudalism and the mandarin bureaucracy, the charge remains unproven. Ritualism's high valuation of spontaneity was not a matter of empty words; and it would be a mistake to impute to defective or wicked institutions what should really be blamed upon wars, foreign invasions, and imbalances between population growth and the growth of productivity, all of which have played their part in the crises which punctuate Chinese history, and especially the history of the last century of imperial rule.

My second observation relates to the persistence of China's a-juridical tradition in the political practice of the People's Republic. It is well known that contemporary Chinese constitutional doctrine denies all value to the bourgeois theory of the separation of powers. Chinese theory recognizes only the separation of functions between the organs of the state explicitly charged with the elaboration of laws (the National People's Congress), the application of the laws (the government), and the judicial control of respect for the law (the courts). None of these organs are invested with any independent powers, since they are all subordinated to the leadership of the Party. We find here once again the only fundamental division established in former times between the power of decision—now vested in the Party rather than in the emperor —and the power of execution—vested in the state apparatus as a whole, made up of various specialized organs. What does the Party take as its guide in exercising its decision-making power? Marxism-Leninism and Mao Zedong Thought, in other words the scientific laws of historical materialism, which play here the same role as that of cosmological speculation in the past.

Nevertheless, with the movement toward a greater emphasis on legality

24

which has developed in recent years, a new principle has emerged: that of the separation of the Party and the state. Does this amount to a true separation of powers? No, for the degree to which this principle is respected, and the way it is interpreted, remain entirely within the discretion of the Party itself. More exactly, the concrete significance of this principle depends on the balance of forces between those among the leaders of the Party who occupy the top positions in the state apparatus, and those who occupy the top positions in the Party apparatus, and in particular between the Standing Committee of the National People's Congress and the Political Bureau. Recently, there have been indications that the first of these two has assumed somewhat greater importance. This situation offers a certain analogy with the phenomenon which can be observed periodically in the history of imperial China, when the leadership of the administrative apparatus strengthens its position in the face of the sovereign power held by the council within the palace, whatever the form or the name of these two organs at any given time.

2. State and Power in Juxtaposition: An Assessment of Ming Despotism

Tilemann Grimm

I. PRELIMINARY REMARKS*

The source material for Chinese history is conceptualized according to a cyclical model and many a Chinese dynasty offers itself as an illustration of this model. Take the six chapters on "food and goods" (*shihuo zhi* 食貨志) from the official Ming history (*Ming-shi* 明史 chapters 77 to 82) as an example. Here one has the quite regular sequence from Ming *chu* 初 (i.e. the beginning of Ming) to Xizong 熹宗 *shi* 時 (i.e. the time of the penultimate Ming emperor Zhu Youjiao 朱由校 with the reign title Tianqi 天敢) to represent the rise and fall of a great dynasty from beginning to end. A 1658 compilation of the history of the Ming (*Mingshi jishi benmo* 明史紀事本末) organized topically, recording specific events (*jishi* 紀事) which are explained in a critical way, remains a simple account "from beginning to end" (*benmo* 本末), and requires some personal remarks by the compiler in order to bring home his critique. Chinese traditional judgements on history were expressed through the story teller's craft, recounting everything of political import from beginning to end, and the two criteria of good versus bad government expressed in the terms *bao* 褒 and *bian* 貶 (eulogize and censure) are the yardsticks of historical criticism.

Another feature of cyclical import is also historiographical in nature, namely the existence of just three outstanding collections of documents in Ming times which marked the beginning (Hongwu 洪武 26th year: 1393), the middle (Hongzhi 弘治 16th year: 1503), and the late period (Wanli 萬曆 15th year: 1587).[1] This leads the compilers of institutional history to a cyclical

---

*This essay got its first impulse from a narrative section in the first of two Ming volumes in the *Cambridge History of China* written by the same author. There the period 1435-1464 has been described as narrative history, while the three cases here (including the Zhengde 正德 period until 1521) are used in the analysis to highlight aspects of so-called "Ming despotism."

[1] *Zhusi zhizhang* 諸司職掌 (1393; Statutes for the organization, i.e. handling, of all offices in the central government) covering the early Ming period; *Da Ming huidian* 大明會典 (1503; *Collected Statutes of the Great Ming* in 180 chapters) covering the period

27

understanding of Ming history in three phases: the strong beginning, the diffuse mid-Ming, and the endangered late Ming. In reality, Ming China as a socio-economic process was as complex a phenomenon as any other major dynasty. It built on Southern Song and Yuan precedents, and passed through stages of development in terms of real economic growth and intellectual diversification. The somewhat one-sided judgment on Ming China as a sort of bureaucratic (or even "totalitarian") despotism is too narrow to assess a society of some 90 or 100 million people and a culture of tremendous multiplicity marked both by the persistence of tradition and by gradual change. And yet, the despotism was there, and "bureaucratic" is a good descriptive term to cover government procedures of various kinds in Ming China. The Hongwu emperor (1368-98), who came from the lowest levels of China's agrarian world, did inaugurate the tone of despotism. He grew from village hunger through warlord experience to an imperial pride of universalistic style. In a way, one may think of him as having defeated and expelled the Mongols in order to imitate them, but his universalism was clearly that of everything "under heaven" based on China's villages, and not on the grand view of the limitless horizons of the steppe. His son, the Yongle 永樂 emperor (1402-24), may have had something of the latter, but after his death things reverted to normal in terms of China's agrarian basis and her commercial instinct (whatever that may signify). In terms of systematic analysis, it seems quite appropriate to have a sequence of weak emperor-despots from Yingzong 英宗 down to Wuzong 武宗 in order to bring out more clearly the institutional side of Ming "despotism."

This introductory passage in Ming-style historical terms should be understood as providing the foundation for the subsequent analysis, which aims to transcend the syndrome of Ming history. Further, the three cases presented here are recognized by Ming historians as comparatively important events in the flow of history,[2] but they may also serve as historical examples for political model-building.

One further historiographic remark may be added: "mid-Ming" is an historiographical invention for the reader's convenience. It begins with the

---

until 1502; *Da Ming huidian* (1587) covering the period until 1585. Cf. Wolfgang Franke, *An Introduction to the Sources of Ming History* (Kuala Lumpur: University of Malaya Press, 1968), p. 178.

[2] Cf. *Ming-shi* ch. 81, sect. "Commercial duties" dated 1529: "Beginning with the Chenghua 成化 period [1465-1487] commercial taxes were collected in silver kind . . . ; in the 8th year [of the Jiajing 嘉靖 period, 1529] this was done again, and made the regular system . . . ," cf. Wada Sei 和田清 (ed.), *Min-shi shokkashi yakuchū* 明史食貨志 譯註, 2 vols. (Tokyo: Toyō Bunko, 1957), Vol. II, text section p. 133; for the Japanese commentary see pp. 867 and 869ff.

moment the Mongol banners had receded and were kept at a safe distance for some time (1424), and the sea-going expeditions came to a halt (1433). It is characterized by the growing influence of the eunuchs, through their close contact with the emperor-despot, by an enduring military system and consistent military measures to keep the context of China's provinces intact, and by a slow yet steady economic growth which would be gradually stabilized on the basis of a silver standard in the early sixteenth century.[3] "Mid-Ming"-China would end where a multi-faceted mechanism of challenge and response led to new developments creating a Chinese empire which remains the fundamental basis of China even today, in the economic, cultural, and political spheres. At the same time an East Asian cultural and economic sphere began to take shape, and foreign influences from Europe, which would henceforth never cease to make themselves felt, first came to bear. The Manchu conquest would eventually settle into the same mould. What I shall deal with in this essay is the prehistory of these developments.

II. THE FIRST CASE

The first "despot" in this context was an eight-year-old boy, Zhu Qizhen 朱祁鎮 , whose father, the Xuande 宣德 emperor (who ruled from 1425 to 1435), had died at the age of only 36. This boy would rule for a period of almost thirty years (1435-64), interrupted by a seven-year interregnum when the throne was occupied by his younger brother Jingtai 景泰 (1450-56), and ending in a phase of destablization. A regency was established at the outset comprising (*a*) members of the dynastic family, acting as *de facto* regents for the eight-year-old emperor-despot, who came into his own when he married; (*b*) the gentry-bureaucrats[4] as represented by the grand secretaries (the "three Yangs" 楊, so-called because they had the same family name, without being related to one another) with practically no one among the ministers who was of equivalent status except the then minister of personnel; (*c*) the eunuch-bureaucrats,[5] foremost among them Wang Zhen 王振 (died 1449) together with some other influential eunuchs; and (*d*) the commanders of the

---

[3]*Ibid.*

[4]This combined term is specifically used here for scholar-officials from "good" families, to differentiate them from other bureaucrats such as eunuch-bureaucrats. Fairbank and Reischauer, *East Asia, The Great Tradition* (Boston: Houghton Mifflin, 1958/60), pp. 309ff.

[5]Eunuch-bureaucrats usually came from lower-status families or families of which nothing further is known. Because they could have no posterity, they were something like a special class. Cf. Fairbank and Reischauer, *op. cit.*, pp. 315ff.

so-called Embroidered-uniform Guard (*jinyiwei* 錦衣衛) as the power sustaining the palace and the court.

All of these together made up what may be taken as the government. While the empress-dowager and the gentry bureaucrats, who were in their late sixties and seventies, represented old age, the eunuch-bureaucrats were still young, generally in their thirties. They had become literate through studies in the palace eunuch school (*neishutang* 內書堂) and thereby developed expertise in political and bureaucratic procedure. Wang Zhen, who dominated the court scene in Beijing from about 1442, was the ablest among them. He had gained the trust of the young emperor, whose teacher he had been for many years. Among other things the eunuch made him familiar with military life, by taking him to the Beijing garrison's training grounds. This approach contrasted favourably with the drab Confucian teaching by strict gentry-bureaucrats.

The pattern of the game was thereby set: (1) the imposing old lady and the old bureaucrats died or receded one by one, (2) the succeeding court secretaries were experienced paper workers, but unskilled in political manoeuvre and decision-making, (3) the eunuch director of ceremonial (*sili taijian* 司禮太監), Wang Zhen, stood behind the young reigning emperor, and more or less imposed his will on the government, thanks to the fact that he had two ministers of war, one vice-minister of works, one commander, and one co-commander of the Embroidered-uniform Guard as his supporters or even henchmen. This was the first time that the Guard, too, was participating in politics. Of the four political forces constituting sources of power, three—emperor, eunuchs, and Guard—formed a dominant bloc for some seven years (1442-49). One, the secretaries, receded into its bureau which lay, to be sure, within the precincts of the palace. No one was strong enough to influence or halt this dangerous trend, particularly as all of them underestimated the threat of a renewed Mongol aggression in the years 1448-50. The results of this were an emperor made captive, and the death of the chief eunuch, together with a host of high dignitaries, but not the fall of Beijing, which the Ming army was strong enough to hold.

The following two reign periods (Jingtai and Tianshun 天順, 1457-64) belong to the same *Yingzong shilu* 英宗實錄 complex:[6] Jingdi 景帝, the younger brother of Yingzong, tended to favour some reform measures especially in the military sphere, but his main interest was in building a new ancestral line. After the *coup d'Etat* of 1457,[7] Yingzong turned out to be an

[6] The two reign periods Zhentong 正統 and Tianshun, with the Jingtai period in between, were put together in one group of *Veritable Records* comprising 361 chapters from 1435 to 1465. Cf. Franke, *op. cit.*, p. 31.

[7] The *coup d'Etat* in 1457 which brought Yingzong back to his throne is called

emperor-despot in the true sense. Three palace guard commanders competed for influence, the Secretariat managed to hold its place, and eunuch power was somewhat subdued after the debacle of 1449, for which Wang Zhen, still leading eunuch, was held responsible. Indeed, it was his dominant influence which in the end led to his death (probably in a brawl following the Mongol onslaught on the imperial convoy), and this power was based on two factors: the young emperor's unimpaired trust down to the bitter end and beyond (he later had him rehabilitated posthumously), and close connections with one or the other commander of the Embroidered-uniform Guard. In other words, his position rested on political power borrowed from above (from the emperor-despot), which was institutionally backed by the centralized autocracy created by the dynastic founder, and military power from below (including police and judicial competences), based on an understanding with the Guard commanders.

Nevertheless, this constellation of forces did not deteriorate into a simple dictatorship of the chief eunuch. At no time did the emperor-despot, with his ritual and family background, lose his primary decision-making power, which overrode any other possible one. Neither the eunuch nor his friend, the commander of the Guard, could or would curb the imperial power. The uppermost limit to the exercise of authority by someone outside the imperial family involved acting in complete agreement with the emperor. This could ensure high honours, since he was the favourite of the Son of Heaven. But the very moment this status was impaired, the emperor's partner in such an alliance was lost. In the case of gentry-bureaucrats he would be dismissed or banished (hardly ever executed). Eunuch-bureaucrats were often treated more harshly, almost according to the rule: the closer the connection, the bitterer the separation. To sum up: in this four-party power game, the gentry-bureaucrats had so far been the weakest, although they represented the stablest and therefore most important segment of China's traditional society; the emperor with his ritualized legitimacy was by far the strongest (in spite of his belonging to the "weak" emperors of this dynasty); the power of eunuch-bureaucrats and Palace Guard commanders was a function of his, the position of the Guard being once again slightly below that of the eunuchs.

III. WHAT DO WE MEAN BY BUREAUCRATIC POWER?

Any large power structure must be based on written materials. Means of

duomen 奪門 ("to force the Palace gate") thereby naming the period. Yu Qian 于謙, the defender and saviour of Beijing in 1449-50, was killed during the incident.

communication are necessary whenever orders are to be promulgated, or proclamations made known which must have gone through a process of suggestion, acceptance, deliberation, and formulation of the relevant text. The Ming bureaucracy did not depart from this general pattern. It could even be characterized as more detailed and more formalized, in a word, more clerical in its procedures than former bureaucracies on Chinese soil. The theme is evoked by a description of the Office of Transmission (*tongzheng si* 通政司)[8] which may be called a sort of "message centre" where all kinds of messages with a political import would be registered and transmitted to the competent government agency.

There is a great variety of types of document which need not be discussed here. But two types are relevant, as in Qing times: suggestions, addressed to the government (*diben* 題本), or memorials, addressed to the emperor (*zouben* 奏本).[9] The former were of a more general scope, and their authors were content that they should be handled by one of the government offices, usually one of the ministries or the military commissions. The latter, of greater urgency, were to be presented to the emperor at the very next morning audience, or even more immediately. The decision was reached by different methods. The usual one was by rescript proposal on a slip of paper called *tiaozhi* 條旨 ("decree in sections") or *piaoyi* 票擬 ("warrant to determine") which was handled between the secretariat and the emperor. Otherwise, ministerial discussions or court deliberations could be convoked by the throne. The rescript proposal was written in black ink and sent to the emperor (usually the eunuch secretary who was in charge of the vermilion ink) for endorsement. The *Veritable Records* (*shilu* 實錄) registered such rescripts with the formula "To be followed" (*zongzhi* 從之).

By this differentiated use of black and red (vermilion) ink the two clerical staffs within the palace, the Grand Secretariat (or Inner Cabinet, *neige* 內閣) and the Inner Directorates (*neijian* 內監), were set apart as power of initiative (the secretaries), and power of decision (the eunuchs), the latter, of course, acting always on behalf of, or even with the direct participation of the emperor. Both had separate headquarters in the palace, one, the *neige*, outside the Wenhua Men 文華門, and one, the eunuch yamen, inside the palace apartments. Both staffs had also clerks similar in number and function. The Cabinet staff was made up of so-called "clerks for the Central Secretariat" (*zhongshu*

---

[8] Charles O. Hucker, "Governmental Organization of the Ming Dynasty," in J. L. Bishop (ed.), *Studies of Governmental Institutions in Chinese History* (Cambridge, Mass.: Harvard University Press, 1968), pp. 59-124. See also *Daxue yanyi bu* 大學衍義補 (*Supplement to commentaries to the Great Learning*), ed. Qiu Jun 邱濬 (1420-95).

[9] Cf. chapter 76 in *Collected Statutes of the Great Ming* (228 *juan* edition).

sheren 中書舍人),[10] the Directorate staff was made up of eunuch secretaries in the "document bureau" (*wenshu fang* 文書房). The clerks of the secretariat often came from eminent families of high officials; the Directorate clerks were selected from among the bright students of the palace eunuch school (*neishutang*, founded 1429). Apart from location and bureaucratic competence, the two were distinguished by their degree of closeness to the emperor-despot. The one who was more *"nei"* (inside) could wield his influence more effectively. This closeness also implied a certain degree of informality, which sustained political influence and power. Discussions about certain matters were therefore often held in the emperor's private quarters, in many cases deep in the night.

But in the last analysis the fine bureaucratic line of division between the two agencies (Grand Secretariat and eunuch Directorates) close to the emperor was in fact the line of a deep rift. The secretaries and their clerks were only the top of an iceberg representing the large bureaucratic hierarchy extending through all offices in the capital, and outside in the provinces. The term "gentry-bureaucrats" is therefore used for this group. The eunuchs, for their part, lived and worked inside the palace precincts, but also in the imperial villas (*huang zhuang* 皇莊), the princely households, and in some top rank military or economic agencies and commissions. The gentry-bureaucrats represented so to speak the bureaucratic faction, the eunuchs the imperial faction. The former felt themselves responsible more to the empire and to the population as a whole; the latter felt themselves responsible to the emperor-despot. The gentry-bureaucrats could live on their own in their clans and families. The eunuchs as individuals were totally dependent on their imperial patron; socially weak, they could exert a maximum of political strength.

Within the gentry-bureaucracy one may notice a certain antagonism between the staff of the palace secretariat and the ministerial staff outside the palace. The former came from the top list of successful examination candidates, passed through the ranks of the Hanlin academy 翰林院 (which, though located in the outer court, had the role of collaborating closely with the Inner Cabinet), and reached the ranks of grand secretaries after a couple of years. The term "cabinet elders" (*ge-lao* 閣老) was fitting for them. The ministers and their vice-ministers came from administrative experience in the regions and in the ministerial sphere; they would look askance at these "central secretaries" and try to bypass the cabinet elders, working if possible with the emperor (and his eunuchs) directly. Such was the case during the Hongzhi reign (1487-1505) and later during the early Jiajing 嘉靖 years (from 1522).

[10] An old title dating as far back as the Wei 魏 dynasty (220-265); in Ming times secretaries of the *zhongshusheng* 中書省 (Central Secretariat), thereafter the Grand Secretariat or *neige.*

Such a division of powers with strong and competent ministers would be regarded as a good style of government. Long terms in office of ministers were considered as marking periods of stability.

IV. DESCRIPTIVE ASSESSMENT OF THE FOUR FORCES EXERCISING SUPREME AUTHORITY

The emperor-despot was created by an arbitrary action on the part of the Hongwu emperor and dynastic founder who, in what is thought to have been a power struggle with his chancellor (and former protegé) on largely trumped up charges, had him killed and the Central Secretariat (*zhongshusheng* 中書省) abolished altogether "to safeguard against future abuse of his authority,"[11] a measure which remained in effect for the rest of the dynasty's history. The dual chief government agencies of Song times (the Board of Academicians and the Board of Military Affairs) were dispersed into the Six Ministries (dating from Tang times) and five Chief Military Commissions. Power was thereby effectively diversified, and there remained only one person, male, of paternal descent, Son of Heaven, autocrat, source of all power within the empire, surrounded by a palace staff of various origins and grades. His honorific names encompass the wealth of Chinese evaluations of exalted persons. To take just one example, Yingzong (Zhengtong 正統 and Tianshun reigns) was characterized as follows: "Exemplifying Heaven and establishing the Way, benevolent, clear, sincere, reverent, bright in culture and lawful in war, of highest virtue and extensive filial piety, the sagacious emperor (法天立道仁明誠敬昭文憲武至德廣孝睿皇帝)." These seventeen characters to which we may add the first term "eminent" (*ying* 英), encompass the field of ritual pathos with its heavenly and earthbound rhetoric. The Ming emperor was in fact Son of Heaven and political despot at the same time. His ritual and government duties constituted a "full time job," and for the successful implementation of decisions he depended more than anything else on competent ministers and counsellors.

To this extent, Chinese administration was predominantly one of personnel. Wu Han in his biography of Zhu Yuanzhang remarked that from Tang times onward the style of government work and of imperial behaviour had changed. High officials used to sit with the emperor during the Tang; they stood in front of the sitting emperor during the Song; and they had to prostrate themselves and kneel in front of the emperor during Ming and Qing.[12] This, at

[11] Cf. chapter III in E. L. Farmer, *Early Ming Government: The Evolution of Dual Capitals* (London, 1976), esp. p. 81; see also Wu Han 吳晗, *Zhu Yuanzhang zhuan* 朱元璋傳 (Hong Kong, 1948), pp. 160ff.

[12] Wu Han, *op. cit.*

least to a certain extent, defines the court style in Ming China.

Public beating of officials was another feature of despotic rule, as was wanton arrest or even killing in the prison of the palace guard. The wealth of power Zhu Yuanzhang had left to his descendants was a steady source for the highhanded use of power as the emperor-despot deemed fit. And yet, with two exceptions (Chengzu 成祖 in 1402 and Yingzong in 1457), there was no usurpation of the throne (in spite of two misguided attempts) and no tyrannicide.[13] The will of the emperor was respected. His person was so-to-speak sacrosanct. His ritual position between heaven and earth as bearer of the heavenly mandate instilled in his subjects' minds a readiness to accept his decisions as fate, and palace guard officers carried them out as if they were the rightful executors of fate.

The palace eunuchs, to proceed to the next political force in Ming China, belong to an age-old tradition. Already during the Warring States period (481-221 B.C.) eunuchs meddled in politics, and during the later Han and Tang, especially, the political influence of the eunuchs was strong. In number and influence, Ming eunuchs seem to have surpassed all others, and this in spite of the dynastic founder's strict prohibition on their participation in politics. "Eunuchs are not allowed to intervene in political affairs, interveners will be beheaded," read the text of an iron board in front of the main gate of the palace halls.[14] Wang Zhen, whose role is discussed above in Section II had it torn down as soon as he felt powerful enough. The main reason for the eunuchs' growing influence in Ming times was the altered policy of the Yongle emperor (and his descendants) who welcomed eunuchs to his camp when they fled Nanjing because of an even stricter anti-eunuch policy under the Jianwen emperor. It was he, Zhu Di 朱棣, the Yongle emperor, who started to entrust important assignments to eunuchs, the best known being the Moslem and admiral Zheng He 鄭和 (of probable Mongol-Arab origin, lived 1371-1433). These early eunuchs were often used in foreign policy: they were sent as imperial envoys to various relatively important "tributary" states. Some of them, however, became governors in Northwest China or in Annam, while others were included in military staffs. Furthermore, the great grandson of the dynastic founder, the Xuande emperor, cancelled his ancestor's second law prohibiting the schooling of eunuchs by founding a special school for them within the palace precincts (the *neishutang*), where a grand secretary taught and trained them. Thus they became familiar with letters, versed in history, and clever enough to countenance the transformation of a prince into

[13] The probable elimination of the Jianwen 建文 emperor (r. 1398-1402) may be taken as the one exception.

[14] See *Mingshi*, ch. 304 (eunuchs i); cf. also *Mingshi jishi benmo*, ch. 28 "Wang Zhen yong shi" 王振用事 ("Wang Zhen usurps power"), year 1442.

a villain.[15] This retrospective judgment is biased, to be sure, as is the sentence according to which there was one useful eunuch for a hundred baleful ones.[16] The emperor-despot made them, and no one would ever be as loyal to the emperor as these persons who had changed their very lives in order to serve him. Their closeness to their patron, the sole source of awe-inspiring power, established theirs. One or the other among the emperor-despots may have preferred the counsel of outsiders such as ministers or high commanders, but in the long run insiders would eventually prevail. A grand secretary could be among them. There were times when grand secretaries even prevailed in the imperial council for a long time. But the eunuchs never vanished. Within and around the palace there existed a whole hierarchy, with thousands of retainers in the service of the "exalted one" (shang 上). They could have luxurious premises with male and female servants. They used to live in a kind of imitation family, and sometimes palace women were even formally married to them, they adopted children or took over nephews and nieces and tried to promote their careers or status. The eunuchs, and above all the high-ranking eunuchs, formed an important channel of social mobility in Ming times. Former prisoners-of-war or slaves belonging to national minorities could become eunuch directors, generals, or high commissioners, and thereby influence court policy. Even serving imperial princes in their provincial households could provide a career. Looked at from outside, emperor and eunuchs seemed to form a single whole. In fact, the body of palace eunuchs was an enduring and reliable instrument in the emperor-despot's hands.

The learned imperial secretaries with their new title of grand secretary (da xueshi 大學士) linked to one or the other imperial audience hall, were first installed after the founder abolished the Central Secretariat, as noted above. They formed the third political force in Ming China's leadership as a whole. Apart from the Six Ministries and the Five Chief Military Commissions, the secretaries were selected to give informal and direct counsel to the one central figure of the régime. For this purpose, learned men with a long-standing experience in Confucian doctrine and literary studies were chosen. In the case of the three Yang secretaries, the Secretariat inaugurated a literary style that was imitated among the literati, the so-called "style of the Secretariat," which was superseded only around 1500. The grand secretaries' rank was mediocre at first (rank five); only after 1425 was their rank elevated so as to equal that of the ministers or even surpass them. But even this could not compare with the former Central Chancellery. The new grand secretaries were technically

[15] Cf. *Mingshi*, ch. 168, under Liu Ji 劉吉. The whole passage reads: "In that time, there was a slander against the three paste and paper cabinet elders, and the six ministers modelled in mud and clay."
[16] *Mingshi*, ch. 304.

equal among themselves. Each of them could give counsel, draft an imperial rescript, or advise on ritual affairs. As a rule, however, one of them would also take responsibility for the drafts written. The start of this career was characterized as "to enter the palace library" (*ru wenyuange* 入文淵閣) and "handle important matters" (*canyu jiwu* 參與機務), thereby expressing the direct counterposition to what the eunuchs at first were held to do, or rather not to do, namely "intervene in political affairs." The grand secretaries occupied an important position at court, they prepared the morning audiences, they used to stand directly at the left side of the throne, they would have the first say in suggesting solutions for particular problems or names of ministers who should deal with them, etc. A few dominant figures among them, especially after the year 1500, may have held a position almost equivalent to that of a prime minister. Otherwise, however, the political rank of the grand secretaries depended entirely on the emperor-despot's personal wishes. Since he often left them alone, sometimes even for years (as in the 1480s) the secretaries were called the "paste and paper cabinet elders."[17] In such periods the necessary day-to-day informal contact with the emperor definitely passed to the leading eunuch directors, while the secretaries sat at their table and drafted rescripts. Only after Liu Jin's fall, discussed below, did the Secretariat develop something of a stable and influential position. The Jiajing emperor did not like to work with or through eunuchs, so their influence receded for about half a century.

The Embroidered-uniform Guard belonged to the eight metropolitan brigades called "personal troops" (*qin jun* 親軍) who were under the command not of the Chief Military Commissions but of the emperor personally. In their case, the role of the minister of war was limited to supervising the keeping of the necessary documentary records. The Guard was founded in the same year the imperial secretaries were established, in 1382. The guards served the emperor by providing personal protection; they also assumed duties in all ceremonial affairs, and acted as a special police under the guidance of leading eunuchs. The Guard's special court (*zhenfu si* 鎮撫司) which originally dispensed military justice, served as a special prison for political offenders. Familiarly named the "decree prison" (*zhao yu* 詔獄) it became one of the institutions most frightening to the bureaucracy of Ming China. Thus a military unit, the *jinyiwei*, serving purposes mostly of internal politics, could easily become a fearsome police instrument in the hands of the emperor-despot and his authorized agents, sometimes coming close to modern instruments of terror.

On the other hand, this highly efficient and powerful institution in the central sphere also attracted ambitious young men anxious to make a career.

[17]See n. 15.

In this way the Embroidered-uniform Guard became another major channel of mobility in the society of Ming China. (To this, and to the eunuchs already mentioned, one may add the Ministry of Works.[18]) Sons and relatives of families close to the emperor and his clan, to high eunuchs, to renowned military leaders and other prominent persons would often establish their social standing through an officer's career in the Embroidered-uniform Guard,[19] even if it was a titular patent only.

Guard officers were not controlled by the Ministry of Personnel; their career data were kept in the War Ministry. The half dozen staff commanders had the privilege of memorializing to the emperor directly. Officers were entitled to have their personal runners (often corvée men) who could act as spies, as secret couriers, even as police in arresting people. The ranks of the guard were made up of soldiers (from military families), strong fellows (*li shi* 力士), constables (*xiao wei* 校尉), and pretorians (*jiang jun* 將軍), the latter comprising some 1,500 persons for the special duty of protecting the emperor. Centurions, chiliarchs, and the commanding staff made up the commissioned officers' corps. Some 2,000 cadets, many thousands of craftsmen, and up to 10,000 "surplus men" (*yu ding* 餘丁) belonged to the Guard. A specialist's estimate for the Guard's strength arrives at a minimum of 16,000 (for the first decades), and a maximum of 75,000 (in later periods); between 40,000 and 45,000 may be the reasonable average for mid-Ming. If we include also the craftsmen, the surplus men, and the cadets, the maximum may have been over 120,000 men.[20]

Political power was in the hands of the Guard commanders. But it did happen now and again that the emperor chose his own trusted person and moved him up to the commanding level. The main power instrument was undoubtedly the "decree prison"; no regulations of criminal procedure could protect persons who had provoked the emperor's wrath (or that of his agents). On the other hand, this was no institution for carrying out clandestine assassination, but rather a prison for investigating under so-called "special treatment." Death did ensue in some cases, but the responsible commander who was notorious for such treatment risked his own head. Of ten noted Guard commanders from Yongle to Tianshun times only two died in office, three were executed, two were killed in other ways, and three were banished. In the end, it was always the imperial person himself who would decide his subject's fate.

[18]Cf. Heinz Friese, "Zum Aufstieg von Handwerkern ins Beamtentum während der Ming-Zeit," *Oriens Extremus* VI (1959), pp. 161-72.

[19]Even Wang Shouren 王守仁, a famous high official from a gentry family was honoured with a Guard command for his son. Cf. *Dictionary of Ming Biography*, p. 1412.

[20]Peter Greiner, *Die Brokatuniform-Brigade (chin-i-wei) der Ming-Zeit von den Anfängen bis zum Ende der T'ien-shun-Periode (1368-1464)* (Wiesbaden, 1975), pp. 129ff.

The Ming history includes two exemplary biographies of *jinyiwei* commanders. These appear in chapter 307 ("deceitful adventure hunters," *ning xing* 佞倖) with overtones of treachery and evilmindedness. Ji Gang 紀綱 (executed 1416) became the gruesome example of all the negative aspects of Ming despotism. Men Da門達, the other type, belonged to the masters of the secret police who would almost irresistibly fall victim to the corruption and struggles for power which permeated court politics. Two other Guard commanders are included, without adding new dimensions to the institution. All of them, however, reflect the despotic nature of the Ming throne and the temptations of centralized power which went with it.

Some further comments should be added to the two foregoing sections. Bureaucratic power is usually thought to be the essence of state activity; indeed, it is sometimes considered to be identical with it. This must be qualified in one way or another. In contrast to the idea of the "*polis*," which leads to our concept of politics, one of the basic Chinese ideas is the distribution and maintaining of orders. The leading administrative figure in the provinces under the Ming was precisely so defined: "commissioner for distributing matters of order" (*buzhengshi* 布政使). The two related offices were the controlling and judicial, as well as the regional military authorities. Also, the function of the provincial governor (*xunfu* 巡撫) is based on the idea of pacifying the populace wherever he came along, until this was later condensed into a genuine governor's yamen.[21] This office was later superseded by a so-called "comprehensive supervisorship" (*zongdu* 總督) which became a fixed institution in Qing times called "governor-general" in Western sources. Local agents of public order, furthermore, were the administrative heads of the prefecture, the sub-prefecture, and the district. The Chinese idea of their function was "the one who administers a certain regional unit by a set of knowledge and experiences derived therefrom." The lowest of these officials was even called "father and mother of the people," a social and moral idea, perhaps, but not a political or judicial one. The basic social order in China's vast agrarian world was maintained by appropriate measures on the spot within the horizons of the village and market town. In other words, while the concept of law and order characterized the West, with its central emphasis on the role of the law (implemented whatever way), the Chinese concept of order is consistently one of tax and tributes. Highly organized as the Chinese administration may have been with its command structure and elaborate

[21] See C. O. Hucker, "Governmental Organization of the Ming dynasty," *Harvard Journal of Asiatic Studies*, Vol. 21 (1958), pp. 39f., who writes: "Beginning in 1430, the sending of metropolitan dignitaries on . . . temporary commissions fell into a stable pattern." Such "Touring Pacifiers" with long tenure may, he suggests, be called "Grand Coordinators."

clerical work, it is doubtful whether any idea of the state, as defined within secure borders and legitimized by legal norms, underlay this traditional reality.

The other qualifying remark to be made regarding patterns of rule in Ming China has to do with the power syndrome as such. The emperor-despot, his secretaries, eunuchs, and Guard commanders (backed by a strong Beijing garrison) converge to form a strongly dominant central power. But the Han and Tang emperors, not to forget those of the northern and southern Song, were all in possession of effective means to exercise their own power and curb that of others. One has to be cautious in assessing Ming despotism. There was indeed a gruesome reality, but did it exist throughout the whole of the dynasty? How far did it radiate into the provinces horizontally, and how far vertically into China's agrarian world? The capital city may have felt much of what the sources convey, and the arbitrary way in which the instruments of power were used may have contributed to an atmosphere of fear and insecurity, but, once again, this was not an altogether exceptional case in world history. A highly centralized system such as this perhaps tends to a weakening of "human rights." Yet, many values were not affected. Filial piety, loyalty, conjugal and brotherly solidarity, as well as friendship between people of the same age and between elder and younger, teacher and disciple, lived on further into later centuries. In this respect, there was no need for a state as a framework for social order, and it seemed as if traditional China could do without it.

V. TWO MORE CASES

While the case of Wang Zhen was the first in Ming history and contained features of real drama, with a tragic end of its protagonist and his posthumous rehabilitation, the second among these three cases represents a "mature" situation: the eunuch bureaucracy in full vigour, the Grand Secretariat separately organized (though utterly powerless) as a bureau for imperial orders (zhichi fang 製敕房), and for letters patent (gaochi fang 誥敕房) in the literary pavilion or library (wenyuange 文淵閣); the Guard commanders under the Tianshun reign executing whatever their imperial master's distrust dictated; and an intelligence service which perhaps never drew its net so tight as under Men Da's and Lu Gao's 逯杲 guidance.

In this case the cast was somewhat more complicated. There was first the emperor with his favourite consort Wan 萬 (1430-87) dominating the court in the years between 1464 and 1475, and the palace household (after 1476). Secondly, there was a eunuch clique led by a director of the Directorate of Imperial Utensils (yuyong jian 御用監) named Liang Fang 梁芳, running a trading company of national and international dimensions (through the tribute trade), with Taoist and Buddhist adherents, and in collaboration with the consort Wan. There was, thirdly, a joint clique comprising the chief intelligence officer (in charge of the so-called Western Depot) who became a general later on, namely Wang Zhi 汪直, together with certain military leaders of northern origin. Fourthly, there was a somewhat powerless Grand Secretariat with a Sichuanese who came from ministerial service, Wan An 萬安 as its senior figure. Finally, there was the Guard under the dominant influence of two eunuchs, Wang Zhi between 1477 and 1482, and a certain Shang Ming 尚銘 before and after.

The Chenghua 成化 period, 1464-87, followed the unhappy periods of emperor Yingzong, and started with a relatively sober and stable political trend which saw control of the northern border reestablished and the empire pacified within the fifteen provinces. At court, the favourite consort Wan, seventeen years older than her imperial mate, dominated the scene, but not so much externally as inside the palace walls. It is interesting to note that her loss of influence within the court led to a new economic interest outside. Under conditions of economic growth and expansion, including an increase in the money supply, predominantly in silver, the court should have been able to afford a luxurious life. But the resources turned out to be insufficient, as a result of a certain period of recession thus far difficult to explain. In these circumstances, the consort Wan collaborated with eunuch director Liang Fang, and three of his agents, of whom one became provincial supervisor with the title of grand defender (*zhenshou* 鎮守) in Yünnan, one port inspector, and the third collector of silver and valuables in southern China. They built up something like a trade emporium, with precious stones, luxury goods, and other valuables which were partially sold on the Beijing market to bolster up court finances. Another device was the so-called "transmitted service patent" (*chuan feng* 傳奉), by which a eunuch transmitted a (possibly sanctioned) imperial order to the letters patent office of the Grand Secretariat to establish a new office or effect a promotion. No Ministry, Censorate, or other office outside was in the know. The recipient would express his gratitude by selling something valuable for a low price, or vice versa. Last but not least, the land holdings of the imperial family are said to have comprised no less than 2.3 million acres by the year 1500. And yet, expenses at court were so high as to consume all these resources. Expensive undertakings in the fields of alchemy and aphrodisiacs, as well as the swelling numbers of Taoist and Buddhist priests, exempt from taxes and provided with free maintenance, the building of new temples, and other expenditures for court luxury, defeated all efforts to fix a budget for the imperial household.

The Chenghua period may be divided into two halves, one until the mid-seventies, and one after that. The first is commonly regarded as balanced, the second may be judged erratic. Wang Zhi's dominance over court and capital came together with certain economic activities of the Liang/Wan "consortium," and this again went with a growing influence of representatives of various religions at court. A magician named Li Zisheng 李子省 was able to satisfy the emperor's interest in magic arts; he was therefore promoted to be chief of the Court of Imperial Sacrifices (*taichangsi* 太常寺), and later director of imperial parks. But the emperor had also elevated a craftsman to a palace function, apparently out of esteem for his competence. The sources tell us of a combination of eunuch (Liang Fang) and favourite (Li Zisheng) meddling in the politics of personnel. While the latter was promoted to vice transmission commissioner, hundreds of adherents of quite different backgrounds were given rank and promoted. Their influence in court and outside persisted until the next emperor ascended the throne. This turn of events (1487) brought down some 1,500 people, among them more than 400 Buddhist practitioners, about 800 Lamaist priests, some 120 Chinese Buddhists, and another group of 120 Taoist magicians. One leading Buddhist, Ji Xiao 繼曉, was promoted "master of state" (*guoshi* 國師). A temple constructed at his instigation and at the usual high cost, required the removal of many private homes.

It seems virtually certain that such information has been included in the official history by the gentry-bureaucrats as proof of "bad times." When eunuchs, favourites, and parvenus held sway, the empire must, in their view, have been in danger. Even the emperor is tacitly criticized by accusing his entourage. And yet, although the eunuchs never lost the stigma of illegitimate political interlopers, notwithstanding their being the emperor's agents, they brought in somewhat unorthodox methods for activating the economy in mining and metallurgy, in the crafts of weapon-making, and other fields. With this went a general enlivening and diversifying of China's economy. Interest in, and the promotion of, economic and religious endeavour of a nonconformist kind can in this case be interpreted as a new trend in otherwise "Confucian" China. The court atmosphere in Chenghua times may thus be seen in another light than that cast on it by Confucian historiographers. Further research is certainly required.

The next case to be discussed is characterized by an apex of court domination. Since this essay is not a contribution to the study of Chinese economic development, but an attempt to understand problems of the Chinese state, what is at stake is the central imperial power and how it functioned over time. After the Hongzhi reign (1487-1505) which is hailed in our sources as a spectacularly good reign, simply because the gentry-bureaucrats were at the helm, and eunuch-bureaucrats kept at bay, a new reign followed with the euphemistic reign title "Correct Virtue" (Zhengde 正德).

While the Hongzhi emperor had displayed some good points, by gathering to-gether the administrative competence of five or six seasoned civil officials and taking their advice, his successor apparently lacked any interest in politics. Re-cent research appears to reveal the image of an emperor-despot who looked askance at his imperial heritage. This included Confucianism, which he held in disdain. His grandfather, the Chenghua emperor, had developed a serious interest in non-Confucian religions, Taoism and Buddhism equally, but the grandson seems to have had a nihilistic point of view. His only interest was apparently in amusement and drama in various forms. He also seems to have developed a fantastic heroic image of himself, to which he sought to give substance by warlike excursions to the frontier or, later, to South China. Perhaps his ancestor, the Yongle emperor, was his model. The judgment on this emperor-despot (and he was a despot just the same) is uncertain. To put it in strong terms, was he a maniac or a tragic genius?

These personal traits set the context of one of the most vivid power struggles in mid-Ming times, with a eunuch director as main figure. The story comprises an exceptional dramatis personae including (*a*) a gifted eunuch-bureaucrat named Liu Jin 劉瑾 who must have castrated himself as a boy;[22] (*b*) a eunuch faction of eight persons (including Liu) surrounding the emperor (called the "eight tigers") who derived their influence and power from their closeness to their patron and their willingness to amuse him as best they could;[23] (*c*) a group of elder eunuchs who were sceptical or downright inimical towards the dominant influence of the Liu Jin clique, such as Li Rong 李榮, Zhang Yong 張永, and others; (*d*) a gentry-bureaucrat faction combining individuals from the Secretariat, from the ministerial offices, and from among the censors who bitterly fought against Liu's dictatorial power; and (*e*) a group of civil and military officials who followed and collaborated with Liu Jin (Jiao Fang 焦芳, Liu Yu 劉宇, and others).

Liu Jin, first among the "eight tigers," started as a sort of *maître de plaisir* for the emperor in the so-called "leopard house." He was not a teacher, as Wang Zhen had been to his boy-emperor, but he was the one who served him most zealously. The gentry-bureaucrats' resistance to the degradation of the state (which they manifestly saw themselves as representing) was plainly in evidence at court. Liu Jin had the audacity to ask for the post of eunuch director of ceremonial, from which the resistance could be best fought and overcome. He thus controlled the imperial landholdings and, above all, the Beijing Training Divisions, the most effective military unit in and around the

[22] See *Dictionary of Ming Biography*, p. 942, the entry on Liu Jin: "Like many eunuchs of his time, Liu as a youth had submitted himself to castration."

[23] *Ibid*. Cf. also *Wuzong shilu* 武宗實錄 31.778ff. and 41.960.

capital. His internal power was implemented through the Depot for Conduct and Ways in the Internal Apartments (*neixing chang* 內行廠), an office to control the two notorious intelligence agencies, the Eastern and the Western Depots; he also controlled the various categories of palace women. His well-developed capacity for handling political business made him master of the government machine. He is said to have been a sharp talker, although his formal education was insignificant. He must none the less have had some skill in the documentary style, and some training in political history as well. He received and dealt with the daily incoming documents. Formally, he did ask his emperor-patron to offer his opinion on reports and memoranda, but the emperor is said to have often replied that he should leave him alone and get the boring business done in his name. With this authority, Liu Jin started to build up his power. At first, he was anxious to get other officials' consent and collaboration. But since he was ambitious and conceited, he was inclined to get those who criticized him demoted, banished, or put in jail. Some of them were beaten to death. By such methods he was able to form a power clique helping him exercise authority. To the group of his supporters belonged, among some less well-known henchmen, a high official like Jiao Fang (1436-1517), grand secretary 1506-10, a northerner like himself, a censor and coordinator along the northern border (Liu Yu) who became minister of personnel, and another minister and member of the Secretariat named Cao Yuan 曹元 who controlled military affairs. With such collaborators, Liu Jin managed to carry out a thorough change of personnel, ousting important gentry-bureaucrats, and conferring new letters patent on more than 1,500 people and several hundred palace guard officers. Three of his friends held ministerial posts (Personnel, War, and Works) and controlled the *neige* at the same time. He promoted a national minority leader to become surveillance commissioner in Sichuan. He saw to it that craftsmen could enter the ladder of success in Ming bureaucracy. He endeavoured to change administrative usages, as they related to 24 items in the sphere of personnel, 30 items in the field of revenue, 18 in the sphere of war, and 30 in the sphere of works.[24] A new man with a new style, Liu Jin aroused considerable interest in his time and later, because he achieved a genuine change in the power centre: his rescripts, which his henchmen drafted and Jiao Fang put into elegant style, went directly to the ministers, as if he were acting emperor or a sort of new chancellor. So far, eunuch power had been exercised through the person of the emperor, but now, although during a comparatively short period (about three and a half years), the palace lay so-to-speak in the shadow of an emperor in voluntary eclipse.

[24] See *Dictionary of Ming Biography*, p. 944. Cf. also vol. 64 of *Wuzong shilu*.

It seems that it was Liu Jin's informal way of dealing with political matters that beguiled some of the gentry-bureaucrats. For the rest, his dominance was apparently the result of sheer fright inspired by brute force. Liu Jin had political talent, he knew the border problems well, he urged stricter control of the salt gabelle, and he had a sense of central authority as such. His trusted fellow-eunuchs held many of the "grand defender" posts (military and political supervisors of the provinces, but not actual governors), and the lucrative maritime trade superintendencies in Quanzhou 泉州, Mingzhou 明州, and Guangzhou 廣州. He went some lengths to put in order the law regarding inheritance of military offices, and interestingly enough, his proposals in this domain were partially kept after his execution.[25] Liu Jin even thought of carrying out a sort of cultural revolution by having widows remarry, and by burning corpses instead of the usual costly burials.[26] Apparently, there was no overall concept, no integrated plan of reform, but what did the renowned Hongzhi ministers do except economize? The *Shilu* recorders called his proposals *bianfa* 變法, possibly in an ironic tone, and they were kept in the text, although after Liu Jin's execution decrees were adopted making them null and void.[27]

This is the first and perhaps a unique case of a eunuch powerholder attempting something like positive political action. The furious opposition on the part of the gentry-bureaucrats underscores the fact that such things were not all trifles. Most of the fury was clearly aroused by new methods of handling personnel. As things developed, the constant threats of cruelty and merciless repression eventually inhibited the broader collaboration he would have needed in order to succeed. So, when his downfall was brought about (in September 1510), in particular by some of his fellow-eunuchs, there seems to have been a sentiment of "back to normal" accompanied by a great sigh of relief. It would certainly be going too far to compare these small and practical attempts with other reform measures in China's history, yet it seems that the sole fact of being "only" a eunuch put him outside the pale of any legitimate comparison as far as Chinese historians were concerned. He was bound in the fetters of Ming bureaucratic society, and at the same time remained outside. When he fell, he fell quickly, and the gentry-bureaucrats' revenge was prompt, after fellow-eunuchs had committed their part of treachery.

Let us sum up the main trend of events during the period discussed above. At first, there seems to be a certain trend of waxing eunuch power from Wang Zhen's time up to Liu Jin's period of "holding authority" (about 1440 to

---

[25] *Wuzong shilu* 68.1499.
[26] *Ibid.*, 41.958.
[27] *Ibid.*, 61.1476ff., 1481ff., 68.1499ff.

1510). The latter's power is documented as the most cruel, but also the most constructive during the seventy years considered here. The combination of eunuch power with that of the Palace Guard resembles former cases. But Liu Jin was more strongly allied with gentry-bureaucrats, whose real state of mind is not easily ascertained. Willy-nilly they must have collaborated—not only Jiao Fang, the grand secretary, Liu Yu, the minister of personnel, and Cao Yuan, the minister of war, but beyond them other bureaucrats and literati like the poet Kang Hai 康海 (1475-1541). A moment of instability cannot be overlooked. The emperor's extravagance and idiosyncrasies provoked tendencies towards usurpation of the throne, and two such attempts were made in 1510 and 1519.[28]

A second point in this context is the growing gentry-bureaucratic opposition. Already at the end of the Chenghua and beginning of the Hongzhi period (1487/88) we notice a determined anti-eunuch tendency. This was dramatized in 1506 when the two old grand secretaries Liu Jian 劉健 (1453-1526) and Xie Qian 謝遷 (1450-1531) were demoted and humiliated. This is conveyed historiographically by the two terms "lord and ministers during Hongzhi" emphasizing good government in Confucian terms, and "Liu Jin wielding power" (*yong shi* 用事), exemplifying illegitimate rule.[29] For the first time an anti-eunuch faction began to take shape. The ministers, as well as the grand secretaries in early Jiajing (from 1522), managed to weaken eunuch power and re-establish gentry-bureaucrat administration, because the new emperor did not like to work with eunuchs as his cousin and uncle had done. The late Ming factional strife between eunuch-director Wei Zhongxian 魏忠賢 and the Donglin 東林 party may have had its prelude in these affairs.[30]

A third point of interest is the unweakened state of emperor and empire in spite of disruptions during this time. The administrative structure remained stable. The armed forces were strong enough to keep border and provinces intact. The economic picture even looked hopeful, and rural unrest in some areas would never really shake the empire. Above all, the emperor retained overriding power, and used it whenever he thought necessary.

[28] Zhu Zhifan 朱寘鐇 in Ningxia 寧夏 launched a rebellion which was put down after eighteen days. See *Dictionary of Ming Biography*, p. 310; thereafter, the rebellion of Zhu Chenhao 朱宸濠 from Nanchang 南昌 was put down by Wang Shouren after forty days. See *ibid.*, p. 312.

[29] *Mingshi jishi benmo*, ch. 43.

[30] Cf. C. O. Hucker, "The Tung-lin Movement of the Late Ming Period," in J. K. Fairbank (ed.), *Chinese Thought and Institutions* (Chicago: University of Chicago Press, 1957), pp. 132-62; see also Heinrich Busch, "The Tung-lin Academy and Its Political and Philosophical Significance," *Monumenta Serica* XIV (1949-50), pp. 1-163.

VI. CONCLUSION

We seek to deal with the state in China. This contribution is based on a sceptical view of the Chinese state. Traditional power structures and the self-sustaining social order in village and urban life form a balance of socio-political and socio-cultural forces which can be understood in terms of social and cultural anthropology. The methods of historical-critical research, as developed in particular by A. J. Toynbee, and the Germans Dilthey, Meinecke, Gadamer, and others must also be applied. We call "despot" or "emperor-despot" what is named *huangdi* in Chinese—"the emperor"—from 221 B.C. onwards, and what is termed *shang* in Chinese—"the exalted one"—in the *Ming Veritable Records*, because the dynastic founder had set apart the occupant of the throne to be the sole fount of power, with no exceptions whatsoever. This led the Ming emperors to bring the Son of Heaven down into the muck of practical politics, and was perhaps one of the main structural reasons for what is often called Ming despotism.

Eunuchs and grand secretaries were those groups of bureaucrats who had direct access either to the imperial person or at least to the original documents pertaining to him. They derived from this a maximum of information, and a clear advantage in the process of communication, which was organized on a centralized basis around the highest decision-making organ in the very heart of the empire; the emperor, sitting in audience within the "great internal" (*da nei* 大內) the imperial palace. The consequence of this pattern was a steady competition for power and influence in which eunuchs usually took the lead, while the elderly secretaries saw themselves in the frustrating role of admonitor and pleader.

The institution of one sole fount of power lured ambitious members of the dynastic clan to vie for the throne. Thus a persistent instability, fed by conflicts over the imperial succession and by the weakness of one or another occupant of throne, was directly linked to the immanent problem of despotic power. The direct instrument of such power was the Embroidered-uniform Guard and its special prison. But the implementation of power always found institutional backing. Both the new Secretariat and the twenty-four eunuch Directorates, Offices and Bureaus which had been organized during the first six decades of Ming autocratic role (1380-1440), and were put to good use during the following seven (1440-1510), the period on which this essay focuses, guaranteed a certain bureaucratic "correctness," however much this might be manipulated. There is the problem of the institutional correlation between regional and central leadership in Ming China. The provinces did not yet have a provincial coordinator invested with power on a regular basis or a supreme commander as in Qing times. As yet, these institutions were still in the stage of development. The Ming government was more centralized (hence the many eunuchs!) and therefore also weaker than the Qing government, with its greater tendency towards decentralization in the exercise of power. The Ming picture shows a rather strong group of ministers, perhaps stronger than under the subsequent dynasty. A powerful instrument for consolidating central power in the throne was the Imperial Guard, which exercised quite unusual authority: in connection with the protection of the emperor's person, they could approximate the yamens, or even more modern organs of totalitarian suppression.[31]

Paramount in our analysis of mid-Ming government, and of the state in China during this period, is the problem of eunuchs, or more correctly of the eunuch-bureaucrats. Socially it is apparent that, irrespective of the moral and ritual problem of stepping out of the family chain, Chinese families in Ming times did vie for getting castrated sons into high positions in order to enhance their social and political status. Since the established gentry families would not usually have their sons castrated, trusting to their self-sustaining status, it would rather be the rising merchant, specialized craftsman or a member of the "managerial" class (to use a modern term) who tried to get connections in this way with higher circles around the throne. One should not overestimate this tendency, however, since a great number of eunuchs came from aborigines, criminals, prisoners-of-war, or favourites within the court sphere, and thus enjoyed only an individual parvenu status without a specific class background. It was not only the emperor who had his eunuch advisers, helpers, and servants. The princely households of which there were dozens, were also entitled to have a staff of eunuchs. By the end of the fifteenth century there were reported to be no less than 10,000 eunuchs in and around the palace precincts. Among these, of course, only a small fraction would belong to the group really exercising and sustaining power. The majority were servants and craftsmen, sometimes little more than slaves. Even in the military domain they were important, in the command structure of the Ming army, along the border, in the provinces, and in some trading ports.

This leads to the socio-political side of the problem. Through his castration the eunuch had skipped direct social contacts in the family context, although as already indicated the more powerful among them would build up a pseudo-family in various ways. Their enforced celibacy had the primary function of allowing them to serve the imperial or princely patron with even greater and more boundless loyalty. A eunuch could thus be more useful to the emperor-despot than any of the other officials, civilian, or military. The only other institution which could be trusted by the despot was his Guard. Not a few

[31] Greiner, *op. cit.*, pp. 142ff.

members of eunuch families entered it. There was a certain intermingling between eunuchs, Guard officers, favourites and other upstarts. The Ming court thereby encouraged a certain social mobility, which has not often been noted. In a more general sense, eunuchs tended to take over functions of a non-gentry kind such as commercial, technological, or managerial activities. Also, they would tend to develop a non-Confucian attitude towards life, and take up rather Taoist or Buddhist practices, which would find support in the imperial family. As a whole, eunuchs, by their specific type of existence, would be apt to contribute to achievements outside the social norm, and sometimes of an innovative kind. This had already been the case in Song times.[32]

The triangle consisting of the emperor-despot, with his eunuch-bureaucrats, the grand secretaries as representatives of the gentry-bureaucracy and the world of literati, and the Embroidered-uniform Guard, constitutes the central problem of this essay. One may reduce the triangle to the age-old juxtaposition of emperor versus his Confucian pleaders, power versus human or moral norms, but not legal ones. We have the judicial services to clarify certain conflicts in the shadow of the court; they convey the semblance of juridical regularity which is sometimes exercised, but this never came close to the idea of a state founded on the rule of law. Indeed, the "Chinese state," if we may use this term, is an organizational problem in the first instance, rather than an institutional one. Institutions are something more than offices and yamens from which power may emanate through the emperor's sanction. In traditional China, institutions belong to the ritual sphere, and thus reflect a socio-cultural or even socio-religious reality.

In order to qualify as a state, a regime must, in my opinion, have more than a power structure with certain executive agencies, and a certain number of bureaucratic procedures, and more too than a specific territory with armed forces to retaliate when "barbarians" happen to intrude. A state must be governed by fixed legal norms, which bind those who control it and those who depend on it alike. In late imperial China what we have is a system of precedent and social order which is controlled by district officials called "father and mother of the people," but enforced largely through the members of the local elite. The term *guan* 官, "official" and "office," is a vague form of defining and delimiting the "state."[33] In reality, the latter was torn by influence groups and power rifts and amounted to hardly more than a fluctuating sum of group conflicts which were held at bay more or less

---

[32]*Mingshi*, ch. 72, and *Songshi*, ch. 466 to ch. 469.
[33]In order to take the discussion of this problem further, the significance of "Legalism" has to be considered once again.

successfully. On top of all this, there were emanations of real political power, invested with a semblance of justice and shrouded in ritual liturgy of a very ancient descent usually called Confucianism. Below the *guan*, the district magistrate (*zhi xian* 知縣), there was society with its inbuilt economic and political pressures, as well as culture with its religious worship and festivities. Whether or not political power in such a system can be called a "state" remains a subject for discussion.

3. The Structure of the Financial Institutions of the State in the Late Qing

Marianne Bastid

It is well known how in various European countries the growth of the modern state corresponds to the development of the financial state, imposing itself on the judicial state and gradually crushing it with its weight. In contrast to such historical development on the European continent, the financial administration in China had from ancient times always been an essential aspect of the machinery and of the functions of the central power, linked to the economic responsibilities of the emperor. The Classics moreover transmitted an ideal of government corresponding to this practice. Indeed, accounts in the *Shu Jing* 書經 concerning Yu 禹 the Great illustrate the close and fundamental relationship between the economic intervention of the ruler and the establishment of a rather complex fiscal system as early as the mythical origins of the empire.[1]

It is also the case that the Chinese empire set up very early the institutions that form the basis of financial administration in modern Europe. Direct annual taxation, which only became common under European monarchies at the beginning of the sixteenth century, has been the rule in China from earliest times. A clear distinction between the public exchequer and the ruler's private wealth is already apparent in the *Zhouli* 周禮.[2] This distinction was not established in Europe until the thirteenth and fourteenth centuries, while in China it applied from the Qin to the Qing.[3] Furthermore, it has been shown that through the intermediary of Arab travellers and of the Norman kingdom of Sicily the financial administrations of modern European states borrowed part of their techniques from China.[4]

Thus at the end of the nineteenth century the administration of public finances in the Chinese empire was deeply rooted in a tradition by which, for

[1] *Chou King*, trans. S. Couvreur (Sien Hsien: Imprimerie de la mission catholique, 1935), pp. 35, 86.

[2] *Le Tcheou-li ou rites des Tcheou*, trans. E. Biot (Paris: Imprimerie nationale, 1851), Vol. I, pp. 22, 27-32, 75, 84-86, 121-136.

[3] Philip Y. K. Fu, *A Study of Governmental Accounting in China: With Special Reference to the Sung Dynasty (960-1279)* (Ann Arbor: University Microfilms, 1968), pp. 77, 83, 92, 163. The distinction was, however, abolished for a period under the Tang.

[4] H. G. Creel, *The Origins of Statecraft in China*, Vol. I: *The Western Chou Empire* (Chicago: The University of Chicago Press, 1970), pp. 12-17.

more than two thousand years, it had always constituted an integral part of the state system. The period from the suppression of the Taiping Rebellion to the great administrative reform of 1906 constitutes the last stage of development of the imperial state. How was the financial administration of the empire organized then? How did it function and what were its importance and role in the state machinery? Did it appear as a major pole for the development of state power? Such are the points to be discussed here, while purely financial matters and the question of the relationship between public finance and the general economy of the empire are left aside, since these relate rather to the action of the state than to its structure.

I. THE STRUCTURE OF FINANCIAL INSTITUTIONS: AN UNEVENLY SPECIALIZED HIERARCHY

At the close of the nineteenth century there no more existed than in earlier times a separate, specialized administration responsible for the overall management of public finance from the central to the local levels. In financial matters, the only specialized departments and offices were to be found above prefectural level, in the shape of grain, salt and customs intendants, superintendants of the salt trade, provincial treasurers, and the Board of Revenue. At the top, moreover, such specialization was not very strict. Indeed, the Board of Revenue (*hubu* 戶部) has functions not directly related to financial management, such as hearing appeals for certain civil cases. Moreover, the role of the Board of Revenue in matters of trade regulation, forestry protection and sericulture, or even in organizing the agricultural ceremonies performed by the emperor[5] at the beginning of each year, is more that of a Ministry of Trade or Agriculture—*nongbu* 農部 is after all one of the literary titles of the *hubu*—than that of Ministry of Finance. Such functions, however, are too limited for the *hubu* to be regarded as being responsible for management both of the economy and of finances. On the other hand, the Board of Revenue shares financial authority in various fields with other administrations: with the Censorate for inspecting provincial accounts;[6] with the Board of Works for the mints and inland customs.[7] From 1861 the administration of the maritime customs, whose origin goes back to 1854 was put under the charge of the Bureau of Foreign Affairs (*zongli geguo shiwu yamen* 總理各國事務

[5] *Qin ding Da Qing huidian* 欽定大淸會典 (*Collected statutes of the Qing dynasty*) (Shanghai: Commercial Press, 1908; preface of 1899, 100 *juan*), 13.1.
[6] *Ibid.*, 69.1-1b.
[7] *Ibid.*, 62.1, 23.1.

衙門) and confined itself to passing copies of its accounts to the Board of Revenue.[8]

In the higher provincial administration also there was only a rough specialization. Many offices retained functions inherited from previous developments or resulting from special historical circumstances. Thus, apart from his financial powers, the provincial treasurer (*buzhengshi* 布政使) had administrative control over the whole body of lower ranking civil officials within the territory of the province.[9] The salt controller for Lianghuai (Lianghuai *yanyunshi* 兩淮鹽運使) was simultaneously responsible for local military defence; the salt intendants in Nanjing, at Pingxiang in Jiangxi, at Pingliang in Gansu, and at Fengbin in Shanxi, also exercised the powers of circuit intendants.[10]

Finance was nevertheless a sector in which side by side with administrative centralization, both vertical specialization and the division of labour were carried farther than in other domains. Indeed, the Board of Revenue was (together with the Board of Punishment) the only central department where internal organization was modelled to some extent on the territorial divisions of the empire. Fourteen offices (*qinglisi* 清吏司) bearing the names of different provinces shared between them the task of auditing accounts and fiscal reports according to their geographical origin.

Although one cannot speak of a financial administration in the true sense of the term, state finances were, none the less, managed by a whole hierarchy of more or less specialized institutions whose structure should be described briefly to facilitate an understanding of their working and interactions.

In Beijing, the Board of Revenue, of which the presidency and the two vice-presidencies, all of them bicephalous, were shared equally by Manchus and Hans, was from the reign of Yongzheng 雍正 effectively headed by a member of the Grand Secretariat who, in the decrees of appointment, was specifically described as "charged with the affairs of the Board of Revenue" (*guanli hubu shiwu* 管理戶部事務).[11] This personage, for whose powers there is no provision in the Collected Statutes of the dynasty, was generally selected from among the former presidents of the Board, ensuring coordination

---

[8]*Ibid.*, 99/2, 3. See also Prince Gong's order of 30 June 1861 in H. B. Morse, *The Trade and Administration of the Chinese Empire* (Shanghai: Kelly & Walsh, 1908), pp. 357-59, 361.

[9]*Qingshi gao* 清史稿 (*A draft history of the Qing dynasty*), ed. Zhao Erxun 趙爾巽 (1st ed. 1928, re-ed. Beijing: Zhonghua shuju 中華書局, 1977, 48 vols.), p. 3346.

[10]*Ibid.*, p. 3353-55.

[11]Ming and Qing archives from the Imperial Palace, Beijing, *Shangyudang* 上諭檔 (Collection of imperial edicts), no. 3289.3.1381.1.267, fol. 265, Edict appointing Yan Jingming 閻敬銘 of the 29th day of the 11th month of the 11th year of the Guangxu 光緒 reign (3 January 1886).

between the latter and the decision-making centre, that is, the emperor.

The Board comprised three types of departments, some common to the whole body of boards, others existing only in some of them, and still others which resulted from powers particular to the Board of Revenue and which were special to it.

In the first category, that of general departments, belong the Chancery (*siwuting* 司務廳), the Office of the Expediter (*ducuisuo* 督催所), the Office of Registration (*dangyuechu* 當月處), the Seal Office (*jianyinchu* 監印處), and the Record Department. The latter was in fact divided into two offices (*beidangfang* 北檔房 and *nandangfang* 南檔房) with separate functions, some of which, such as checking the triennial census of the population of the Eight Banners, the distribution of pay, and accounting for provincial receipts and expenditures, are related to the specific functions of the Board.[12]

To the middle category belongs the Office of Food Costs (*fanyinchu* 飯銀 處),[13] which received from the provinces and discharged to the parties concerned sums allocated as payment of the maintenance allowance to Board personnel on duty.[14] Here also one can class the Coinage Department (*qianfatang* 錢法堂), which had a counterpart in the Board of Works.[15]

The Three Storehouses (*sanku* 三庫),[16] on the other hand, properly belong in the third category, that of offices specific to the Board of Revenue. These Three Storehouses received the major portion of fiscal returns in money and precious goods sent to Beijing by the provinces. Together with the huge Department of Granaries (*cangchang yamen* 倉場衙門), which ensured the transport of grain tribute on the Beihe, its storage in the public granaries of the capital and in Tongzhou as well as its distribution,[17] this ensemble constituted the central treasury of the imperial state.

[12] *Da Qing huidian*, 19.6.

[13] Similar agencies operated in the Grand Secretariat (*ibid.*, 2.6), in the Board of Rites (*ibid.*, 26.3-3b), in the Board of Punishments (*ibid.*, 57.5), and in that of Public Works (*ibid.*, 61.6b).

[14] Although less important, this indemnity was somewhat similar to the *yanglian* (養廉 reward for honesty) which territorial officials received. But it was given in addition to the ordinary salary to officials sent out on duty only.

[15] *Da Qing huidian*, 62.1.

[16] Bullion Store (*yinku* 銀庫), Satin and Silk Store (*duanpi ku* 緞匹庫), Dyes and Paper Store (*yanliaoku* 顏料庫). Unlike these three storehouses, the storehouses dependent on the Grand Secretariat and the Board of Rites did not include money reserves and affected only supplies destined for the use of these organizations themselves (books, fabrics etc.). As for the storehouses of the Board of Works, they had far less importance than those of the Board of Revenue: the main money store, the Warehouse of Thriftiness (*jieshenku* 節慎庫) served as a link treasury for the Board of Revenue but lacked any real financial autonomy; *Da Qing huidian*, 61.6.

[17] *Ibid.*, 25.1ff.

Changeable in composition, the Office of Inquiry (*xianshenchu* 現審處) heard appeals of land cases among bannermen.[18] The Office of Contributions (*juannafang* 捐納房), which had a larger staff, received sums from the sale of official degrees and titles, and issued the corresponding certificates.[19] The administrative departments which constituted the real framework of the Board, however, were the fourteen provincial offices (*qinglisi*). In addition to registration and auditing of land tax returns, each being responsible for one or more particular provinces, these offices shared, rather unequally, the various other tasks necessary to financial management. Thus the Zhejiang office was charged with drawing up the annual reports of the population census and grain reserves of the empire, while the Sichuan office provided the annual report on the harvest. The Fujian office was responsible for government aid in case of famines, the Shandong office had primary authority over the salt tax, and the Yunnan office supervised the transport of tribute for the whole country.[20]

At the provincial level, the provincial treasurer was responsible for tax collection and the consignment to Beijing and in some cases to other provinces of sums due, and for the management of the provincial exchequer.[21] He had to submit regular fiscal and financial reports to the Board of Revenue as well as the census from the area under his jurisdiction, documents which were examined by the fourteen provincial offices. The provincial treasurer was assisted by a team of a few statutory officials,[22] to which were added personal aides whom he recruited himself for their special abilities and who were assigned to particular duties, assisted by clerks and copyists. His yamen, however, involved no really technical services other than the provincial treasury (*fanku* 藩庫).

For Manchuria there existed the so-called Shenyang Board of Revenue (Shengjing *hubu* 盛京戶部), a legacy of the political organization that existed

---

[18]*Ibid.*, 24.1.

[19]*Ibid.*

[20]The powers of each office are detailed in the *Da Qing huidian*,. 20-23. See also the summary chart drawn up by E-tu Zen Sun, "The Board of Revenue in Nineteenth-Century China," *Harvard Journal of Asiatic Studies*, Vol. 24 (1962-63), pp. 182-83. These offices numbered thirteen under the Ming, but a fourteenth, the Jiangnan office, was added at the beginning of the Qing.

[21]Each province had one, except for Jiangsu, which had two, one at Nanjing, the other in Suzhou. One post was added for Gansu and Xinjiang in 1884, and for Taiwan in 1887, bringing the total to twenty-one.

[22]Namely an archivist (*jingli* 經歷), a secretary or a chancellor (*liwen* 理問, *dushi* 都事, *zhaomo* 照磨), a treasury keeper (*kudashi* 庫大使), and in certain cases a granary keeper (*cangdashi* 倉大使).

before the Qing conquest of the empire.[23] This board collected the revenues from the imperial domains and sundry taxes, oversaw the surveying and assessment of the Banner lands in the north-east, paid the expenses of the civil administration in Shenyang as well as the official expenses of military governors, and heard civil cases involving Manchus. In all these duties the Shengjing *hubu* enjoyed complete autonomy. However the ordinary land tax did not pass through its hands, but was collected by local officials and sent direct to the Board of Revenue in Beijing, the accounts being checked by the Shandong office. Thus the Shengjing Board of Revenue had only restricted local powers rendering it more comparable to a provincial treasury than to its namesake in Beijing.

Below provincial level, the financial powers of the intendants (*dao* 道) were limited to a defined fiscal area: the salt tax, grain tribute or customs. These powers were exercised either alone or together with other administrative responsibilities, in the latter case covering usually only one section of the provincial area.

Five of the salt-producing provinces had a salt controller (*yanyunshi* 鹽運使), nine had a salt intendant (*yanfadao* 鹽法道).[24] These officials were responsible for the accounts and collection of monopoly receipts and the salt tax for a given area, and for the control of the distribution, sale, and (where called for) the production of salt. They were assisted by a few deputies, and particularly by an important number of subordinates, so many that the yamen of a salt controller or intendant usually employed a larger staff than that of a provincial treasurer.

The thirteen grain intendants, responsible for checking, transporting or storing of grain tribute taxes levied in kind or in cash equivalents were shared among twelve provinces.[25] Eight came under the authority of the director-general of grain transport (*caoyun zongdu* 漕運總督); the others under the authority of the provincial governor. The statutory subordinates with whom they were provided in areas from which the tribute grain had to be sent to Beijing were mainly concerned with the policing and technical control of

[23] It is described in the *Da Qing huidian*, 35.3b-4b.

[24] In fact, Jiangsu was divided between the authority of a salt controller stationed in Tongzhou (Lianghuai *yanyunshi* 兩淮鹽運使) and that of a salt intendent based in Nanking (Jiangnan *yanxundao* 江南鹽巡道). Cf. P. Hoang, *Exposé du commerce public du sel*, Variétés Sinologiques No. 15 (Shanghai: Imprimerie de la mission catholique, 1898), 17pp.

[25] *Da Qing huidian*, 6.4. Huang Benji 黃本驥 , *Lidai zhiguan biao* 歷代職官表 (*Historical table of posts*) (Shanghai: Zhonghua shuju, 1965; this edition comprises three sections: an introduction by the modern editors, Huang Benji's text which dates from 1846, and an explanatory list of official titles by Qu Tuiyuan 瞿蛻園), 2.262, 303, 3.162.

transport rather than with strictly financial matters.[26]

Of the twenty-six customs houses which were spread through nine provinces and which collected taxes from trade in the interior and on the coast, sixteen were entrusted to officials whose main duties lay elsewhere (usually circuit intendants); only ten were headed by an official especially appointed for the task, whose title and powers varied. In fact the three customs houses in the capital were headed by an imperial commissioner (*qinchai dachen* 欽差大臣), and six others were administered by an inspector of customs (*haiguan jiandu* 海關監督), three of whom were appointed with the approval of the emperor and three on the direct initiative of the Ministry of Revenue. The Tianjin house was under a customs intendant (*haiguandao* 海關道) subordinate to the provincial treasurer of Zhili.[27] These customs houses did not involve any other statutory office, but included a large subordinate staff of inspectors, assessors, clerks, and various servants.[28]

Below the provincial treasurers and the intendants, financial administration was only one of the many responsibilities of prefects and district magistrates.

In the prefectures and divisions of comparable level (the *zhilizhou* 直隸州) some of the statutory deputies of the chief magistrate were entrusted specifically with financial work.[29] Besides such officials, who had to hold seventh to fifth official rank, some subordinate officials were charged solely with financial administration. These were the treasury keeper (*kudashi* 庫大使), the granary keeper (*cangdashi* 倉大使), the receiver of dues and miscellaneous taxes (*shuikesidashi* 稅課司大使), the inspector of miscellaneous taxes (*xuankesizhengdashi* 宣課司正大使), the deputy inspector of miscellaneous taxes (*xuankesifudashi* 宣課司副大使), the subinspector of miscellaneous taxes (*xuankefensidashi* 宣課分司大使), the inspector of salt and tea

[26] These subordinates bore the titles *guanliang tongzhi* (管糧同知), *guanliang tongpan* (管糧通判), *yayun tongzhi* (押運同知), *yayun tongpan* (押運通判), *Li dai zhiguan biao*, 3/89, 171; *Qingshi gao*, pp. 3576-77.

[27] *Da Qing huidian*, 23/1.

[28] *Ibid.*, 23/2-2b.

[29] They were then designated by the epithets *guanliang* (管糧 charged with payments for the army); *duliang* (督糧 inspector of grain tribute) or *yancao* (鹽漕 charged with the salt convoy), coupled with their title *tongzhi* (同知 first class sub-prefect), *tongpan* (通判 second class sub-prefect), *zhoutong* (州同 first class assistant to the department magistrate), *zhoupan* (州判 second class assistant to the department magistrate): thus *duliang tongpan* (督糧通判 second class sub-prefect, inspector of grain tribute). Cf. *Huangchao jingshi wen sanbian* 皇朝經世文三編 (*Third collection of essays of the ruling dynasty on statecraft*), ed. Chen Zhongyi 陳忠倚 (Shanghai: Baowen shuju 寶文書局, 1898; repr., Taibei: Guofeng 國風, 1963, 80 *juan*), 33.7b. H. S. Brunnert and V. V. Hagelstrom, *Present-day Political Organization of China* (Shanghai, 1911; repr., Taibei: Book World, 1961), pp. 427-31.

(*yanchadashi* 鹽茶大使), the inspector of customs (*guandashi* 關大使).[30] Every prefecture did not necessarily have all these officials, and their numbers varied. Their role was to aid the prefect in the financial matters which fell to his charge, namely overseeing district accounts, drawing up fiscal reports concerning the prefecture as a whole, collection of certain commercial taxes, management of their receipts and the accounts of the prefectural administration.[31] The real work, however, was done by an unofficial staff attached to the administration of the prefectural yamen under various titles.

Unlike the prefect, the district magistrate had no subordinate official assigned to finance, and thus depended even more than his superior on the staff of his yamen for assistance in fulfilling his financial duties. Among the six departments (*fang* 房) into which, modelled on the divisions of the central government, the prefectural and district yamen were divided, one was particularly concerned with financial matters, the revenue office (*hufang* 戶房 or *huliangfang* 戶糧房). To this were usually appended the following offices: a treasury (*kufang* 庫房), which stored receipts, paid salaries, kept a daily balance sheet (of great importance when the magistrate handed over to his successor); a granary office (*cangfang* 倉房) to manage storehouses and ensure the distribution of aid in time of disaster, the supply of food to prisons, provision of fodder to the army and to the postal service, in addition to looking after visiting officials. In areas where the so-called "Banner" lands were important, there was also an office for the census of the banners (*huqifang* 戶旗房), responsible for fiscal matters in these areas and sometimes also for checking copper currency.[32]

The staff of the *hufang* comprised compilers (*dianli* 典吏) and copyists (*tiexie* 貼寫). The number of the former was determined by the Board of Personnel, that of the latter being suggested by the governor-general or governor.[33] They were overseen and their work coordinated by two or three

[30] Brunnert and Hagelstrom, *op. cit.*, p. 429.

[31] *Qin ding hubu zeli* 欽定戶部則例 (*Imperial collection of the Jurisprudence of the Board of Revenue*), ed. Huixiang 惠祥 and Zailing 載齡 (1874, 100 *juan*), 9.17-17b, 10.10b-11. *Shinkoku gyōseihō* 清國行政法 (*Administrative Law of the Qing Empire*), ed. Rinji Taiwan kyūkan chōsakai 臨時臺灣舊慣調查會 (Provisional Committee of the government of Taiwan for the study of Ancient Chinese customs) (Tokyo 1905-14; repr., Tokyo: Daian 太安 , 1965-67, 6 vols.), 1.257. *Zhongguo jingji quanshu diyiji* 中國經濟全書第一輯 (*Encyclopedia of the Chinese economy*) (Nanjing: Lianghu zongdushu cangban 兩湖總督署藏板 , 1908, 762p; a translation of part of the Japanese work in 12 vols. published by the Tōa Dōbunkai 東亞同文會 in 1907-1908), pp. 474-75.

[32] *Zhongguo jingji quanshu*, p. 481.

[33] They were recruited from the common people for a term which, according to the regulations, should not exceed five years (*Da Qing huidian*, 12.4). In fact many employees managed to remain in their posts by changing names or by giving the position to a member of their family.

personal servants of the magistrate ("domestics" in the seventeenth-century French sense), responsible specifically for financial matters.[34] These latter gathered the information required by the secretary of taxation (*qiangu* 錢穀 : literally "money and grain," i.e. responsible for fiscal affairs), who supervised assessment and collection of taxes, the issuing of receipts, the expenditure and delivery of government funds, and who drew up the reports and financial returns demanded of the magistrate.

Unlike the personal servants, who were selected from among the commoners, the secretary of taxation was a literatus and therefore closer in social rank to the magistrate than the other yamen employees, though he too was recruited and paid by the magistrate. He belonged to the category of personal advisors (*muyou* 幕友 or *mubin* 幕賓 or *shiye* 師爺), with whom the territorial officials surrounded themselves in order to fulfill the technical duties with which they were charged. Indeed, to their classical education some of these literati had added a highly specialized administrative training, acquired through personal study, from the instruction given by more experienced elders, and from practical experience in yamen offices. In important districts several secretaries would share responsibility for financial affairs: a *qiangu* (who in this case would deal only with accounting), a *zhengbi* (徵比 responsible for tax collection), a *qianliangzong* (錢糧總 in charge of land tax), and a *zhangfang* (賬房 charged with account registers) who made payments.[35]

It was these secretaries who were really competent and effective. Obliged to be relatively honest because of their personal ties with the magistrate, they helped ward off state bankruptcy by assuring a minimum of stability and coherence in the operation of the financial machine.

II. FINANCIAL INSTITUTIONS IN OPERATION: AN INSTRUMENT OF REGULATION RATHER THAN OF UNIFICATION

How was the administration of public finance carried out by this hierarchy of institutions?

In order to make plain the special characteristics of the workings of the financial machinery at the end of the nineteenth century, a distinction will be

[34] The generic term for this category of personnel recruited and paid by the magistrate is *changsui* (長隨 permanent attendant). According to the particular responsibilities with which they were charged, these attendants were called *qianliang* (錢糧 charged with land tax), *qiancao* (錢漕 charged with grain tribute), *shuiwu* (稅務 charged with sundry taxes), *sicang* (司倉 supervisor of the granaries). Cf. T'ung-tsu Ch'ü, *Local Government in China under the Ch'ing* (Cambridge, Mass.: Harvard University Press, 1962), pp. 74-76.

[35] *Ibid.*, pp. 97, 101-104.

made between regular business on the one hand, and exceptional matters on the other. By regular business is meant all day-to-day transactions, ordinary and extraordinary, long provided for in edicts and ordinances, and conducted according to established precedents, namely: the levy and collection of the land tax, salt tax, miscellaneous taxes (*zashui* 雜稅), and "special contributions" (*juan* 捐); the assessment of normal state expenditures, the assignment to their payment of given fiscal receipts; the terms of public payments and the minting of coins; and finally, accounts, checks and reports pertaining to all these operations. Most of these matters accorded with the idea of *changli* 常例 ("regular practice") in the Board's administrative vocabulary.

By exceptional matters is meant the standing levy of additional taxes or duties and permanent commitment to new types of public expenditures. For the period with which we are concerned here, between the end of the Taipings and the 1906 reform, the category "exceptional matters" covers essentially the following areas: the *lijin* tax (釐金), the maritime customs, expenditure committed to modernization, foreign loans and repayments, payment of war indemnities. These were transactions designated by the Board of Revenue as *xinzeng* (新增 "newly added").[36]

In regular financial business, as indeed in general administration, each level of the hierarchy exercised rather a function of checking, regulation and transmission than a power of initiative or impulsion with regard to the next lower level. The terms which recur most frequently in official texts and personal descriptions by officials to designate these relationships of subordination are *ducha* (督察 oversee and check), *shi* (視 inspect), *he* (覈 scrutinize), *ji* (稽 investigate), *jiandu* (監督 supervise), *jiancha* (監察 examine). These terms, whose usage is far from strictly defined, imply varying degrees of responsibility with regard to the work and conduct of subordinates. This degree of responsibility can scarcely be measured other than by comparing in each individual case the severity of the punishment incurred by officials of higher ranks when their inferiors committed a mistake.[37]

The legal total for taxes was fixed according to permanent quotas. Each

[36]*Huangchao jingshi wen xubian* 皇朝經世文續編 (*Continuation of the collection of essays of the reigning dynasty on statecraft*), ed. Sheng Kang 盛康 (Sibu lou kanban 思補 樓刊板, 1897, 120 *juan*; repr., Taibei: Wenhai 文海, 1966), 30.70b-71. This text is the memorial from the Board of Revenue, presented to the emperor and approved by him in 1884, leading to modification of the forms and content of the financial reports which the provincial government had to send regularly to Beijing. It was then that the category of *xinzeng* was introduced for both receipts and expenditures.

[37]The complexity of the factors affecting how punishments were determined in each case is analysed, with an example taken from the salt administration, by T. A. Metzger, *The Internal Organization of Ch'ing Bureaucracy: Legal, Normative and Communication Aspects* (Cambridge, Mass.: Harvard University Press, 1973), pp. 294-97.

fiscal return was allocated in advance to the payment of predetermined expenditures either according to equally permanent quotas or, where these did not exist, in accordance with established precedents. The procedures for payment, collection, transfer and allocation of funds, as well as accountability and control were subject to detailed regulation.[38]

Modification of all these regulatory arrangements presupposed imperial approval. In spite of the role of financial advisor which it was supposed to play in relation to the emperor, the Board of Revenue only rarely took the initiative in itself suggesting such changes. When it did so, the matters involved usually concerned the finances of the capital alone, where the Board functioned as paymaster-general. Sometimes changes would be effected on the advice of the Grand Council (*junjichu* 軍機處), but usually the authors of such proposals were local magistrates.

Take the case of the land tax. Yeh-chien Wang's study has shown that since the middle of the eighteenth century the quotas for this tax remained relatively unchanged; in practice, calculations were carried out with regard to taxable area, on a basis established by surveys made at the end of the Ming. In contrast, the surcharges added to this tax and calculated according to this fixed base-rate, frequently varied. The fight against the Taipings provided the occasion for a gradual transfer of decision-making power in this matter from the hands of the district magistrate to the provincial authorities, that is to the provincial treasurer supported by the governor, or where appropriate, by the governor-general, although ultimate sanction remained at the discretion of the emperor. The Board of Revenue intervened only rarely, and then only as the sovereign's adviser, recommending his approval or rejection.[39] Apart from this, although the new scales of surcharges established by governors in the years following the Taiping uprising had received the imperial sanction, they were not incorporated into the statutory regulations governing the land tax. Neither the new regulations for fiscal reports established in 1884 by the Board of Revenue nor the revised edition of the *Da Qing huidian*, begun in 1883 and completed in 1899, refer to them.[40] Thus the annual financial figures issued by local officials and provincial authorities had still to conform to out of date rules, indicating only payments made under the old quotas and not sums that were actually collected. The Board of Revenue was thus

---

[38] The broad outlines of fiscal regulations are recorded in the *Da Qing huidian*, 18-19. But certain arrangements concerning the accounting reports had been modified in 1884 (cf. the text cited in n. 36, 30.69-74b), although the 1899 edition of the *Da Qing huidian* fails to mention this.

[39] Yeh-chien Wang, *Land Taxation in Imperial China 1750-1911* (Cambridge, Mass.: Harvard University Press, 1973), pp. 24-26, 34-36, 70, 75.

[40] *Huangchao jingshi wen xubian*, 30.69-74b.

deprived of all means of institutional control over the surcharges added to the quotas.

The fiscal initiative which the provincial authorities gradually assumed for themselves with regard to surcharges on the land tax extended to other payments as well, the so-called miscellaneous taxes. The surcharges imposed on various types of commercial licence, on duties on land transactions, alcohol and gaming, were often expedient measures devised by ingenious local magistrates, expedients later legalized, standardized and made general by the action of the provincial treasurer and governor.[41]

If the Board of Revenue made so bold as to try to impose its views on the modifications of ordinary fiscal matters it ran into very strong resistance on the part of the provincial governments. Such was the case when in the autumn of 1884 a memorial from the Board, providing for twenty-four measures intended to cover military expenditure, was issued by order of the emperor to all provincial administrations for application.[42] This initiative immediately provoked lively reactions from the latter. Most of the Board's proposals were criticized with arguments varying from province to province, and rejected; other fiscal arrangements were suggested, generally less productive and applicable only within the jurisdiction of the objecting province.[43] The provinces were immediately successful in these appeals.

This episode is quite revealing regarding relations of authority between different levels of financial power. In fact the Board's fiscal programme was

[41]*Guangxu zhengyao* 光緒政要 (*Important policies of the Guangxu reign*) ed. Shen Tongsheng 沈桐生 (Shanghai: Nanyang tushu gongsi 南洋圖書公司, 1909, 34 *juan*), 16/14-14b, concerning a supplementary tax on distilleries in Zhili proposed by Li Hong-zhang in 1890. On the general authority exercised by the provincial government, without reference to the Board of Revenue, in matters concerning the rate scale on the collection of various taxes, cf. the memorial from the governor of Shanxi dated 24th day of the 2nd month of the 14th year of Guangxu (5 April 1888), *Gong zhong dang Guangxu chaozouzhe* 宮中檔光緒朝奏摺 (*Secret palace memorials of the Guangxu reign*) (Taibei: Guoli gugong bowuyuan 國立故宮博物院, 1973, 26 vols.), Vol. 3, pp. 695-96; also the memorial from the governor of Jiangsu dated 28th day of the 2nd month of the 14th year of Guangxu (9 April 1888), *ibid.*, Vol. 3, pp. 701-702.

[42]*Guangxu zhengyao*, 10.20b-21b.

[43]The content of these protests is summarized by Luo Yudong 羅玉東, "Guangxu chao buqiu caizheng zhi fangce" 光緒朝補救財政之方策 ("Emergency financial measures under the Guangxu reign"), *Zhongguo jindai jingji shi yanjiu jikan* 中國近代經濟史研究集刊 (*Bulletin of research on the economic history of modern China*), Vol. 6, No. 2 (May 1933), pp. 200-202, from original reports which he was then able to consult in the imperial palace archives in Peking. Some of the memorials presented by the governor-general of Sichuan, the governor of Shaanxi and the governor of Hunan were translated from the *Peking Gazette* (*Jingbao* 京報) of 11 September, 13 September, and 2 October 1885 in the *North China Herald*, 21 October 1885, p. 468, 18 November 1885, p. 576, and 2 December 1885, p. 629.

not an isolated, extemporary measure, but part of a deliberate effort, from the time of Yan Jingming's 閻敬銘 accession to the Chinese presidency of the Board on 13 March 1882, to put financial management on a sound basis and increase the available resources. Indeed in 1882, a commission of sixteen members, half Chinese, half Manchu, was formed to revise the regulations concerning the financial reports demanded from the provinces. With imperial consent the commission was granted access to records held in the *beidangfang* 北檔房, the office where information sent by the provinces was centralized and which had hitherto been the exclusive domain of the Manchus, thus giving the latter the privilege of sole access to knowledge of the exact state of the public exchequer. The provincial governments were then invited to draw up, with the assistance of inspectors specially assigned by the Board, a complete statement of their revenues and expenditures for the years 1880 and 1881. From this information, an account in eighty-four volumes and a nine-volume summary was compiled and presented to the throne. The new regulations and formulae for financial reports promulgated in 1884[44] were based on this inquiry and the documents submitted by the provinces.

It should moreover be emphasized that the Board's memorial containing the twenty-four fiscal proposals had received imperial sanction. The incident revealed the impotence of the Board, from which the emperor immediately withdrew his support. Nevertheless, the provincial governments did not try actually to usurp the *hubu*'s authority. They did not suggest a single measure valid for the whole empire, but simply solutions to be applied within their own areas of jurisdiction, and moreover agreed, in spite of everything, to an increase in their fiscal burdens. It was a case of what might be considered a kind of "deconcentration" of decision-making. Final sanction in fact rested with the centre, and took the form of the imperial verdict, but the substance of the decision comprised the sum of several separate decisions, of which the content was decided in several places outside the centre. This type of authority relationship can be found in other instances of attempts at fiscal reform suggested by the Board of Revenue.[45]

While in regular financial operations checks and controls at least, if not initiative, were effectively centralized, there was much more fluctuation in cases of "exceptional matters." Whether it be for the levy of *lijin*, commitment to modernization expenditures, or foreign loans, initiative came first from the provincial governments, which only requested imperial approval

[44] *Huangchao jingshi wen xubian*, 30.69-74b.
[45] Luo Yudong, *op. cit.*, and Peng Yuxin 彭雨新, "Qingmo zhongyang yu gesheng caizheng guanxi" 清末中央與各省財政關係 ("Financial relations between the central government and the provinces in late Qing"), *Shehuikexue zazhi* 社會科學雜誌 (*Social Science Review*), Vol. 9, No. 1 (June 1937), pp. 86-89.

once the matter had already been settled.[46]

Only after repeated calls to order, coupled with sanctions, did the provincial authorities agree, from 1892, to request prior authorization from Beijing for all foreign loans; failing this, the *zongli yamen*, pressed by the Board of Revenue, would refuse to entertain any complaints which might be made by foreign creditors.[47] But in so far as they found the necessary resources for themselves, the provinces maintained their freedom of initiative with regard to modernization expenditures. The efforts of the Board of Revenue to control provincial borrowing, however, by no means led it to reserve for itself the right to sign contracts. For the period with which we are concerned, the Board intervened only in the case of one loan, of £1,000,000 in 1905. Most loans continued to be contracted by provincial governments or public enterprises, the largest loans henceforth being negotiated and signed by the *zongli yamen*.

It was also only gradually, and without ever obtaining complete accounts, let alone the profits, that the Board of Revenue came to exercise a certain right to oversee the collection of *lijin*. From 1869 periodic reports were sent

---

[46]It was only in April 1854 that the provincial treasurer of Jiangsu presented a report on the collection of *lijin* which he had established in 1853 at Yangzhou, moreover immediately obtaining imperial approval for this innovation: *Huangchao Dao Xian Tong Guang zouyi* 皇朝道咸同光奏議 (*Memorials to the throne for the Daoguang, Xianfeng, Tongzhi and Guangxu reigns of the ruling dynasty*), ed. Wang Yanxi 王延熙 (Shanghai, 1902, 64 *juan*), 37.1, for the memorial of the provincial treasurer, Lei Yixian 雷以諴, *Da Qing Wenzong xian huangdi shilu* 大清文宗顯皇帝實錄 (*Veritable records of the Xianfeng reign of the Qing dynasty*) (Mukden: Manzhouguo guowuyuan 滿洲國國務院, 1937, 360 *juan*), 125.29-30, for the edict of 21 April 1854. These two texts have been translated into English in E. G. Beal, *The Origin of likin 1853-1864* (Cambridge, Mass.: Harvard University Press, 1958), pp. 84-88.

The first purchases of foreign military and industrial equipment were made by Lin Zexu 林則徐, on his own authority in 1840; his official correspondence does not indicate that he had requested imperial approval even after the deal was made. Zeng Guofan 曾國藩 follows his example, particularly from 1860, although he did inform the throne and received its sanction; the other provincial commanders at the time of the Taipings did likewise. The first foreign loans were contracted at the same time by provincial officials, notably the intendant of Suzhou, Songjiang and Taizhou in Jiangsu, some without any guarantee from Beijing, others with a post facto imperial sanction: cf. the lists of loans and official sources mentioning them in Xu Yisheng 徐義生, *Zhongguo jindai waizhai shi tongji ziliao* 中國近代外債史統計資料 (*Statistical documents on the history of foreign debt in modern China*) (Beijing: Zhonghua shuju, 1962), pp. 4-17.

[47]The imperial decree of 25 November 1891 refusing all responsibility of the Chinese state in cases of failure to observe this rule was officially communicated to foreigners in order to dissuade lenders: Public Record Office (London), Series FO 17, Vol. 1142, fol. 13.

in by the provinces.[48] In 1884 the *lijin* figured in the new categories of receipts (*xinzeng zhengshou* 新增徵收) regarding which the provinces thereafter were obliged to issue an annual report. However the reference figures which were then fixed and served as a basis for the allocation of funds were those of the returns for the year 1881.[49] It was also at the suggestion of the Board that *lijin* was imposed on certain products such as opium and tea, although even there it failed to control more than a share of the profits.[50]

The maritime customs, which was one of the major innovations in public finance in the late years of the empire, partially escaped interference from the financial administration. Its reports were sent to the Board of Revenue, but it received instructions only from the *zongli yamen*. The customs banks in which the duties were deposited, however, were placed under the authority of a Chinese superintendent, who was usually an intendant with territorial responsibilities (*daotai* 道台), directly subordinate to the provincial government and charged with remitting funds to it for report and possible subsequent transfer to the Board of Revenue.[51] It should be noted that, unlike traditional fiscal revenues, the returns of the maritime customs had no fixed allocation. Thus provincial governments were able to take out foreign loans against the takings of the customs over which they had jurisdiction, a situation of which they took full advantage. The 1884 ruling on financial reports demanded from the provincial governments merely obliged the latter to specify amounts received under the heading of the maritime customs.

These arrangements did not, however, leave the provincial governments entirely free to use customs revenues as they pleased. Indeed, from 1866, 40 per cent of these returns, which had until then been earmarked for payment of the indemnity incurred through the second opium war, were thereafter assigned to the budget of the central government. Moreover, the central authorities did not fail to exhort the provinces to deduct from the remaining 60 per cent those funds necessary for any new expenditures decreed by the central government. This applied both to standing expenditures, such as the financing of the admiralty (*haijun yamen* 海軍衙門), subsidies for the imperial household, or funds for building the Summer Palace, and to

---

[48] Beal, *op. cit.*, pp. 76-77. Luo Yudong 羅玉東, *Zhongguo lijin shi* 中國釐金史 (*History of the lijin in China*) (Shanghai: Commercial Press, 1938; repr., Taibei: Xuehai 學海, 1970, 2 vols., 649 p.), pp. 139-42, gives the list of reports actually remitted, from the archives of the imperial palace.

[49] *Huangchao jingshi wen xubian*, 30.70-71b.

[50] Luo Yudong, "Guangxu chao buqiu caizheng zhi fangce," pp. 202-10.

[51] Memorandum of the Inspector-General F. A. Aglen, reproduced in H. B. Morse, *The International Relations of the Chinese Empire* (London and New York: Longmans, 1910-18; repr., Taibei: Book World, 1963, 3 vols.), Vol. 3, pp. 401-403.

short-term expenses such as the military campaigns in Xinjiang and Gansu.[52] But in all these proceedings, the Board of Revenue acted at most as an intermediary, having neither the initiative in matters of expenditure nor any real control over the use of funds requisitioned in this manner.

Among the new matters involving public finance after the Taiping Rebellion, one area alone seems to have been placed entirely under the authority of the Board of Revenue: the sharing out among the provinces of payments intended for servicing loans contracted by the central government and for paying war indemnities.[53] As loan agreements were concluded, the Board fixed the annual amount due from each province. These funds were remitted to the *daotai* of Shanghai (Su Song Tai *dao* 蘇松太道) who was responsible for servicing the debt. Yet although the provincial governments had to submit a report on their execution of this obligation, they were allowed considerable latitude regarding the dates of payments and the resources appropriated thereto.

It should be stressed, moreover, that the new posts created by such operations as *lijin* levy and the creation of official enterprises, arsenals, factories, transport companies and banks, did not become statutory positions but were supplied through the commission system. Unlike office-holders, the commissioners (*weiyuan* 委員) were nominated not by the emperor but by means of a simple letter of commission (*zhawei* 札委) issued by an official usually above the rank of prefect. They were not subjected to the rigorous examination procedures or hierarchical controls presided over by the Board of Personnel. Their nomination did not even have to be announced to higher levels, as did that of personal secretaries, even though they were paid out of public funds. Since they often owed their position to provincial authorities, it was to them that they usually reported, and on their support that they depended for the maintenance of their commission or their promotion to a statutory post.

Thus, the new financial business of the last third of the nineteenth century did not provide the Board of Revenue with the opportunity actually to extend its influence or to impose its central authority to greater effect. Rather, it contributed to a growth in the importance and responsibilities of the provincial governments. This fact seems to have been sanctioned in an edict of November 1889 which authorized provincial treasurers to submit secret reports directly to the emperor.[54] But, judging from currently available

[52] Liu Guangjing 劉廣京, "Wan Qing dufu quanli wenti shangque" 晚清督撫權力問題商榷 ("The limits of regional power in the late Qing period: a reappraisal"), *Qinghua xuebao* 清華學報, new series, Vol. 10, No. 2 (July 1974), pp. 190-91.

[53] Luo Yudong, "Guangxu chao buqiu caizheng zhi fangce," pp. 219-21, gives details of the distribution made in 1896 of the repayment of the Franco-Russian and British loans.

[54] *Guangxu zhengyao*, 15.22-22b.

archival materials, it appears that the provincial treasurers did not make use of this right, which had moreover been conferred on them so that they could, if the situation arose, inform against misappropriations of funds committed by governors or governors-general. The only palace memorials sent by provincial treasurers remained, as before, documents of thanks for their appointment.[55] Palace memorials concerning provincial financial affairs are all written in the name of the governor or governor-general, while the treasurer, who was the most explicitly financial official, never appears except in the role of book-keeping subsidiary. If the treasurer had a proposal or request to make, it was the governor who intervened to present and press for it before the throne. Indeed, it was not uncommon for the more powerful provincial magistrates to have a treasurer of their choosing appointed.[56] The most important fact, without doubt, is that the very procedure by which governors referred provincial matters under their jurisdiction directly to the emperor at the same time as they submitted a routine report to the Board of Revenue singularly weakened the latter's hierarchical control.

Another institutional obstacle inhibited the centralizing influence of the Board of Revenue, but at the same time weakened the authority of provincial governments over the financial organs at various levels under their jurisdiction, namely the lack of a unified treasury. Each administrative division had its own treasury; only a fraction of the returns collected by state agents, the portion allocated for the expenditures of higher ranks, was subject to a one-treasury system and thus to tighter control. But on the level of the Board of Revenue there was no central auditing office. The fourteen *qinglisi* functioned without coordination among one another, concerned only with the areas under their own jurisdiction, while the *beidangfang* contented itself with assembling the reports transmitted to it after approval.

Finally the principle of personal direct responsibility to the emperor of all officials, together with a rapid turnover except in the highest and lowest grades, limited the possibility of developing a body of regulations and conventions specific to financial institutions which would allow such institutions to protect themselves and expand while still assuring their own internal policing. The merits of officials, including those in the financial field, were examined regularly by the Board of Personnel, which administered punishment and rewards. Even if an accommodating or conniving provincial treasurer could, in his reports on the administrative staff under his jurisdiction, conceal

---

[55]Cf. the documents collected in *Gong zhong dang Guangxu chao zouzhe.*

[56]When Zhang Zhidong 張之洞 was appointed governor-general of Huguang in August 1889, he managed shortly after to have Wang Zhichun 王之春 appointed to the position of provincial treasurer of Hubei. Wang Zhichun had been his grain intendant and one of his faithful collaborators in Canton.

misdeeds of some district magistrates, he risked being reported by a censor, or simply by the governor, and referred to the Board of Personnel for punishment.

Just as the means of altering the financial machinery lay to a large extent outside that machinery, financial institutions were far from being masters either of their own management or of the procedures and modes of sanction which affected them.

Without doubt the Board of Revenue did exercise some sort of authority which passed downward through the hierarchy to the districts, while, conversely, financial control passed up the chain to Beijing. Centralization and subordination appear, however, more formal than really effective. One detects no truly systematic, persistent moves effectively to centralize the financial resources of the empire in the hands of Beijing. In organization and operation, financial institutions appear as instruments of regulation and balance rather than of compulsion and unification. Nevertheless, by virtue of its importance and its role in the state apparatus should not the financial administration be regarded as the mainspring of public authority?

III. THE PLACE OF THE FINANCIAL ADMINISTRATION IN THE STATE: A DOMINANT AND PARALYSING ROLE

In the official hierarchy of the Six Boards, precedence was given to the Board of Personnel, the Board of Revenue taking only second place. This order of precedence might be a legacy from the past of no real significance. One notes for instance that even today in French protocol, the Lord Chancellor leads the ministers, although the Ministry of Justice is not the most important and most coveted of the ministerial portfolios. In fact, however, the Board of Personnel remained the Board with the most prestige right up to the 1906 reform because it represented power over men, over the organization and distribution of authority. It is true that the Grand Council (*junjichu*) relieved it of its role in the appointment and evaluation of the merits of the highest-ranking officials,[57] but the governing of careers and promotions remained a crucial means of influence in a society dominated by a bureaucratic class. Whereas after the presidency of the Board of Personnel promotion was usually to the post of grand secretary or to the presidency of the metropolitan examinations, the most common step from the presidency of the Board of Revenue was to that of the Board of Personnel, to the presidency of the provincial examinations in Peking, or to the vice-presidency of the metropolitan examinations; it was rather unusual to move directly from

[57] *Lidai zhiguan biao*, 1.64.

the Board of Revenue to the Grand Secretariat.[58]

In the provinces, the treasurer held the second rank of the mandarinate, judges only the third rank. Whatever their particular responsibilities, all intendants held the same rank. In the private secretariats (*mufu* 幕府), however, the legal secretary took precedence over his financial colleague who was immediately beneath him.[59]

Although not at the top of the hierarchy, the financial offices were accorded a high degree of social esteem. One must note also that from 1864 to 1906, the Grand Council counted almost without interruption one of the presidents or vice-presidents of the Board of Revenue among its members, while membership from the Board of Personnel was less continuous, and that of the other Boards altogether occasional.[60]

These indications of the social prestige of financial offices must be substantiated with a more precise evaluation of the weight of the administration of finances. Two approaches have been chosen for this investigation. In one, which draws on methods recently used in studies of modern Europe,[61] an attempt is made to measure the Chinese "Financial State" quantitatively. The other approach consists in examining the effect of financial control on the rest of administrative management.

The financial administration can be measured first by the number of men it employed. Of the Six Boards, the Board of Revenue and that of Punishments reputedly employed a staff several times larger than that of their counterparts.[62] The total number of posts mentioned in the 1899 edition of the *Da Qing huidian* went up to 145 for the Board of Personnel, but 425 for that of Revenue.[63] The table below allows the reader to compare the number

[58] Cf. the chronological tables of holders of these posts in Wei Xiumei 魏秀梅 , *Qingji zhiguan biao fu renwu lu* 清季職官表附人物錄(*Tables of late Qing officials, with a biographical appendix*) (Taibei: Zhongyang yanjiuyuan jindaishi yanjiusuo 中央研究院 近代史研究所 , 1977, 2 vols.), pp. 63-70, 110-20.

[59] T'ung-tsu Ch'ü, *Local Government in China under the Ch'ing*, p. 108.

[60] Wei Xiumei, *op. cit.*, pp. 46-56. Qian Shifu 錢實甫 , *Qingji zhongyao zhiguan nianbiao* 清季重要職官年表 (*Annual tables of important officials in late Qing*) (Beijing: Zhonghua shuju, 1959), pp. 47-51.

[61] In particular, P. Chaunu, "L'Etat," in P. Chaunu et al., *Histoire économique et sociale de la France*, Part 1, Vol. 1 (Paris: Presses universitaires de France, 1977), pp. 9-228.

[62] *Qingmo choubei lixian dang'an shiliao* 清末籌備立憲檔案史料 (*Documents from the archives relating to the drawing up of the constitution at the end of the Qing*), ed. Gugong bowuyuan Ming Qing dang'anbu 故宮博物院明清檔案部 (Department of Ming and Qing archives in the Imperial Palace Museum) (Beijing: Zhonghua shuju, 1979, 2 vols.), p. 424.

[63] Calculation based on the *Da Qing huidian*, 4-25. The total does not take into account the *yuanwailang* 員外郎 "of indeterminate number."

of statutory posts recorded in Huang Benji's tables in 1846[64] with the actual number of appointees mentioned in the official directory of autumn 1895.[65]

Six Boards	Statutory posts mentioned by Huang Benji	Directory of Autumn 1895		
		Statutory officials	Officials in non-statutory posts	Total
Revenue	354	394	367	761
Punishments	267	268	412	680
Works	230	214	217	431
Rites	138	140	94	234
War	137	135	163	298
Personnel	124	131	97	228
Total	1,250	1,282	1,350	2,632

The calculation of financial staff in the provinces is more difficult since administrative specialization was rather the exception than the rule. Restricting oneself to posts in which financial duties are the dominant element according to the definition given in the *Da Qing huidian* of 1899, one arrives at a total of 377. This includes provincial treasurers and their immediate subordinates, intendants whose main function was to oversee grain, salt or tea, and the staff of the salt and customs administrations. Even if one adds 1,000 persons to this, assuming that about half the deputies and connected officials assisting prefects and district magistrates by virtue of the statutes of the dynasty were occupied essentially in financial work, one arrives at a total of of 1,800 financial posts, which seems few when compared with the 20,000-odd civil posts described in the *Da Qing huidian* of 1899 for a population of about 450 million people. Thus one can estimate one financial post per 250,000 population.

By way of comparison, one may recall that in 1515, of a body of about 5,000 officers for 16 million subjects, the kingdom of France had 1,557 financial officers and nearly 10,000 in 1665 out of a total of about 46,000 officers for 20 million subjects, that is a ratio of one financial officer per 9,634 and 2,000 inhabitants respectively.[66]

[64] *Lidai zhiguan biao*, 2nd section.

[65] These figures, calculated on the basis of the *Da Qing qinshen quanshu* 大清搢紳全書 (*List of officials of the Qing Empire*) for autumn 1895, are taken from Loh Wai-feng's thesis "The Board of Revenue and Late Ch'ing Finance," submitted at Harvard University in 1977 but still unpublished. I am most grateful to the author for allowing me to consult his work on this subject, as no copy of the list of officials is held in a French library.

[66] P. Chaunu, *op. cit.*, pp. 37, 193-94.

Of course, just as the machinery of the Chinese imperial administration was far from consisting solely of a body of 20,000 officials, the execution of financial tasks also required a large full-time staff of subordinate employees, servants, private secretaries, and commissioners. It was a characteristic of the "Financial State" in late Qing times that the number of financial officials remained almost constant, tending rather to decrease[67] while the size of the non-statutory staff increased.

In the absence of reliable sources it is not really possible to measure this growth exactly or to assess its importance in relation to the overall increase in personnel attached to the imperial administration during the same period. The factors presented here are intended mainly to suggest degrees of importance and to point out trends of development.

Right at the beginning of the nineteenth century, Hong Liangji estimated that there would be about 1,000 clerks (*lixu* 吏胥) in an important district, 700 to 800 in a medium-sized district, and at least 100 or 200 in a small one.[68] If one takes an arithmetical average of 500 clerks, the total amounts to about 763,000 for the 1,526 districts and equivalent divisions. By about 1870-80, noting the steady increase in such subordinate personnel, You Baizhuan 游百川 gives total of 2,000 to 3,000 for a large district, with a minimum of 300 to 400.[69] Thus, applying a low estimate of 800 clerks on the average, one arrives at a total of 1,200,000. If one includes yamen clerks of the higher administrative levels, servants and personal secretaries attached to officials,[70] commissioners charged with various duties and persons attached to these last, the total of non-statutory administrators at the end of the nineteenth century quite probably exceeds 1½ million.

Of this number, what might be the proportion of people allocated solely to finance? Very likely about half. The introduction of *lijin* and the growth of miscellaneous taxes contributed to a considerable increase in financial personnel. However, there was also an increase in numbers employed in policing work, administration of judicial matters, education and the maintenance of order. If the financial bureaucracy developed at a faster pace, it was essentially at the lower levels, through the increase in posts, profitable

---

[67]Some posts were abolished, for example the superintendent of customs at Canton in 1904.

[68]Hong Liangji 洪亮吉, *Juanshige wenjiaji* 卷施閣文甲集, 1.22, in *Hong Beijiang quanji* 洪北江全集 (*Complete works of Hong Liangji*) (1877).

[69]*Huangchao jingshi wen xubian*, 28.46b.

[70]On the increase in the numbers of personal secretaries in the second half of the nineteenth century, cf. Zheng Tianting 鄭天挺, "Qingdai de mufu" 清代的幕府 ("The provincial governor's office in the Qing dynasty"), *Zhongguo shehui kexue* 中國社會科學 (*Social Sciences in China*), 1980, No. 6, pp. 127-47.

no doubt to their holders, and dreaded by the taxpayers, but which conferred no real authority since they were not part of the regular hierarchy and did not involve a regular system of promotion. What took place was less an extension of central power, more a proliferation of public powers at provincial, and especially local, level. It was a fairly anarchic proliferation, dictated by the laws of necessity—money was required, a supplementary tax had to be levied, people were recruited to ensure collection and accounting—but one which in certain cases, notably the growth of private secretaries, led to the development of new principles of specialization and rationality. However morally dubious the yamen clerks might have been, their technical competence was scarcely questioned.

Now, how far was this new personnel marked off from either officialdom or ordinary people? One will observe that the heads of the provincial *lijin* offices (*lijin zongju zongban weiyuan* 釐金總局總辦委員) and their subordinates who were in charge of the various stations were, like the Chinese personnel of a certain level in the maritime customs, nearly all recruited from among expectant officials appointed to the provinces without an actual post by the Board of Personnel. They certainly had the same qualifications as officials in charge of regular posts but since they held non-statutory employment their careers, inspection of their work, and their promotions were not subject to the Board of Personnel. On the contrary, the lower fringe of this non-statutory bureaucracy seemed at times quite close to, and little different from, the ordinary population or, to use a Western term, civil society itself. At local level it is not always easy to draw a clear line between extensions of the state machinery and the power structures of the rural or urban communities. There is a certain continuity between these latter and the formal system of public administration, and it is in the management of tax-collection on trade that this continuity is undoubtedly the most striking. It was standard practice that the agents of the *lijin* offices and the collectors of new taxes be recruited from groups close to the merchant community, and even from this community itself, in order to facilitate such collection, or even that the levy of these taxes be subcontracted to a merchant, to an association, or to leading figures of the gentry.

Although many ambiguities exist, it is nevertheless essential to distinguish between two phenomena on which contemporaries held different views. One is that, because of the administration's incapacity and often at its express request, local gentry assumed growing responsibility in the management of local public affairs, including tax collection.[71] The reformers emphasized the

---

[71] Cf. Mark Elvin's study of the administration of waterways in the Shanghai area ("Market Towns and Waterways: The County of Shanghai from 1480 to 1910," in G. W.

effectiveness and legitimacy of such participation, and after 1901 the movement for local autonomy (*difang zizhi* 地方自治) demanded its legalization.[72] The other phenomenon is that where state agents had recourse to individual assistants outside the established administrative framework to offset deficiencies, such assistants had considerable scope to usurp public power for personal ends precisely because regular control was lacking. In many areas, for example, tax collection had become a private commercial matter in which staff of the yamen or *lijin* office acted as capitalist entrepreneurs, advancing the money for tax payments, and then reimbursing themselves from taxpayers with usurious interest, with the support of the forces of public order. It was against the pervasive extent of such abuses of public authority by agents lacking legitimacy, either official or local, that contemporaries vigorously protested.[73]

Apart from the numbers of staff employed in the administration of finance, it would be desirable to assess the amount of money made available through taxation and managed by the financial bureaucracy, in order to ascertain the leverage of such administration. Whatever the minutiae of public accounts, however, the practices of prevarication and corruption here too prevent any exact calculation. The most reliable method for assessing developments is, after all, to start with the officially acknowledged receipts. The table below provides the key data. To facilitate comparisons, the figures in treasury taels (*kupingliang* 庫平兩) have been converted into metric weights of silver.[74]

Skinner [ed.], *The City in Late Imperial China*, Stanford, 1977, pp. 441-73); the author shows how, at the end of the nineteenth century, a "financial symbiosis" existed between the imperial government and the gentry administrators (p. 465). See also P. A. Kuhn, "Local Taxation and Finance in Republican China," in *Select Papers from the Center for Far Eastern Studies* (Chicago: The University of Chicago), No. 3, 1978-79, pp. 100-136: the study stresses that by the end of the Qing period the participation of local gentry in fiscal tasks concerned mainly the surtaxes and excise taxes, levy of the land tax remaining a monopoly of the state, protected by law and, moreover, exciting only moderately the covetousness of the local gentry (pp. 115-16).

[72] Kuhn, *op. cit.*, p. 108.

[73] *Huangchao jingshi wen xubian*, 28.8-9, 16-17, 38-39. *Huangchao jingshi wen sanbian*, 22.2-3, 23.7b-8.

[74] This conversion was made at the rate of 37.31256 grammes of silver per tael, the equivalent recognized by the treaty of Shimonoseki for the central treasury tael when it was used for accounting receipts. Fixed for the last time in 1742, the weight of a treasury tael only varied slightly, by less than 1%: Wu Chengluo 吳承洛, *Zhongguo duliangheng shi* 中國度量衡史 (*History of weights and measures in China*) (Shanghai: Shangwu 商務, 1937), p. 258; H. B. Morse, *The Trade and Administration of the Chinese Empire*, p. 154. The margin of error is certainly greater for periods prior to 1713, when the treasury tael was defined exactly, but probably never exceeds 5 to 10%. This last percentage actually

Date	Value of tax product in tonnes of silver	Source
1682	1,147	Source (a)
1766	1,492.48	Source (a)
1879	between 1,567 and 1,604	Source (a)
1887	3,142	Source (b)
1893	3,085	Source (b)
1903	3,731	Source (c)

Sources: (a) *Qingshi gao*, pp. 3703-3706 (*shihuozhi* 食貨志 , 6).
        (b) Liu Yueyun 劉嶽雲, *Guangxu kuaiji biao* 光緒會計表 (*Statements of account of the Guangxu reign*) (Shanghai: Jiaoyu shijie she 教育世界社, 1901, 4 *juan*), 1.1b, 2b.
        (c) *Zhongguo jingji quanshu*, pp. 392-93. This figure is that of the annual report of the Board of Revenue for 1903.

Of a gross national product (GNP) estimated at 124,575 tonnes of silver around 1880,[75] the state mobilized 1.28 per cent. In 1893, while the GNP remained much the same, the state levied 2.47 per cent. In the opinion of the best informed contemporaries, the sums actually collected as taxes amounted to three or four times the professed returns;[76] taking account of this factor, the percentage of GNP collected works out at 4 to 5 per cent in 1880, and 8 to 10 per cent in 1893, but scarcely more than 11 per cent in 1903, since by that time the growth of mines, industries, transport, and commerce had increased the GNP.

It may be useful to recall here that around 1640 in the kingdom of France, the state probably had 15 per cent of the GNP at its disposal, that is, about 1,000 tonnes of silver, as opposed to only 90 tonnes in 1515 and 283 tonnes in 1588.[77]

In spite of a strong progression, which almost doubled the amount collected

_____

represents the greatest variation between the value of different monetary taels in the nineteenth century. Yet, on the one hand, it does not appear that the fixing of the weight of a treasury tael in 1742 represented a sensible adjustment related to the average weight previously in use, while on the other hand one observes that the accounts of the central treasury continued to refer to values expressed in pre-1742 taels without making any conversion: cf. Wei Jianyou 魏建猷, *Zhongguo jindai huobi shi* 中國近代貨幣史 (*A history of the currency in modern China*) (Shanghai: Qunlian 羣聯, 1955), pp. 34-36.

[75] Calculation based on Chung-li Chang's estimate, *The Income of the Chinese Gentry* (Seattle: University of Washington Press, 1962), p. 296, corrected by A. Feuerwerker, *The Chinese Economy ca. 1870-1911* (Ann Arbor: The University of Michigan Center for Chinese Studies, 1969), p. 2.

[76] *Zhongguo jingji quanshu*, pp. 349, 369, 392-93.

[77] P. Chaunu, *op. cit.*, Vol. 1, pp. 37, 47, 188.

in ten years, Chinese public finance drained only a modest proportion of the nation's resources. The financial powers of the state remained weak. Levying part of the wealth created by the apparatus of production was only one source of state authority among several, and did not make a decisive contribution to strengthening and increasing the state's capacity to influence society. Indeed the bureaucracy born of the growth in public finance was, as we have seen, essentially "irregular," outside the established body of officers admitted to the service of the state. In the eyes of the most clairvoyant contemporaries, far from truly increasing the efficacy of the state, this bureaucracy even threatened its foundations.[78]

It is also significant that in this development the share of fiscal returns administered directly by the Board of Revenue remained modest and relatively stable: 15.9 million taels in 1887, 22.8 in 1893, about 20 million taels, i.e. 746 tonnes of silver in 1903.[79] The proportion works out respectively at 18.78 per cent, 27.5 per cent, and 20 per cent of officially-acknowledged fiscal resources. But if one considers that the actual tax product was no doubt four times greater, and that unlike the local administrations the Board of Revenue had no direct control over collection and therefore over the supplementary profits, the central government's share appears even smaller.

Neither in the allocation of management responsibilities, nor even by the volume of returns, does this financial structure really differ from that which prevailed from the mid-Ming onwards, especially if one takes into consideration the territorial expansion, population growth, and monetary inflation[80] which the empire had experienced since then. Indeed, around 1550 the Board of Revenue siphoned off over four million taels, that is, 12 per cent of the value of fiscal returns.[81]

Thus the new requirements of the state in late Qing did not substantially alter the system of public finance which the Manchu dynasty had borrowed, along with many other institutions, from its Ming predecessors. The essential features of this system remained as follows: the principle of fixed fiscal quotas; multiplicity of treasuries; a single fiscal authority at the top in the

---

[78] Cf. the thorough analysis of Zheng Guanying 鄭觀應, "Shuli" 書吏 ("Clerks"), *Huangchao jingshi wen sanbian*, 23.8-9.

[79] Liu Yueyun, *Guangxu kuaiji biao*, 1/11. *Zhongguo jingji quanshu*, p. 569.

[80] According to the calculations of Matsui Yoshio 松井義夫, "Shinchō keihi no kenkyū" 清朝經費の研究 (Study of the expenditures of the Qing dynasty), *Mantetsu chōsa geppō* 滿鐵調查月報 (*Monthly report of the Manchurian Railway enquiry services*), Vol. 15, No. 1 (January 1935), p. 43, salaries increased eight-fold and prices six-fold between 1660 and 1860, the population having almost quadrupled to reach 430 million, and territory having doubled to 11 million km^2.

[81] Ray Huang, *Taxation and Governmental Finance in Sixteenth Century China* (Cambridge: Cambridge University Press, 1974), pp. 268, 274.

person of the emperor, combined with a certain sharing of initiative at lower levels; lack of a true budget for the operation of the fiscal administration as well as of a sufficient regular staff. As Ray Huang's study[82] has shown, the main concern of the Ming financial administration was to maintain political stability; it was therefore conceived with the aim of preventing the development of provincial financial power but by the same token it also deprived the central government of the means to enhance its own financial potential. Under the Ming, the financial capacity of the state sank to a level far lower than under the Song or even the Yuan; the growth and specialization of the financial administration had been sharply checked at that time.

If a certain financial potential was developed at the end of the Qing, it was above all at the local level, evading to a large extent the control of the regular financial institutions of the state. The maritime customs are a typical example of this. Its administrative dominion expanded rapidly through the creation of new services—lighthouses and beacons, weather forecasting, mail etc.—and even through the absorption of old administrations like the inland customs in 1901, yet the organism itself was not truly integrated into the state apparatus.

Neither for the prestige and number of its staff, nor for the mass of resources which it handled, did the financial administration of late Qing appear as the driving force in a substantial growth of the power of the imperial state. Did it at least exercise a preponderant influence in guiding administrative management as a whole?

It should first be noted that the officials who were the real executive agents, namely the governors-general and governors, prefects and district magistrates, held financial initiative and power, to such an extent that their action in other matters was not subject to external financial control. In this respect finance was subordinated to politics, rather than the reverse. Financial irregularity was not in itself an *a priori* ground for revoking or attacking a decision. A governor who decided to open a factory did not have to submit his plan for the approval of some financial controller before its execution; he ordered the provincial treasurer to make the payment from funds which he himself would have previously set aside for this purpose. The district magistrate was likewise master over the execution of his decisions; control exercised over him by the prefect and provincial treasurer was hierarchical in nature and not strictly financial. The auditing of accounts conducted by the Board of Revenue, and the surveillance of the Censorate intervened *a posteriori*. Where these resulted in revocation, for purely financial reasons (inadequacy or illegality of the resources involved), of certain decisions whose execution had already begun, it was usually not a question of procedural cavil by means

[82] *Ibid.*

76

of which a financial bureaucracy tried to extend its dominance over all government sectors, but rather of a broad political choice relating to priorities which the state must respect. It should be pointed out, moreover, that the Censorate, which played a crucial role in the control of the administration, since it watched over even the highest-ranking mandarins, was in no respect a financial institution, and that its role was above all to check on the honesty of officials and the proper execution of decisions.[83]

When, in the case of an important decision, a provincial governor referred the matter to Beijing before taking action, it was the imperial approval which he sought. The emperor could, if he saw fit, ask the advice of the Board of Revenue. The latter's advice would prevail, however, only if it was approved by the Grand Council and by the emperor, that is by the purely political authorities. Unfortunately, the available sources do not allow us to determine whether in the Grand Council's deliberations the arguments presented by the Board of Revenue or the grand councillors who came from the Board carried relatively more weight than the others. But if one believes the evidence of some of the presidents of the Board of Revenue, such as Yan Jingming and Weng Tonghe 翁同龢, this was by no means the case.

Nevertheless, two facts must be stressed which contrast with this weakness of financial control over political and administrative decisions: on the one hand, the place of financial work in official duties, and on the other, its importance with regard to promotion.

The already burdensome financial tasks that fell to the district magistrate became increasingly difficult to carry out in the situation prevailing at the end of the nineteenth century, so that the magistrate was often nothing more than a mere tax collector. Having scarcely time to devote himself to anything other than collecting taxes and doing the related accounting, he gave the imperial administration, which in the eyes of the populace he embodied, the image of an essentially fiscal institution.

As a result of the importance assumed by financial tasks in the business of the local mandarins and the growing difficulties of the treasury, the evaluation of officials below the third rank, and at times even above, came to depend mainly on their fiscal prowess. To be classed "exceptional" (*zhuoyi* 卓異), a category which opened the way to promotion, it was necessary to have transmitted without too much delay and in their entirety, the fiscal returns due from one's area of jurisdiction.

[83] Cf. the statistical analysis of interventions made by the censorate by Tang Jihe 湯吉禾, "Qing dai kedao zhi chengji" 清代科道之成績 ("Achievements of the censors under the Qing dynasty"), *Zhongshan wenhua jiaoyu guan jikan* 中山文化教育館季刊 (*Bulletin of the Sun Yat-sen Institute for Culture and Education*), Vol. 2, No. 2 (1935), pp. 517-525.

Fiscal administration thus absorbed a large part of the official's energy and attention at the expense of other activities, and thereby shaped the nature of the civil service. Hence one can say that financial administration exercised a dominant influence over general administration. But this influence in fact restricted the state's action and its intervention in social life, and was one of the factors contributing to the crumbling of the imperial state's power.

It is significant that, while recognizing the importance of the problem of public finance, the reform movement, with which the establishment of a new governmental system in 1906 is connected, did not make financial reform its central objective. Moreover, it was before, not during, the period when the government suffered from the greatest lack of funds and when the fiscal burden became heaviest, that the call for reform was put forward.

While it is undoubtedly the case that the prospect of assuring adequate financial means contributed greatly to convincing the court to accept the reforms, the simple desire to retain power over a unified empire was in itself a yet more decisive factor. The guiding idea of the reform movement was the adjustment of relations between the sovereign and his subjects, the uniting of hearts (*yixin* 一心) which would allow the peaceful regulation of society by the state (*zhi* 治) and consequently the prosperity of the population and strength of the country (*fuqiang* 富强).

From the end of the Taiping Rebellion to 1906, the financial administration operated according to a system of deconcentration which was the result neither of a regression nor of an advance in centralization. This decentralization seems to me to be due both to the level of technical means, in particular the uncertainties of the means of communication and information, and to political conceptions, notably the idea that to govern is to regulate, to maintain equilibrium and harmony, not to command or constrain. In this context, the management of public finance did not stimulate the growth and spread of state authority as was the case in the monarchies of Europe. It encouraged only the proliferation of local powers of a semi-official type which made the task of a unitary government even more difficult.

Indeed the anarchic growth of a sub-bureaucracy which evaded regular modes of control, that is the increase in non-statutory personnel at provincial and local levels which characterized the late Qing, had important consequences for the transformation of the imperial state into a new type of state. On one hand, the presence of these agents called into question the legitimacy of public authority in the eyes of the population, and on the other it infringed on the exercise and efficacy of central authority, since it created or reinforced networks of local complicity as well as of regional forces. The machinery of a new state thus could not build directly on the imperial administrative system.

It was obliged not only to grant to ordinary citizens, or at least to some of them, legal participation in government and means of control over the administration, but also to establish effective lines of command from the highest to the lowest level. These two different and often contradictory demands have greatly contributed to the vicissitudes of the evolution of Chinese political institutions until the present day.

The Structure of the Financial Institution of the State in the Late Qing

It was obliged not only to grant to ordinary citizens, or at least to some of them, legal participation in government and means of control over the administration, but also to establish effective lines of command from the bottom to the top level. These two different and often contradictory demands have greatly contributed to the vicissitudes of the evolution of Chinese political institutions until the present day.

4. Decentralization in a Unitary State: Theory and Practice, 1940-1984

Stuart R. Schram

Although in many domains of political and economic work a high degree of decentralization, or of devolution of power and responsibility, has prevailed in China during most of the period since 1949, the unitary nature of the Chinese state has been forcefully asserted, and any hint of the federalism which prevails (in theory) in the Soviet Union utterly repudiated. In this paper, I shall offer a sketch of the evolution of this paradox, with the aim of elucidating the sources of Chinese ideas and practices, as they emerged from the triple matrix of the national heritage, Marxist and Soviet influence, and the concrete problems confronted by China over the past half century.

These three dimensions are all relevant to this problem, as to every other aspect of contemporary Chinese politics. The imprint of traditional practices, and of the Leninist tradition, are relatively easy to identify and define. The practice of investing local officials with wide powers, and at the same time maintaining them under constant control and holding them ultimately accountable, is a well-known trait of the imperial system, from Qin and Han times onward. The many-faceted but pregnant concept of "democratic centralism" is likewise very close to the heart of Chinese interpretations of Soviet theories, as it was at the core of Lenin's own thinking.

The lessons of China's political experiènce in the decades prior to 1949 were somewhat more ambiguous. While Mao Zedong and his comrades shared with all politically-conscious Chinese of their generation an overriding desire to avoid the disintegration of the national polity and the consequent subjection or extinction of the Chinese people, and were therefore inclined to stress the need for a strong centralized state, tactical considerations sometimes led them to offer not only self-determination, but federalism freely entered into, to national minorities in key positions, from the 1920s to the mid-1940s.

To cite only a few instances of this (all of them drawn from the most authoritative possible source, namely Mao's own writings), a proclamation in verse dated January 1929, while giving as the ultimate goal of the revolutionary struggle "to unite China" (*tongyi zhonghua* 統一中華), added that the Manchus, Mongols, Muslims (Hui 回), and Tibetans should "themselves determine their statutes" (*zhangcheng ziding* 章程自定). The use of the term *zhangcheng* indicated that these peoples would decide their own constitutional position within the framework of a united China, but it nevertheless implies a considerable degree of self-determination.[1]

In an interview of 23 July 1936 with Edgar Snow, Mao spoke explicitly of a federation:

> The relationship between Outer Mongolia and the Soviet Union, now and in the past, has always been based on the principle of complete equality. When the people's revolution has been victorious in China, the Outer Mongolian republic will automatically became a part of the Chinese federation, at its own will. The Mohammedan and Tibetan peoples, likewise will form autonomous republics attached to the China federation.[2]

Mao used similar language once again in his report to the Seventh Congress of the Chinese Communist Party in April 1945, where he said:

> The question of the New Democratic state and of New Democratic political power also includes the question of federalism. All the nationalities (*minzu* 民族) within China's boundaries should, on the basis of the principles of voluntariness and democracy, organize the Chinese Federation of Democratic Republics (*Zhonghua minzhu gongheguo lianbang* 中華民主共和國聯邦), and moreover, on this federal basis, organize the Central Government of the federation.[3]

If Mao Zedong thus spoke explicitly of federalism during the Yan'an period, it was no doubt partly in response to the spirit of the times, when the main goal of the Chinese Communist movement was repeatedly said to be "national revolution" (*minzu geming* 民族革命) and "national liberation" (*minzu jiefang* 民族解放). It was also quite obviously a case of following, in this as in other matters, the Soviet example.

But it was no doubt also because he was well persuaded that the smaller peoples who were or had been part of China would certainly choose, when the time came, to resume their rightful place there. The classic example of this is the case of Mongolia. Three years after telling Edgar Snow that when

---

[1] Proclamation of the Fourth Red Army, signed by Mao and Zhu De. Copied from a text on display at the Museum in Ciping on the Jinggangshan. See also Takeuchi Minoru 竹內實 (ed.), *Mao Zedong ji* 毛澤東集 (*Collected writings of Mao Zedong*) (Tokyo: Hokubōsha 北望社 , 1971), Vol. 2, pp. 71-72.

[2] Originally published in the *Shanghai Evening Post and Mercury*, 3, 4, and 5 February 1937. The above extract, reproduced from Snow's typewritten manuscript, was reprinted with his permission in S. Schram, *The Political Thought of Mao Tse-tung* (New York: Praeger, 1963). In the revised edition (New York: Praeger, 1969), it appears on pp. 419-20.

[3] This paragraph was, for obvious reasons, eliminated in the post-1949 edition of the *Selected Works*. The original 1945 version is conveniently reproduced in *Mao Zedong ji*, Vol. 9 (1971), p. 220.

the revolution was victorious in China, the Mongols would "automatically" join the Chinese federation, Mao defined China's boundaries, in *The Chinese Revolution and the Chinese Communist Party*, in such a way as to place the whole of Mongolia on the Chinese side, at least by implication. By 1952, when this text was revised for publication in the *Selected Works*, Mao had discovered that (quite apart from the possible feelings of the Mongols themselves) the relationship between the Outer Mongolian republic and the Soviet Union was not necessarily based on "the principle of complete equality," and that there was no possibility at all of that country's joining the Chinese family of nations. He therefore inserted a sentence referring to China's boundary with the People's Republic of Mongolia.[4]

Thus, Mao's appeals to federalism in the 1930s and 1940s by no means negated his commitment to a strong centralized Chinese state. Circumstances having changed after 1949, there was no longer any hesitation in proclaiming the rigorously unitary nature of the new People's Republic. The problem of the relations between the central authorities and the lower levels (including areas inhabited by national minorities) remained, however, and it is that which forms the subject of this paper.

The line of the Chinese Communist Party in this domain, as in so many others, assumed definite shape during the Yan'an period. The quintessential expression of the Party's administrative philosophy is to be found in the concept of the "mass line." Before discussing the implications of the Yan'an heritage for the relations between the centre and the localities, it will perhaps help to clarify the issues if we first consider briefly another dimension of the "mass line," and of political work generally, namely the relation between the leaders and the led.

Such an effort at clarification may find some justification in the oddly conflicting views of these matters which have prevailed over the past three decades. When the Chinese People's Republic was established in 1949, some people saw it as a carbon copy of the Soviet system; others, such as Karl A. Wittfogel, stressed the indigenous roots of the methods employed by Mao and his comrades. But whether the new régime was characterized as "Stalinist" or as a "stronger Oriental despotism," it was commonly stigmatized in the West as repressive and totalitarian.

Then came the interlude of the Cultural Revolution, during which the pendulum of fashionable orthodoxy swung almost as far in the opposite direction, to such an extent that we heard rather of a sage leader whose

---

[4] See the original text, with the post-1952 variants, in *Mao Zedong ji*, Vol. 7, p. 98. For a slightly fuller discussion of this point, see S. Schram, *Mao Tse-tung* (Harmondsworth: Penguin, 1967), p. 256.

approach to revolution left no place for power or coercion at all, and whose sole concern was to allow the people to liberate themselves and to run things in their own spontaneous way. Such a romanticized, or sentimentalized, version of the Yan'an heritage was sheer myth, the product of a wish-dream on the part of those who propagated it.

Though Mao Zedong saw the process of government as in part an educative process, he had no Spockian notions to the effect that the "students" should be entirely free to decide what they should learn; and if we look at the record of his life as a whole, it is evident that his thought is strongly marked by an insistence on the need for firm leadership by a political elite.

On the whole, this is now recognized, but in many quarters the pendulum has swung back once more to the previous extreme, and China is regarded as an even more hatefully totalitarian country than the Soviet Union. A corollary of this view is that the "mass line," about which so much was heard in the 1960s, is nothing but a sheer imposture.

That is, once again, a biased and simplistic conclusion, but although the "mass line" does have meaning, it must be correctly understood as evoking a particular aspect of "democratic centralism," not as the negation of the latter concept. This is, in fact, evident from Mao's own classic definition of the term, which reads:

> ... all correct leadership is necessarily from the masses, to the masses. This means: take the ideas of the masses (scattered and unsystematic ideas) and concentrate them (through study turn them into concentrated and systematic ideas), then go to the masses and propagate and explain these ideas *until the masses embrace them as their own* (*hua wei qunzhong de yijian* 化爲群衆的意見), hold fast to them and translate them into action, ... [5]

To suggest that ordinary people may be a source of ideas from which correct policies are elaborated, and that they can in turn understand these policies, rather than blindly applying them, marked a very great rupture with one of the central themes of traditional Chinese thought.

According to the *Analects*: "The people may be made to follow a path of action, but they may not be made to understand it."[6] This is one of the Confucian prejudices that Mao strove for half a century to break down. He did not, however, cast doubt in so doing on the Leninist axiom that class consciousness can only be imported into the working class from outside, and more broadly that the Communist Party must provide ideological guidance to society as a whole.

As the words underscored in the quotation from Mao's mass-line directive

---

[5] *The Political Thought of Mao Tse-tung*, pp. 316-17. (Italics added.)
[6] *Confucian Analects*, Book VIII, Ch. ix, in Legge, *The Chinese Classics*, Vol. I, p. 211.

make plain, the people, though taken into the confidence of the leaders of the revolutionary movement, were in the end to be made to embrace, and to internalize, ideas which, if left to themselves, they were quite incapable of elaborating in systematic form. There is an obvious parallel here with Lenin's thinking, and it is therefore not surprising that, at about the same time as he put forward this formulation of the "mass line," Mao should have reaffirmed in its full Leninist rigour the principle of centralized guidance by a revolutionary elite. "Some comrades," he complained in his speech of 1 February 1942, launching the Rectification Campaign, ". . . do not understand the Party's system of democratic centralism; they do not know that the Communist Party not only needs democracy, but needs centralization even more. They forget the system of democratic centralism, in which the minority is subordinate to the majority, the lower level to the higher level, the part to the whole, and the entire membership to the Central Committee."[7]

Within the broad limits defined by Mao's insistence both on a measure of initiative and involvement from below, and on firm centralized guidance from above, there is room for an infinite variety of formulations and shades of emphasis. From Yan'an days to the early 1960s, Mao Zedong rang the changes on these themes. Consistently, however, he regarded centralized leadership as in the last analysis even more important than democracy. The Cultural Revolution saw, at least in its initial stages, the reversal of this emphasis, and appeared to call into question the very need for a locus of power and authority which was not immanent in society itself. Subsequently, we shall consider whether this episode constituted the logical culmination of Mao Zedong's thinking about these matters, or whether it was rather an aberration. There is no doubt, however, that the present Chinese leadership has utterly repudiated the "anarchism" of Mao's last decade, so the Yan'an emphasis on centralism can assuredly be taken as summing up the predominant view of the relation between leadership and democracy over the past four decades.

Although these considerations regarding the relations between the bearers of political power and the population as a whole provide the indispensable background for understanding the administrative philosophy of the Chinese Communist Party, it is the problem of the relation between organs of power at the central, regional, and local level which constitutes the main theme of this essay. Here, too, a knowledge of the Yan'an heritage is indispensable to the understanding of developments after 1949.

The ideas of the Chinese Communist leadership about patterns of organization were strongly influenced by twenty years of military and political

[7] *The Political Thought of Mao Tse-tung*, p. 313.

struggle in the countryside. During the late 1930s and early 1940s, the lessons of this experience were summed up, systematized, and applied to economic work as well as to guerrilla tactics.

The key slogan of the early 1940s was "centralized leadership and dispersed operation" (*jizhong lingdao, fensan jingying* 集中領導，分散經營). Such an approach was particularly appropriate in the conditions of the time, when only a relatively small proportion of the total area controlled by the Communists was located in the main Yan'an base area, and the technical level of the economy was so low that rigorously centralized planning of inputs and outputs was neither possible nor desirable. Even under these circumstances, however, the accent was by no means on continued and unmitigated dispersion of responsibility and effort. Mao Zedong made this point quite unequivocally in his report of December 1942 *Economic and Financial Prblems*.[8]

Asking the rhetorical question why the self-sufficient industry of the Border Region should be run in such a dispersed fashion, Mao replied:

> The main reason is that the labour force is divided among the various branches of the Party, government and army. If it were centralized, we would destroy their activism. For example, we encouraged 359 Brigade to set up the Daguang Textile Mill and did not order it to combine with a government mill because most of the several hundred employees at the mill were selected from the officers and men of 359 Brigade. They work to produce the bedding and clothing requirements of the Brigade and their enthusiasm is high. If we centralized, we would destroy this enthusiasm. . . . Adopting the policy of "dispersed operation" is correct and ideas aimed at centralizing everything are wrong. However, enterprises of the same kind carried out within the same area should be centralized as much as possible. Unlimited dispersal is not profitable. At present, we are already carrying out . . . centralization of this kind. . . . Perhaps this process of dispersal at first and centralization later cannot be avoided.

Later in the same section, listing the economic measures which should be pursued in 1943, Mao placed second (immediately after increased capital investment) that of "establishing a unified leadership for the whole of self-supporting industry, overcoming the serious anarchy which exists now."[9] In order to achieve this result, he called for the establishment of a "unified plan," drawn up under the "unified leadership" of the Finance and Economy Office (*Caijing banshichu* 財經辦事處), but at the same time he specified that

---

[8] Only the first part of this very long work appears in the current canon of the *Selected Works*. The passages quoted below are from Part 7, "On developing a self-sufficient industry." For the sake of convenience, I give the pagination from the Tokyo *Mao Zedong ji*. The translation used is that of Andrew Watson, *Mao Zedong and the Political Economy of the Border Region* (Cambridge: Cambridge University Press, 1980).

[9] *Mao Zedong ji*, Vol. 8, pp. 263-64; Watson, *op. cit.*, pp. 149-50.

agriculture, industry, and commerce should not be "put entirely in the hands of one single official organization for the whole Border Region." Instead, the unified plan should be "handed over to the Party, government and army systems for separate implementation." Nevertheless, Mao's final conclusion was that the problem of unified leadership was "the central problem in advancing self-supporting industry during 1943."[10]

The sentence just quoted poses explicitly the problem of the relation between Party, state, and army, which remained a central and often controversial issue after 1949. A key concept, introduced in Yan'an, conveys the essence of the Party's unifying and guiding role as conceived at that time. The term is *yiyuanhua* 一元化 —literally, "to make one," "to make monolithic." It has sometimes been translated "to co-ordinate," but that is probably too weak a rendering; "to unify," which has also been used, is unsatisfactory because it seems best to reserve this English term as the equivalent for *tongyi* 统一, just as "centralized" is best kept for translating *jizhong* 集中. The English equivalent which I propose to use is "integrate," but this question of translation is less important than the concerns which underlay the adoption of the Chinese expression in the early 1940s. Because this concept has hitherto received far less attention than democratic centralism or the mass line, I shall give a number of illustrations of its use, before summing up my understanding of its significance.

To the best of my knowledge, the *locus classicus* of this term is to be found in the Resolution of the Politburo dated 1 September 1942 "On the Unification of Party Leadership in the Anti-Japanese Bases, and Adjusting the Relations between Various Organizations."[11]

This resolution asserts explicitly and forcefully the link between Party-government and Party-army relations on the one hand, and the hierarchical structure of each individual organization on the other. Paragraph 8 of the resolution begins as follows:

> The *yiyuanhua* of Party leadership is [to be] expressed on one hand in the mutual relations between Party, governmental, and mass organizations at the same level; on the other hand, it is [to be] expressed in the relations between upper and lower levels. In this [latter respect], strict adherence to the principle of obedience

---

[10] *Mao Zedong ji*, Vol. 8, pp. 265, 273; Watson, *op. cit.*, pp. 151, 160-61.

[11] This was one of the documents studied in the course of the Rectification Campaign, and an English translation can be found in Boyd Compton, *Mao's China: Party Reform Documents, 1942-1944* (Seattle: University of Washington Press, 1952; paperback 1966), pp. 161-75. Authorship of the resolution has not been officially attributed to Mao, but the Chinese text is included in the Tokyo *Mao Zedong ji*, Vol. 8, pp. 155-63.

of the entire Party to the Central Committee is of decisive significance in unifying Party leadership.[12]

There follows a forceful lecture on the obligation for responsible Party organs at lower levels to seek instructions from the Central Committee in important matters, and not to "endanger the unified leadership of the entire Party by setting up strange new standards and making decisions on their own." The resolution sums up as follows the relation between the Party and other organizations:

> The Party is the vanguard of the proletariat and the highest form of proletarian organization; it should lead all other organizations whether military, governmental, or mass. The unification (*tongyi*) and *yiyuanhua* of the leadership in the bases should be expressed in each base in the existence of a unified Party committee exercising leadership over everything. . . . Consequently, it has been decided that organs representing the Central Committee (Central Committee bureaux and sub-bureaux) and Party committees at each level (district and local committees) are to be the highest leading organs in the districts, that they are to unify (*tongyi*) the leadership in all Party, governmental, military and mass work.[13]

A somewhat clearer definition and explanation of the meaning of the elusive term *yiyuanhua* is to be found in the decision of 1 June 1943, drafted by Mao Zedong, from which I quoted the well-known paragraph on the "mass line." In an immediately following passage (paragraph 7) of this directive, Mao declares:

> In relaying to subordinate units any task . . . , a higher organization should in all cases go through the leader of the lower organization concerned, so that he may assume responsibility, thus achieving the goal of combining division of labour with integrated leadership (*yiyuanhua*). A department at a higher level should not go solely to its counterpart at the lower level (for instance, a higher department concerned with organization, propaganda or counter-espionage should not go solely to the corresponding department at the lower level), leaving the person in overall charge of the lower organization (such as the secretary, the chairman, the director or the school principal) in ignorance or without responsibility. Both the person in overall charge and the person with specific responsibility should be informed and given responsibility. This *yiyuanhua* method, combining division of labour with unified (*tongyi*) leadership, makes it possible, through the person with overall responsibility, to mobilize a large number of cadres . . . to carry out a particular task, and thus to overcome shortages of cadres in individual

---

[12] Compton, *op. cit.*, pp. 171-72; translation modified on the basis of the Chinese text in *Mao Zedong ji*, Vol. 8, p. 161.

[13] Compton, *op. cit.*, pp. 162-63; *Mao Zedong ji*, Vol. 8, p. 156. Roughly the same passage is quoted and analyzed by Mark Selden, *The Yenan Way in Revolutionary China* (Cambridge, Mass.: Harvard University Press, 1971), pp. 223-34, who gives the best available account of the circumstances in which these policies were adopted.

departments and turn a good number of people into cadres for one's own work. This, too, is a way of combining the leadership with the masses.[14]

It will be seen (as well as such things can be seen in translation) that *yiyuanhua* is here used as an appositive for "combining division of labour with unified leadership." The sense, plainly, is that the necessary division of labour between various organs can exist without posing a threat to the unity of the movement only on condition that the whole system be penetrated and controlled by a unifying force in the shape of the Party. To convey this function, I have chosen the English equivalent "to integrate" (which I shall also use in the participial form, e.g., "integrated Party leadership").

The use of the term *yiyuanhua*, with its strong verbal force, reflects the perception, on the part of the Chinese Communist leadership, of the situation that prevailed in the early 1940s in the base areas, which were fragmented, often isolated, and exposed to enemy attack. Under such circumstances, the various agencies of political, economic, and administrative control could scarcely be effectively integrated. They stressed, therefore, the necessity of *making* monolithic or monistic (*yiyuanhua*), because excessive dispersal in fact prevailed.

This interpretation, which had suggested itself on the basis of the written materials of the Yan'an period, was confirmed by Liao Gailong 廖蓋隆, Deputy Director of the Institute of Marxism-Leninism-Mao Zedong Thought of the Chinese Academy of Social Sciences, in a conversation of 26 June 1980. Replying to my question about the nuance between *yiyuanhua* and *tongyi* (as in *"dang de yiyuanhua/tongyi lingdao"* 黨的一元化／統一領導, "the integrated/unified leadership of the Party"), Professor Liao stated that, when "dispersionism" (*fensanzhuyi* 分散主義) prevailed, there was a tendency to talk about *yiyuanhua*; when unity had been effectively established and was no longer threatened, it was more common to speak of *tongyi lingdao*.[15]

One might assume that, once the Chinese Communists had established their authority throughout the whole of the country and set up the People's Republic of China, dispersionism would no longer be a threat. In fact, for

[14] *Selected Works*, III, pp. 120-21, revised on the basis of *Mao Zedong ji*, Vol. 9, p. 29, to take account of changes in the official Chinese text as compared with the 1943 version (which are not particularly extensive).

[15] Conversation at the Chinese Academy of Social Sciences between the Director of the Institute of Marxism-Leninism-Mao Zedong Thought, Yu Guangyuan 于光遠, Liao Gailong, and other members of the Institute, and the "North American Delegation to Investigate Problems of the Chinese Revolution," which visited China from 16 June to 15 July 1980. The other members of the delegation were Ed Friedman (leader), Jerome Ch'en, Angus McDonald, Maurice Meisner, Ross Terrill, and Tsou Tang. For the significance of these comments in the context of 1980, see below.

many complex historical and practical reasons, the problems of fragmentation and of divided authority by no means evaporated in 1949, and the concept of "integrated leadership" therefore did not become irrelevant. But the whole context did, of course, change radically with the conquest of power.

I. FORM AND CONTENT OF THE PEOPLE'S DEMOCRATIC STATE

In characterizing their new régime, the Chinese themselves made use of a distinction which Mao had employed in *On New Democracy* between the "state system" (*guoti* 國體) and the "system of government" (*zhengti* 政體).[16] Not surprisingly, since they viewed the matter in a Marxist framework, Chinese writers in the early 1950s defined *guoti* primarily in class terms. Thus, one reference work for political study by basic-level cadres, first published in 1952, said in part:

> The state system is the class essence of the state. The question of the state system is the question of the place of the various social classes in the state, i.e., it is the question of which class controls the political power of the state. For the most part, the state systems of the various countries of the world at the present time can be divided into three types: (1) the capitalist state system, marked by the dictatorship of the reactionary bourgeoisie; (2) the socialist state system, marked by the dictatorship of the working class; and (3) the new-democratic state system, marked by the joint dictatorship of the various revolutionary classes, led by the working class and with the worker-peasant alliance as the foundation.[17]

This had been the classification laid down by Mao in 1939-40. The state established in 1949 was called a people's dictatorship, rather than a proletarian dictatorship, because it was seen as a hybrid form adapted to the circumstances prevailing during the "period of transition" from postwar reconstruction to the building of socialism. While it was an axiom of Marxism that power, in a society where capitalism had begun to develop, could be exercised only by the proletariat or by the bourgeoisie, and not by any intermediate class or combination of classes, Lenin had put forward, in 1905, the formula of the "revolutionary-democratic dictatorship of the workers and the peasants" to characterize the political system under which certain reforms could be carried out in Russia prior to the establishment of a full-blooded proletarian dictatorship. Mao's "people's democratic dictatorship" was a lineal descendant of this Leninist concept, which had been

[16] Mao Tse-tung, *Selected Works*, II, pp. 351-52.

[17] Chen Beiou 陳北鷗, *Renmin xuexi cidian* 人民學習辭典 (*People's study dictionary*), 2nd ed. (Shanghai: Guangyi shuju 廣益書局, 1953), pp. 288-89.

applied to China and other Asian countries by the Comintern in the 1920s and 1930s.

On the eve of victory, Mao Zedong defined the locus of sovereignty in such a state in terms of what has often been called a concentric-circle metaphor. The "people" who were to exercise the dictatorship would be composed of the working class, the peasantry, the urban petty bourgeoisie and the "national bourgeoisie." These are the four categories making up the famous "four-class bloc" invented by Stalin in the 1920s. Of these classes, the workers were to exercise hegemony, and the peasants constituted the most reliable allies. The petty bourgeoisie were to be largely followers, while the national bourgeoisie had a dual nature: they were part of the people, but at the same time exploiters. Consequently, those elements among them who behaved badly could be re-classified as "non-people," and find themselves on the receiving end of the dictatorship, the objects rather than the subjects of revolutionary change.

Mao made no mystery at all of the type of state which was to represent these four classes. Replying to imaginary critics who complained that the Communists were "autocrats," he declared:

> My dear sirs, you are right, that is just what we are. All the experience the Chinese people have accumulated through several decades teaches us to enforce the people's democratic dictatorship—which one could also call the people's democratic autocracy (*renmin minzhu ducai* 人民民主獨裁), the two terms mean the same thing—that is, to deprive the reactionaries of the right to speak and let the people alone have that right.[18]

Since *guoti* was thus made to include not only the class nature of the state, but the mode of rule ("dictatorial" or "autocratic"), what realm of meaning was left to be covered by *zhengti*? Most definitions of the *zhengti* of the Chinese People's Republic in its earliest years[19] refer back to Mao's formulation in "On New Democracy," where he wrote in part:

> As for the question of the "system of government,"[20] this is a matter of how political power is organized, the form in which one social class or another chooses to arrange its apparatus of political power to oppose its enemies and protect

---

[18] *The Political Thought of Mao Tse-tung*, p. 234.

[19] See, for example, *Renmin da xianzhang xuexi shouce* 人民大憲章學習手冊 (*Study handbook on the people's charter*) (Shanghai: Zhanwan Zhoukan 展望周刊 , Nov. 1949), p. 135; *Renmin da xianzhang xuexi ziliao* 人民大憲章學習資料 (*Materials for the study of the people's charter*) (Tianjin: Lianhe tushu chubanshe 聯合圖書出版社, Oct. 1949; repr. 1950), p. 31.

[20] In the original version, this reads "political power" (*zhengquan* 政權) rather than "system of government" (*zhengti* 政體), but the latter term is used in the first sentence of the ensuing paragraph, so the overall sense of the passage is not substantially affected. (See *Mao Zedong ji*, Tokyo, Vol. 7, pp. 165-66.)

itself.... China may now adopt a system of people's congresses, from the national people's congress down to the provincial, county, district and township people's congresses, with all levels electing their respective governmental bodies. But if there is to be a proper representation for each revolutionary class according to its status in the state, a proper expression of the people's will . . . then a system of really universal and equal suffrage, irrespective of sex, creed, property or education, must be introduced. Such is the system of democratic centralism. . . .

The state system, a joint dictatorship of all the revolutionary classes and the system of government, democratic centralism—these constitute the politics of New Democracy.[21]

This passage was, of course, written in 1940, when Mao was still operating within the context of the United Front with the Guomindang and the position of the Chinese Communist Party was relatively weak. By 1949, his idea of a "republic of New Democracy" stressed rather the need for dictatorship over the "reactionary" classes than direct elections based on universal suffrage as the key to genuine democracy. The affirmation of "democratic centralism" as the basic organizational principle of the new state remained, on the other hand, intact.

If we turn now from the realm of theory and definition to more concrete aspects of the political and administrative organization of China in the earliest years of the People's Republic, the general picture at this time can be summed up in two complementary propositions. On the one hand, the slogan of "centralized leadership and dispersed operation" (or variants thereof) remained in honour, and in other respects institutions and policies were adapted to the requirements of a country which had not yet been fully integrated politically and militarily, and in which political and economic conditions were widely divergent from one region to another. But on the other hand, the whole effort of the Chinese leadership was bent toward transforming this existing national reality in such a way as to lay the foundations for effective centralized planning on the Soviet model.

An important and characteristic feature of the political order established in 1949, which illustrates the interaction of the two aspects of the situation to which I have just alluded, was the division of the country into six "Greater Administrative Regions." As the most recent studies of the problem have convincingly argued, this institutional device, which might appear at first glance to contain germs of federalism (or even of "warlordism," since the regions were military as well as political), was designed not to perpetuate the existing regional differences, but to bring central authority effectively to bear at the lower levels.[22]

[21] *Selected Works*, II, p. 352.

[22] See Ronald C. Keith, "The Pattern of National Political Integration in China, 1949-1954: The Role of the Greater Administrative Regions" (Ph.D. thesis, University

The political framework into which these regions were inserted in December 1949 was unitary and in no sense federalist, as the terse reference to relations between central and local authorities in the "Common Programme" of September 1949 (which served as the fundamental law of the state until the adoption of a formal constitution in 1954) made perfectly clear. The relevant passage (Article 16) reads as follows:

> The jurisdiction of the Central People's Government and the local people's governments . . . shall be prescribed by decrees of the Central People's Government Council so as to satisfy the requirements of both national unity and local expediency.[23]

Thus the various entities below the national level—people's congresses and people's governments—were to enjoy only such powers as were explicitly conferred on them by the national government. There could not be a more complete negation of the very principle of federalism. At a meeting of the Central People's Government Council on 2 December 1949, a fortnight before the formal establishment of the Greater Administrative Regions and the political and military organs administering them, Mao justified this development, in a speech to the Central People's Government Council, in terms of his usual argument in favour of combining "national unity and local expediency":

> China is big. . . . We must establish this kind of level of forceful local organ; only then can we manage affairs well. What ought to be unified must be unified . . . , but we must combine unification and local expediency.[24]

It is not surprising that such an intermediate level should have been created in 1949, in view of the conditions prevailing at the time, nor is it surprising that the region should have been abolished in 1954, as the First Five-Year Plan was getting under way. What *is* curious and striking is that the regions should have been weakened in March 1950, only a few months after they had been set up, and then reinforced, and their importance re-asserted once again, in March 1951.

The provisional institutions of September 1949 provided for a two-tier "Central People's Government," comprising the "Central People's Government Council" (*zhongyang renmin zhengfu weiyuanhui* 中央人民政府委員會), which had overall responsibility for major decisions regarding policy and

---

of London, July 1977); and also Dorothy Solinger, *Regional Government and Political Integration in Southwest China, 1949-1954* (Berkeley: University of California Press, 1977).

[23] English text conveniently reproduced in T.H.E. Chen, *The Chinese Communist Regime: Documents and Commentary* (London: Pall Mall, 1967), p. 38.

[24] *Renmin ribao* 人民日報, 4 December 1949; quoted in Solinger, *op. cit.*, p. 29.

organization, and the "Government Administrative Council" (*Zheng wu yuan* 政務院), which was in charge of the day-to-day running of affairs. (Mao Zedong was Chairman of the first, and Zhou Enlai *zongli* 總理 or Premier of the second.)[25] It was in fact the Government Administrative Council which adopted, on 16 December 1949, the "Organic Regulations of the Greater Administrative Region People's Government Councils" defining the structure and functions of these bodies, although the "Organic Law of the Central People's Government" of September 1949 had contained a reference to such a regional level,[26] and the Central People's Government Council had approved in principle the setting up of regional political authorities.

These regulations gave the regional authorities (which were ultimately to take the form of elected People's Government Councils, but would consist in the immediate future, in the aftermath of the civil war, of appointed Military Administrative Committees) fairly wide powers at their own level and below it, subject to the approval and/or control of the Central People's Government in important matters.[27]

As for the substantive powers of action of the regional authorities, they were, as Dorothy Solinger has put it, "both local power organs and central agents."[28] The regional authorities were to obtain the approval of the Government Administrative Council in matters of "national importance," act first and then report to the Centre on "important" matters, and deal with lesser problems on their own, including the appointment and removal of subordinate officials at the provincial and lower levels.[29]

The successive policy reversals of March 1950 and March 1951 related primarily to financial matters. Here, the Common Programme had, while calling on the Central People's Government to draw up a "general plan for rehabilitating ... the economy ... ," also stressed that, under the unified leadership of the Centre, the economic departments of local governments should "give full play to their creativity and initiative."[30] The "Organic Law" of 16 December 1949 provided that, "within the scope of overall state budgetary estimates," the Military Administrative Committees were to prepare regional budgets for submission to the central government for approval.[31] Less than three months later, on 3 March 1950, a decision of

[25] "The Organic Law of the Central People's Government of the People's Republic of China," in Chen, *op. cit.*, pp. 46-51.
[26] *Ibid.*, Article 7, par. 9b, p. 47.
[27] Keith, *op. cit.*, pp. 112-13.
[28] Solinger, *op. cit.*, p. 36.
[29] *Ibid.*, pp. 31-33, and Keith, *op. cit.*, pp. 112-20.
[30] Article 33, text in Chen, *op. cit.*, p. 41.
[31] Solinger, *op. cit.*, p. 32.

the Government Administrative Council on the unification of national financial and economic work called for the centralization of revenue and expenditure in terms which largely deprived the regions both of their policy-formulating role and of the material basis for any degree of autonomy, by requiring that all grain, tax money, etc., should be handed over to central control.[32] Then, only a year afterward, on 29 March 1951, a complete reversal was operated, and a three-level plan for tax sharing was introduced, which Zhou Enlai justified on the basis of a slight variant on the Yan'an slogan, "unified leadership and divided responsibilities" (*tongyi lingdao, fenji fuze* 統一領導，分級負責).[33]

The reasons for these abrupt reversals must lie at least in part in the interaction of divergent views among the leadership. The term *yiyuanhua*, discussed above, was very close to the centre of this debate. On 13 March 1950, ten days after the turn away from the earlier policies of relative decentralization, Gao Gang 高崗 gave a report at a conference of Party workers from the North East Region in which he put forward an interpretation of *yiyuanhua* very different from that which had prevailed in Yan'an. In the course of a defence of the Soviet-style policies of "one-man management" in factories, he made the following remarks:

> There are some comrades amongst us who consider that the secretary of the Party committee or Party branch can replace the system whereby the factory general manager enjoys overall responsibility. This idea is manifestly wrong. Party committees and Party branches are not administrative organs within factories. . . . They may make timely suggestions when necessary, but cannot replace the factory general manager. . . . Each state enterprise must work under the economic plan for the whole country and that plan is formulated by state organs under the leadership of the Party Central Committee or representative organs for the Central Committee. The responsibilities of the factory general manager are given him by higher organs of state and are determined not only by the needs of his own factory, but also by the integrated (*yiyuanhua*) requirements of the national plan. If the factory general manager is made responsible not to leading organs of state or organs responsible for enterprises at a higher level, but to a Party committee or Party branch within the factory . . . then there will no longer be any "integrated leadership" (*lingdao yiyuanhua*), but on the contrary integrated leadership will be split and shattered. We must understand that Party organs should not and cannot replace state organs.[34]

---

[32] *Ibid.*, pp. 34-35; Keith, *op. cit.*, pp. 125-26.

[33] Keith, *op. cit.*, pp. 126-34.

[34] *Ganbu xuexi ziliao* 幹部學習資料 , No. 10 (July 1950), pp. 73-74. The above translation is taken, with minor changes, from William Brugger, *Democracy and Organisation in the Chinese Industrial Enterprise* [1948-1953] (Cambridge: Cambridge University Press, 1976), p. 78. It was Dr. Brugger's work which called this speech by Gao Gang to my attention, and his discussion of the issues raised by the above quote (continued on

By putting "*yiyuanhua*" in quotation marks, Gao plainly intended to turn their own slogan against those who still had a nostalgic attachment to Yan'an patterns of organization. Such people, he suggests, *talk* about integration, but real integration consists in firm control from the Centre. A similar argument, in a broader context than Gao's discussion of leadership in factories, was made in a *Changjiang ribao* editorial of December 1950, which reads in part:

> Today, we have set up a people's political power of nationwide character, we have taken over the cities, we are responsible for complicated tasks of running various aspects of the people's political, economic, and cultural life. This is already completely different from the previous era of base areas in the countryside, when the main thing was leading the revolutionary war. . . . The simple leadership organs of that period of the base areas are no longer appropriate today. . . .
>
> What we need today is to insist that the whole country be united under the integrated (*yiyuanhua de*) leadership of the Centre, and that it not be dispersed under the integrated leadership of the localities. . . .

Certain tasks, the editorial continued, such as land reform and the suppression of bandits, could still be dealt with in a decentralized fashion, under local leadership. Economic construction, however, should be under the control of the specialist departments, on a national basis. "We must distinguish between these two types of tasks, and combine unified leadership by the local Party and direct leadership by the various specialized systems, uniting both of these under the leadership of the Centre. This is the new system of leadership and of organization which must be adopted following the establishment of a unified political power in the whole country."[35]

Clearly, what is envisaged here is not "dual rule," as practised in Yan'an, i.e., a system in which responsibility for a given factory or other unit is shared between the relevant specialized department or ministry in the Centre and the Party committee at the appropriate level. It is rather a system split into two, with some activities (such as industrial development) under direct and exclusive central control, and other matters such as land reform handled by the local political authorities, with the two pyramids coming together only in the Centre. Such a pattern of leadership would be "integrated" to the extent that the Centre ultimately controlled everything, but it would not provide for the conduct of national affairs in a uniform and integrated fashion.

March 1951 saw, as already indicated, a sharp turn back toward a policy

---

pp. 235-37) is of considerable interest. (On p. 78, he wrongly identifies this text as a passage from Gao Gang's speech of 2 June 1951, which dealt with similar matters; the words quoted here were in fact spoken on 13 March 1950.)

[35] *Changjiang ribao* 長江日報, 16 December 1950, reproduced in *Ganbu xuexi ziliao*, No. 26 (February 1951), pp. 47-48. See also the discussion in Keith, *op. cit.*, pp. 126-27, which first called my attention to this text.

of combining "unified leadership and divided responsibilities," actively promoted by Zhou Enlai. This orientation, in turn, could not prevail in the face of the contrary logic of the Soviet-inspired system of economic develop-ment to be introduced from January 1953, with the beginning of the First Five-Year Plan. A wholesale reorganization of the state structure, in which the governments of the Greater Administrative Regions were replaced by mere administrative committees and their standing thus downgraded, there-fore took place on 15 November 1952. These steps were explicitly justified by the need to "meet the new situation and new task of nation-wide large-scale planned economic construction." Finally, on 19 June 1954, the Central People's Government Council took the decision to dismantle the entire regional military, Party and state machinery.[36]

And yet, only a very few years later, regional patterns of organization were reborn phoenix-like from their ashes, both in economic and in Party affairs. But before tracing this evolution and considering the reasons for it, it is necessary to say something about the nature of the constitutional arrange-ments introduced in 1954, which excluded much more categorically and explicitly than those of 1949 any element of federalism.

II. THE CONSTITUTIONAL PERIOD, 1954-1965

This paper is not concerned with constitutional law for its own sake, and the aspects of the 1954 Constitution most significant for our purposes can be summed up very briefly. Three points are particularly worthy of note.

First, and most importantly, all legislative powers are exclusively reserved to the National People's Congress (Article 22). People's congresses at lower levels, from the provinces down to the *xiang* 鄉, have only the power to "adopt and issue decisions within the limits of the authority prescribed by law" (Article 60). Moreover, people's congresses at *xian* 縣 level and above are authorized to "revise or annul inappropriate decisions of people's con-gresses at the next lower level" (Article 60); thus, the National People's Congress can, under the 1954 Constitution, nullify the acts of provincial assemblies.

Secondly, as regards the executive organs, people's councils at levels below the Centre are "responsible and accountable" not only to the people's congresses at the same level, but to the administrative organs at the next higher level; the whole pyramid of local people's councils are "administrative organs of state under the unified leadership of, and subordinate to, the State

[36]Keith, *op. cit.*, pp. 136-42.

Council" (Article 66).

Finally, although the Constitution provides for various forms of autonomy for national minorities, it is made very plain that such limited local powers do not in any way detract from the unitary character of the state. Article 3 lays down that the People's Republic of China is a "unified, multi-national state," and further underscores the point by stipulating that "national autonomous areas are inalienable (*buke fenli de* 不可分離的) parts of the People's Republic of China."

And yet, this quite clear and forceful repudiation of federalism, and assertion of the absolute primacy of the central government, by no means settled all the problems relating to the *de facto* balance of power between the Centre and the localities.

On 13 January 1953, the Chinese government had set up a Committee for Drafting the Constitution, headed by Mao. In 1953, while this body was busy with its task, an eight-line rhyme was coined to characterize the proper functioning of the political and administrative system. This jingle read as follows:

> Great power is monopolized,
> Small power is dispersed.
> The Party committee takes decisions,
> All quarters carry them out.
> Implementation also involves decisions,
> But they must not depart from principles.
> Checking on the work
> Is the responsibility of the Party committee.[37]

Five years later, Mao explained that this rhyme had been invented in 1953 "for the purpose of opposing the dispersionism which existed at that time."[38] There were, indeed, particular reasons in 1953 to be concerned about the unity of the state. Although the powers of the Greater Administrative Regions had been reduced at the end of 1952, they still constituted a possible basis for the emergence of "independent kingdoms." One of them, in particular, the North East Region, had long been the fief of Gao Gang, and Mao in 1956 said that the mis-use of the regions by Gao and his "anti-party alliance" had been one reason for their abolition.[39] The verses were, however, not

---

[37] "Sixty Articles on Work Methods," *Current Background*, No. 892, p. 9; Chinese in *Mao Zedong sixiang wansui* 毛澤東思想萬歲 (*Long live Mao Zedong Thought*) (hereafter *Wan-sui*), Supplement, p. 34.

[38] *Loc. cit.*

[39] See the official version of "On the Ten Great Relationships," in *Selected Works*, V, pp. 293-94.

regarded as relevant only to the situation in 1953. In January 1958, Mao reaffirmed them as a succinct statement of his administrative philosophy, and expounded their meaning at some length.[40]

The fact that a formulation first put forward at the beginning of the First Five-Year Plan should thus have been refurbished precisely at the moment, on the eve of the Great Leap Forward, when Mao was consciously preparing to move away from the Soviet model of economic planning and development, is a striking symbol of the continuity of Chinese administrative philosophy over the past three decades. The general thrust both of the eight-line rhyme quoted above, and of Mao's 1958 commentaries, is clear enough. It can be summed up in two points: major decision-making power is concentrated at the top, though the lower levels must be consulted; leadership of all political, economic, and cultural work is vested in the Party. There were, on the other hand, significant variations in the years 1953-58 both in the exact balance between Centre and regions, and in the forms of Party control.

I shall deal first with the problem of the relations between the Centre and the lower levels in the political hierarchy, which is relatively straightforward, and then with the much more complex issue of the way in which decentralized authority is exercised in the localities.[41] The starting-point for any serious discussion of these issues must be the ideas put forward by Mao Zedong in April 1956, when he was just beginning to turn his mind to the radical re-structuring of the Chinese model which led, two years later, to the "Great Leap" policies.

Mao's speech of 25 April 1956 to the Politburo, entitled "On the Ten Great Relationships," is unquestionably one of his half dozen most important utterances after 1949, and one of the two or three most authoritative statements of his administrative philosophy. Section V, on the relationship between the Centre and the localities, must be interpreted in the context of the speech as a whole, which tended above all to argue that the one-sided and

---

[40]*Current Background*, No. 892, p. 9; Talk of 11 January 1958 at the Nanning 南寧 conference, *Wan-sui* (1969 edition), p. 148, translated in *Miscellany of Mao Tse-tung Thought* (Arlington, Va.: Joint Publications Research Service, 1974), pp. 79-80 (JPRS No. 61269).

[41] There is no fully satisfactory English translation for *difang* 地方, as contrasted with *zhongyang* 中央 (centre). The Chinese term covers the whole spectrum from *xiang* and natural village up to province (or region when that administrative level existed). One possible English equivalent, "locality," has the disadvantage that it evokes rather the lower end of this range; for this reason, in *Mao Tse-tung Unrehearsed* (Harmondsworth: Penguin, 1974) I preferred "region." That term can, however, easily lead to confusion between levels below the Centre in general, and the supra-provincial level in particular. For that reason, I have chosen in the following discussion to avoid it, and have replaced "region" by "locality" in all quotations taken from *Mao Tse-tung Unrehearsed*.

doctrinaire pursuit of any policy goal was self-defeating. Thus, if you really wanted to develop heavy industry, you must not neglect light industry and agriculture, and in order to build up new industrial centres in the hinterland, it was necessary to make proper use of the existing industry in the coastal areas. Reasoning in similarly dialectical fashion, Mao said, on the question which concerns us here:

> The relationship between the Centre and the localities is also . . . a contradiction. In order to resolve this contradiction, what we now need to consider is how to arouse the enthusiasm of the localities by allowing them to run more projects under the unified plan of the Centre.
> As things look now, I think that we need a further extension of local power. At present, it is too limited, and this is not favourable to building socialism.[42]

In the last analysis, Mao continued to attach supreme importance to the cohesion and efficiency of the state as a whole, and he valued decentralization and grass-roots initiative within the limits thus set. Summing up his discussion in Section V of "On the Ten Great Relationships," he declared:

> There must be proper enthusiasm and proper independence. . . . Naturally we must at the same time tell the comrades at the lower levels that they should not act wildly, that they must exercise caution. Where they can conform, they ought to conform. . . . Where they cannot conform . . . then conformity should not be sought at all costs. Two enthusiasms are much better than just one. . . . In short, the localities should have an appropriate degree of power. This would be beneficial to the building of a strong socialist state.[43]

The emphasis on centralism is even stronger in the official version than in the unofficial text from which I have been quoting. The new text adds, at this point: "In order to build a powerful socialist state, we must have strong and united leadership by the Centre, we must have unified planning and discipline throughout the whole country; disruption of this necessary unity is impermissible."[44]

But, despite the abiding emphasis on a strong centralized state, Mao's immediate concern in 1956 was with widening the scope of local authority, since he regarded the existing degree of centralization as self-defeating. In another talk at the same April 1956 Politburo meeting, he said: "The relationship between the lower echelons and the higher echelons is like that

---

[42]This quotation is taken from the version of Mao's speech first circulated within the Party in 1965, and reproduced by the Red Guards in 1967-69, as translated in *Mao Tse-tung Unrehearsed*, pp. 71-72. On the differences between this text and the official version of 1976, see my research note in *The China Quarterly*, No. 69 (March 1977), pp. 126-35.

[43]*Mao Tse-tung Unrehearsed*, p. 73.

[44]*Selected Works*, V, p. 294.

of a mouse when it sees a cat. It is as if their souls have been eaten away, and there are many things they dare not say."[45]

But how was effective centralization to be combined with an "appropriate degree" of local power? This problem, in Mao's view, was inextricably linked to the issue of dual versus vertical control, which is explicitly raised in Section V of "On the Ten Great Relationships":

> At present dozens of hands are meddling in local affairs, making them difficult to manage. . . . Since the ministries don't think it proper to issue orders to the Party committees and people's councils at the provincial level, they establish direct contact with the relevant departments and bureaux in the provinces and municipalities and give them orders every day. These orders are all supposed to come from the central authorities, even though neither the Central Committee of the Party nor the State Council knows anything about them, and they put a great strain on the local authorities. . . . This state of affairs must be changed.
>
> . . . We hope that the ministries and departments under the central authorities will . . . first confer with the localities on all matters concerning them and issue no order without full consultation.
>
> The central departments fall into two categories. Those in the first category exercise leadership right down to the enterprises, but their administrative offices and enterprises in the localities are also subject to supervision by the local authorities. Those in the second have the task of laying down guiding principles and mapping out work plans, while the local authorities assume the responsibility for putting them into operation.[46]

The last paragraph of the above quotation refers to the policy, adopted in 1956-57, of keeping only large-scale or important enterprises, especially in the field of heavy industry, under the direct control of the central ministries, and handing other industrial and commercial enterprises over to the lower levels. The complex pattern which resulted has been the subject of many studies. Two decades ago, Franz Schurmann drew a distinction which remains useful between what he called "decentralization I," involving the transfer of decision-making power to the production units themselves, and "decentralization II," signifying the transfer of power to some lower level of regional administration. He viewed Chen Yun 陳雲 as an advocate of the former view, which would have led China in the direction of a Yugoslav-type economy, and Mao Zedong and Liu Shaoqi 劉少奇 as partisans of the second. He finds, however, that Chen Yun's approach constitutes a "contradictory" combination of centralization, decentralization I, and decentralization II. Harry Harding, who uses a six-fold set of criteria for approaching the problem,

---

[45] *Wan-sui* (1969), p. 35; translation in *Miscellany of Mao Tse-tung Thought*, p. 30.

[46] This version is based primarily on the official Chinese text, as translated in *Selected Works*, V, p. 293, but the translation has been modified in places, sometimes making use of the phrasing employed in *Mao Tse-tung Unrehearsed*, p. 72.

likewise concludes that the policy (in fact drafted by Chen) adopted by the Third Plenum in the autumn of 1957 was an "eclectic" one, combining centralization and decentralization. Such a contradictory or "eclectic" approach was, in reality, characteristic of everyone in the leadership at the time; the differences were matters of emphasis. During the Great Leap Forward, Schurmann added, this policy of combining centralism and democracy in a "unity of true opposites" consisted in "centralization of general policy impulses and decentralization of specific policy impulses."[47] Plainly, what he calls here "general policy impulses" are in essence what Mao's 1953 jingle referred to as *da quan* 大權 or "great power"; "specific policy impulses" (or the right to generate them) can be equated with *xiao quan* 小權, "small power."

On 31 January 1958, Mao revised the "Sixty Articles on Work Methods," the directive constituting in effect the blueprint for the Great Leap Forward. In article 28 of this directive, the 1953 jingle is first quoted, and then explained in the following terms:

"Great power is monopolized" (*da quan dulan* 大權獨攬) is a cliché which is customarily used to refer to the arbitrary decisions of an individual (*geren duduan* 個人獨斷). We borrow this phrase to indicate that the main powers should be concentrated in collective bodies such as the Central Committee and local Party committees, we use it to oppose dispersionism. Can it possibly be argued that great power should be scattered? . . . When we say, "All quarters carry them out," this does not mean that Party members do so directly. It is rather that there must first be a phase in which Party members enter into contact with those who are not Party members in government organs, enterprises, co-operatives, people's organizations, and cultural and educational organs, discuss and study things with them, and revise those parts [of higher-level directives] which are inappropriate [to the particular conditions]; only then, after they have been approved by everybody, are they applied.[48]

This text, it will be seen, deals both with relations between levels, and with the co-ordinating role of the Party. Mao's deliberate emphasis on the parallel between the current maxim *daquan dulan* and the term *duduan*, which

[47] Schurmann, *Ideology and Organization in Communist China* (Berkeley: University of California Press, 1966), pp. 86-87, 175-76, 196-98. See also Harry Harding, *Organizing China. The Problem of Bureaucracy 1949-1976* (Stanford: Stanford University Press, 1981), pp. 107-15, 175-82. Both Schurmann and Harding rely to a great extent on secondary sources for Chen Yün's views; Chen's own words, including an extract from his speech at the Third Plenum, can now be read in N. Lardy and K. Lieberthal (eds.), *Chen Yun's Strategy for China's Development* (Armonk: M. E. Sharpe, 1983). See, in particular, the editors' summary of his views, pp. xix-xxii, and the endorsement, in a November 1957 regulation drafted by Chen, of "dual rule" (*shuangchong lingdao* 雙重領導), p. 78.

[48] *Wan-sui* (supplement), pp. 34-35; my translation.

normally refers, as he says, to the arbitrary or dictatorial decisions of an individual, shows once again that he did not shrink back from asserting the need for strong, centralized rule—or from implementing such ideas in practice.

How could such centralization be combined with the exercise of real and significant, though subordinate "small power" at lower levels? Primarily through the co-ordinating role of the Party, to which the greater part of Mao's commentaries on the 1953 jingle are devoted. Although he did not here employ the term *yiyuanhua*, it is clear that the impulse expressed in this concept was at the centre of his thinking. In remarks of April 1956, he recalled that, in response to the emergence of excessive decentralization and local independence in the base areas of the Yan'an period, the Central Committee had adopted a resolution on strengthening the "party spirit" (*dangxing* 黨性, a translation of the Russian *partiinost'*). "*Yiyuanhua* was carried out," he continued, "but a great deal of autonomy was preserved."[49]

In another comment of January 1958 on the 1953 jingle, Mao referred to the fact that the system of one-man management had been discredited, and included among the most basic organizational principles to be observed "the unity of collective leadership and individual role," which he equated with "the unity of the Party committee and the first secretary."[50] This can be taken as a reaffirmation of Mao's Yan'an-style understanding of *yiyuanhua* or integrated leadership, as opposed to Gao Gang's ideas on the subject, discussed earlier. For Gao, as we have seen, *yiyuanhua* had a sense very close to its literal meaning of "to make monolithic." A monolithic pattern of organization implied, in his view, that each entity such as a factory could be responsible to only one outside authority, which in practice meant the relevant ministry in Peking. The factory manager, as the agent or point of contact of this authority, must therefore have unchallenged authority within the factory. According to Mao's view, which was the prevailing view in the late 1950s, integration or *yiyuanhua* had to be carried out not merely at the national level, but in the localities. Otherwise, even "small power" could not be dispersed without leading to confusion. And the agent of integration could only be the Party committee at each level.

A particular case illustrating the meaning and limitations of dual rule is

---

[49] *Wan-sui* (1969), p. 36; translation in *Miscellany of Mao Tse-tung Thought*, p. 31. The "Resolution on strengthening the Party spirit" adopted by the Politburo on 1 July 1941 (Compton, *Mao's China*, pp. 156-60), did not in fact use the term *yiyuanhua*, but referred to the importance of centralization, and of "unified will, action and discipline." Manifestly, Mao regarded this decision as the first step in a process of establishing integrated Party control which found further expression in 1942 and 1943.

[50] *Wan-sui* (1969), p. 148; *Wan-sui* (Supplement), pp. 34-35.

that of cadres who have been "sent down" (*xiafang* 下放). Such cadres, it was stated in the spring of 1958, while they should maintain links with their original units (to which they might return), were exclusively under the authority of the local Party committee, and *not* subject to "dual leadership" (*shuangchong lingdao* 雙重領導) by Party and ministry. The Yan'an resolution of 1941 on *yiyuanhua* was explicitly recalled, thus suggesting that the cohesion of the political system might once again be open to doubt.[51]

The Great Leap Forward of 1958, in which Mao's ideas, outlined above, found their fullest and most dramatic expression, involved the juxtaposition of many diverse inspirations and imperatives. In the domain of organization and leadership methods which concerns us here, the most flagrant contradiction was that between the stress on unified and integrated Party leadership, and the fragmentation of economic initiative and control to such an extent that, as Mao later recognized, effective planning largely ceased to exist.

This situation was prefigured by the procedures laid down by Mao himself in the "Sixty Articles" of January 1958, of which Article 9 read as follows:

> There are three sets of production plans. The Centre has two sets. One is the plan that must be fulfilled and is made public; the other is the plan that is expected to be fulfilled and is not made public. The local administration also has two sets. The first set of the local administration is the second set of the Centre, and this is the one which must be fulfilled by the local administration. Appraisal and comparison should be made with the Centre's second set as the criterion.[52]

In this pyramid of plans, the lower the administrative level, the higher the targets. Thus the Centre's second plan, which was not made public, set higher targets than were publicly announced, and these higher targets were binding on the local authorities, who for their part were invited to set privately and to strive for even more ambitious objectives. When, in the atmosphere of euphoria which swept across China in the summer of 1958, local authorities at various levels and the leaders of the newly-established communes began to vie with each other in setting increasingly inflated targets, the third set of plans became in fact the only meaningful one for them. And since appraisal and comparison were to be made with the Centre's second set as the criterion, there was no effective basis for the co-ordination of production.

---

[51] Liu Shoupeng 劉壽彭, Zhu Zhen 朱眞, and Bi Feng 畢風, "Xiafang ganbu bixu fucong dangdi dangwei de tongyi lingdao" 下放幹部必須服從當地薰委的統一領導 ("Sent-down cadres must accept the unified leadership of the local Party Committee"), *Xuexi* 學習, No. 6, 1958, pp. 22-23. Like Mao in 1956, this article identifies the 1941 resolution with *yiyuanhua* even though it did not use the term.

[52] "Sixty Articles on Work Methods," quoted in S. Schram, "Mao Tse-tung and the Theory of the Permanent Revolution," *The China Quarterly*, No. 46 (April-June 1971), pp. 232-33.

Articles in the Chinese press at the time praised this procedure as a "revolution in planning methods," which would liberate the energies of the masses and prevent the stifling of their creativity as in the past.[53] Mao himself, however, admitted subsequently that this "revolutionary" method had failed to provide for the necessary co-ordination of efforts on a national scale. In July 1959, in addition to expressing his regrets at what he had now come to regard as the ill-advised adventure of the backyard furnaces, Mao took responsibility for the dismantling of the planning system in the previous year. At the Beidaihe meeting of August 1958 (which officially approved the creation of the communes) a directive had been put out, said Mao, which was called a directive on planning, but which was tantamount to doing away with planning altogether. "By doing away with planning," he went on, "I mean that they dispensed with overall balances and simply made no estimates of how much coal, iron and transport would be needed. Coal and iron cannot walk by themselves: they need vehicles to transport them. This I did not foresee."[54] Despite the fact that he was a "complete outsider when it comes to economic construction," Mao acknowledged that the main responsibility for this failure to co-ordinate inputs and outputs was his, and indicated that his comrades should "take him to task" for it. In the ensuing years, the emphasis was therefore shifted toward a firmer insistence on centralized control, symbolized by the slogan "The whole country a single chessboard."

Even in this new context, however, the principle that power must be in some way shared between the Centre and the localities was preserved. Thus, for example, in comments written in early 1960 on the Soviet *Textbook of Political Economy*, Mao declared:

> One good thing about Europe is that all its countries are independent. Each of them does its own thing, and this makes it possible for the European economy to develop at a fast pace. Since the Qin dynasty, our country has taken shape as a big nation. Over a long period of time, the country has kept a more or less unified appearance. One of the defects of this was bureaucratism, which kept the country under very tight control, so that each locality could not develop independently. Procrastination was rampant and economic development was at a very slow pace. Today the conditions are completely different. We want to attain unification for the whole country and independence for the different provinces. It will be relative unification and relative independence.[55]

Still, the emphasis remained, in the early 1960s, on the crucial and decisive role of the decision-makers at the Centre. The definitive formulation of Mao's

[53] See, for example, Wei Yi 未易, "Jihua fangfa de geming" 計劃方法的革命 ("A revolution in planning methods"), *Xuexi*, No. 8, 1958, pp. 10-12.
[54] Speech of 23 July 1959 at Lushan, in *Mao Tse-tung Unrehearsed*, pp. 142-43.
[55] *Wan-sui* (1967), p. 226; *Miscellany of Mao Tse-tung Thought*, p. 296.

105

ideas on this subject, prior to the Cultural Revolution, is that to be found in his speech of January 1962, in which he drew together the problem of the structure of power, and that of the relation between the leaders and the led, in a broader definition of the concept of "democratic centralism." After asserting that centralism and democracy must be combined "both within the Party and outside," and stressing once again, as he had in Yan'an, that centralism was even more important than democracy, Mao went on to say:

> Without democracy, there cannot be any correct centralism because people's ideas differ, and if their understanding of things lacks unity, then centralism cannot be established. What is centralism? First of all it is a centralization of correct ideas, on the basis of which unity of understanding, policy, planning, command and action are achieved. This is called centralized unification. If people still do not understand problems, if they have ideas but have not expressed them, or are angry but have still not vented their anger, how can centralized unification be established? If there is no democracy, we cannot possibly summarize experience correctly. If there is no democracy, if ideas are not coming from the masses, it is impossible to establish a good line, good general and specific policies and methods. Our leading organs merely play the role of a processing plant in the establishment of a good line and good general and specific policies and methods. Everyone knows that if a factory has no raw material, it cannot do any pro- cessing. . . . Without democracy, you have no understanding of what is happening down below; the general situation will be unclear; you will be unable to collect sufficient opinions from all sides; there can be no communication between top and bottom; top-level organs of leadership will depend on one-sided and incorrect material to decide issues, and thus you will find it difficult to avoid being sub- jectivist; it will be impossible to achieve unity of understanding and unity of action, and impossible to achieve true centralism.[56]

Here the term "democratic centralism" is made to cover both the funda- mental dilemma of combining effective "centralized unification" with active support and initiative from below, and the problem of the upward and downward flow of ideas evoked by the slogan of the "mass line." Mao's overall view of this whole cluster of issues is clearly reflected in the metaphor of the "processing plant." To be sure, this plant is incapable of producing anything meaningful if it is not constantly fed with information and sug- gestions, but in the last analysis the correct line can only be elaborated by the brain at the centre. The deprecatory adverb "merely" before "processing plant" does not change the fact that this is where the decisive action takes place.

---

[56] *Mao Tse-tung Unrehearsed*, pp. 163-64.

III. THE CULTURAL REVOLUTION DECADE, 1966-1976

Suddenly, in the spring of 1966, we find Mao Zedong saying something startlingly different from his ideas of 1962. "I have always advocated," he asserted on 28 March 1966, "that whenever the central organs do bad things, it is necessary to call·upon the localities to rebel, and to attack the Centre."[57] So far as can be determined from the available materials, Mao had never in the past advocated any such thing. In seeking an explanation of why, at the time of the Cultural Revolution, Mao adopted a stance so much at variance with his own previous position, it is necessary to look beyond the domain of administrative philosophy to the political situation of the time, and above all to the arguments within the Party about the changing role of classes in Chinese society, and the class nature of state power.

We have already noted that the state established in 1949 was called a people's dictatorship, rather than a proletarian dictatorship, because it was seen as a hybrid form adapted to the circumstances prevailing during the "period of transition" from postwar reconstruction to the building of socialism. And though it began to be said in 1953, and was officially proclaimed in 1956, that the people's democratic dictatorship was "in essence identical" with the dictatorship of the proletariat, the Chinese state continued to be designated as a "people's democratic state" until the Cultural Revolution, and the overwhelming majority of the population was thus guaranteed, at least in principle, some sort of symbolic involvement in national affairs.[58]

Throughout the 1950s, Mao continued to define the threat to the people's dictatorship from "enemy classes" essentially in terms of the surviving influence of the privileged strata of the old society and their ideas. He repeatedly and fiercely attacked bureaucratic tendencies in the Chinese Communist Party, but he saw these, even during the "anti-Rightist" campaign of 1957, essentially as a defect in work style, and not as the manifestation of a change in the class character of the Party and its cadres. Suddenly, in the early 1960s, Mao began to talk about the emergence of something akin to the "new class" denounced by Milovan Djilas a decade earlier.

[57] *Wan-sui* (1969), p. 640.

[58] The assertion of the essential identity between the people's dictatorship and the proletarian dictatorship is commonly thought to date from 1956. See, however, for a statement that Chinese theorists began to draw this conclusion with the beginning of the Five-Year Plan in 1953, the article by Gao Fang 高放, "Guanyu woguo wuchanjieji zhuanzheng jianli de tedian" 關於我國無產階級專政建立的特點 ("On peculiarities of the establishment of China's proletarian dictatorship"), *Xin jianshe* 新建設, No. 12, 1956, pp. 1-7, discussing the decisions adopted at the Eighth Party Congress.

His reflections on this theme were inspired not only by his observations of conditions in China, but by developments in the Soviet Union. It is not surprising, therefore, that one of the earliest formulations occurs in his reading notes of 1960 on the Soviet *Textbook of Political Economy*, where he argued that, though a socialist society had abolished classes, it would probably have, in the course of its development, "certain problems" with "vested interest groups" attached to their privileges.[59] In his speech of 30 January 1962, Mao took the decisive step of referring to such defenders of their own personal interests as "new *bourgeois* elements," which might still be produced in socialist society. "During the whole socialist stage," he continued, "there still exist classes and class struggle, and this class struggle is a protracted, complex, sometimes even violent affair." From this he drew the conclusion that China's "instruments of dictatorship" should not be weakened but rather strengthened.[60]

As is apparent from this last statement, while Mao seemed to be criticizing the same phenomenon as Djilas, he disagreed with the latter regarding the remedy, calling for the strengthening of the proletarian dictatorship rather than for Yugoslav-style "producers' democracy." For the existence of such elements in society could, in his view, cause the indefinite survival and perpetual renewal of "bourgeois" thinking long after the old bourgeoisie had disappeared, thus turning what had previously been seen as a problem of re-education during a transitional period into a life-and-death struggle between the forces of socialism and capitalism.

We obviously cannot deal here in any detail with Mao's ideas on the nature and role of class differences in China at this time, still less with related topics such as his attitude toward survivals of "bourgeois right."[61] I have introduced this theme in order to explain why Mao's hitherto consistent attachment to a strong central authority vacillated in 1966.

A further problem, directly related to conflicts within the leadership in the early 1960s as to how the country should be run, is that of the role of the various echelons of the administrative and party hierarchy. It has been argued, by Franz Schurmann in particular, that the Chinese Communist Party (and indeed other Communist Parties) exhibits its greatest strength at intermediate levels, notably at the provincial level. This phenomenon, he suggests, may be explained in part by the fact that at the regional level "the Party faces less competition from state administrative organizations than at

[59] *Wan-sui* (1967), p. 192; *Miscellany of Mao Tse-tung Thought*, p. 267.
[60] *Mao Tse-tung Unrehearsed*, p. 168.
[61] For a systematic discussion of these issues, see my article "Classes, Old and New, in Mao Zedong's Thought, 1949-1976" in J. L. Watson (ed.), *Classes and Social Stratification in China Since 1949* (Cambridge: Cambridge University Press, 1984), pp. 29-55.

the central level." He adds, however, that there may be another reason:

> Regional governments, in contrast to the state ministries, have control over a wide range of different administrative and managerial units. The kaleidoscopic nature of regional administration is partly due to the fact that light industry and agriculture constitute one of their major economic domains. Factories are small and very different, and the farms each have their local peculiarities. Thus one of the major functions of the Party is coordination.[62]

Co-ordination or *yiyuanhua* is and has been, undoubtedly, not only one of the main functions of the Party at levels below the Centre (as noted above), but one of its main sources of strength. Schurmann then goes on, however, to suggest that the conflict between Party power in the provinces, and the power of the ministries in Peking, had been resolved by 1959 in favour of the Party. Such a tension there may well have been, but in the early 1960s it had been succeeded, at least in Mao's perception, by an alliance between state power at the Centre and Party power in the regions, both of them working, despite some divergences of interests, to take China down what he regarded as the "capitalist road." The dichotomy defined by Franz Schurmann remained relevant, however, to the extent that, in setting out to destroy the "capitalist roaders" in the Party, it was important to Mao to know where the chief strength of the Party bureaucracy lay.

In addition to the provincial level, there was also, by the early 1960s, once more a supra-provincial regional level. Even before the launching of the Great Leap Forward in 1958, there had existed something called "co-ordinated areas" (*xiezuo qu* 協作區), which apparently served primarily an economic function, and did not involve the formal delegation of political decision-making or executive powers.[63] In January 1961, the establishment of six regional Party bureaux was formally announced. These were not paralleled, as they had been a decade earlier, by regional agencies of state power, but they clearly played an important role in the integration or co-ordination of economic work. Their significance as a bastion of Party power is underscored by the violent Cultural Revolution attacks on the first secretaries of these regions as "capitalist roaders" and builders of "independent kingdoms." There is, however, some uncertainty as to whether these bureaux were themselves important *loci* of authority, or whether they were in fact primarily a mechanism through which the dominant province in each region

[62] Franz Schurmann, "Politics and Economics in Russia and China," in D. Treadgold (ed.), *Soviet and Chinese Communism: Similarities and Differences* (Seattle: University of Washington Press, 1967), p. 317.

[63] These "areas" were mentioned by Mao Zedong in his speech of 20 March 1958 as something which was already in existence. *Mao Tse-tung Unrehearsed*, p. 106.

imposed its will on the rest.[64]

To resume the discussion of Mao's motives for launching the Cultural Revolution, and the implications of these developments for his administrative philosophy, the essential point is that, because a majority of the leadership did not share Mao's views, he was obliged momentarily to jettison the axioms of centralized authority and of obedience to the majority which he had always hitherto preached. But in spite of this, he was no believer in anarchism or anything approaching it, so very rapidly the emphasis on centralism re-emerged once again in his thinking, in altered form.

In August 1966, when the Red Guards first burst upon the scene, Mao gave it as his view that "we should let disorder reign for a few months," adding: "Even if there are no provincial Party committees, it doesn't matter; aren't there still district and *xian* committees?"[65] Such words, and the policies which Mao effectively pursued in 1966, do not signify that he had ceased to believe in the need for effective leadership. They do confirm, however, that he saw the provincial level as one of the main bastions of the Party bureaucracy, and therefore as expendable. They also indicate that, if he had not turned his back on Leninism altogether, he had moved far enough away from a Leninist stance so that he was prepared deliberately to take the *risk* of swamping the Party in an effort to purge and purify it.

In any case, when he was confronted explicitly, in February 1967, with a sharp choice between Leninism and anarchism, Mao had no hesitation in coming down on the side of the former. Speaking to the Shanghai leftists Zhang Chunqiao 張春橋 and Yao Wenyuan 姚文元, he noted that the Shanghai People's Committee had demanded the abolition of "heads" (*zhang* 長), and commented: "This is extreme anarchism, it is most reactionary. If instead of calling someone the 'head' of something, we call him 'orderly' or 'assistant', this would really be only a formal change. In reality there will still always be 'heads'."[66] Mao then proceeded to discuss the various objections to establishing communes, like that which Zhang and Yao had just set up in Shanghai, throughout the rest of the country, and ultimately changing the name of the state to "People's Commune of China." One of these was that communes were "too weak when it comes to repressing counter-revolution," in other words that they did not provide that "strong socialist State" in which Mao had always believed. A more basic objection was that they left no role for integrated Party leadership:

[64]For a detailed argument along these lines, see David S. G. Goodman, "Centre-Province Relationships in the PRC: Sichuan and Guizhou, 1955-1965" (Ph.D. thesis, University of London, 1981), especially Chapter 9.

[65]*Wan-sui* (1969), p. 653.

[66]*Mao Tse-tung Unrehearsed*, p. 277.

If all [*of these organizations*] are changed into communes, what will we do with the Party? Where will we put the Party? In the committees set up under a commune, there will be members who belong to the Party, and others who don't. Where will we put the Party Committee? There will still have to be a Party! There has to be a nucleus, it doesn't matter what it's called, it is all right to call it a Communist Party, it is all right to call it a social-democratic party, it is all right to call it a social-democratic workers' party, it is all right to call it a Guomindang, it is all right to call it the Yiguandao 一貫道 , but in any case there has to be a party. In a commune there has to be a party; can the commune replace the party?[67]

The history of the ensuing nine years made it abundantly clear that in the Chairman's view it could not. Throughout the remainder of his life, Mao strove to combine in some fashion the need for leadership with the anti-elitism and encouragement of initiative from below which had constituted the justification (if not the sole motive) for the Cultural Revolution. Over this enterprise there continued to hang, however, a fundamental ambiguity, resulting from the fact that the right of the masses to "rebel" against the Party hierarchy and state bureaucracy was guaranteed only by a figure exercising personal authority of a kind which soon came to be officially likened to that of the first Qin emperor.

The veritable cult of Qin Shihuang belongs to the last and saddest period of Mao's life. Those final three or four years stand out in even more singular relief because just previously, in 1970-72, a new compromise appeared to be emerging in China on many of the policy issues, including patterns of leadership and of political and economic organization, which had split the Party since the early 1960s.

One significant symbolic expression of the trend toward the re-building of some kind of coherent organizational structure was the re-emergence of the term *yiyuanhua*, to which I devoted so much attention in summing up the Yan'an heritage. The Party Constitution adopted at the Ninth Congress in April 1969, at which Lin Biao 林彪 played a dominant role, declared in Article 7: "Party committees at all levels shall set up their working bodies or dispatch their representative organs in accordance with the principles of integrated (*yiyuanhua*) leadership, close ties with the masses, and simple and effective structure." It was also stated in Article 5: "The organs of state power of the dictatorship of the proletariat, the People's Liberation Army, and the Communist Youth League and other revolutionary mass organizations, such as those of the workers, the poor and lower-middle peasants and the Red Guards, must all accept the leadership of the Party."[68] It was not

---

[67] *Wan-sui* (1969), pp. 670-71; *Miscellany of Mao Tse-tung Thought*, pp. 453-54.

[68] Chinese text in *Hongqi* 紅旗, No. 5, 1969, p. 37; translation (here slightly modified) in *Peking Review*, No. 18, 1969, p. 38.

explicitly stated, however, that the Party must exercise *integrated* leadership over all these other organs and organizations.

In August 1973, at the Tenth Congress, Article 7 of the Party Constitution was revised to incorporate this term: "State organs, the People's Liberation Army and the militia, labour unions, poor and lower-middle peasant associations, women's federations, the Communist Youth League, the Red Guards, the Little Red Guards and other revolutionary mass organizations must all accept the integrated leadership of the Party." Commenting on this provision in his report on the revision of the Party Constitution, Wang Hongwen 王洪文 declared:

> Organizationally, the Party's integrated (*yiyuanhua*) leadership should be given expression in two respects: First, as regards the relationship between various organizations at the same level, of the seven sectors—industry, agriculture, commerce, culture and education, the Army, the government and the Party—it is the Party that exercises overall leadership. The Party is not parallel to the others, still less is it under the leadership of any other. Second, as regards the relationship between higher and lower levels, the lower level is subordinate to the higher level, and the entire Party is subordinate to the Central Committee. This has long been a rule in our Party and it must be adhered to.

Wang's forceful assertion of the ultimate authority of the Centre was, of course, merely a repetition of what Mao had, indeed, been saying since the 1940s. As for the significance of the concept of *yiyuanhua* at this time, we have seen that this idea was born in the Yan'an context as the expression of the will to invest the Party with the mission of unifying the widely-separated base areas, which had a tendency to become "independent kingdoms." In the early 1970s, the Party was called upon to play a similar role with regard to centres of power which were not regional, but functional.

Wang Hongwen paid lip service to this goal in 1973, but his formulation displayed elements of ambiguity. Thus, in the continuation of the passage just quoted, he declared: "We must strengthen the Party's integrated leadership, and the leadership of the Party committee must not be replaced by a 'joint conference' of several sectors. But at the same time, it is necessary to give full play to the role of the Revolutionary Committees."[69] Given that, at the outset the Revolutionary Committee had been destined to take over all power from the Party as well as from other organs within its geographical sphere of competence, the effect of this qualifying phrase was to blur the issue once again, even if in practice the Party secretary and chairman of the Revolutionary Committee were often one and the same.

In my introduction, written early in 1973, to a collection of essays by a

[69]Chinese text of the 1973 Party Constitution and of Wang's comments in *Hongqi*, No. 9, 1973, pp. 27, 22; English in *Peking Review*, No. 35/36, 1973, pp. 28, 25.

European Study Group, I concluded that, despite earlier impressions according to which the Revolutionary Committees might provide an alternative to Party control, it had become plain that the whole network of political and economic authority at all levels would once again be effectively subordinated to the Party, not only in theory but in fact.[70] As regarded the organizational issues which concern us specifically here, Marianne Bastid put forward the view, in her contribution to the same volume, that in accordance with the principles of unified Party leadership (*dang tongyi lingdao* 黨統一領導) and democratic centralism, which were being vigorously asserted once again, no level below the Central Committee had absolute decision-making power on any matter. In practice, she added, the Centre did effectively intervene to modify decisions already made by lower levels. At the same time, she concluded that there had been changes since the Cultural Revolution, in the shape of a trend toward the "transfer of responsibility down to lower levels," even if this took rather the form of the devolution of the "right of impulse," i.e., the right to initiate policy proposals, though not to take final decisions.[71]

As it happened, at the very moment when these words were being written, forces were at work undermining the still-fragile compromise of which Zhou Enlai had been the principal architect. All recognition of the importance of professional skills was soon swallowed up once again in an orgy of political rhetoric, and all things foreign were regarded as counter-revolutionary. As far as patterns of rule were concerned, the new hero and model became, as already noted, the first Qin emperor.

It is impossible today to say with certainty which of the initiatives taken in his name, during the last four years of his life, Mao did or did not endorse, wholeheartedly or with reservations. It is a fact, in any case, that a large proportion of the statements, both about Legalism and about Confucianism, published from the autumn of 1972 to the autumn of 1976, in the context of the "Movement to Criticize Lin Biao and Confucius," amounted at best to a crude caricature of Mao's previously-expressed ideas on Chinese history and Chinese thought. Moreover, though the promoters of this campaign, and of the subsequent movement to study the theory of the proletarian dictatorship, claimed to be struggling against bureaucracy, and against the "new class," Mao must have been conscious, by the early 1970s, of the problem of the "new new class," i.e., of the fact that "rebels," once they acquire power and status, tend to become bureaucrats too. Indeed, the ultra-leftists went out of their way to underscore their own ambitions, by the importance they

[70] S. Schram (ed.), *Authority, Participation and Cultural Change in China* (Cambridge: Cambridge University Press, 1973), p. 103.

[71] M. Bastid, "Levels of Economic Decision-making," in *ibid.*, pp. 189, 194, 196-97.

attributed to the "Legalist leading group around the emperor"—in other words, to themselves rather than to the Party organization. It is in this light that one must interpret Zhang Chunqiao's comment, in his report of January 1975 on the new state Constitution, that the provision making the chairman of the Chinese Communist Party the commander of the armed forces (in the absence of a chairman of the People's Republic) would "certainly help to strengthen the Party's integrated (*yiyuanhua*) leadership over the state structure."[72] Zhang was not in fact interested in the relation between organizations at all, but in making use of Mao's personal authority to extend his own influence and that of his faction.

And yet, though the continuing instability which prevailed in China during Mao's last years undoubtedly resulted in part from his inability, old and ill as he was, to control the actions of his wife and her associates, it cannot be denied that this situation grew also out of deep and irreconcilable contradictions in Mao's own approach to revolution. He, too, perceived authority in the first instance as a personal attribute rather than the prerogative of an organization. He, too, in the course of the last decade of his life, promoted something very much like anarchy, and at the same time continued to assume his own absolute right to direct events.

In one of the very last directives published in his lifetime, Mao was quoted in May 1976 as saying that revolutions would continue to break out in future because "junior officials, students, workers, peasants and soldiers do not like big shots oppressing them."[73] There is no way of verifying the authenticity of this brief text, which was published in the context of the campaign against Deng Xiaoping 邓小平, but it sounds very much like the irrepressible Mao. On the one hand, he remained committed to the need for "heads," but at the same time he could not resist the temptation to challenge them and shake them up.

Throughout his career, from Jinggangshan and Yan'an to the 1960s, Mao Zedong treated democracy and centralism as two indissolubly-linked aspects of the political process, one of which could not be promoted without reference to the other. The Cultural Revolution saw the emergence of two quite different concepts. Democracy was replaced by "rebellion"; centralism was replaced by *zhong* 忠, personal loyalty to the great leader and helmsman. No doubt Mao Zedong saw these tendencies as bound together in a dialectical unity, like democracy and centralism, which he had not in principle repudiated. Nevertheless, he allowed a situation to develop in which the "heads,"

---

[72] *Hongqi*, No. 2, 1975, p. 17; translated in *Peking Review*, No. 4, 1975, p. 19.

[73] Quoted in a *Renmin ribao* editorial of 16 May 1976; translated in *Peking Review*, No. 21, 1976, p. 9.

of which he had himself acknowledge the necessity, at all levels of society and the economy, could not in fact function as heads because, though they were held accountable, they had no power to take decisions. The alliance of the leader and the masses took the form, on the national level, of an un-structured plebiscitary democracy, sadly reminiscent of earlier examples. At lower levels, it produced a mixture of arbitrary rule by *ad hoc* committees, military control, apathy and confusion. This, too, is part of Mao's objective legacy to the Chinese people.

IV. RECENT TENDENCIES

Although the primary concern of this essay is with the relation between central and local authority, this aspect of the political system is, as I have stressed throughout, shaped to a significant extent by the spirit and structure of the polity as a whole. In this respect, the changes since Mao's death, and especially since mid-1978, are altogether remarkable, and merit discussion before we turn once again to the narrower topic of the locus of political and economic decision-making.

In a word, China's present leaders have repudiated the political ideas and methods which held sway during the last ten years of Mao's life for two distinct, though complementary reasons. On the one hand, they argue that the Cultural Revolution led to a situation of "anarchy," that is, to the dissolution of the cohesion and centralized control necessary to a strong socialist state. But at the same time, not only the so-called "dissidents," but official spokesmen (though in more prudent terms) have denounced the arbitrary, tyrannical, and undemocratic nature of political life in China from 1966 to 1976, and indeed from the late 1950s onwards.

A distinction is, of course, drawn between Mao Zedong on the one hand, and Jiang Qing 江青 and her supporters on the other, but at the same time it is freely recognized that Mao's approach to political leadership was, if not "fascist" in character, then strongly marked by influences from China's "feudal" or "pre-capitalist" past.

An article in the first issue of a new scholarly journal devoted to Chinese history, published in January 1979, begins with the observation that "China's despotic feudal state with a centralized structure (*fengjian zhuanzhizhuyi zhongyang jiquan guojia*封建專制主義中央集權國家) played a progressive role in history, but its negative effects on China's historical development are also very obvious."[74] We saw earlier that Mao, too, despite his admiration

---

[74] "Pipan fengjianzhuyi, wei shixian sige xiandaihua er fendou buxie 批判封建主義，

for Qin Shihuang, frequently commented on the negative effects of an overly rigid and bureaucratic system in imperial times. But Chinese writings of the past few years explicitly recognize that the Chinese political system suffers from the persistence of "feudal" or "pre-capitalist" influences. The article quoted above made this point as follows:

> China is a country which was ruled for a long period by feudal despotism, and which is still lacking in a modern democratic tradition. From the time when Qin Shihuang united the six countries, a system of monarchical absolutism [based on] a centralized feudal structure (*fengjian zhongyang jiquan de junzhu zhuanzhi zhidu* 封建中央集權的君主專制制度) continuously dominated the political life of two thousand years of Chinese feudal society.

Not only did the spirit of "feudal absolutism" continue, after the 1911 revolution, to be manifested in the autocracy of Yuan Shikai 袁世凱 and Chiang Kai-shek 蔣介石. Ever since the establishment of the People's Republic of China, the author argued, the system had all too often been characterized not by genuine democracy, capable of guaranteeing the people's rights, but by feudal despotism in socialist garb, manifested in particular in the "idolization" (*ouxianghua* 偶像化) of Mao Zedong, and his "deification in stereotyped images" (*xingxiang shenhua* 形象神化).[75]

Five or six years ago, it was, of course, said that all these things took place against Mao's own wishes, and were the fault of the "gang of four." Even then, in texts for internal circulation, Mao's own responsibility was recognized, and this was soon strongly underscored in the resolution adopted by the Central Committee on 27 June 1981 regarding certain questions in the recent history of the Party.[76]

Wherever the explanations may lie, it is today accepted by many Chinese in responsible positions that socialist democracy remains still in large measure to be invented. There have been considerable fluctuations in the climate of opinion in China since the search for new directions in theory and policy was formally launched at the Third Plenum in December 1978, and many

爲實現四個現代化而奮鬪不懈 ("Struggle unrelentingly to criticize feudalism, in order to carry out the four modernizations"), *Zhongguo shi yanjiu* 中國史研究 , No. 1, 1979, p. 14. (The article is by a member of the journal's editorial staff [*benkan pinglunyuan* 本刊評論 員].) The characterization of the Chinese political system from Qin times onwards as a "despotic feudal state with a centralized structure" (or, as the *Selected Works* translate the Chinese expression given above, an "autocratic and centralized feudal state"), is taken straight from Mao's "The Chinese Revolution and the Chinese Communist Party," *Selected Works*, II, pp. 107-108. (Chinese in *Mao Zedong ji*, Vol. 7, p. 100.)

[75] *Zhongguo shi yanjiu*, No. 1, 1979, p. 13.

[76] For a discussion of the evolving Chinese view of Mao's role, especially during the last twenty years of his life, see my article "To Utopia and Back: A Cycle in the History of the Chinese Communist Party," *The China Quarterly*, No. 87 (September 1981).

observers take the view that any significant impulse to genuine democratic reform has by now been snuffed out. This is, in my opinion, too one-sided an assessment of the situation.

The most authoritative document defining the reasons why a more democratic system is needed, the means by which it can be promoted, and the frontiers which cannot be transgressed, remains Deng Xiaoping's speech of 18 August 1980 to an enlarged session of the Politburo. The goal, forcefully proclaimed, is "to reform and perfect, in a practical way, the Party and state systems, and to ensure, on the basis of these systems, the democratization of the political life of the Party and the state, the democratization of economic management, and the democratization of the life of society as a whole."[77]

Concretely, this means, in the political domain, "to develop in full measure people's democracy, and to ensure that the people as a whole truly enjoy the power to supervise (*guanli* 管理) the state in a variety of effective ways, and especially to supervise political power at the basic level, as well as all enterprises and undertakings."[78] The fact that such rights have not, during the previous three decades, been adequately guaranteed to the people Deng blames, apart from over-centralization and the confusion of functions between Party and state (to which I shall turn in a moment, since they constitute the main theme of this essay), on excessive powers enjoyed by individual leaders, and in particular by Mao Zedong himself. This phenomenon, in turn, is of course explained by the fact that "What the old China has left to us is rather a tradition of feudal autocracy than a tradition of democracy and the rule of law."[79] But Deng also adds that, in addition to the "tradition of feudal despotism (*fengjian zhuanzhizhuyi* 封建專制主義) in Chinese history," this phenomenon also reflected the "tradition of concentrating power to a high degree in the hands of individual leaders in the work of parties in various countries in the days of the Communist International."[80] These influences, Deng argues, led to a bad system, and when the system is

---

[77]Deng Xiaoping, speech of 18 August 1980, reproduced in *Zhonggong yanjiu* 中共 研究, Vol. 15, No. 7 (15 July 1981), pp. 108-39; translated in *Issues and Studies*, Vol. 17, No. 3, 1981, and reprinted in *Communist Affairs*, Vol. 1, No. 1, 1982, pp. 101-18. This English version is clumsy and sometimes inaccurate, but for the sake of convenience I have cited it, in addition to the Chinese text, even though the translations used here are largely my own. The passage just quoted appears on p. 130 of *Zhonggong yanjiu*, and on p. 113 of *Communist Affairs*. For the official Chinese version of this speech, which has been only slightly modified, see *Deng Xiaoping wenxuan* 鄧小平文選 (Beijing: Renmin chubanshe, 1983), pp. 280-302, and also the translation, *Selected Works of Deng Xiaoping (1975-1982)* (Beijing: Foreign Languages Press, 1984), pp. 302-25.

[78]Chinese, p. 111; translation, p. 103.

[79]Chinese, p. 124; translation, p. 110.

[80]Chinese, p. 120; translation, p. 108.

bad, even great figures may be encouraged in evildoing rather than restrained by it:

> When Stalin gravely disrupted the socialist legal system, Comrade Mao Zedong said that this kind of thing could not have happened in Western countries such as England, France and the United States. But although he himself recognized this point, because the problem of the system had not really been solved . . . , there none the less came about the ten years of calamity of the "cultural revolution".[81]

It is hardly necessary to remark that this comment of Mao's, and Deng's evocation of it, do not imply in the case of either man a feeling that perhaps, in some respects, the capitalist system is superior. The campaign against "bourgeois liberalization," and the harsh repression of the dissidents since 1981 underscore this point, but it was plain enough in Deng's speech of August 1980. The explicit criticism of the Soviet and Comintern inheritance is, however, of profound significance. This theme is developed very much more fully in a report of October 1980 by Liao Gailong, which can be seen in many respects as an elaboration of the ideas sketched out by Deng Xiaoping in his relatively brief speech of the previous August.[82]

In this report, Liao not only criticized the influence of "unwholesome political theories" propagated in the world communist movement; he actually traced these errors back beyond Stalin to Lenin himself. Lenin's theory of party-building, he said, as first formulated in *What is to be done?*, took shape under the autocratic rule of the tsars, and an overemphasis on centralism, together with a neglect of inner-Party democracy, was necessary at that time. But, comments Liao, "after the Russian Communist Party had become the ruling Party, he did not place the Party organization on a democratic basis." Similarly, "Lenin's political theories overemphasized the aspect of violent suppression of the dictatorship of the proletariat, and neglected the democratic aspect. He even did so to such a degree that he said the proletarian dictatorship was an iron dictatorship not bound by any laws," thus negating any notion of socialist legality.[83]

---

[81] Chinese, p. 126; translation, p. 111.

[82] Liao Gailong, "Historical Experience and Our Road of Development" (Report of 25 October 1980 at a meeting of Party schools throughout the country to discuss the history of the Chinese Communist Party), Chinese text in *Zhonggong yanjiu*, Vol. 15, No. 9 (15 September 1981), pp. 108-77; translation in *Issues and Studies*, October, November, and December 1981.

[83] Chinese, pp. 142-43; translation, *Issues and Studies*, November, pp. 92-93. For a more extended discussion of the views of Liao Gailong, Deng Xiaoping, Hu Yaobang 胡耀邦 and others on problems of democratic reform, see my monograph, *Ideology and Policy in China since the Third Plenum, 1978-1984* (London: Contemporary China Institute, School of Oriental and African Studies, 1984). ("Research Notes and Studies, No. 6")

On the relation between decentralized economic and political management or supervision, and the insistence on unified leadership, Deng Xiaoping declared:

> Bureaucratism is a complex historical phenomenon which has existed for a long time. The bureaucratic phenomenon which exists in our country at the present time, apart from the fact that it has some points in common with the bureaucratism which has existed in history, also has its own peculiarities, and is thus different both from bureaucratism in old China, and from bureaucratism in the capitalist countries. It is intimately linked to our long-standing belief that a socialist system, a system of planned management, necessarily implies a high degree of concentration of power at the Centre over the economy, politics, culture and society. Our leading organs at various levels have all managed a great many things which they should not manage, could not manage well, and indeed were unable to manage. Provided only that there are certain rules, all these things can be handed down to lower levels, to the enterprises, the undertakings, and social units, for them to deal with by themselves, on the basis of the genuine application of the system of democratic centralism. Thus they can all be handled very well, whereas if they are all taken to the leading organs of Party and state, to the ministries at the Centre, they become very difficult to handle.[84]

The two domains evoked here—local government and economic management—are those most frequently mentioned in all the recent discussions of what, concretely, is meant by "high-level democracy." The central and crucial place of these two aspects of the question in the current official view is underscored in the resolution of 27 June 1981, which after asserting the need for Party leadership and for "vigilance" against those hostile to socialism, goes on to declare:

> A fundamental task of the socialist revolution is gradually to establish a highly democratic socialist political system. . . . It is necessary . . . gradually to realize direct democracy for the people (*renmin de zhijie minzhu* 人民的直接民主) at the grass roots of political power and community life and, in particular, to stress democratic management by the working masses in urban and rural enterprises over the affairs of their establishments.[85]

In the economic domain in particular, as crucial, perhaps, as the degree of centralization is the medium through which it is imposed. For several years, there has been a strong negative bias against interference in the day-to-day running of plants by lower-level Party organs, on the grounds that participation in decision-making by economic actors on the part of political organs inadequately informed as to the economic and technical realities on which such decisions should be based can only lead to precisely that subordination

[84] Deng Xiaoping, speech of 18 August 1980, Chinese pp. 118-19; English, p. 107.

[85] "Resolution on Certain Questions in the History of Our Party Since the Founding of the People's Republic of China," *Renmin ribao*, 1 July 1981; translated in *Beijing Review*, No. 27, 1981, pp. 10-39. (The above quotation is from par. 35.)

of facts to theories, or to utopian visions, from which China suffered so much during the two decades after 1957. But if guidance from the Centre is not to be transmitted through local Party organs, then it can only be exercised by the state bureaucracy. If so, what becomes of the Party's function of integration or *yiyuanhua* of the entire political and economic system? Is this to take only the form of the Central Committee laying down general guidelines for the government? And if so, was Gao Gang right after all?

This problem of "integrated leadership" has been the object of considerable discussion during the past four or five years, and here, once more, the positions taken have been neither uniform nor unchanging. In his report of October 1980, Liao Gailong declared that it was necessary "to overcome the phenomenon of failing to distinguish between Party and government, and substituting the Party for the government, and to carry out a division of labour between Party and government." And he added: "So-called 'integrated leadership' (*yiyuanhua lingdao*), the failure to distinguish between Party and government, the substitution of the Party for the government, all these [practices] are so many refuges for arbitrary and despotic rule by individuals, they all have the effect of sabotaging the principles of a lively and vigorous socialist democracy in the political life of the state."[86]

Liao Gailong, who had stressed in 1980 the advantages of a bicameral National People's Congress, which would allow for the representation both of regions and of social categories, and of which the two houses could act as a check on one another,[87] justified in May 1982 the decision in favour of a unicameral system, embodied in the Draft Constitution published on 28 April (and reproduced in the final draft adopted in December) on the grounds that such an "integrated system for the National People's Congress (*yiyuanhua de renmindaibiao dahui zhidu* 一元化的人民代表大會制度) would allow the more effective exercise of the powers of the Congress as the "sole legislative organ and the sole organ of state power."[88]

If the Party, despite its ultimately supreme role, is to be discouraged from meddling in the day-to-day running of the affairs of state, a crucial instrument for guaranteeing the implementation of this principle is the effective establishment of the rule of law. Since 1979, there has been consistent emphasis on the importance of "socialist legality," and there has also developed a more wide-ranging debate on the role of law in the political system, centred in particular around the question of the rule of law versus

[86] Liao Gailong, "Historical Experience and Our Road of Development," Chinese, p. 166; English, December, p. 89.

[87] *Ibid.*, Chinese, p. 164; English, December, p. 87.

[88] Conversation with the author, 7 May 1982.

arbitrary personal rule.[89]

The fact that the Party is not above the law is now explicitly proclaimed in the Statutes of the Party itself, as adopted at the Twelfth Congress in September 1982. The key sentence in the "General Programme" reads: "The Party must conduct its activities within the limits permitted by the Constitution and the laws of the state."[90] This provision was explicitly singled out for emphasis by Hu Yaobang in his report of 1 September to the Congress. On the same occasion, Hu called for continued reform of China's political institutions and system of leadership so that "the people are better able to exercise state power," and for the extension of democratic management to all enterprises and institutions, and the encouragement of "self-management of community affairs by the masses at the grass-roots level."[91]

As regards the arrangements laid down for the organs of political power at the lower levels, the Constitution of December 1982 once again defines the People's Republic of China as a "unitary multinational state," and asserts that "all the national autonomous areas are inalienable parts of the People's Republic of China."[92] People's congresses at *xian* level and above once again have the power to annual "inappropriate resolutions" of their counterparts at the next lower level, and local people's governments (called "people's councils" in 1954) are once again responsible both to the people's congress at the same level, and to the government at the next higher level. And all local governments are, once again, "administrative organs of state under the unified leadership of, and subordinate to, the State Council."[93]

And yet, in several important respects, there are significant changes as compared to the system established three decades ago. There is, first of all, the attempt, from top to bottom of the state structure, to introduce a real separation between legislative and executive powers, not only in theory but in practice. A key device for achieving this is the very considerable increase in the power of the Standing Committee of the National People's Congress, and the provision for the establishment of standing committees in all people's congresses at *xian* level and above.[94] This provision is complemented, at the local as at the national level, by the stipulation that no

---

[89] See, in this volume, the contribution of Harro von Senger, Ch. 6.

[90] *Beijing Review*, No. 38, 1982, p. 10.

[91] *Beijing Review*, No. 37, 1982, p. 27.

[92] For the Constitution of 4 December 1982 see *Beijing Review*, No. 52, 1982, pp. 10-29. Because of the many different forms in which this document has been published, I shall refer here, as I did earlier in discussing the Constitution of 1954, to Article numbers rather than pages. Here, see the Preamble and Article 4.

[93] Articles 104, 108, 110.

[94] Articles 67, 70, 71, etc., and Articles 96, 104.

member of such a standing committee shall hold "any post in any of the administrative, judicial, or procuratorial organs of the state."[95] Plainly, the intention is that these standing committees (and the various specialized committees and *ad hoc* committees of enquiry which the National People's Congress is instructed or authorized to establish) will be able to supervise the executive far more effectively than the unwieldy, and infrequently-convened, plenary sessions of the people's congresses at various levels can possibly do.

Nevertheless, of greater weight, presumably, than this system of checks and balances in determining the relation between central and local power in the future will be the expansion of the functions of the lower-level bodies. The scope of action of local people's governments is spelled out in rather wide-ranging terms. They shall (within the limits of their authority, of course), "conduct the administrative work concerning the economy, education, science, culture, public health, physical culture, urban and rural development, finance, civil affairs, public security, nationalities affairs, judicial administration, supervision and family planning in their respective administrative areas."[96] It could be argued that all this is implied by the 1954 formulation "administer their respective areas," but the new language does appear to have been chosen to convey the message that these are active and significant organs.

Another innovation is the establishment of residents' committees and villagers' committees among the urban and rural population, as "mass organizations of self-management at the grass-roots level." These committees are to deal with mediation, public security (!), public health, and other matters, and to "convey residents' opinions and demands and make suggestions to the people's government."[97]

The real significance of this new institution, and of other changes not laid down in the Constitution, but left to legislation, such as the direct election of deputies to people's congresses at the *xian* level and below, will, of course, be decided by the spirit in which such provisions are implemented. Of fundamental importance in this respect will be the new political climate which emerged in the spring of 1984, after the bleak winter of 1983-84, dominated by a witch-hunt against "spiritual pollution." The trend set in April 1984 ran in the direction of greater responsibilities for individuals and groups, and in a very broad and as yet ill-defined sense, toward greater political and intellectual pluralism.[98]

[95] Articles 65, 103.

[96] Article 107; cf. Article 64 of the 1954 Constitution.

[97] Article 100.

[98] For an extended discussion of this problem, see *Ideology and Policy in China since the Third Plenum.*

The most basic factor in the matrix out of which this orientation emerged was unquestionably the logic of economic reform, which found its fullest expression in the Decision of the Third Plenum on the Reform of the Economic Structure, adopted on 20 October 1984. The call to build a "planned socialist commodity economy" raises both economic questions ("Will it work?") and ideological questions ("Is it socialist?") which do not concern us directly here. The following paragraph illustrates graphically, however, the connection between these new ideas and the issues discussed in this article:

> Especially because of the influence of "left" deviationist errors in the Party's guiding ideology after 1957, various correct measures for enlivening the economy and developing a socialist commodity economy were regarded as "capitalist". As a result, the problem of excessive centralization and unification (*jizhong tongyi* 集中統一) in the economic structure (*tizhi* 體制) not only failed to be resolved for a long time, but constantly grew more acute. During this period, power was transferred to lower levels on many occasions, but in every instance this was limited to adjusting the administrative power of the Centre and the localities, and of different departments and regions. The critical issue of giving enterprises decision-making power (*zizhu quan* 自主權) was not addressed, so it was impossible to break out of the old conventions.[99]

The whole thrust of this passage, and of the 20 October Decision as a whole, is in the direction indicated by Deng Xiaoping in August 1980 when he complained that leading organs had "managed a good many things which they should not manage," thus bringing about an excessive concentration of power at the Centre. More precisely, it is evident that the passage just quoted amounts to an explicit repudiation of the concept of "dual rule," in the form in which it was advocated by Mao, and practised in Yan'an and during the Great Leap Forward.

None the less, though the Party at various levels is not supposed to run things directly, it is evident that ultimate authority still resides in the Party, and that basic policy guidelines are laid down by the Party. That being the case, the hope for democracy, at all levels, high and low, depends in large measure on the progress of democracy within the Party itself. An article published in 1979 put the problem as follows:

> In order to carry out the four modernizations, we must strengthen Party leadership. But we must absolutely not turn Party leadership into bureaucratic leadership. A noteworthy phenomenon under the conditions of the dictatorship of the proletariat is the frequent appearance of bureaucratism in the guise of "Party leadership," "Party directives," "the interests of the Party," and "Party discipline." Because of the prestige of the Party among the masses, and its position

---

[99] *Beijing Review*, No. 44, 1984, p. v; translation modified after comparison with the Chinese in *Renmin ribao*, 21 October 1984.

as the ruling party (*zhizheng dang* 執政黨), such bureaucratism often becomes, in many respects, even worse (*hai lihai* 還厲害) than old-style feudal bureaucratism. ... Hence the more we stress strengthening Party leadership, the more we must pay attention to inner-Party democracy and people's democracy, and combat bureaucratism.[100]

In other words, only to the extent that the Party itself abandons the obsession with centralization criticized by Deng Xiaoping in August 1980 will there be hope for the successful development of the impulses toward less rigid forms of control and more effective devolution of power which have emerged, tentative and fragile, in recent years.

The signs in this respect are somewhat ambiguous. Apart from giving over-all guidance in the domains of policy and ideology, the Party exercises effective control over the political system as a whole by retaining the ultimate power of decision as regards all senior appointments to the state as well as to the Party hierarchies. Until recently, this power extended down in principle two levels below that of the Party committee in question, though in practice lower levels could shape such decisions in a variety of ways. In mid-1984, the system was changed so that control over appointments extended down only one level.[101] In the case of the Rectification campaign of 1984, the Organization Department at the Centre took decisions (apart from those relating to the personnel of central Party and state organs) only regarding the first secretaries and their deputies at provincial level, leaving it to the newly-constituted provincial leaderships to carry the process further down.[102] Moreover, in some instances, provincial Party leaders were able to make use of their links to the central authorities to secure the annulment of decisions concerning them.

These facts serve to underscore once again the obvious fact that decentralization or devolution of certain decision-making functions cannot in itself be equated with democracy. On the other hand, not only have direct elections, involving (despite bureaucratic interference) significant freedom of choice, been carried out for lower-level people's congresses, but experiments were conducted in late 1984 in the election of provincial Party secretaries. The franchise for these was, of course, restricted, and the Central Committee

[100] Jia Chunfeng 賈春峰 and Wang Mengkui 王夢奎, "Guanliaozhuyi, fengjian zhuan-zhi yu xiao shengchan" 官僚主義、封建專制與小生產 (Bureaucratism, feudal despotism, and small-scale production), *Zhexue yanjiu* 哲學研究 , No. 3, 1979, p. 16.

[101] For an authoritative discussion of this whole problem, see the article by Melanie Manion, "The Cadre Management System, Post-Mao: The Appointment, Promotion, Transfer and Removal of Party and State Leaders," *The China Quarterly*, No. 102 (1985).

[102] Conversation of 11 April 1984 with Li Rui 李銳, then First Deputy Head of the Organization Department of the Central Committee.

retained the ultimate right to endorse or reject the choice of the majority, but the symbolic importance of such a development remains very great.

Moreover, there was continued and systematic emphasis on the importance of devolution of decision-making power. In an authoritative statement of February 1985, a spokesman for the Organization Department stressed that one of the key problems at present was to "resolve the problem of overconcentration as regards the boundaries of authority for managing cadres" (*jiejue ganbu guanliquan xian guoyu jizhong* 解決幹部管理權限過於集中). Since the Central Committee had decided in 1984 to push down this authority to lower levels, the number of cadres directly controlled from the Centre had, he noted, been reduced by two-thirds. The spokesman endorsed a new four-character "principle," "*jianzheng fangquan*" 簡政放權 ("Simpler administration and extending power downwards"), combining half the Yan'an slogan "Better troops and simpler administration" with the new idea of devolution of authority.[103]

In a word, while the primacy of the Party and of the Centre still remain, in the last analysis, absolute, processes are under way which may yet lead to greater degrees of decentralization, and greater freedom of choice for the citizens. The result will be largely determined, however, by the success of the partisans of democratic reform in securing the acceptance of their ideas by the central Party organs themselves.

[103]"Zhongyang zuzhibu fuzeren da . . . benbao jizhe wen" 中央組織部負責人答······本報記者問 ("A responsible person from the Organization Department of the Central Committee answers . . . our reporter's questions"), *Renmin ribao*, 11 February 1985. The spokesman in question may well have been the head of the Organization Department, Qiao Shi 喬石.

5. The System of "Class Status"

Jean-François Billeter

I. INTRODUCTION

If some perspicacious and unprejudiced souls had had the leisure freely to observe Chinese society over these last thirty years, if they had been able to describe its customs as did Montesquieu's two Persians, they would certainly have devoted a large amount of space to a system which directly affected the daily life of all Chinese and quite clearly influenced all their social relationships. Borrowing a term from everyday language, they would have called it the "class status" system. But no such thing happened and this system has in fact almost completely escaped our attention. An explanation for this oversight can be found in the fact that only a very small number of Westerners writing on the new régime over the last thirty years have really experienced daily life in China and been able to describe it, not as it was for them, foreign visitors or residents, but as it was for the Chinese. Since they lacked direct experience, they could not have noticed the importance of this system. Our ignorance can also be explained by the fact that though official sources frequently alluded to the system, they deemed it inadvisable to provide a complete picture of it and were even less anxious to analyse its real functioning. Moreover, those who were familiar with the system, citizens of the People's Republic, émigrés, or overseas Chinese, did not talk about it for the simple reason that it seemed natural to them. For the class status system to appear as an institution both important and problematic, a dual evolution had to occur: on the one hand, the system had to start being openly discussed in China itself; on the other hand, we ourselves, weary of purely political analyses of Chinese reality, had at last to set about examining this reality from new vantage points.

The paradox is that, just as the class status system has become an object of study, its importance within Chinese society is diminishing. Since 1978, its role has become less central as a result of various factors, and in the long run, these factors might even bring about its gradual extinction. Nevertheless, because of its importance over the last thirty years, we can rest assured the system will necessarily die hard. And even if it were to disappear in the very

127

near future, it still remains a fascinating object of study in terms of the recent history of Chinese society and in terms of comparative sociology and social anthropology.

Several authors have already studied the class status system.[1] No doubt, other research work will be carried out in the future; other works will appear and shed light on this vast and complex question. For several years, the official Chinese press, the main literary journals, the journals of the demo-cratic movement and those from Hong Kong have published many first-hand accounts and documents which help us better to perceive and understand this aspect of reality. In the present article, I do not aim to present and analyse this new material, nor to bring any new facts to the reader's attention. Rather, I intend to give a concise account of the class status system, and to define the part it played and continues to play in Chinese society. Through this attempt at synthesis, which is necessarily tentative, I wish to demonstrate the significance of the general problems that this system poses.

II. THE GENESIS AND DEVELOPMENT OF THE SYSTEM

The term *chengfen* 成份, usually translated by "status" in the context which concerns us here, literally means "component part." It can refer to "the components" or, by a slight shift in meaning, "the composition," as of a chemical compound, for example. At the time of land reform, the Com-munist Party adopted the term to refer to the exact economic condition of each peasant family and hence to its relative position on a socio-economic scale which included, in ascending order, agricultural workers, poor peasants, middle peasants, rich peasants, and landlords. In 1955, in the context of cooperativization, the middle peasants were divided into "upper" and "lower" middle peasants, and great importance was henceforth attached to

---

[1] In 1976, Gordon White devoted an excellent monograph to the debates which took place on the notion of class status during the Cultural Revolution: *The Politics of Class and Class Origin: The Case of the Cultural Revolution* (Canberra: The Australian National University, 1976). ("Contemporary China Papers 9"). Richard C. Kraus is the author of a thesis whose main results appeared in digest form in "Class Conflict and the Vocabulary of Social Analysis in China," in *The China Quarterly*, No. 69 (1977), pp. 54-74. The thesis itself has recently appeared in a revised version as *Class Conflict in Chinese Socialism* (New York: Columbia University Press, 1981). In July 1980, the Contemporary China Institute in London organized a conference on the theme: "Class and Social Stratification in Post-Revolutionary China." A selection of the papers presented on that occasion has been published in J. L. Watson (ed.), *Class and Social Stratification in Post-Revolution China* (Cambridge: Cambridge University Press, 1984) ("Contemporary China Institute Publications").

this distinction. Since it was a matter of the specific economic status of each household within the social class, the composite term "class status" (*jieji chengfen* 階級成份) seemed perfectly natural.

This classification provided the criteria needed to carry out two separate operations. First, it allowed the "enemy camp" to be distinguished from the "friendly camp"; in other words, the camp likely to be expropriated from the one likely to benefit from the reallocation of confiscated property. Secondly, it was used to organize this reallocation on a detailed basis. In the first instance, it served a function which can be considered standard from the standpoint of Marxist revolutionary theory: it prepared for the exploited classes' reappropriation of the means of production held by the former ruling classes. In the second instance, it was taken as a basis for a redistribution under conditions of shortage and therefore it served a function that had never been granted to class analysis by any Marxist text. But it was still an economic function. Some of the designations introduced into the classification, however, such as "revolutionary fighter" or "family of a revolutionary martyr," did not arise from relations to the means of production and were not of an economic nature. Rather, they conferred prestige and rights, and hence status. But, in reality, did not the other classifications very soon come to play a similar role? Did not the landlords and the rich peasants, deprived of their civil rights, "objects of the dictatorship of the proletariat," see themselves assigned negative status, while the poor peasants, the lower-middle and the upper-middle peasants saw bestowed upon themselves positive status which brought with it prestige and carefully graded rights?

In the early fifties, the work which the Party had undertaken of transforming social and economic relationships was extended to the cities. The Party applied the methods which it had worked out in the countryside to determine the condition of each city dweller. In many cases this condition was economic in the Marxist sense of the term, that is, it was defined by the person's relation to the means of production: "pedlar," "craftsman," "worker," "capitalist." But in the city, too, there appeared less conventional designations belonging not to traditional Marxist class analysis but rather to an indefinitely extendable nomenclature of socio-professional categories. Some of these, for example the term "cadre," were attended by rights and special prestige and thus conferred status.

Like the agrarian reform in the villages, the "Three Antis" and the "Five Antis" campaigns of 1951 provided the opportunity for carrying out this systematic work of naming and classifying in the cities as well. In 1952, practically the whole Chinese population was classified in this manner and the system included over sixty designations. Every Chinese citizen knew his own. In all his papers and in all the files which concerned him, his class status was inevitably listed. This appellation could take on great importance at any time, in the working world, in social relations and especially in political life. If he was a "cadre," "worker," or "poor peasant" for example, this appellation made him *a priori* into a representative of the people, the proper beneficiary of socialism's achievements. If he was an "intellectual," it would make him into an unreliable ally whom one would tend to mistrust. If he was a "landlord," it would make him into an enemy, an outsider. In each case, class status directly affected his position in the new society, his relationship with the revolutionary authorities, the ambitions which he could legitimately nurture in the political or professional sphere, the degree of protection with which he could provide others, and therefore his social prestige; it determined his freedom in choosing a spouse and his children's opportunities for social promotion. Class analysis had been applied in an extraordinarily systematic and meticulous way. It had produced a system which determined to a large extent the life of each individual and all of his relationships with others. Should it not be acknowledged that in making itself so concrete, it had changed its function and taken on a role that no Marxist would ever have dreamed of giving it? That it had given birth to a system of status, that is to say a system of social categories enjoying unequal rights and prestige? That it had served, in other words, to organize a new system of inequalities?

The fact that this sytem of organized inequality could develop in the space of a few years and soon be accepted by the greater part of the social body, no doubt indicated that it corresponded to the wishes and hence, in the last analysis, to the interests of a large segment of Chinese society. It is also because it was inspired by an ideal of justice which many people shared: the time had come for the former exploited classes to take their revenge on the exploiters and reverse the old relationships of inequality to their advantage. Was not the whole Marxist theory of revolution centred on the idea of this necessary reversal as summarized in the notion of the dictatorship of the proletariat? It is under the banner of this theory that the new inequality was organized: a transitory inequality, fated to wither away and transform itself into true equality. No doubt, the organization of this inequality could be accomplished all the more easily because it was founded on an egalitarian eschatology.

III. PARADOXICAL FEATURES

Neverthelsss, the new system rapidly took on a number of features that are not easily compatible with Marxist theory. We are going to single out three. The first is the *permanence* of the system.

The collectivization of agriculture and the "socialist transformation" of industry and commerce, essentially completed in 1955-56, profoundly altered the relations of production and therefore made most of the designations established several years earlier outdated. Logically, a new class analysis should have been made and the designations should have been changed accordingly. A capitalist who became an employee should have been classified as "employee"; a poor peasant who became a member of a higher level agricultural cooperative should have been classified as "cooperative member" and no more. But this did not occur and everyone kept his former status. Why? The question is important and several factors must be taken into account. Perhaps at first, it seemed useless to change designations that were fated to wither away in any case, according to theory. The Party also explained that subjective attitudes changed less rapidly than objective factors and that the danger with which the dispossessed classes still threatened the new régime made it necessary to keep the first designations, at least for a certain period of time. To some extent this vigilance was no doubt justified. None the less, the old class status system still constituted an anachronism. It was becoming necessary to account for the new situation in a more adequate way. In his address at the Eighth Party Congress, Deng Xiaoping admitted that the system "had lost or was losing its importance."[2] In 1955-56, hierarchies were created in the Party, the administration, industry, the army, and other sectors that defined the position and function of a sizeable part of the population far more accurately. In 1957, in "On the correct handling of contradictions among the people," Mao Zedong offered a picture of Chinese society where new types of contradictions were supplanting the old antagonisms, advocating that the old language be adapted to the new reality. But in September 1962, at the time of the Tenth Plenum of the Central Committee, he did the opposite. He asked for a return to basics, to the "classic" class struggle, putting forward the call: "Never forget class struggle."[3] He asserted that the antagonism between the bourgeoisie and the proletariat, between landlords and poor and lower-middle peasants still constituted the pivotal factor in this class struggle and had lost none of its acuteness in spite of the transformations which Chinese society had undergone.

Another paradoxical feature that asserted itself very quickly and which was incompatible with Marxist theory was the *hereditary nature* of class status. It had become hereditary owing to a confusion the Party had originally intended to avoid. In 1950, during the agrarian reform, the Party had specified

[2] *Renmin ribao*, 18 September 1956.

[3] Cf. "Speech at the Tenth Plenum of the Eighth Central Committee," in Stuart Schram (ed.), *Mao Tse-tung Unrehearsed* (Harmondsworth: Penguin Books, 1974), pp. 188-96, especially 189-90.

that no class status would be attributed to children and that only family origin (*jiating chushen* 家庭出身) would be mentioned. But in practice, this origin was defined by the father's class status, so that the distinction generally made no sense and was hardly taken into account. In the city as well as the country, children were soon considered branded by their parents' class status, especially their father's, and they experienced all its advantages or disadvantages. They served their apprenticeship of having prestige or being discriminated against at school, and when they became integrated into the working world and adult political life, they could clearly see the implications of the status which they had inherited. Naturally, ostracism was most severe in the villages. There, former landlords and their children were treated as pariahs. How had things reached this stage? There had been no debate, no consultation, directives, laws, at least at the beginning. The hereditary nature of status seems to have asserted itself spontaneously. In other words, it seems to have resulted from the convergence of numerous and powerful social interests. The Party certainly had a great stake in it and, if it was not actually responsible for the phenomenon, in practice it surely encouraged it since it was bound to benefit directly from it. By their status, the children of cadres would be privileged people. The play of interests which had made status hereditary also guaranteed its permanence. Those who had a privileged or relatively favourable status married "in their milieu" so as not to jeopardize their advantages. Those at the other end of the social scale were obliged to intermarry because of the ostracism which befell them. Even in intermediary zones, where the stakes were less significant, marriages generally seemed to take place within specific categories and to have contributed to the preservation of the system.[4]

When Mao Zedong in 1962 reaffirmed the role of the former social classes,

[4] As a former Red Guard who emigrated to Hong Kong points out: "Most of the children of upper cadres (including the local, civil, and military cadres) and of high-ranking intellectuals marry among themselves, especially the children of intellectuals because they benefit from family surroundings, an education, a life style, connections, and career opportunities which make them into people fundamentally different from ordinary mortals" (Jean-Jacques Michel and Huang He, *Avoir vingt ans en Chine* [Paris: Le Seuil, 1978], p. 95). Real behaviour is complicated by the fact that male status prevails over female status. Secure in his positive status, a worker can very well marry the daughter of a former landlord without any negative consequences. But he does not always evade these consequences. The Red Guard already quoted estimates, for example, that "if a worker, who is furthermore a member of the Party, marries a girl from a bourgeois background, then one can say that that's the end of his political future" (*op. cit.*, pp. 95-96). For women who marry, on the other hand, things are perfectly clear: their future depends on their husband's status. They can escape the fate of a bad status through marriage, as men cannot.

and hence of class status as it had been defined in the early fifties, he must have realized that his position was likely to favour a hardening of social stratifications based on status and create dangerous tensions. Specifically, it was necessary to avoid excluding from political life, in too obvious a fashion, young people from middle-class families and denying them any hope of upward mobility. It was better to make the most of their abilities than to have them become opponents of the régime. A similar problem existed in the countryside. Mao Zedong therefore proceeded to stress the subjective factor: of course individuals had to be judged according to their class status, but their subjective attitude (*sixiang* 思想) toward the socialist regime and their individual behaviour (*biaoxian* 表現) also had to be taken into account. He considered it normal that a hostile attitude toward socialism be transmitted within families of the former dispossessed classes, but he did not want to accept a strict determinism in this matter: all those who were born into such families had to be convinced that they were free to redeem themselves through their personal commitment. Mao Zedong's innovation had still other implications: it gave the Party a means of criticizing people who were protected by a positive status such as "cadre," "worker," or "poor peasant." The Party could henceforth accuse them of having "objectively," by their words or deeds, rallied to a class other than their original class or even, in the case of workers, to a class other than the one to which they actually belonged economically. If the Party leadership wanted to fight against bureaucratization and privilege, or simply against the most blatant manifestations of these, this kind of argument was essential.

Thus powerful forces were at work within China seeking to impose a closed society, in which status would be hereditary in fact, if not in law, while other forces were acting in favour of a more open society in which class status would have only relative importance, or would have no importance at all, and would not interfere with upward mobility. It is easy enough to see that the main members of the first group were the cadres. They favoured a hereditary conception of status for two reasons: first, because it guaranteed that their privileges would be transmitted to their children, and secondly because it made their work easier. Indeed, by basing themselves on the objective criterion of class status in the countless decisions which they had to make on a daily basis (awarding student places or jobs, promotions, nominations, cooptations, delegations, the selection of persons to be criticized or of "objects of struggle," etc.), they were guarding themselves against any possible criticism. If they used the uncertain criteria of subjective attitude and behaviour, they could be wrong at any time and be accused of having been insufficiently firm in their class position, indeed of having betrayed the Party line and the higher interests of socialism. Admittedly, the objective criteria were not always the fairest, but they were the most reliable. As for the forces which favoured an easing of the system, they included, among others, the intellectuals and the student youth of middle-class origin. This youth demanded the right to prove its loyalty to the new régime by individual political commitment. The intellectuals wanted to be recognized for their professional competence and their intellectual, scientific, and technical contributions and, by virtue of these, be given the right to be considered fully-fledged members of the new society.

They asked that professional competence (*zhuan* 專, literally "to be an expert") be recognized at least as much as revolutionary virtue (*hong* 紅, literally "to be red"). Others, who were aspiring to greater power but were unable to claim technical or intellectual competence, played up revolutionary virtue—in other words, militancy, political activism, indeed radicalism—by maintaining, on the one hand, the superiority of virtue (*hong*) over technical competence (*zhuan*) and, on the other, the superiority of personal commitment in the new struggles over formerly acquired rights or rights inherited through parents. These radical forces tried to impose themselves during the Cultural Revolution by using violence against both the intellectuals and the former cadres. Their spearheads were those from the Red Guards and rebellious organizations who stressed revolutionary virtue and the need for each person to prove it then and there by the "living application" (*huoxue huoyong* 活學活用) of Mao Zedong's thought. The former cadres defended themselves by actively helping their children organize themselves into opposing Red Guard factions, occasionally called "loyalists," and by putting significant means at their disposal. These factions forcefully reasserted the primacy of historically acquired class status and did something which no one had yet dared do: for the first time, they *openly* defended the idea that status should be considered hereditary. They did so brutally by spreading everywhere the slogan "When the father is a hero, the son is one too; when the father is a reactionary, the son is a good-for-nothing" (*Laozi yingxiong er haohan, laozi fandong er hundan* 老子英雄兒好漢，老子反動兒混蛋). This frankness provoked heated reactions. Yu Luoke 遇羅克, a young man from Peking who was then twenty-four, denounced the outrageousness of this position from the point of view of Marxist theory in a scathing manifesto that immediately spread throughout China. This manifesto, entitled *On Family Origin* (*Chushenlun* 出身論), was published by the Red Guards in the capital in December 1966. Yu Luoke was arrested in January 1968, by order of Xie Fuzhi 謝富治, minister of public security, and though he defended his loyalty to the thought of Mao Zedong, he was shot in March 1970.[5] His tragic end

[5] Yu Luoke was recently rehabilitated. The Chinese press published detailed articles

well illustrates the violence of conflicts during that period and the important stakes that revolved around the definition and role of class status.

I have singled out two characteristics of the class status system that are not compatible with Marxist conceptions: the preservation of status beyond the social transformations which should have made it obsolete, in other words, its anachronism, and its tendency to become hereditary in practice. A third, equally problematic characteristic has to be pointed out: its *heterogeneousness*. I noted the existence of such heterogeneity among the status categories laid down in the countryside and in the cities in the early 1950s, but at the same time I suggested that it was only apparent, since all the designations adopted at the time, whether derived from the standard class analysis or referring to socioprofessional categories, had the common function of attributing certain rights and privileges, positive or negative. A much more obvious heterogeneousness appeared in the course of the 1950s, when the list of recognized statuses took on novelties such as "counter-revolutionary," "rightist," or "bad element." The first, introduced at the time of the "Three Antis" and the "Five Antis" in 1951, was a legally-defined offence. That of "rightist," created in 1957 and applied to hundreds of thousands of people in the course of that year and the next, was again political.[6] But these labels had from the outset the same function as a class status, to which they were likened. Witness the formula *di-fu-fan-huai-you* 地富反壞右 which had unmatched political fortune and which combined in an abbreviated form the "five bad categories" (*huaiwulei* 壞五類), in other words, the landlords (*dizhu* 地主), the "rich peasants" (*funong* 富農), the "counter-revolutionaries" (*fangemingfenzi* 反革命份子), the "bad elements" (*huaifenzi* 壞份子), and the "rightists" (*youpai* 右派), also referred to collectively as the "elements from the five categories" (*wulei fenzi* 五類份子). These five bad categories were contrasted with the "five red categories" (*hongwulei* 紅五類), which included workers, peasants (poor or middle), cadres, martyrs, and

---

about him that constitute extremely interesting documents. See particularly "Huapo yemu de yunxing—Ji sixiang jiefang de xianqu Yu Luoke" 劃破夜幕的隕星——記思想解放的先驅遇羅克 (A meteor which has pierced the darkness—To the memory of Yu Luoke, precursor of the liberation of thought), published in the *Guangming ribao* 光明日報 of 21 and 22 July 1980, and "Nifeng elang zhong de xiongying—Yu Luoke" 逆風惡浪中的雄鷹——遇羅克 ("Yu Luoke, a bold eagle in the midst of the evil winds"), *Xin shiqi* 新時期, No. 4, 1980, pp. 13-22.

[6] No exact figure has yet been published to my knowledge. In *The Wilting of the Hundred Flowers* (New York: Praeger, 1962), Mu Fu-sheng estimates that the number of people treated as "rightists" was 300,000 (p. 173). Some official figures that include categories other than "rightists" suggest a lower estimate, but they may well be smaller than the true figures; cf. Jacques Guillermaz, *Le Parti communiste chinois au pouvoir, 1949-1972* (Paris: Payot, 1972), p. 149.

revolutionary intellectuals. The new designations, like status, justified denying the people who were so classified their rights and prestige. They also revealed most clearly the fundamentally arbitrary nature of the system. "Arbitrary" here is not meant to refer to the arbitrary exercise of power, but is used in the more fundamental and abstract sense it has in the concept of "cultural arbitrariness" (*arbitraire culturel*). Theoretically, the status system was justified because it was seen as derived from Marxist class analysis, which was reputed to be scientific and objective. Actually, it originated from the determination to organize social relationships according to a rational and controllable order—a determination which no doubt must be interpreted both as the resurgence of a very ancient Chinese tradition and as a specifically contemporary phenomenon.

The arbitrary nature of the status system stands out most obviously in the fact that an individual could belong to two or more categories simultaneously; in those cases, it was up to the Party cadres to decide according to which status he would actually be treated. In extreme cases such as that of a rich peasant become worker, or of an intellectual, son of a martyr, accused of right-wing deviation, the cadres' decision could be the object of all sorts of bargaining.[7]

This survey of the three "abnormal" features of the class status system— its anachronistic character, its hereditary tendency, and its heterogeneousness —has made obvious its arbitrary nature and its main function, which is distributive. We have seen that its function is to allow the political authorities to regulate the distribution of property, rights and prestige. Prestige may be taken as simply the symbolic expression of these various rights and privileges.[8]

[7] In the title story of the collection *The Execution of Mayor Yin and Other Stories from the Great Proletarian Cultural Revolution* (London: Allen and Unwin, 1979), Chen Jo-hsi 陳若曦 [Chen Ruoxi] cites a characteristic example of this kind of bargaining. Someone is talking about the hero, a former Guomindang officer who rallied to the Communists on the eve of Liberation, and says: "Now, as you know, class status determines everything: a good class origin will always get you promoted above the heads of others. Well, at the time of the agrarian reform, the work team classified his mother in the 'poor peasant' category; but he objected immediately and suggested a stricter classification for, said he, when his father was alive they would often hire farm workers at the time of the harvest; therefore, strictly speaking and in order to respect the Party's instructions, they should be classified as 'rich peasants', he insisted. Finally, they were labelled 'middle peasants' " (pp. 8-9; see also pp. 21-22). It might be argued that in a study like this one it would be better to quote first-hand sources or interviews rather than a literary work. But one of the great qualities of Chen Ruoxi's short stories is the richness and accuracy of her sense of observation, which make her work a particularly valuable testimony to Chinese reality.

[8] This conception of prestige derives from Pierre Bourdieu's analyses; cf. *Esquisse d'une théorie de la pratique* (Geneva and Paris: Droz, 1972), particularly pp. 227-43,

We must specify that we are talking about official prestige as sanctioned by ideology and the Party's various forms of propaganda. This type of prestige, it should be pointed out, does not necessarily coincide with the prestige accorded spontaneously by public opinion.

IV. THE CENTRAL QUESTION

These findings bring us to the central question. Up to now, inside and outside China, everyone had assumed that the system of class status was a natural corollary of the Marxist regime. This view was spontaneously adopted by almost all the sympathizers of the régime, whether Marxist or not, as well as by its detractors. It was only in the recent past that several China specialists, political scientists, and sociologists, all Anglo-Saxon, got down to studying and describing in detailed and concrete fashion the real functioning of this system. Of course they noted the abnormal features the system presented from the Marxist point of view. But, instead of viewing these as the sign of a break with Marxism, they interpreted them as phenomena of adaptation required by the changing reality of a rapidly evolving society.[9] Personally, I think it more useful to adopt another point of view and to consider that, under a Marxist cloak, a *sui generis* system was born in China which must be understood as such.

It seems to me that the expression "class status," used to translate *jieji chengfen*, contains a very revealing ambiguity in this respect. In the social sciences, a distinction is made between caste, order, status, class and still other types of social division. Usually, "class" is given Marx's purely economic definition. "Status" on the other hand is a social condition defined by certain rights and prohibitions, involving a certain amount of prestige, that may or may not be linked to certain concretely defined activities. The term is vague and takes on different connotations depending on the historical context. It seems to me perfectly suited to present-day China. The fact that it is joined to the word "class" is a logical paradox which conceals an actual paradox. Indeed, as pointed out, the status system grew out of the sort of class analysis to which all Marxist parties adhere, and which the Chinese Communist Party

"Le capital symbolique." See also *Le sens pratique* (Paris: Les Editions de Minuit, 1980), pp. 191-207. Bourdieu was concerned with the function of prestige in the economy of certain pre-capitalist societies. It would of course be necessary to examine to what extent or with what qualifications his analyses would be applicable to present-day Chinese society.

[9] This is the case with Richard C. Kraus, for instance. Susan L. Shirk, whose work will be referred to below, is a notable exception.

applied systematically during the régime's first years. But as far as their real function was concerned, the *jieji chengfen* very soon became a status system which can quite justifiably be compared to other similar systems that have existed in history or still exist today. Considered from this angle a whole series of problems that seemed insoluble is easily resolved. We cease being surprised by the fact that the system survived the radical transformations of the fifties and played a growing part in daily life when logically it should have withered away; that it should have become so diversified as to include the condition of each individual, no individual being able to escape it; that it should have combined economic, professional, political, and legal notions without the slightest compunction; that, beyond a language that remained Marxist, it demonstrated an obvious indifference toward the scientific study of social facts. We are, in fact, dealing with a system of designations by means of which the political authorities regulate all important social relationships—those that concern ideological authority, the devolution of power and the distribution of goods. It can be justly stated, as Jean Daubier has done, that the ruling principle of this system is "to each according to his rank."[10]

In the following pages, I no longer wish to present the status system negatively, as an anomaly or deviation, but positively as an institution that has played an absolutely central role in Chinese social life for thirty years. I hope that this presentation will shed some light on its genesis, its functioning and the historical part it has played hitherto.

V. THE PARTY'S CONCEPTION AND PEASANT REALITY

The work teams that were sent into the villages to carry out land reform and who set about determining the economic condition of each peasant family, also had as a mission to lay the foundations for a policy of alliance. In applying class analysis as it had been defined by Mao Zedong to village society, they had to provide an objective and detailed answer to the opening question of the first volume of the *Selected Works*: "Who are our enemies, who are our friends?" Mao Zedong had explained: "To distinguish real friends from real enemies, we must make a general analysis of the economic status of the various classes in Chinese society and of their respective attitudes towards the revolution."[11] Once these points had been clarified on a scientific basis, the Party would be able to decide with precision and full knowledge of the

[10] J. Daubier, *Les nouveaux maîtres de la Chine* (Paris: Grasset, 1979), p. 65.

[11] The original 1926 version of this article also called for an analysis of the "class nature" and "numerical strength" of the various classes.

facts who were its opponents and who were its allies and therefore to conduct a perfectly rational policy. This was the idea, apparently simple. But in applying this idea to peasant reality, the work teams encountered difficulties.

One of the most significant difficulties stemmed from the fact that often the initial expropriation of the landlords in 1950, or of the landlords and rich peasants in the more radical phase of 1947-48, did not provide the peasants with enough land and goods to satisfy their needs. The poor peasants, who benefited directly from the support of the Party, were then tempted to expropriate not only the rich peasants, but also the middle peasants, and were very likely to provoke among the latter an opposition which the Party wished to avoid at all costs. This major problem is very clearly apparent in *Fanshen*. But problems also arose because the relatively simple criteria which the Party had defined in 1933, in the context of the "Land Verification Movement," which aimed to check on how land reform had been carried out during the previous two years, were insufficient to determine the exact limits between classes. In *Fanshen* we read:

> By far the most important dividing line was that between the middle peasants and the rich peasants. The Draft Agrarian Law of 1947 had made this the great divide between friend and enemy, between the people and their oppressors, between revolution and counter-revolution. It was absolutely essential that this line be clear and unequivocal. Yet here the Juichin documents were most ambiguous. In describing middle peasants the document said, "Some of the middle peasants practice a *small* amount of exploitation, but such exploitation is not of a *constant* character and the income therefrom does not constitute their *main* means of livelihood."
>
> Anyone using these standards would have to know exactly what *small, constant,* and *main* meant in order to carry out the intent of the law.
>
> In regard to the difference between poor peasants and middle peasants the same kind of difficulty arose.[12]

In May 1948, the Central Committee issued a substantially revised version of these regulations which provided somewhat more detailed criteria (and also took a more moderate line, no longer defining the Party's goal as "the annihilation of the landlord class"), but in practice it remained difficult to draw with precision the line between the various social classes. The Party, which sought to discern enemy classes whose opposition Marxist theory had explained in advance, was faced with a great variety of economic conditions. Taken together, these formed a continuous spectrum instead of separating neatly into two antagonistic camps.

Moreover, these "classes" were not stable, and a peasant family might

[12]William H. Hinton, *Fanshen: A Documentary of Revolution in a Chinese Village* (New York: Vintage Books, 1966), p. 286.

belong to a given class only for a brief period of time. To account for this, the Central Committee was obliged to add to the regulations an article that defined the period to be considered in the determination of class. As Mark Elvin has remarked:

> Chinese rural society in the nineteenth century and early twentieth century was thus one of the most fluid in the world, lacking any of the status or caste restraints which typified late pre-modern Japan or India. The Communist land-reform documents of the 1930s again give proof of this. According to a Communist party ruling it took only three years to establish "landlord" or "rich peasant" status. . . . Everywhere there was a constant competition, without benefit to society as a whole, in which the fortunes of individual peasant families continually rose and fell. It was a society that was both egalitarian and riven with mutual jealousies. The economic closeness of exploiter and exploited, and the lack of any ideologically sanctioned inevitability in the social differences between them made for hostility rather than harmony.[13]

The third difficulty encountered in the course of the debates that preceded the distribution of confiscated goods, stemmed from the exclusively economic definition that the Party wanted to apply to social reality. The reduction of real-life experience to purely economic categories was not self-evident for the peasants, as Hinton notes in the following passage:

> With a "well bottom" view of the world still limiting their vision, most peasants found it hard to separate their personal problems from the basic economic situation that was the root of their misery. . . .
> Time and again, Little Li, Ch'i Yun, and the other work team cadres who sat in on the meeting had to bring the discussion around to objective economic facts and warn against classifying some family in the upper brackets because the family head had collaborated with the Japanese, habitually beat his wife, or sided with his wife against his mother.[14]

This suggests that the Party employed a conception of peasant society that was not entirely adapted to reality. This problem seems to me not to be due to a lack of knowledge of the rural milieu, but to originate rather on a deeper, conceptual level. The Party considered as an axiomatic truth the idea that Chinese society was divided into two enemy camps and that these two camps confronted each other on a demarcation line that necessarily ran through the whole of society, and moreover that this line could be objectively defined and clearly traced. But in spite of the injustices and conflicts which made up rural society, it was difficult, if not impossible, to draw such a line. As a result, the Party hedged in applying its own criteria, and class analysis seems often to have been determined through wholly unscientific bargaining.

[13] Mark Elvin, *The Pattern of the Chinese Past* (London: Methuen, 1973), pp. 258-59.
[14] *Fanshen*, p. 279.

The Party based its action, its programme, the very definition of its mission, on a series of ideas which had great authority because they were rooted in Marxist theory. The difficulties encountered in applying these ideas to pre-1949 peasant reality were not likely to throw doubt on their general validity. Instead of revising them in the light of the facts, the Party merely solved the problems raised by their failure to match sociological reality, in a completely pragmatic manner. After 1949, its new position of power not only gave it the means of pressure and manipulation, but completely exempted it from revising its ideas. It could now impose them. It imposed its ideas and its language on its own members first and then on all parts of Chinese society. E. Vogel discusses the new dilemmas which confronted the cadres in the following way:

> In Chinese society it has traditionally been considered virtuous to honour old personal ties. The betrayal of local ties went against the sentiment of the local population and hardly endeared the cadres or the Communist Party to the masses. ... During the period preceding Liberation many local Communists had persuaded village leaders that if they cooperated with the guerillas they could expect favourable treatment after Liberation. Cadres had fully expected that they would be able to make good these promises, but now they were being told by their superiors that they must break these ties and draw class lines sharply.[15]

The last sentence clearly shows that a choice had to be made, not only between two languages' or two systems of thought, but also between two value systems.[16] For his part, C. K. Yang points out in *A Chinese Village in Early Communist Transition*: "Communist strategy in the transition period was to concentrate intensive indoctrination upon the elite, both old and new. This meant ideological remolding of the former leadership portion of the population in pre-Communist society and intensive indoctrination for the younger activists marked for leading the new social order." The author discusses the former village ruler who, through reeducation, withdraws into mute opposition to the new régime, as well as the successes of the education lavished on the young generation:

> If the adult villagers were still quite ignorant of and disinterested in Communism, pupils from the elementary schools in 1951 were already enthusiastically singing Communist songs and parroting Communist slogans, and many of them acted as informants for the Communists on affairs of the village and even of their own families. Indoctrination sessions and general propaganda carried on within the

[15]E. Vogel, *Canton under Communism* (Cambridge, Mass.: Harvard University Press, 1969), pp. 105-106.

[16]On the problems that arose because of this choice on another level, see Lin Yü-sheng, *The Crisis of Chinese Consciousness* (Madison: The University of Wisconsin Press, 1979), especially the excellent chapter on Lu Xun and his attachment to the notion of *nian jiu* 念舊 (fidelity to old ties).

new organizations such as the peasants' association and the Youth League were already producing a crop of young leaders who could follow the Communist directives with at least superficial understanding of the new terminology.

As for the peasants, they were more reserved in accepting the new language:

> If the young activists showed considerable genuine conviction in the new ideological line, it was partly due to the concrete benefits they reaped from the change, including prestige and material gain from being elevated to the new status of leadership. But the common peasants generally did not share these benefits, and they were still pressed by the problem of eking out a bare subsistence for themselves and their families. . . . The early impact of Communism on the ideology of the great majority of the Nanjing peasants left them apathetic, skeptical, and submissive rather than showing any genuine enthusiasm and conviction toward Communism.[17]

This brief survey shows how different social group either rejected, or sceptically accepted, or, on the contrary, adopted the new language and, through it, the ideas and values advocated by the Party. In the beginning of the 1950s, all Chinese society used this language with greater or lesser reticence.

VI. ON THE ORIGIN OF THE PARTY'S CONCEPTIONS

We are so accustomed to Marxist language—terms such as "revolution," "class struggle," "economy," "production," "policy," "Party," "State"—that there is a great temptation to take it for granted and see it as universally applicable. We are all the more inclined to do so because this terminology belongs not only to Marxism, but more generally to contemporary Western society. These notions are so common that it is difficult for us to stand back from them and view them with a critical mind. Yet, this is precisely what we have to do if we are to understand what the adoption of Marxist terminology has meant for China.

Marxist theory is a critical interpretation of the capitalist system and, by implication, of the social formations which preceded it historically. At the same time, it is an interpretation that is deeply rooted within the capitalist system. Marx was a great demystifier, but only within the framework and limits of his own period and his own society, whose basic tenets he shared in certain fundamental ways. Like his contemporaries, he saw economics as an autonomous area, where objective rationality prevailed, a rationality that operated independently of the wills of social protagonists. Like them, he

[17]C. K. Yang, *A Chinese Village in Early Communist Transition* (Cambridge, Mass.: M.I.T. Press, 1959), pp. 198-99.

142

thought that a scientific analysis of economics and its laws would generate of itself a policy and, more generally, behavioural guidelines that would be completely rational. In spite of his critical acuity, he did not see that he was relying on categories which appeared to him to be the expression of a rational reality, but were in fact the product of cultural arbitrariness.

Karl Polanyi demonstrated this last proposition in *The Great Transformation*.[18] He showed that, in the words of Louis Dumont, "the liberalism which dominated the nineteenth century and the first decades of the twentieth, essentially the doctrine of the sacrosanct role of the market and its concomitants, is based on an unprecedented innovation: the complete separation of the economic aspects of the social fabric and their construction into an autonomous domain."[19] According to Polanyi, what distinguishes European industrial society of the nineteenth and twentieth centuries from all other known forms of societies, is that it thought it could substitute an impersonal economic regulation for the old forms of social regulation—religious, customary, ethical, political. This regulation was to be carried out through the market, and all elements of social activities were to be redefined in market terms.

European industrial society was therefore born of a fiction, in other words, of an arbitrary reinterpretation of social reality that permitted specific interests to manipulate it as they saw fit. These new interests make their appearance along with industrial ventures, which require costly investments and therefore involve high risks. Industrialists had to be sure that they could buy all the ingredients of the production process. For this, labour, land, and capital had to be transformed into commodities:

> They could, of course, not be really transformed into commodities, as actually they were not produced for sale on the market. But the fiction of their being so produced became the organizing principle of society. Of the three, one stands out: labor is the technical term used for human beings in so far as they are not employers but employed; it follows that henceforth the organization of labor would change concurrently with the organization of the market system. But as the organization of labor is only another word for the forms of life of the common people, this means that the development of the market system would be accompanied by a change in the organization of society itself. All along the line, human society had become an accessory to the economic system.[20]

The transformation was thus carried out. This resulted, first in England during the first half of the nineteenth century, then in France, Germany, and

[18] Karl Polanyi, *The Great Transformation: The Political and Economic Origins of Our Time* (Boston: The Beacon Press, 1957).

[19] Louis Dumont, *Homo aequalis: Genèse et épanouissement de l'idéologie économique* (Paris: Gallimard, 1977), p. 1.

[20] *Op. cit.*, p. 75.

other European nations, in societies where industry subjugated virtually the whole of society and put it at its service. Between the holders of capital who commanded and the new proletarian class, an opposition took shape whose clear-cut nature had no parallel in earlier societies. This opposition appeared as purely economic. The very fabric of society was viewed in economic terms. Political economy was the major science of the period, a period which now saw politics as an area where only economic conflicts of interests were expressed and arbitrated. One of the paradoxes pointed out by Polanyi is that the free market, presumably a purely economic institution, and the labour market specifically, were imposed through political violence, and maintained through continual state intervention.[21] The contemporary world has its main origin in this revolution which, while industrial, was also political, social, ethical, and intellectual.

The more hindsight history gives us, the more clearly we see the extent to which Marx remained, on certain essential points, a prisoner of his time. It is true that he analyzed with great lucidity the revolution which was taking place in the nineteenth century. One has only to cite the following well-known passage from *The Communist Manifesto*:

> The bourgeoisie, wherever it has got the upper hand, has put an end to all feudal, patriarchal, idyllic relations. It has pitilessly torn asunder the motley feudal ties that bound man to his "natural superiors", and has left remaining no other nexus between man and man than naked self-interest, than callous "cash payment".[22]

These words are perfectly in keeping with Polanyi's analysis. But on one important point, Marx and Engels' thought differs from that of Polanyi. For they go on to say: "In one word, for exploitation, veiled by religious and political illusions, it [the bourgeoisie] has substituted naked, shameless, direct, brutal exploitation."[23] Thus the advent of the new age is accompanied by the revelation of a fundamental and objective fact which had remained hidden. Marx and Engels regard the laying bare of this objective truth as in itself progressive, and as the condition for all future progress.

It is clear where Marx remained a prisoner of his time. He wrongly took as objective and universal truths notions which actually resulted from an arbitrary interpretation of social reality and violated that reality. Like his contemporaries, he regarded political economy as an objective science. Like them, he accepted its anthropological corollary, the idea that in the final analysis, everywhere and always, men's actions are determined by economic

[21]*Ibid.*, p. 127 (see also p. 102).
[22]Karl Marx and Friedrich Engels, *The Communist Manifesto* (Harmondsworth: Penguin Books, 1967), p. 82.
[23]*Loc. cit.*

interests. He deduced from this that the radical transformation of the relations of production would suffice to establish a viable society. Like his contemporaries, he thought that political problems were derivative problems and that, when all was said and done, only the good organization of the "infrastructure" counted. I am well aware that Marx's thought is not simple, that several inspirations intersect within it, that his works contain pages which display great philosophical audacity, rare sociological intuition, and remarkable acuity in political analysis. But from the standpoint of the present discussion, what counts is that his thought, and even more the simplifications to which it gave rise, remained stamped by the specific historical universe of nineteenth century European industrial society, and never ceased serving as a vehicle for its fundamental categories. By the way in which it reduces the social to the economic and regards the economic as an area ruled by objective laws, and its way of confining itself to a simplifying conception of man and of denying the autonomy of political and ethical questions, Marxist ideology is a variant of liberal ideology.

It is therefore hardly surprising that it had the same effects on traditional societies as liberal ideology. It also "liberated" the individual from the customary network of social relations which protected him; it rent the tight fabric of hierarchical status, rights and obligations, representations and beliefs and replaced them with abstract economic relationships on the one hand, and an equally abstract ideology on the other, whose key concepts were so general that they did not easily relate to individual experience.

The difficulties which the Party encountered during the agrarian reform cannot be fully understood, it seems to me, unless all of this is taken into account. Having accepted the universalist pretentions of Marxism, the Party could easily believe that it had available a scientific and culturally neutral instrument of analysis. In fact, it was using a language that was deeply imbued with a completely different sociocultural universe from the peasant world with which it was dealing. It did not, and no doubt could not, notice this at the time, since the determination to transform society took precedence over all other considerations. In any case, the fabric of traditional social relationships had no value in its eyes. It was only an obstacle that had to be overcome.

VII. THE DISTRIBUTIVE FUNCTION OF CLASS STATUS IN THE NEW RÉGIME

We are now in a position to account for the genesis of the status system in a more precise way. This system originated in a transformation which consisted of a negative stage and a positive stage, intimately linked. The negative stage lies in the reduction of social reality to purely economic terms. This reduction condemns traditional social relationships, whose logic is infinitely more complex than economic logic, to wither away more or less rapidly: they can no longer be considered other than as anachronistic remnants of an abolished universe. This kind of reduction is the same as that which is at the origin of capitalist society.[24] In Europe, where it was carried out for the first time, modern individualist ideology developed with it.[25] There is harmony between this reduction, first postulated and then imposed on social reality, and individualism. The two phenomena are concomitant. Individualism is the adequate expression of what man has become in a market society.

But, unlike the English liberals at the beginning of the nineteenth century, the Communist Party did not seek to submit society to the laws of the market. Consequently, the negative stage of the transformation was immediately combined with the positive. The Party redistributes the confiscated goods and property. In so doing, it favours the social categories that it considers as its allies and penalizes the others. It establishes a hierarchical order, placing the most reliable, trustworthy, and revolutionary categories at the top and those that are most suspicious and reputed to be opposed, in varying degrees, to the revolutionary enterprise, at the bottom. This order very rapidly takes on decisive importance, for the Party has the monopoly on distribution in all areas, or is on the way to securing it, and can therefore ensure that this order materializes, where necessary by constraint. It will be able to impose it on society, just as the English liberals imposed the laws of the market in their time.

The same radical transformation takes place in the cities. It is carried out slightly differently and to some extent more easily because the capitalist economy has already left its mark and dislocated part of the traditional social relationships. But in the end the revolution is the same everywhere: a system of representations claiming to be derived from class analysis, in other words, from the analysis of civil society, imposes itself on this civil society and subjects it to its own logic.

The Party has the monopoly of distribution in all areas. It determines by

[24] Cf. Polanyi, *The Great Transformation*, as well as *Primitive, Archaic and Modern Economies: Essays of Karl Polanyi* edited by George Dalton (Boston: Beacon Press, 1971). For a very accurate analysis of the incompatibility of the traditional peasant mentality with the mentality imposed by the market economy, see Pierre Bourdieu, *Algérie 60: Structures économiques et structures temporelles* (Paris: Les Editions de Minuit, 1977).

[25] Dumont devoted a series of important studies to the genesis and definition of this individualistic modern ideology. See especially the Introduction to *Homo hierarchicus: Essai sur le système des castes* (Paris: Gallimard, 1966) and his *Homo aequalis*.

various means the distribution of property, rights, opportunities, power, and prestige. The issue of the general principles according to which it regulates this distribution is of course pivotal both for itself and for the society it dominates. These principles have to be accepted as fair by the social body as a whole and, particularly, by those penalized by the distribution. It is sufficient that the losers admit to being penalized for morally valid reasons for the régime to be justified and guaranteed stability. Generally speaking, among the criteria which help regulate distribution in different societies, past and present, the main ones are qualification, birth and virtue. *Qualification* can be intellectual, professional, or technical; the social regimes that adopt it as their main criterion for selection are run by a mandarinate, a bureaucracy, or a technocracy. Those that favour *birth* will be dominated by an aristocracy, a caste, or a race. Those that opt in favour of *virtue* are governed by the best from the moral point of view, by an elite organized into a party or sect, or some other structure.[26]

From its beginnings and until quite recently, that is for almost thirty years, the Chinese regime belonged, unquestionably, to the third type. Everything was brought into play to substantiate the idea that all those who benefited from preferential treatment or enjoyed some privilege had deserved it because of their revolutionary virtue, their devotion to the revolutionary cause. This virtue, this devotion could take many forms, display itself in the most diverse manner, take different names. These were best summarized in the epithet of "revolutionary" (*geming* 革命) or "red" (*hong* 紅), which acquired a near magical power as a result. Virtue was the principle which justified the status hierarchy which we discussed above—a hierarchy which was moral as well as political. The most revolutionary were at the top, the most reactionary were at the bottom.

Not only does this distribution according to virtue shed light on one of the structural features of the régime, it also sheds light on certain aspects of its evolution, certain crises it underwent. Indeed, social régimes based on virtue are naturally unstable given the fact that, unlike qualification or birth, virtue is not objectively measurable or certifiable. In this kind of régime,

---

[26]This and the three following paragraphs owe a great deal to Susan Shirk's remarkable contribution to the July 1980 conference (see above, note 1), "The Decline of Virtuocracy in China," now published in the volume edited by James L. Watson. She made me discover the link between the principle of virtue and the class status system that I am studying here. The distribution criteria she cites correspond to the three types of authority singled out by Max Weber: that of qualification corresponds to rational authority, that of birth to traditional authority, and that of virtue to charismatic authority. Cf. Max Weber, "The Types of Authority and Imperative Co-ordination," in Talcott Parsons (ed.), *The Theory of Social and Economic Organization* (New York: The Free Press, 1964), pp. 324-423.

everyone had better be virtuous, or at least seem virtuous, so that very soon all virtue comes to appear suspicious. Virtue and self-interest being hand in glove, suspicion, hypocrisy, and opportunism settle in. Everyone is in danger of being justifiably or unjustifiably accused of hypocrisy or opportunism. A defence is sought in refusing to take risks or in refusing to expose oneself to any criticism whatsoever, in other words, in conformism. This is all the more true since the surest way of displaying revolutionary virtue is to denounce the lack of revolutionary virtue in others. In short, a pathology of virtue develops which can take extreme forms, catastrophic for the society.[27] In order to protect itself, society quite naturally tends to make the régime of virtue evolve into a régime based on qualification or birth. In China, this tendency was obvious and permanent. We have already discussed the forms it took. Intellectuals, technicians, certain administrators tried to get professional competence recognized as a selection criterion at least equal to that of virtue. On the other hand, cadres and other categories, the military for example, always leaned in favour of the birth criterion.

The régime opted for the primacy of virtue. This choice emerged quite naturally and for several reasons. It allowed attitudes that were considered favourable to the development of a new society to be encouraged and an egalitarian spirit, devotion to the common good, activism and "political consciousness" to be rewarded. In a backward country that had to mobilize all its labour reserves but did not have the means to pay, materially, for the effort invested, appealing to each person's virtue was a practical necessity. Finally, virtue was a potent instrument for consolidating the new authority. Indeed, it allowed the Party to promote its partisans and downgrade its opponents, or simply its likely opponents. From now on political support for the regime was the necessary condition of all upward social mobility. This allowed the Party to control tightly the social groups that might have claimed the right to participate in government by virtue of their birth or qualifications, namely the merchants, industrialists, technicians, and intellectuals. For example, it could effectively reduce the hold of these groups over higher education, in favour of workers' or peasants' children who presumably had a higher level of "political consciousness." But above all, the principle of virtue justified the power of the Party itself, for what was the Party, if not

[27] The analysis of this pathology of virtue is one of the most interesting contributions of Shirk's study. This took on the most extreme and vicious forms during the Cultural Revolution. Shirk sees the Cultural Revolution as an attempt on the part of Mao Zedong to remedy the ills of a régime founded on virtue by restoring virtue; having increased the ill he wanted to heal to the point of absurdity, he provoked, in due course, the definitive rejection of "virtuocracy" and the conversion of the Chinese régime to the principle of meritocracy.

the association of all those who had made personal sacrifices in order that the revolution might take place, who had devoted themselves body and soul to the cause of socialism? Their past commitment testified to their revolutionary virtue and legitimized their present position. From a sociological point of view, it could be said that virtue was the fulcrum of Maoism. And the relinquishing of virtue in favour of the guiding principle of qualification signified the end of Maoism.

Thus, from 1949 to 1976, social mobility, which had been one of the most striking features of Chinese society during the first half of the century, was reduced and, above all, channelled. While it had previously taken the most varied, and sometimes the most unexpected courses, it was now firmly placed under Party control. In this solidifying of the social organism, class status played an essential role. It is not surprising that all the demands relating to social mobility henceforth took the shape of discussions on the proper interpretation of status.

To this function of *distribution*, three other more abstract but no less important functions of the class status system can be added: concealment, exclusion, and repression.

VIII. THE CONCEALMENT FUNCTION

The concealment function started to manifest itself fully in 1957. Having carried out a radical transformation of all social relationships in the early fifties, the Party had had to face a new type of conflict, produced by these very transformations. It had had to deal with a part of the peasantry which refused to deliver or sell to the state all of the grain it had requested. Because of this, it had been obliged to undertake collectivization very rapidly, a measure which was badly received. On the other hand, the measures the Party had taken to guarantee its control over the working class, and the increase in productive effort which it had required without adequate compensation, had also provoked resistance. Its stranglehold on the educational system and on intellectual and artistic life was considered too severe by segments of the student youth and the intellectuals, even those who were Communist. The monopoly it claimed in the areas of politics and information was deemed excessive, indeed dangerous, by a growing fraction of public opinion. These different conflicts combined to create the régime's first big crisis, in 1956-57.

In January 1956, Mao Zedong had called for a more understanding and conciliatory attitude toward the intellectuals, and a greater effort to integrate them into the new society.[28] The editorial "On the Historical Experience of

---

[28]*Mao Zedong sixiang wansui* 毛澤東思想萬歲 (n.p., 1969), pp. 28-34.

the Dictatorship of the Proletariat," published in April 1956, which constituted the Chinese response to Khrushchev's secret speech regarding Stalin, stressed the continuing existence of contradictions under socialism, and in May 1956 Mao launched the slogan "Let a Hundred Flowers Bloom."

Nevertheless, by this time, a substantial segment of Chinese society had condemned the Party's policy with sufficient clarity so that the Party felt its freedom of action threatened. The Polish October and the events in Hungary made the Party more sensitive to the dangers it could face. At first it compromised. In February 1957, Mao Zedong admitted the continuing existence of "contradictions among the people," stating that these could be solved peacefully as long as the Party and the other social protagonists acted with discernment. But, he said, these contradictions could also turn into "antagonistic contradictions," in other words, into a confrontation between the people and its enemies.

This is where class, and hence status, came into play again, for who were the enemies, if not, by definition, Guomindang reactionaries, bourgeois, or landlords? In the summer of 1957, when the Party concluded that the protest movement was taking a turn that was no longer tolerable, an unprecedented wave of repression fell on those who had participated in the movement. The first to be condemned were the officials of bourgeois democratic parties, but all those condemned in their wake were characterized, like them, as "right-wing deviationists." Their guilt was said to consist in adopting the positions of the bourgeoisie. A new type of conflict, engendered by the new régime, was thus presented as a classic conflict between the revolutionary forces and the reactionary forces of the old régime. Its real nature was concealed.[29]

In 1962, when Mao Zedong reaffirmed that the antagonisms between the bourgeoisie and the proletariat, between the landlords and the poor and lower middle peasants still constituted the main contradiction, he was resorting to the same method. He was concealing the real problems, that is the discontent of the intellectuals and the disaffection of the peasantry, badly hit by the consequences of the Great Leap Forward, toward the new régime. In the autumn of 1966, once again, when the Red Guards were launching an assault on the positions held by "those within the Party who had taken the capitalist road"—in other words the positions of the higher Party cadres who were opposed to Mao Zedong's policy—these cadres deflected the

[29] "La lutte des classes en Chine bureaucratique," a long article by Pierre Brune in *Socialisme ou barbarie*, Vol. IV, No. 24 (May-June 1958), pp. 35-103, remains, in spite of much new information, the best analysis of this crisis published in French; see also P. Brune's sequel in the same journal (Vol. V, No. 29, December 1959-January 1960, pp. 58-90), and Jean-Luc Domenach, "Une crise sociale en Chine populaire," *Annales*, Vol. 34, No. 5 (Sept.-Oct. 1979), pp. 1069-93.

attack against themselves by identifying for the rebels "classic" victims, former bourgeois and landlords who were then beaten and despoiled. But at the same time some rebel organizations argued that the existing proletarian dictatorship had become a bourgeois organ and must be overthrown. In 1968, after two years of confusion, Mao Zedong took sides openly, under pressure from the army. Once again, he stood up for conventional notions. Later, at the end of his rule, his ultra-leftist allies put forward the argument that the bourgeoisie was to be found in large part within the Communist Party, thus placing the emphasis once again on "new bourgeois elements" rather than on the survivors of the old reactionary classes. Yet they too remained cautiously ambiguous.[30]

After Mao Zedong's death, and the fall of the "gang of four," the Party did not relinquish the continuing usefulness of the most hackneyed language. The Party's struggle against the clique was described as a life and death struggle between the proletariat and the bourgeoisie. Wang Hongwen 王洪文 was now a representative of the "new-born bourgeoisie" (*xinsheng zichanjieji* 新生資産階級) and Yao Wenyuan 姚文元 an offspring of a reactionary big landlord and capitalist family.[31] This kind of language seems absurd, mad, divorced from the facts. But one must not forget that for thirty years, the reality of such categories, which could have been challenged from the historical or sociological standpoint, was artificially maintained through the institution of class status. Landlords, bourgeois, counter-revolutionaries had to exist, since whole categories of Chinese were defined as such in their papers and known as such by the authorities and their entourage. Therefore this language upholds a connection not with the facts, but with the logic of an institution still very real which veils (though progressively less and less) existing social relationships.

IX. THE EXCLUSION FUNCTION

Mao Zedong's leading question, "Who are our enemies, who are our friends?" not only inspired all the class analyses made by the Party before and after taking power. It also defines the essential spirit of the class status system, and for thirty years continued to haunt Chinese society. This society included not only categories that were simply hostile to the régime—this would have been a real fact—but rather those *declared* to be enemies, considered as such

[30] See specially Yao Wenyuan's article "On the Social Basis of the Lin Piao Anti-Party Clique," *Hongqi*, No. 3, 1975, translated in *Peking Review*, No. 10, 7 March 1975.
[31] Speech by Wu Teh 吳德, in *Peking Review*, No. 44, 29 October 1976, and *Peking Review*, No. 1, 1 January 1977; see *China Quarterly*, No. 69 (March 1977), pp. 195-203.

a priori and treated accordingly by the government. They were "objects of the dictatorship of the proletariat," deprived of their civil rights and, in some cases, of their freedom, constantly under suspicion and almost permanently subjected to ideological reeducation. These categories included the "landlords" first of all and, to a lesser degree, the "rich peasants" and "bourgeois." Next and foremost were the "counter revolutionaries," the "bad elements," and the "rightists." Taken together, these categories constituted "the class enemy" (*jiejidiren* 階級敵人). All the others constituted "the people" (*renmin* 人民) or "the popular masses" (*renmin qunzhong* 人民羣衆). The importance of this dichotomy is well known, as is the absolutely fundamental role it has played in the life of the new régime, both in the sphere of the most abstract and general representations and in that of the most everyday practice, in the most prosaic social relations and in the psychology of the individual.

Though in some cases "enemy" status was hereditary and acquired simply through birth, in other cases it was determined by the Party and imposed with or without legal justification. Whoever showed opposition to the régime or brought attention to himself by behaving in a way that suggested such opposition could be declared a "counter-revolutionary." He was then the object of a purely political condemnation, a kind of political, and hence social excommunication. Any individual who committed a common law offence and who could rightly or wrongly be accused of deliberate anti-social behaviour, could find himself classified in the "bad element" category. As for the rightists, they were guilty, as already noted, of having adopted "bourgeois" positions—that is, enemy positions—no matter what their original status. These three status categories could be attributed to anyone, especially the first, which was based on both the most serious and the vaguest accusation. The counter-revolutionaries were sent to camps from which they never returned, even those with limited sentences.[32] Their fate was a warning to all. Even if the camps were a taboo subject, their existence was always sufficiently well known to have a powerful dissuasive effect on any citizen who might have been tempted to come into conflict with the Party. The cloak of mystery made the threat even more diffuse. It conveyed the feeling that there was no defence. On the other hand, the idea that counter-revolutionaries were present in the body of society was carefully fostered in literary works (including children's literature), comic strips, films, and other forms of propaganda.[33]

No Chinese could ignore the fact that, unless he was very cautious, any

[32]This fact was revealed by Jean Pasqualini among others, in *Prisoner of Mao* (New York: Paul R. Reynolds, 1973).

[33]On this subject, see Jean-Pierre Diény, *Le monde est à vous: La Chine et les livres pour enfants* (Paris: Gallimard, 1971).

difficulty he encountered in his relations with the Party could escalate to the point where he could run the danger of being condemned as a counter-revolutionary. Even if he was only dimly conscious of this possibility, it gave rise to an obsessive fear, all-pervasive, though variable in degree, and fostered a compensatory need for security. This need could only be satisfied by identifying as much as possible with the positive camp, the "popular masses" or "revolutionary masses." Naturally, for this security to be assured, one's affiliation with the positive camp had to be recognized by the Party. The individual could only obtain this Party recognition if he recognized the authority of the Party. Thus the Party had the power of awarding the luxury of a sense of security to those who rallied round it and accepted its supremacy. Of course, security was never absolute, the Party being free to change its mind in changing circumstances.

The importance of this mechanism should not be underestimated. The assurance of belonging to the people's camp provided not only great psychological comfort, but also the advantage of freedom from responsibility. This freedom was quite naturally part of the lot of those who enjoyed an enviable class status, the workers, for example. Since the "good" categories were in the majority, it was the lot of a large segment of society. This is, no doubt, one of the reasons the status system remained alive: it gave the majority of the population the right to abdicate political responsibility, coupled with the right to a good conscience and psychological security.

For the cadres, the system presented a similar advantage. When they had to decide if they should give someone a position or a mission, or if they should demote or condemn him in some way, they could judge him according to his status. They could consider a person worthy of trust *a priori* because his status was good, or suspicious *a priori* because it was bad. This way they knew that whatever happened, they would be covered. The following anecdote, told by a young Chinese refugee in Hong Kong, is typical:

> I think that basically the relations that the cadres have with the educated young people are determined by their political interests. In our village, there was an educated young woman who knew Mao's works better than anyone. The cadres had a lot of esteem for her. One day, activists had to be chosen for the study of Mao's works. Everyone expected her name to be mentioned. Not at all. She had doubtful social origins and the cadres prefered to abstain.[34]

Another anecdote shows the reverse mechanism. The cadres, who consider it dangerous to trust someone whose origins are doubtful, make those whose origin is "good" benefit from what could be called "class immunity." Another young refugee tells the following story:

[34] *Avoir vingt ans en Chine*, p. 124.

I knew a cadre who got off lightly. Twice he tried to rape a young educated woman of the village. The first time, the girl put up a struggle and finally he gave up. She had not wanted to lodge a complaint, but had told several of her girl-friends what had just happened to her. One day, the same cadre came back and tried to rape her again. The girl called her friends and they threw themselves on him and beat him black and blue. . . .

I don't know what he went and told the local leaders, but whatever it was, they demanded that the young educated women acknowledge their mistake: had they not beaten a cadre? Then there was an investigation: all the young educated girls implicated in this affair came from worker families, their social origins were irreproachable. The same was true of the cadre. Finally, things were ironed out.

But maybe if one of these girls had had a bad social origin, the issue of *class vengeance* would have been raised and the affair would have had untold repercussions.[35]

These two examples, which could be multiplied at will, well illustrate the status system's advantages for the cadres: it exempts them from taking upon themselves the responsibility of a judgement on people or facts. In other words, it relieves them of an important part of their moral responsibility. These anecdotes also illustrate the dreadful inequality that the system creates between the beneficiaries of a positive status, who are practically assured of being socially and politically integrated, and the others, on whom the threat of being excluded weighs permanently, though in varying degrees.

It would seem that the régime could not maintain itself without excluding. It used exclusion in order to eliminate certain conflicts. It used the threat of exclusion in order to obtain allegiance and create a consensus in its favour. Since contemporary Chinese society had previously been exceptionally mobile, and moreover since the new régime, by its very nature, engendered serious tensions, it had to maintain this consensus and restore it when it was in danger of losing it. To do this, it had to make the threat real and demonstrate its reality by other than mere propaganda means. In official language this was called "reactivating the class struggle" (*zhua jieji douzheng* 抓階級鬥爭), "mobilizing the masses" (*fadong qunzhong* 發動羣衆) to launch a "revolutionary campaign" (*geming yundong* 革命運動). For thirty years these campaigns followed one another almost uninterruptedly, separated by lulls lasting at most a few months. Each one of these big mobilizations had a specific objective, or sometimes even several simultaneously: economic, ecological, sanitary, educational, or civic. Usually they were primarily or exclusively political, aimed at "driving out the class enemy," and thus "purifying the class ranks" (*qingli jieji-duiwu* 清理階級隊伍), at demonstrating through large-scale manoeuvres that the class struggle was the mainspring of history. These purely political mobilizations were the most dreaded

[35] *Ibid.*, p. 109.

of all, for each of the countless organized groups that made up the fabric of Chinese society was expected to carry out its own "class struggle." The Party committee of each of these groups had to itemize the victories it had won in this struggle. If the Committee was unable to claim a positive result, it was in a vulnerable position. This is when status was inestimably valuable to it. The "class enemies" had already been designated in advance. The village "landlord" would serve as a scapegoat. Accused of some anti-socialist remark or activity, he would be exposed to popular condemnation and subjected to new humiliations. In the cities, things were carried out in the same way. Among intellectuals treatment was sometimes milder. The people who had been condemned as rightists in 1957 would take the initiative, make some fitting confession and thereby do their colleagues and the Party committee a favour; in exchange, they would be spared ill treatment. These were the routine solutions.

In other cases, people would openly or secretly denounce one another. It could also happen, however, that no "object of struggle" (*douzheng duixiang* 鬪爭對象) would appear and that the cadres would be obliged to manufacture one in order to fulfil the task the Party had assigned to them and defend their position. In order to do this, they developed procedures which they perfected over the years until they formed a very smooth technique. First they created an atmosphere of "class struggle." Then, in meetings which they organized, they would force each member of the group to express himself, criticize himself and criticize others, by clearly dissociating himself ("drawing the line," *huaqing jiexian* 劃清界限) from others who might be suspect.[36] By using various forms of pressure, the cadres would make the members of the group select an enemy out of self-protection, fabricate a trial and under the cadres' control, condemn him. In theory, the cadres were only recording the verdict delivered by the "revolutionary masses." This they would do with a concern for form and a documentary meticulousness whcih were meant to obliterate completely the original arbitrariness of the procedure. They themselves would appear in a favourable light: they would unload on to the group the ungrateful task for which they were responsible, transforming an innocent man into a "counter-revolutionary" and ruining his life and that of his relatives.[37]

[36] It is this guilt by association, always possible, that makes class status "contagious." It was not unusual for divorce to be the only convincing way of dissociating oneself.

[37] The journal *Huanghe* 黃河 published a detailed account of one of these trials, in which the victim was a young peasant named Deng Qingshan 鄧青山. The testimony, which at first might strike many Western readers as an Orwellian invention, should, precisely because it is so extreme, be regarded as a precious document of political anthropology. See "Fangeming-an yili" 反革命案一例 ("An example of a counter-revolutionary affair"), in *Huanghe* (Hong Kong), No. 1 (May 1976). A French translation of this document, which is signed Mu Zhong, appeared in *Esprit* (July-August 1977), pp. 66-78.

In every campaign of political mobilization, large or small, which took place in the People's Republic of China until the very recent past, this mechanism was at work. It was the underlying impetus in a variety of circumstances and occasions. It is useless to point out the degrading effects it had on the cadres and on normal citizens who were all obliged to become accomplices to falsehood. It is useless to mention that it destroyed group cohesion and made the social fabric disintegrate in those places where the fabric had kept, or regained, some vigour. Clearly, no positive unity, no real kind of harmony could arise from a mobilization that derived from the fear of being excluded. The mechanism established a vicious circle. However, gradually, a consensus developed within Chinese society: the increasingly conscious and common rejection of this very mechanism.

Public opinion began to consider that a large proportion of the cadres, particularly the grass-roots political cadres, and even more specifically those who had joined the Party between 1966 and 1976, were incapable of doing anything but engaging in the destructive activity of "political struggle." It was commonly said that "they make their living by intimidating others" (*kao zhengren chifan* 靠整人吃飯).[38] Recognizing the irreversibility of this rejection, the present leaders set themselves the task of converting these purely "political" cadres into a body of managers capable of ensuring China's modernization. They must succeed at this if they wish to create the conditions for a true modernization, conditions that would allow China to take better advantage of her human and physical resources and give herself structures open to change.

X. THE REPRESENTATION FUNCTION

The last of the important functions of the class status system, the function of representation, is the hardest to understand. The functions that we have examined so far—distribution, concealment, and exclusion—all manifested themselves in a direct and concrete way in political life, social relationships, and the fate of individuals. Their effects were observable; one merely had to

[38]The verb *zheng* 整 rarely appears in political documents, but plays a very great role in real political life. Its primary meaning is "to put in order." In the official language of the Party, it has taken on the sense of "rectify" (the line, work style, etc.), as in the "rectification campaign" of 1942-43. In everyday life, it has a much more concrete sense. A person is "rectified," or it is said that so-and-so "got himself rectified" (*ai zheng* 挨整). The implication is that he was given a warning or a reprimand *of a political character*. To translate, as I have done, *zhengren* 整人, "rectifying people," as "intimidation" is a rendering which, although somewhat free, I regard as accurate in terms of the sociological reality it expresses.

abstract the principle from the effects. The representation function, on the other hand, has always remained implicit, at least for the majority of the social protagonists. With few exceptions, it never entered clearly into their calculations and strategy. It was never made into an issue except in a partial and round-about way. We shall see that this is part and parcel of its very nature and that its importance lies precisely in the fact that its principle remained hidden.

In his study *Esquisse d'une genèse de l'idéologie*, Claude Lefort noted: "In all pre-capitalist formations, it is the mode of production which is conservative. In capitalism, it is the ideology that is conservative and has the task of covering up the revolution which inhabits the mode of production."[39] Lefort sees bourgeois ideology as an attempt at denying the permanent revolution in which the social body is caught, at denying what Marx called "the continual upheaval of production, the uninterrupted perturbation of all the social categories," by imposing on thought a set of immutable notions. The transformations inflicted on society were so swift and brutal that the old symbolic systems were collapsing and the nature of the social reality, which is essentially indefinite, unstable, open, *historical*, was in danger of manifesting itself too directly. The new notions (Humanity, History, Progress, Science, Society, State, Order, Property, Individual, Family, Fatherland, etc.) allowed the new reality to be accounted for while they also enclosed it in a system of reassuring certainties. But while the old symbolic systems were concrete and in keeping with the real-life experience of social relationships, the notions which made up bourgeois ideology were abstract. For Lefort, this divorce between representations and experience—between immutable and abstract representations and the experience of a social reality subjected to permanent mutations—is a characteristic trait of ideology, which he considers as a specifically modern phenomenon.

From this broad viewpoint, it is clear that, in China, we are dealing with the same modern phenomenon of ideology, but in a different form. Sudden and violent transformations made the traditional symbolic systems obsolete and made any finite and stable vision of social reality lack credibility. It is true that in contrast to bourgeois ideology, revolutionary ideology justifies the permanent transformation of society and even demands it. But it resembles bourgeois ideology by the fixity and abstract nature of its representations. It is also based on immutable, hence reassuring, creatures of reason: the social classes. These classes are supposed to constitute the most trustworthy aspect

[39]"Esquisse d'une genèse de l'idéologie dans les sociétés modernes," in Claude Lefort, *Les formes de l'histoire: Essais d'anthropologie politique* (Paris: Gallimard, 1978), p. 296.

of reality, on which reasoning can with certainty rely, on which political thinking can unquestionably base itself. The power of the Party is justified by the scientific knowledge it has of social reality. Now, class is the most fundamental element of the Party's knowledge. This knowledge could be said to be based entirely on the axiomatic assertion that *there are* classes, allied or opposed to one another, that these well-known classes are the peasants, the workers, the bourgeoisie, the landlords, etc. This assertion is the rock on which the whole revolutionary ideology is built. These classes, invoked continually and represented everywhere, have a striking fixity. They are not subject to the laws of time or to the vicissitudes of real history. They are not affected by the social transformations which have been taking place for thirty years. They form a timeless representation of social reality, as the Party wishes this reality to be perceived. Other abstract categories are just as important (the Party and the masses, the reactionaries and the people) and play just as decisive a role in the political language; but these are only conceivable in reference to class, and unlike class, they cannot be directly represented. "A mass," as they say in Chinese (*yige qunzhong* 一個羣衆), in other words a person belonging to the popular masses as opposed to the Party, is necessarily represented by the concrete features of a peasant, a worker, an employee, or a revolutionary intellectual. A reactionary must necessarily take on the traits of a bourgeois, a landlord, or one of their acolytes. Class constitutes both the bedrock of reality and reality as it is truly incarnated.

We are dealing with a remarkable type of philosophical realism. Classes are considered *a priori* as substances. They are creatures endowed by thought with the highest degree of reality and permanence. Individuals do not enjoy the same dignity, and attain a completely meaningful existence only by belonging to a class. This conception runs completely counter to view of modern individualist ideology, according to which the individual is a basic datum and enjoys the highest reality coefficient. To us, class and society are derived realities resulting from the more or less voluntary association of individuals; to use the philosophical terminology of the Middle Ages, they do not seem like realities to us, but ideas, or "names." While revolutionary ideology is realist, ours is nominalist. But beyond their opposition, these two conceptions have in common their ideological, i.e. simplifying, character. Since both have the function of providing a reassuring vision by reducing the complexity, ambiguity, and instability of the social realm to a few simple and consistent ideas, their connection with empirical reality is necessarily uneasy. The complexity of reality is likely to contaminate them at any time. Ideologists must defend their views against this kind of danger. In China in 1962-65, they did so by fighting the "middle characters" (*zhongjian renwu* 中間人物) in literature, protagonists whose attitudes and feelings were not restricted to those of their class, were not elementary and transparent, revolutionary or counter-revolutionary. They also did so during the same period and for the duration of the entire Cultural Revolution by condemning absolutely the notion of "human nature" (renxing 人性). The idea that people belonging to enemy classes might have something basic in common was fiercely rejected and only "class feelings" (jieji ganqing 階級感情), inevitably either revolutionary or counter-revolutionary, were accepted. Nothing human was to escape a reality conceived in terms of classes. In defending this vision, the ideologists were accomplishing a task that was essential to maintaining the system of class status.

Because we are accustomed to reasoning within the framework of our individualist ideology, we might be tempted to reject class ideology *a priori* as arbitrary and monstrous. We would in any case be inclined to consider it as artificial, to see it as a particularly schematic form of propaganda and imagine it as having been imposed on a society against its will. We would certainly not be entirely wrong. We saw how the Party imposed its language and conceptions in the countryside during the agrarian reform. But we would be failing to understand that at a certain point, class ideology became the natural expression of a vast coalition of interests. The power of the ideology was such that even those to whom it was fundamentally detrimental often accepted it, at least until the period of the Cultural Revolution.

We should not underestimate the importance of one factor, the need to understand. At a time of great upheaval, when the traditional system of references has collapsed, when individuals no longer know how to interpret their own fate, when they feel at the mercy of blind forces, the need to find a system of clear certainties, shared by all, can be profound. Class ideology corresponded perfectly to this need. It offered a vision of society that was both comprehensive and concrete. Intelligible interrelationships were established between the great themes of the nation's history, the revolutionary struggle, political life, and individual or community existence. The appeal of this vision was proportionate to the uncertainty that had taken hold of people during the preceding four decades of unprecedented cultural crisis.

Under the *ancien régime*, the family had been the matrix of all social relationships. A child's apprenticeship of social life within the family made him competent in all life's circumstances, before a school master, a manager, a civil servant, or the emperor himself (as well as conversely, before students, employees, citizens, or subjects). All areas of social life were organized according to the family scheme. Family structure was very closely connected to deep-seated and very ancient religious, philosophical and cosmological conceptions.[40] Because of all this, the Chinese naturally tended to consider

---

[40] For an attempt at a concise overview of these conceptions, see Jean-François

the system of relationships which they maintained among themselves, within the family and without, as the product of a superior civilization, of universal relevance. All relationships were hierarchical and ritualized. The ritualization of all social relationships turned them into a perfectly codified game in which each participant's behaviour was predictable. The art of living reduced friction, held conflicts in check and guaranteed everyone a noteworthy psychological security. The inequity of hierarchy was compensated for in various ways, in particular by the respect shown to age, which everyone could hope to enjoy at the close of his life.

These remarkably coherent conceptions were demolished as the market economy, with or without foreign dependence, gave rise to forms of power unconnected to tradition (racketeers, financiers, speculators, impotent and irresponsible civil servants), as free from the notion of the common good as from traditional reciprocal relationships, and started to dislocate the fabric of ancient relationships and impose impersonal, purely economic abstract relationships which were no longer integrated into an overall view of man and the world. Traditional holism was condemned before an individualistic ideology had been able to develop.

In France and England, where the advent of the market society had sprung from an internal evolution, the individualist conception which was its necessary expression had been able to develop, evolve, progressively assert itself and fit into the customs and behaviour. In other European countries, and later outside Europe, the market society imposed itself in a more brutal way, without giving representations and mentalities the time to adapt. In every instance, it provoked phenomena of rejection. The first great anti-individualistic reaction occurred in Germany during the romantic period.[41] An analogous reaction left a profound mark on the history of Russia in the nineteenth century.[42] In each case there followed a crisis in traditional social relationships, and a weakening of the old regulatory mechanisms. In reaction, authoritarian, and in some cases totalitarian régimes appeared which had in common the function of substituting the external authority of the state for the failing regulatory mechanisms. This substitution took different forms in Russia, Germany, Italy, Spain, Japan, and elsewhere. In some of these countries, the ruling power claimed to be upholding the threatened traditional

---

Billeter, "La civilisation chinoise," in *Histoire des moeurs* (Encyclopédie de la Pléiade, Paris: Gallimard, forthcoming).

[41] This is the subject of recent research, as yet unpublished, by Louis Dumont, who has given a preliminary sketch of his ideas in "L'Allemagne répond à la France: Le peuple et la nation chez Herder et Fichte," *Libre* (Paris), No. 6 (1979), pp. 233-50.

[42] See Alain Besançon, "La Russie et l'esprit du capitalisme," in *Présent soviétique et passé russe* (Paris: Le livre de poche, 1980), pp. 51-81.

order. In the USSR, it set about solving the crisis by instituting a new, revolutionary order. It is not really surprising that the totalitarian phenomenon made its appearance in countries where the ruling power claimed to restore old conceptions, as well as in countries where it meant to wipe the slate clean of the past, such as in Germany and the USSR. Seen in its broadest sense, the problem was the same and the solutions corresponded to very similar requirements.

China experienced both tendencies. During the thirties, the Nanjing régime tried to create a Chinese fascism. It was diverted from doing so only when it finally found itself caught in the anti-fascist camp during the Second World War. From 1949, the Communist Party was prepared to solve the problems of a society in crisis by applying the Soviet model and creating a revolutionary regime. It sought to wipe the slate clean of all the traditional social institutions that were still operating, and institute a new, unique, regulatory system, completely subordinated to the political power. To achieve these ends, it *redefined the social reality* entirely and, through the status system, subjected each individual to this new reality.

The importance of what we have called the "representation function" is now apparent. In order to have civil society submit to its policy, the Party had to make it accept a certain representation of itself, in which class and class status played an essential role. This was accepted because, as we have seen, it corresponded to numerous interests, but also because it was simple, seemed true, and created an intelligible order. Its innate heteronomy could not be perceived, at least in the beginning. And yet, heteronomy was its essential characteristic. This representation could never have been so perfectly unitary and all-inclusive if it had not come from a source exterior to the society that was represented. But because it came from such an exterior source, the Party, and society had no hold on it, it constituted a remarkable instrument of domination.

XI. THE NEW RÉGIME AND THE CHINESE PAST

In 1949, the need for a ruling power capable of defending China's independence, assuring its unity and maintaining civil peace was felt by all. The need to create a new consensus, a new public spirit, new social relationships and new institutions was also felt, and required measures which only a determined ruling power could take. The Communist Party, which presented the accomplishment of these tasks as the first stage of an even more ambitious revolutionary programme, benefited from large reserves of public trust. It was able to act with speed and achieve much in just a few years. It set up a strong

161

ruling power and extended its control everywhere. It succeeded so well that, in the process, it prevented society from adapting itself, on its own, to the complex requirements of modern society, or rather from pursuing the process of adaptation that had already begun. The Party trapped society, and itself along with it, in a vicious circle that determined the whole history of the last thirty years. The external regulation of social activity by an *authoritarian* power was justified on a temporary basis, as long as failing internal mechanisms had to be compensated for and new ones had to be gradually promoted. But its power became *totalitarian* in the sense that it tried relentlessly to control everything, virtually abolished the autonomy of civil society, and paralysed it. Having paralysed it, it had to expend absurd efforts to "mobilize" it, while at the same time fearing the mobilization might become real and go beyond its control. For all Chinese, order had seemed like the prerequisite to the march toward a better future, but the Party now created an order which was essentially constricting and static.

One of the many questions that arise as a result of this transformation is whether to view the establishment of such an order as the inevitable result of a revolution directed by a Leninist one-party state; or whether it should be seen as a return to older forms of social organization, the two causes possibly working in conjunction up to a point. For an adequate answer to this complex question, we would have to proceed comparatively, by examining the new Chinese régime and the Soviet régime and determining, beyond their deep kinship, a certain number of features that distinguish one from the other. These distinctive features would then have to be related to the histories of the two societies.[43] Here I shall limit myself to a few brief remarks.

First, during China's entire history, from the beginning of the Zhou dynasty to the beginning of the present century, that is for nearly three thousand years, the Chinese ruling classes were always organized according to a meticulously determined hierarchical order. During the first centuries of the Zhou dynasty, it was feudal and religious; it expressed itself in the ancestor worship of the seigniorial families. When the centralized State, inspired by the Legalists, appeared in the fifth and particularly the fourth centuries B.C., the hierarchical principle was applied to the organization of the State machinery.

---

[43] To the best of my knowledge, the two principal studies in comparative history at present are Barrington Moore, *Social Origins of Dictatorship and Democracy* (Boston: Beacon Press, 1966), and Theda Skocpol, *States and Social Revolutions: A Comparative Analysis of France, Russia and China* (Cambridge: Cambridge University Press, 1980). The first deals only in passing with the Soviet Union, and examines only the pre-history of the new régime in China. The second is undoubtedly of some interest, but in my opinion does not underscore clearly enough the points which distinguish both the Soviet and the Chinese régime from that which grew out of the French Revolution.

A person's position no longer depended on birth, but on the decision of the sovereign. Later, during the imperial era, the sovereign retained the power to determine positions within the hierarchy.

Under the Song, and later the Ming and Qing dynasties, he ruled the mandarinate, one of the largest and most elaborate hierarchically organized status systems the world has ever known. It could be said that, during three thousand years, nearly all Chinese political thought gravitated around this hierarchical model, which it strained to justify, adjust, or criticize. Chinese political thought never detached itself from the monarchical idea which was that model's necessary complement.[44]

Secondly, in the course of history, the ruling classes gradually organized all of society hierarchically. Under the Zhou, only the nobility was subjected to a hierarchical order. The Legalists responded to the dissolution of the traditional aristocratic order by a recruitment that contributed to making a state-controlled hierarchical order penetrate civil society. The idea of society as a whole being structured by a single hierarchical order was retained later under the empire. The division of society into "scholars," "peasants," "craftsmen," and "merchants"—always referred to in that order of decreasing dignity—was established under the Han and later remained one of the foundations of imperial ideology. Legal thought developed and imparted its hierarchical notions to the social body with ever greater depth, by way of criminal, as well as sumptuary laws. This legal thought reached its first apogee under the Tang. Later the Mongols divided the population of the empire into four classes, unequal before the law; professions became hereditary. They remained so at the beginning of the Ming dynasty, an age when peasant, soldier, and craftsman families were subjected to different administrations. While these institutions did not long survive the founder of the dynasty, it is nonetheless true that under the Ming and Qing, control of the population progressed steadily and, concomitantly, neo-Confucian ideology entered more and more into the mentality of the entire population. Hierarchical conceptions eventually penetrated all the pores of Chinese society.

It is clear which traditional features re-emerged in the People's Republic status system: first and foremost, the idea of a society fashioned entirely on a hierarchy of status. But this old conception could not openly assert itself, for it was incompatible with that other fundamental representation which is the class struggle, a representation which opposes the "people" and its enemies horizontally, so to speak. Also, it could not really assert itself because the Party's privileged position would no doubt have been in danger of being too

---

[44] On the origins of these conceptions and the way in which they influenced Chinese society in the past, see Billeter, *op. cit.*

clearly revealed. Finally, it was counterbalanced by the modern representation of a social body governed by the purely rational division of work among equal citizens. These are the contradictions, the ambiguities that can be observed on the level of representations.

On the other hand, in everyday behaviour, particularly that of the bureaucracy, hierarchical formalism asserted itself in the most patent manner.[45] Another traditional feature lies in the Party's power to modify the status of individuals and groups, in its way of using the status system as a means of government and as an instrument for regulating social mobility. But on this point also, the differences with the past are noteworthy. The mandarinate, founded on the institution of State examinations, constituted for a long time such a regulatory instrument, but it was more open than the class status system, at least in principle; exceptions aside, no one could be prevented from standing as a candidate for the examinations because of his social origin. The hereditary nature of class status must be seen as the resurgence of a third traditional feature. This feature does not originate in the system of the mandarinate, which normally did not recognize hereditary status, but in the primordial part played by the family and in the deeply-rooted idea that an individual's life was primarily a link in the chain that connected him to his ancestors and descendants and that his destiny was inseparable from the destiny of the whole chain.

These limited observations give an idea of the complexity of the problems raised by these kinds of comparisons between the new régime and the old; they also suggest how subversive such comparisons could be to the new régime, which claimed to be completely severed from the past. These kinds of comparisons were taboo for nearly thirty years. It is only after Mao Zedong's death, when the Party leadership belatedly took note of the deep crisis affecting the régime, that they could be mentioned: if, all things considered, the régime and Chinese society as a whole had made so little progress in modernizing—this was the new question—was it not because they were perhaps still profoundly affected by "feudal remnants"? Since 1978, a great deal has been written on this question and sometimes, in the press and among intellectuals, it has given rise to very instructive debates.

At the end of his life Mao Zedong himself inspired another comparison between the past and the present during the anti-Confucius campaign of

---

[45] Everyday speech is rich in expressions which reveal a hierarchical conception of social relationships. This is the case, in particular, with compound verbs such as *gaoshang-qu* 告上去 , literally, "go up and report," i.e., to report something to higher levels, or *xiadao qunzhong zhong qu* 下到羣衆中去 , literally, "go down among the masses," in other words, join with the masses, or become one with the masses. It would be worthwhile to devote a small socio-linguistic study to expressions such as these.

1973-74. At that time, the régime openly claimed to draw its inspiration from a great historical precedent, that of the centralized state as conceived by the Legalists of antiquity, as developed in the Qin kingdom starting from the fourth century B.C. and as applied to the entire empire from 221 B.C. on. During this campaign, the Legalists and Qin Shihuang were extolled as great revolutionaries and contrasted with the Confucianists, representatives of reaction. Now, if it can indeed be said that the Legalist statesmen and the first emperor were revolutionaries, it should be stressed that they were revolutionaries in a very special sense. According to Jean Levi's thesis,[46] which I find very convincing, the goal of the Legalists' action was to solve a major crisis in Chinese society, a situation of growing anarchy, by using an all-powerful State to create a social order of which the functioning would be perfectly controllable and predictable. No social mobility would be allowed, except as authorized by the State. Each citizen would have his status, to which above all he would have to be faithfully committed, but which could be modified by the State, should the case arise, either to reward merit or to penalize bad conduct. This system of reward and punishment was meant to create, in all subjects, behaviour patterns which, in becoming natural, would guarantee the social order's automatic preservation and reproduction. War would take care of destroying the surplus and hence would also become part of the mechanism for reproducing an order which was supposed to be definitive. Though forcefully rejected by the whole subsequent Confucian tradition, this system, frightening in its rigour and logic, had a lasting influence on Chinese political conceptions and practices. In 1973, when the Chinese leaders set about rehabilitating and praising it, many observers viewed it as a pretext. They were not wrong, for the anti-Confucius movement during which Legalism was so extolled, was above all a huge political manoeuvre. But in identifying themselves with the Legalists of antiquity and identifying Mao Zedong with Qin Shihuang the ideologists of the period were revealing, perhaps in spite of themselves, the profound analogy which existed between the revolutionary order they were themselves defending and the state-controlled order which the Legalists had set up in bygone days. Both orders were just as radical in their break with the past as completely conservative in their desire for enclosure, their refusal to allow civil society to evolve, innovate, or produce the unpredictable, in short their rejection of history. In a certain sense, the eulogy of Legalism was a confession on the part of Maoism; it was also its swan song.

[46]His argument is developed in the introduction to his translation of the *Shangjun shu* 商君書 ; see Shang Yang, *Le livre du Prince Shang*, traduit et présenté par Jean Levi (Paris: Flammarion, 1981), pp. 9-50.

165

XII. CONCLUSION

The status system and class ideology will remain forever linked to the name of Mao Zedong. As his authority declined, they began to decline as well. During the Cultural Revolution, status began to be discredited because of the violence of the conflicts to which the issue gave rise. It became more and more apparent during those crisis years that status was powerless to establish a stable order. About two years after Mao Zedong's death, from 1978 on, status began to dwindle in importance. In some areas it was even openly abandoned. This development is still too recent and too fraught with uncertainty and ambiguity for us to say anything definitive on it. But by way of conclusion, let us nevertheless make a few comments.

One of the constants in Mao Zedong's thought was his preference for virtue as a distributive criterion. As we have seen, distribution according to virtue involves such drawbacks and conflicts that a shift to one of the other criteria is inevitable. The Cultural Revolution attempted to solve the problems which the reign of virtue had given rise to by returning to a purer virtue, an attempt that was bound to be disastrous and exacerbate the evil it was meant to cure. Later, the need for a straightforward conversion to the competence criterion asserted itself strongly. It was under Deng Xiaoping's energetic leadership that this conversion took place. Important interests were thus violated, in particular those of a large number of cadres belonging to the middle and lower levels of the apparatus. These cadres are opposed to the new development; they are slowing it down but have so far been unable to reverse it. Naturally, it also relegates the criterion of birth to second place and therefore makes the status system lose much of its importance. At the beginning of 1979, the Party leadership announced it was proceeding with the rehabilitation of nearly all the "landlords," "rich peasants," "counter-revolutionaries," "bad elements," and "rightists." In other words, it would rehabilitate nearly all the people who had been assigned to these status categories during the first years of the régime, as well as all those who had afterwards inherited such status. No other decision could have shown with greater ostentation the leadership's determination to break with the practices of the Maoist era.[47] But the break was far from complete, since each individual

[47] Some of the citizens concerned, those who had been wrongly classed in one of the categories beyond the pale, were rehabilitated. Others had their "hats removed" (zhai maozi 摘帽子), because the condemnation inflicted on them had attained its goal and they were considered to have been reeducated. A minority, considered as not yet reeducated, retained their negative status. The two main articles announcing these measures appeared in Renmin ribao on 29 January 1979 (p. 4) and 30 January 1979 (p. 2). For a detailed analysis of this political event and fuller references, see China News

case had to be treated according to an unchanged procedure involving several levels in the Party organization, and in a number of cases, status was preserved. It was also made clear that though the class struggle would no longer be unduly broadened, nevertheless it still existed. During the same period, status information ceased being required on official papers, employment application forms, etc. But we must not take this to mean the actual disappearance of the system: people suspect the cadres of preserving all the information needed for possibly restoring earlier practices. However, the new orientation is clear. It signifies an evolution which is most probably irreversible in the long run and will lead to the replacement of the reign of virtue, class ideology and the status system by other regulatory mechanisms.

In the minds of the present leaders, these mechanisms should be distribution according to competence, application of the law, and respect for the "objective laws of economics." Time will tell whether they will succeed in making these mechanisms prevail, since they are incompatible with the prerogatives claimed by the Party and which it considers as guarantees of its power. If the principle of distribution according to competence is to be generalized, it will have to become possible to judge the Party and its members too according to competence, that is, according to their aptitude at governing the country and assuring its development. The application of the law will only become a standard feature of life if the Party openly accepts the principle of equality before the law. Respect for what are today known in China as the "objective laws of the economy," and what we would call "economic rationality," presupposes that the demands of effective administration take precedence, should the occasion arise, over the political interests of the party.

The more the status system loses its distributive function, the less it fulfils its concealment function. Stereotypes are disappearing. The Party no longer evokes the spectre of the old class struggles at the drop of a hat. The leaders, or at least some of them, speak a language that is more and more direct and refers to real present-day problems with greater and greater candidness. For example, citing Chen Yun 陳雲, Hu Yaobang 胡耀邦 declares that "whether the Party in power lives or dies will depend on that Party's spirit": the Party will have to pull itself together, as far as discipline and morality are concerned, if it wants to guarantee its longevity.[48] This warning is directed, clearly enough, at the whole Party, not at "class enemies" within its ranks.

The exclusion function is also losing ground, or rather being transformed.

Analysis (Hong Kong), No. 1152 (13 April 1979). See also "Class Status in the Countryside: Changes over Three Decades," *Beijing Review*, No. 3, 21 January 1979, pp. 14-21.

[48]This weighty phrase is the title of an important speech by Hu Yaobang before the Disciplinary Investigation Committee of the Central Committee. For the full text, see *Renmin ribao*, 11 December 1980.

The blackmail of excommunication is gradually being replaced by more modern means of control and repression, through the police and the legal process. The Party is delegating much of its power in this area to specialized agencies, though it still reserves the right to exclude individuals from society without resorting to the courts.

Above all, the status system no longer provides an overall representation of social reality. Previously, in the official imagery, in the films, the theatre and novels, each character was marked by status and indeed completely defined by it; he therefore always entertained perfectly predictable relationships with the other protagonists. Now, in the imagery, characters are represented in a vague manner, without any avowed social connotations, or simply as members of a profession. In the films, the threatre, novels and short stories, their personal history defines them much more; this history may be determined by status, but it no longer reduces itself to status. For several years, literary works have no longer been illustrating the conventional vision of reality imposed by ideology; they have begun exploring, within certain limits, true life experience. This contributes to the undermining of former certainties and to the revelation that reality is different—complex and not to be enclosed in any simplistic system of representation. Hence literary creation helps destroy the remains of an overall representation which served for thirty years as the basis for any authorized interpretation of social reality and as the régime's main justification. This general development is creating a vacuum which the Party is at a loss to fill. The theme of the four modernizations is inadequate to the task. The homage which the leaders continue to pay to the thought of Mao Zedong seems to aim at conjuring this vacuum, but will not serve to fill it either.

Chinese society is entering a new phase in the gigantic and uninterrupted crisis it has known since its entry into contemporary history. The question which arises today is whether the Party is ready to acknowledge that it must allow individual autonomy, group autonomy and the autonomy of civil society as a whole to assert itself and allow a complex and open society to develop. Though a society of this kind may need a strong state, it can in no way put up with a totalitarian one; therefore, the Party's own power will have to be limited by various forms of counter-power as well as by the law. Can it accept the fact that a complex and open society must continuously elaborate a plurality of self-representations and can no longer be reduced to one, single, overall, permanent representation? Conversely, will the various forces wishing to conquer their autonomy know how to make the Party accept this fact? On these essential questions, and in spite of lessons being widely drawn from a substantially negative assessment of the past thirty years, the situation remains uncertain. It is possible that an evolution of this kind is incompatible with the Party's interests and that the Party will succeed in preventing it, as it did in the Soviet Union. It is also possible that the evolution will be carried out in one way or the other and that, several years from now, the class status system and all its concomitants will appear as a mere historical curiosity, a kind of corset imposed on Chinese society during a transitional period.

6. Recent Developments in the Relations between State and Party Norms in the People's Republic of China

Harro von Senger

Time and again the state and the Party are mentioned in the same breath in the contemporary literature of the People's Republic of China (P.R.C.), and as a rule the Party is placed first, in such phrases as "Party and state" (*dang he guojia* 黨和國家),[1] "the Party and the government of China" (*Zhongguo dang zheng* 中國黨政),[2] "the CCPCC and the State Council" (*Zhong gong zhongyang, guowuyuan* 中共中央‧國務院),[3] "the Party Centre and the State Council" (*dang zhongyang guowuyuan* 黨中央國務院),[4] "the Party committees and governments at all levels" (*ge ji dangwei he zhengfu* 各級黨委和政府)[5] and so forth.

"Resolutely support the leadership of the Chinese Communist Party and the Government of the People's Republic of China . . ." Thus begins the first of the four articles of the "Soldiers' Oath"[6] issued by the General Staff and the General Political Department of the Chinese People's Liberation Army to

---

[1] "Dang he guojia lingdao zhidu de yi xiang zhongyao gaige" 黨和國家領導制度的一項重要改革 ("An important reform of the leadership system of the Party and state"), *Renmin ribao* 人民日報 , 28 October 1980.

[2] *Zhonghua Renmin Gongheguo guowuyuan gongbao* 中華人民共和國國務院公報 (*Bulletin of the State Council of the People's Republic of China*), No. 5, 1980 (23 June 1980), p. 143.

[3] "Zhong gong zhongyang, guowuyuan fachu guanyu jinyibu zuohao jihua shengyu gongzuo de zhishi"中共中央、國務院發出關於進一步做好計劃生育工作的指示("The Central Committee of the CCP and the State Council put forward directions regarding the further development of work on family planning"), *Renmin ribao*, 14 March 1982.

[4] "Dang zhongyang guowuyuan fachu tongzhi yaoqiu jiji fazhan duozhong jingying" 黨中央國務院發出通知要求積極發展多種經營 ("The Party Centre and the State Council issue a circular calling for the active development of a diversified economy"), *Renmin ribao*, 6 April 1981.

[5] Referred to in: "Quanmian shixing he jianjue guanche tiaozheng fangzhen" 全面實行和堅決貫徹調整方針 ("Carry out in all respects and resolutely implement the general policy on readjustment"), *Renmin ribao*, 2 December 1980.

[6] "Jiefangjun ge budui juxing 'junren shici' xuanshi he jiaoyu huodong" 解放軍各部隊舉行〈軍人誓詞〉宣誓和教育活動 ("All units of the PLA carry out activities relating to the taking and teaching of the 'soldiers' oath' "), *Gongren ribao* 工人日報 , 7 April 1981.

all units. What are the relations between the two wielders of power, Party and state? This essay attempts to provide an answer to this question from the point of view of the different roles played by the state and the Party in the normative realm. It does not pretend to deal fully with all problems, but seeks rather to single out some key issues for discussion.

I. THE STATE AND ITS NORMS

As far as the emphasis on the concept of the unitary state is concerned, the theory of the state universally held in the P.R.C. can be traced back as far as the Legalists of the Warring States period (fifth to third century B.C.), in accordance with whose teachings Qin Shihuang established the first unitary state (221-206 B.C.) on Chinese soil. In addition to the heritage of China's own past, the Chinese theory of the state is also fundamentally shaped by the theses outlined by Lenin in his *State and Revolution*. During the past three decades, the state has been defined primarily as

> an instrument of class rule, an organization for exercising violence consisting in the main of an army, a police force, courts and prisons to carry out the dictatorship of the dominant class over the dominated classes.[7]

Thus Article 1 of the Constitution of the P.R.C. of 5 March 1978 stated that the P.R.C. is a "socialist state of the dictatorship of the proletariat,"[8] a formulation which was replaced in Article 1 of the Constitution of the P.R.C. of 4 December 1982 by "socialist state under the people's democratic dictatorship." This is, in accordance with the Preamble of the Constitution of 4 December 1982, "in essence the dictatorship of the proletariat." At the Second session of the Fifth National People's Congress (18 June-1 July 1979)[9] and in the Preamble, paragraph 8, of the Constitution of the P.R.C. of 4 December 1982, it was officially proclaimed that the "exploiting classes" as such had already been eliminated on the Chinese mainland. To be sure, the idea of continuing "class struggle" in China and abroad has, as the Preamble of the Constitution of 4 December 1982 shows, been retained, but it is no longer expressed in the same lurid terms as during the Cultural Revolution. There is a clear trend toward speaking only of "dictatorship" over isolated,

[7] *Xiandai Hanyu cidian* 現代漢語詞典 (Beijing: Shangwu yinshuaguan 商務印書館 , 1979), p. 418; compare further *Falü zhishi wenda* 法律知識問答 (*Questions and answers regarding basic legal knowledge*) (Beijing: Beijing chubanshe 北京出版社 , 1979), p. 49.

[8] This term was taken over from Article 1 of the Constitution of the P.R.C. of 17 January 1975.

[9] Hua Guofeng 華國鋒 , "Report on the Work of the Government," *Beijing Review*, No. 27, 1979, pp. 9-11.

172

numerically insignificant "counter-revolutionaries," "degenerates in Party and government organizations" who "cause tremendous damage to economic construction and upset social stability" and other "hostile anti-socialist elements," rather than of "dictatorship over classes."[10] The term "socialist state of the people's democratic dictatorship" in Article 1 of the Constitution of the P.R.C. of 4 December 1982 is interpreted in accordance with an observation made by Mao Zedong in 1949[11] as a combination of "democracy for the people" and "dictatorship over the reactionaries,"[12] and is equated with the term "people's democratic state,"[13] an expression already embodied in Article 1 of the Constitution of the P.R.C. of 20 September 1954. At the same time, there is a growing interest in a closer examination of the implications of the "form of state" (*guojia xingshi* 國家形式) established in China in 1949, the "people's republic." During the Cultural Revolution the discussion had in contrast been almost exclusively about the "nature of the state" (*guojia benzhi* 國家本質) that is, about its function as an "instrument of class dictatorship."[14]

In the P.R.C., the norms promulgated by the state organs are collectively known as "*fa*" 法 or "*falü*" 法律. The term "*fa*" is defined as follows in the largest existing encyclopaedic dictionary of the P.R.C.:

> Legal term. 1. Overall designation for the behavioural norms promulgated or approved by the state embodying the will of the ruling class, the observance of which guarantees the state's coercive power. Into the sphere of "*fa*" fall all *falü* (laws), *faling* 法令 (decrees), *tiaoli* 條例 (rules), *guize* 規則 (regulations), *jueding* 決定 (resolutions), *mingling* 命令 (orders), *panli* 判例 (precedents), *guanli* 慣例 (practices), etc. One of the instruments of class dictatorship. . . .
> 2. Identical to "*falü*."[15]

Probably the most concise definition for the term "*falü*" is as follows:

[10] Hu Yaobang 胡耀邦 , *Beijing Review*, No. 37, 13 September 1982, p. 28.

[11] "On the People's Democratic Dictatorship," *Selected Works*, Vol. 4 (Peking, 1969), p. 418.

[12] Guo Yuzhao 郭宇昭 , "Renminminzhu zhuanzheng shi wo guo de guoti" 人民民主專政是我國的國體 ("The People's Democratic Dictatorship is our country's state system"), *Renmin ribao*, 23 December 1982, p. 5.

[13] Xu Chongde 許崇德 , "Xiugai xianfa shi yi" 修改憲法十議 ("Ten points about the revision of the Constitution"), *Minzhu yu fazhi* 民主與法制 , No. 3, 20 March 1981, p. 8.

[14] Yan Jiaqi 嚴家其 , "Shehuizhuyi guojia ye yao jiejue hao zhengti wenti—tan tan Makesi guanyu 'shehui gongheguo' de sixiang" 社會主義國家也要解決好政體問題——談談馬克思關於 '社會共和國' 的思想 ("A socialist country must also solve well the problem of the political system—on Marxist thinking regarding a 'socialist republic' "), *Guangming ribao* 光明日報 , 8 December 1980.

[15] *Cihai* 辭海 (Shanghai: Shanghai cishu chubanshe 上海辭書出版社, 1979), Vol. II, p. 2071.

Guize (regulations, norms) enacted and promulgated by the state to protect the interests of the ruling class.[16]

In the P.R.C., the terms *fa* and *falü* hence fall within the meaning of positive statute law, and can be translated only with reservations by the far more comprehensive German and French words *Recht* or *droit*.

II. THE PARTY AND ITS NORMS

What are the relations between the state, which formally enacts statute law, and the CCP? The Constitution of the P.R.C. of 5 March 1978 states in Article 2 Section 1:

> The Communist Party of China is the leading core of the whole Chinese people. The working class leads the state through its vanguard, the Communist Party of China.

Article 56 of the Constitution further stipulates:

> Citizens must support the leadership of the Communist Party of China.

At the suggestion (*jianyi* 建議) of the CCPCC, the Fifth NPC at its Third session on 10 September 1980 set up a committee to draft a complete revision of the Constitution of the P.R.C. of 5 March 1978.[17] The revised draft of the Constitution of 21 April 1982 produced by this committee was further completed and amended in some 100 places following discussion throughout the country,[18] and it was approved on 4 December 1982 by the Fifth National People's Congress. Thereupon it entered into force as the fourth Constitution of the P.R.C. It dispenses with the two above-mentioned articles of the Constitution of 5 March 1978. But this change appears to be largely formal. In practice the leading role of the Chinese Communist Party

[16] *Xin Hua cidian* 新華辭典 (31st edition, Beijing, April 1980), p. 111.

[17] "Zhongguo Gongchandang Zhongyang weiyuanhui guanyu xiugai xianfa he chengli xianfa xiugai weiyuanhui de jianyi" 中國共產黨中央委員會關於修改憲法和成立憲法修改委員會的建議 ("Proposal of the Central Committee of the Chinese Communist Party regarding the revision of the Constitution and the arrangements for a Committee on the Revision of the Constitution"), 30 August 1980; also, "Zhonghua Renmin Gongheguo di-wu jie quanguo renmin daibiao dahui di-san ci huiyi guanyu xiugai xianfa he chengli xianfa xiugai weiyuanhui de jueyi" 中華人民共和國第五屆全國人民代表大會第三次會議關於修改憲法和成立憲法修改委員會的決議 ("Decision of the Third Session of the Fifth National People's Congress regarding the revision of the Constitution and the arrangements for a Committee on the Revision of the Constitution"), 10 September 1980, in *Zhonghua Renmin Gongheguo guowuyuan gongbao* 中華人民共和國國務院公報, No. 12, 1980 (18 November 1980), pp. 375-77.

[18] See Peng Zhen's 彭眞 report in *Beijing Review*, No. 51, 1982, p. 10.

remains intact. Thus the Preamble of the Constitution of 4 December 1982 declares: "Under the leadership of the Communist Party of China and the guidance of Marxism-Leninism and Mao Zedong Thought, the Chinese people of all nationalities will continue to adhere to the people's democratic dictatorship and follow the socialist road, steadily improve socialist institutions. . . ."[19] "The force at the core leading China's cause of socialism" is the CCP, emphasise the Party Statutes passed on 6 September 1982 by the Twelfth Congress of the CCP (1-11 September 1982) in the opening paragraph of the "General Programme."[20] The Constitution of the P.R.C. for its part lays down in Article 1 of its first chapter, "General Principles," that "The People's Republic of China is led by the working class . . ." But the "Vanguard of the Chinese working class" is the CCP, and Hu Yaobang, General Secretary of the Central Committee of the CCP, confirmed in his report of 1 September 1982 at the Twelfth Party Congress of the CCP: "Our party is now the leading core of nationwide political power."[21]

According to the texts, the National Party Congress and the Central Committee (CC) appointed by it are the highest executive bodies of the CCP. But real power lies with those groups which during the period between the meetings of the Central Committee exercise its powers: the Politburo of the CC and its Standing Committee, as well as the General Secretariat of the CC, which was re-introduced by the Fifth Plenary Session of the Eleventh CCPCC (23-29 February 1980).

The Party statutes of 6 September 1982 stipulate in Article 10 Section 2:

> The Party is . . . organized according to the principles of democratic centralism . . . each Party member must obey the Party organization, the minority obeys the majority, the lower levels of organization obey the higher levels and all levels of organization as well as all Party members must obey the National Party Congress and the Central Committee of the Party. . . .

According to the concluding paragraph of the "General Programme" of the Party Statutes,

> The Party members are in a minority of the whole population, and they must work in close co-operation with the masses of the non-Party people. . . .[22]

The relationship with "cadres who are not Party members" is laid down in detail in Article 36 of the Party Statutes of September 1982. As early as spring 1981 the Chinese press reported that loyal non-Party members (*dangwai renshi* 黨外人士) were also being appointed to prominent offices at

[19] *Beijing Review*, No. 52, 1982, p. 11.
[20] *Beijing Review*, No. 38, 1982, p. 8.
[21] Hu Yaobang, in *Beijing Review*, No. 37, 1982, p. 14.
[22] *Beijing Review*, No. 38, 1982, p. 10.

the regional governmental level.[23] But by far the largest number of cadres working in the governmental bodies at all levels are members of the CCP,[24] and they form Party branches (*dang zhibu* 黨支部) in their spheres of operation, controlled by a Party committee (*dangwei* 黨委).

The Party Centre in Beijing is obviously not in a position to assess or direct in detail the daily and hourly work performed by the innumerable Party branches and Party members working under its control in the agencies of the state. And yet the aim is for all Party officials to act in unity. For this purpose the Party Centre employs certain guidelines based on "Marxism-Leninism and Mao Zedong Thought" which unite all Party members, and which I wish to call collectively "Party norms."

Three types of Party norms must be differentiated, which are usually listed in a fixed order in contemporary Chinese literature, such as for example, the last paragraph of the General Principles of the Party Statutes of 6 September 1982:

1. *zhengzhi luxian* 政治路線, often simply "*luxian*";
2. *fangzhen* 方針 ;
3. *zhengce* 政策 .

Deviations from this terminology, which is not definitive in every respect in the P.R.C., are sometimes discerned, but these cannot be further discussed in this context.

During the period 1949-78 the largest encyclopaedic dictionary in the P.R.C. defined the term "*zhengzhi luxian*" (political line) *inter alia* as follows:

> Expression of the political task formulated by the party of the proletariat [=CCP] for the purpose of achieving its political objectives during a specific historical period. . . . The "*fangzhen*" and "*zhengce*" which are in effect for specific work are laid down in accordance with the political line.[25]

The same dictionary explains the term "*fangzhen*":

[23] "Chongfen fahui dangwai renshi zai si hua jianshe zhong de zuoyong" 充分發揮黨外人士在四化建設中的作用 ("Develop in full measure the role of non-Party people in building the four modernizations"), *Tianjin ribao* 天津日報 , 1 April 1981.

[24] Song Zhengting 宋振庭 , "Jiaqiang he gaishan dang de lingdao shi wenbu jinxing si hua jianshe de baozheng" 加强和改善黨的領導是穩步進行四化建設的保證 ("To strengthen and improve Party leadership is the guarantee of steadily carrying forward the four modernizations"), *Gongren ribao* (Beijing), 23 February 1981; "Qingli 'zuo' de sixiang, jiashen dui san zhong quanhui luxian de lijie" 清理'左'的思想，加深對三中全會路綫的理解 ("Eliminate 'leftist' thinking, and deepen understanding of the line of the Third Plenum"), *Renmin ribao*, 8 April 1981.

[25] *Cihai* 辭海 , *Zhengzhi falü* 政治法律 (Shanghai: Zhonghua shuju 中華書局 , 1961), p. 23. In the main the same as *Cihai, Zhengzhi falü fence* 政治法律分冊 (Shanghai: Shanghai cishu chubanshe, 1978), p. 48.

176

Direction-indicator which shows the course for a task or venture.[26]

Zhengce refers among other things to

> measures and procedures laid down by a political party for the realization of its political objectives, which serve as the basis of and guidelines for action.[27]

The common English translations of the words [*zhengzhi*] *luxian*: "[political] line," *fangzhen*: "orientation," also "general policy," and *zhengce*: "policy," like the original Chinese meanings, point to the increasingly more specific contents of the three types of Party norms, and hence to the increasingly narrower spheres which they govern. This aspect is emphasized by Marianne Bastid in her essay "Levels of Economic Decision-Making."[28] Neither the Chinese nor the cited English terms give an indication of the underlying philosophy of the three Party norms:

> Dialectical materialism and historical materialism are . . . the theoretical basis on which our Party established its *luxian, fangzhen, zhengce*.[29]

None of the three types of Party norms shows the traces of its dialectical origins more distinctly than the *fangzhen*, of which Mao Zedong wrote in his essay "On Contradiction":

> The study of the various states of unevenness in the development of contradictions, the study of the principal contradiction and the secondary contradictions, as well as the principal and secondary aspects of the contradictions, is an essential method by which a revolutionary party correctly determines its strategic and tactical *fangzhen* in the political and military realm.[30]

In order to express the particularly marked dialectical nature of *fangzhen*, the term "duality norm" [*Polaritätsnorm*] has been chosen for it in this essay, to complement the conventional English translation cited above. The latter retains its validity with regard to the intended effect of *fangzhen* as a general guiding aid for Party cadres. In the European Marxist-Leninist vocabulary "polarity" describes the relationship of pairs of dialectical opposites to one another. It is said of the two poles of a dialectical contradiction that they are opposites, and that the existence of one presupposes and necessitates that

[26] *Cihai, Zhengzhi falü fence*, p. 46.

[27] *Cihai, Zhengzhi falü*, pp. 22-23.

[28] In *Authority, Participation and Cultural Change in China, Essays by a European Study Group*, edited and with an Introduction by Stuart R. Schram (Cambridge: Cambridge University Press, 1973), p. 160. Also compare Franz Schurmann, *Ideology and Organization in Communist China* (Berkeley: University of California Press, 1968).

[29] Chen Jinyu 陳進玉, "Zhongshi he gaohao Makesizhuyi zhexue de xuexi" 重視和搞好馬克思主義哲學的學習 ("Emphasize and carry out well the study of Marxist philosophy"), *Jiefang ribao* 解放日報, 21 May 1981.

[30] *Selected Works*, Vol. I, p. 337.

of the other. However, from the point of view of the dialectic as practised in the P.R.C., there are in addition to contradictions with two also contradictions with more than two poles, and the expressions "bipolar" (*liangji* 兩極) and "multipolar" (*duoji* 多極) are entering foreign policy analyses. Thus the Party organ *People's Daily* writes:

The "bipolar" world is on the point of changing into a "multipolar" world.[31]

The following eight basic elements of the so-called "Eight Point Charter" for increasing agricultural output devised during the Great Leap are, for example, explicitly designated as constituting a "multipolar contradiction" (*duoji maodun* 多極矛盾): *shui* 水 (irrigation); *fei* 肥 (fertilizing); *tu* 土 (soil improvement); *zhong* 種 (seed selection); *mi* 密 (close-planting); *bao* 保 (plant protection); *gong* 工 (improvement of agricultural tools) and *guan* 管 (agricultural management).[32] Whether Western Europeans find the idea of bipolar and multipolar contradictions convincing is neither here nor there. The only thing that matters in this context is the fact that the method of analyzing contradictions is regarded as "the basic method of Marxism, the most fundamental method of understanding things"[33] in the P.R.C. and is indeed put into practice by the Party Centre when promulgating *fangzhen*.

The *fangzhen* prescribe the course for a work or undertaking by regulating the basic aspects of this work or undertaking which are understood to be in a mutually dialectical relationship. Depending on the type of regulation, two types of "duality norms" can be distinguished: those which prescribe "struggle," and those which prescribe the "identity" of the opposite aspects of contradictions.

Some examples of duality norms of the first kind follow. One duality norm for political-ideological education in schools enjoins (or enjoined): "Advance the proletarian, eliminate the bourgeois!"[34] "Both red and expert!"

---

[31] Pei Monong 裴默農 , "Lüe lun fandui Sulian baquanzhuyi de zhanlüe guanxi" 略論反對蘇聯霸權主義的戰略關係 ("A brief discussion of strategic relations concerning the struggle against Soviet hegemonism"), *Renmin ribao*, 8 July 1981, p. 7.

[32] Liu Weihua 劉蔚華 , "Maodun jiegou de duoyangxing" 矛盾結構的多樣性 ("The manifold nature of the structure of contradictions"), *Shehui kexue zhan xian* 社會科學戰線, No. 2, 1979, p. 93; compare also, "Tongyixing de shizhi ji qi juti xingtai" 統一性的實質及其具體形態 ("Maintaining unity, and its concrete form"), *Guangming ribao* 光明日報, 21 April 1981.

[33] Sun Shuping 孫叔平 , *Lishi weiwuzhuyi he bianzheng weiwuzhuyi* 歷史唯物主義和辯證唯物主義 (*Historical and dialectical materialism*) (Shanghai: Shanghai renmin chubanshe 上海人民出版社, 1980), p. 111.

[34] "Jiaqiang dui qingshao nian jiaoyu, peiyang you hong you zhuan rencai" 加強對青少年教育，培養又紅又專人才 ("Strengthen the teaching of young people about becoming persons who are both red and expert"), *Nanfang ribao* 南方日報 , 25 May 1979; Chen Zhihai 陳志海 , " 'Xing wu mie zi' de tifa wu ke feiyi" '興無滅資' 的提法無可非議 ("The

is likewise in force for the Chinese education system, as well as in other domains.

Liao Jianming interprets these *fangzhen* on the philosophy page of the *Guangming ribao* of 26 June 1980: "Party Centre wants to regulate the two contradictions between 'red' and 'not red,' as well as between 'expert' and 'not expert.' "[35]

The duality norm "Let a hundred flowers bloom!", oriented toward the development of socialist culture and art, governs the contradiction between "let bloom" (*fang* 放) and "rein in" (*shou* 收) as Mao shows in his analysis of the dialectical nature of these *fangzhen*.[36] In contrast to the duality norm usually also quoted in this connection, "Let a hundred schools contend!", the course "Let a hundred schools keep silent!" was adopted during the Cultural Revolution, according to the current view.[37]

The general guiding duality norm for political work is: "Let [ideologically incorrect thoughts first] flow and [then] channel [them]!"[38] It negates the tendency to block crudely (*duse* 堵塞) and to suppress (*yazhi* 壓制) unpopular currents of thought instead of thoroughly discussing and refuting them.

A duality norm concerning propaganda work is directed against the "giving of prominence to individuals" (*tuchu geren* 突出個人): "Take increasingly the masses, and less often individual Party leaders as the subject of propaganda!"[39]

As late as 1976, during the campaign against the "wind from the right," the postulate that the level of the Chinese economy had to be raised was attacked as the "theory of the exclusive importance of the productive forces"

---

formulation 'advance the proletarian and eliminate the bourgeois' cannot be repudiated"), *Renmin ribao*, 3 August 1979. Article 24 of the Constitution of the P.R.C. of 4 December 1982 reflects the spirit of this duality norm.

[35] Liao Jianming 廖劍鳴, "Hong yu zhuan shi yi dui maodun ma?" 紅與專是一對矛盾嗎? ("Are red and expert a pair of contradictions?"), *Guangming ribao*, 26 June 1980; see also the articles of Hu Qirui 胡啓銳 and Luo Rongquan 羅榮泉 in *Guangming ribao*, 14 August 1980.

[36] Mao Zedong, *Selected Works*, Vol. V, p. 432.

[37] Liao Mosha 廖沫沙, "Tan fang yu shou" 談放與收 ("On letting bloom and reining in"), *Xin Hua yuebao* 新華月報. *Wenzhai ban* 文摘版 4, 1980, p. 146.

[38] "Xiaochu 'zuo' de yinxiang jianchi shudao fangzhen" 消除'左'的影響，堅持疏導方針 ("Eliminate 'leftist' influence and resolutely maintain the orientation of letting flow and channelling"), *Renmin ribao*, 15 March 1981.

[39] "Jianchi shao xuanchuan geren de fangzhen" 堅持少宣傳個人的方針 ("Firmly grasp the orientation of carrying out less propaganda about individuals"), *Guangming ribao*, 11 March 1979; "Zhong gong zhongyang fachu zhishi jianchi shao xuanchuan geren" 中共中央發出指示堅持少宣傳個人 ("The Central Committee of the Chinese Communist Party issues a directive insisting on less propaganda about individuals"), *Renmin ribao*, 12 August 1980.

(*wei shengchanli lun* 唯生產力論).[40] The "Eight-Character duality norm" (*ba-zi fangzhen* 八字方針), issued by the Party Centre in the spring of 1979, (which Hu Yaobang, in his report of 1 September 1982 to the Twelfth Party Congress of the CCP, said provided guidelines for the sixth Five-Year Plan in 1981-85), is diametrically opposed to the course pursued prior to, and to some extent even during the two years following the fall of the "Gang of Four":

Readjust [the economic disproportions]!
Reorganize [the existing enterprises including their leadership teams]!
Renew [the economic administrative structures]!
[All this with the aim to] raise [productivity and the level of the overall national economy]![41]

Duality norms of the second kind try to harmonize the opposite aspects of specific contradictions, for instance by laying down definite priorities or by decreeing an equilibrium between the poles of the contradiction.

With regard to one duality norm "essential to the construction of socialist modernization"[42] namely "Regard agriculture as the foundation, industry as the leading factor!" Yao Bomao writes on the philosophy page of the *Guangming ribao* of 17 January 1980:

[40] "Pipan wei shengchanli lun" 批判唯生產力論 ("Criticize the theory of everything depending on the productive forces"), in *Zhua jieji douzheng zhe ge gang* 抓階級鬥爭這個綱 (*Grasp the key link of class struggle*) (Changsha: Hunan renmin chubanshe, 1976), pp. 48ff.; "Zhuazhu xiuzhengzhuyi sixiang zhengzhi luxian zhe ge yaohai, shenru pipan Deng Xiaoping shouyi paozhi de 'tiaoli' " 抓住修正主義思想政治路綫這個要害，深入批判鄧小平授意炮製的'條例' ("Grasp the harmfulness of the political line of revisionism, deepen the criticism of Deng Xiaoping's 'articles' "), *Renmin ribao*, 23 August 1976.
[41] "Gongren jieji yao daitou dahao zhongdian zhuanyi di-yi zhang" 工人階級要帶頭打好重點轉移第一仗 ("The working class should take the lead in the first battle to shift the emphasis [to modernization]"), *Renmin ribao* editorial, 1 May 1979; "Zhengdun jiu shi yao fadong qunzhong hen jie maodun jiejue wenti" 整頓就是要發動羣衆狠揭矛盾解決問題 ("Rectifying the situation means mobilizing the masses resolutely to expose contradictions and resolve problems"), *Renmin ribao*, 20 June 1979; Hu Yaobang's report, *Beijing Review*, No. 37, 1982, p. 16; for a summary of the Plan, see *Renmin ribao*, 13 December 1982, p. 1.
[42] Yu Guangyuan 于光遠, "Yi nongye wei jichu shi wo guo shehuizhuyi xiandaihua jianshe de yi ge jiben fangzhen" 以農業爲基礎是我國社會主義現代化建設的一個基本方針 ("Agriculture as the foundation is a basic orientation of our country's socialist modernization and construction"), *Jingji yanjiu* 經濟研究, No. 3, 1979, p. 2; *Makesi zhuyi zhexue yuanli* 馬克思主義哲學原理 (*Principles of Marxist philosophy*) (Jilin: Jilin renmin chubanshe, 1980), p. 229.

As far as the contradiction between industry and agriculture is concerned, one should in the socialist system stress the striving after the identity in the contradiction.[43]

The booklet *Historical Materialism and Dialectical Materialism*, published in 1980, offers the following chain of reasoning in a paragraph entitled "Under certain conditions the two aspects of a contradiction are mutually interdependent":

> The system of the socialist economy is a unity of opposites, such as industry and agriculture, . . . large, small and medium-sized enterprises, national and regional enterprises. All these . . . opposite aspects are mutually interdependent, the existence of one aspect is the precondition for the existence of the other. For the construction of socialism, the Party has prepared a number of *fangzhen* concerning the economic organization, based precisely on this objectively given unity of contradictory aspects.[44]

An allusion is made here to a series of duality norms which prescribe "walking on two legs" (*liang tiao tui zou lu* 兩條腿走路), such as

> Industry and agriculture are to be promoted simultaneously!
>
> Heavy industry and light industry are to be promoted simultaneously!
>
> National and regional enterprise are to be promoted simultaneously![45]

These duality norms, stemming from the Second session of the Eighth Party Congress of the CCP (5-23 May 1958), have in the meantime been revised. Thus one now stipulates:

> Planning the national economy in the order of priority agriculture, light industry, heavy industry![46]

The following two norms signal reversals in the sphere of economic construction:

> Gradual transition from extensive to intensive economy![47]

---

[43] Yao Bomao 姚伯茂 , " 'Douzheng zhexue' bixu chedi paoqi" '鬥爭哲學' 必須徹底 抛棄 ("The 'philosophy of struggle' must be thoroughly abandoned"), *Guangming ribao*, 17 January 1980.

[44] Sun Shuping, *op. cit.*, pp. 104-105.

[45] *Cihai, zhengzhi falü*, p. 24; *Zhengzhi jingjixue xiao cidian* 政治經濟學小辭典 (Jilin: Jilin renmin chubanshe, 1980), p. 185; *Cihai, jingji fence* 經濟分冊 (Shanghai, 1980), p. 67.

[46] "Zijue an nong qing zhong fangzhen fazhan jingji" 自覺按農輕重方針發展經濟 ("Develop the economy by relying consciously on the priority agriculture, light industry, heavy industry"), *Renmin ribao*, 17 July 1979.

[47] "Wei tigao jingji xiaoguo zuochu geng da gongxian" 爲提高經濟效果作出更大貢獻 ("Make greater contributions to raising the level of economic results"), *Renmin ribao*

Change from "steel as the key link" and the preferential development of heavy industry to stressing the development of consumer-goods production while striving for a balance between the production of the means of production and the production of consumer goods![48]

Another duality norm in effect for the national economy states:

With priority to control through the planned economy, simultaneously attach importance to regulation through the market economy![49]

In the sphere of culture and science "Make the past serve the present!" and "Make foreign things serve China!" are invoked time and again.[50]

The relationships among three aspects considered to constitute a three-polar contradiction, are governed by the "*fangzhen* guiding the healthy growing-up of the young generation" formulated by Mao Zedong in 1953 and which is still invoked today, according to which young people should "remain in good health, study well and work successfully [for the construction of socialism]!"[51] A commentary on this norm states that it "fully expresses the dialectical unity of physical, intellectual, and moral development".[52]

---

editorial, 16 April, 1981; "Ruhe lijie gongye shengchan de waiyan he neihan..." 如何理解工業生產的外延和內含······("How shall we understand what is meant by extensive and intensive [methods for developing] industrial production?"), *Renmin ribao*, 5 May 1981: "Zenyang lijie jianshe fangzhen de gaibian?" 怎樣理解建設方針的改變 ("How shall we understand the change in the orientation of [economic] construction?"), *Gongren ribao*, 23 May 1981.

[48] *Renmin ribao*, editorial cited, 16 April 1981.

[49] Jiang Yiwei 蔣一葦, "Jingji tizhi gaige de yi ge genben wenti" 經濟體制改革的一個根本問題 ("A basic question in the reform of the economic system"), *Renmin ribao*, 14 August 1979. Also compare, "Zhuyi yanjiu jingji gongzuo zhong de bianzhengfa" 注意研究經濟工作中的辯證法 ("Pay attention to dialectics in the study of economic work"), *Hongqi* 紅旗, No. 15, 1982 (1 August 1982), p. 35; a provision in accordance with this duality norm is to be found in Article 15, para. 1 of the Constitution of the P.R.C. of 4 December 1982.

[50] Ye Shuifu 葉水夫, "Pipan 'wenyi heixian zhuanzheng' lun, nuli zuohao waiguo wenxue gongzuo" 批判'文藝黑綫專政'論，努力做好外國文學工作 ("Criticize the 'theory of the dictatorship of the black line' in literature, strive to carry out well our work on foreign literature"), *Wenxue pinglun* 文學評論, No. 1, 1978, p. 48; "Guanche gu wei jin yong fangzhen, kaizhan wo guo gudai wenyi lilun gongzuo" 貫徹古為今用方針，開展我國古代文藝理論工作 ("Implement the general policy of using the past to serve the present, develop theoretical work on ancient Chinese literature"), *Guangming ribao*, 14 April 1979.

[51] Mao Zedong, *Selected Works*, Vol. V, p. 96 (translation modified).

[52] *"Mao Zedong xuanji" diwu juan, xuexi wenda* (4) "毛澤東選集" 第五卷學習問答（四）(*Questions and answers in studying volume 5 of Mao Zedong's* Selected Works [4]) (Beijing: Beijing renmin chubanshe, 1977), p. 29.

It can be demonstrated that the other two kinds of Party norms are also based on Mao's theory of contradictions, which is in turn governed by the notion of development. This notion shapes the thought of all tendencies or factions within the CCP. Everything develops. Like humanity as a whole, so Chinese society, too, develops. It is now passing through the socialist period, on the way to communism. Development toward the final objective is divided into various stages. Each of the various stages is distinguishable by a specific kind of principal contradiction that dominates all other contradictions to be solved at the same time. By means of the Party political line, the Party Centre "identifies" and defines the principal contradiction or the principal problem which is to be solved during a specific period, and thus the dialectical stage, the stage of development, through which Chinese society is passing.

The evaluation of the principal contradiction made by the Party Centre, and hence the Party's political line, have changed several times during the last fifty years. In essence, the sequence of the principal contradictions covered by the various political lines was as follows:

From 1937 to 1945 the contradiction between the entire Chinese nation, including Chiang Kai-shek's Guomindang government, on the one hand, and Japan wanting to conquer China on the other, was considered as the principal contradiction; the principal task was the defeat of Japan.

From 1945 to 1949 the contradiction between the CCP and Chiang Kai-shek's Guomindang government was, in the final analysis, considered as the principal contradiction; the principal task was the defeat of Chiang.

From 1949 in fact until October 1976, the date the "Gang of Four" was smashed, but formally to the Third Plenum of the Eleventh CCPCC (18-22 December 1978) the principal contradiction was: the Chinese "proletariat" against the Chinese "bourgeoisie"; the principal task was the so-called "class struggle" of the "proletariat" against the "bourgeoisie," and since the start of the Cultural Revolution primarily against the so-called power holders taking the capitalist road within the CCP.

Since the Third Plenum of the Eleventh CCPCC (18-22 December 1978) the contradiction between the need to modernize and backwardness, especially in the four sectors of agriculture, industry, national defence, and science and technology, is considered as the principal contradiction in China;[53] the principal task is the "four modernizations."

According to the Party political line now prevailing, the P.R.C. is passing through a stage of development which is shaped by the principal contradiction

[53] See the communiqué of the Third Plenum in *Renmin ribao*, 24 December 1978, p. 1; and also "General Programme" of the Party, *Beijing Review*, No. 38, 1982, p. 9.

between the need to modernize and backwardness. This principal contradiction is to be resolved before the year 2000. To this end numerous so-called secondary contradictions (*feizhuyao maodun* 非主要矛盾, also *ciyao maodun* 次要矛盾)[54] must be solved, and that in all possible spheres, *inter alia* also in the sphere of relations with foreign countries and of external trade. These concrete contradictions are regulated by the Party's duality and political norms. The relationship of these to the legal system of the state will be illustrated by the example of foreign trade.

III. THE PARTY NORMS PERMEATE THE ENACTED STATE LAWS

The call for *socialist* modernization of the P.R.C. by the year 2000 provides that the country is to be modernized in a manner appropriate to China, and modernization is not to be bought at the expense of independence and sovereignty. Thus the basic orientation laid down by Mao Zedong in 1958, "self-reliance as primary and striving for foreign aid as secondary" is maintained.[55]

The contradiction between China and foreign countries is governed in the most general manner by the duality norm: "Let foreign things serve China, while China specifies the course!" Another duality norm handles the contradiction between export and import:

Exports in first place;
combine imports with exports;
proportion imports to exports;
achieve a balance between imports and exports!

Imports must be used to increase the export capacity.[56]

So much for the handling of contradictions in the area of basic policy issues. But in concrete terms, the following alternative arises: Should the

[54] Chen Yangjiong 陳揚炯, *Zhexue mantan* 哲學漫談 (*Random notes on philosophy*) (Beijing: Zhongguo qingnian chubanshe 中國青年出版社, 1980), pp. 164ff.

[55] The slogan "The Chinese road to modernization" (*Zhongguoshi de xiandaihua daolu* 中國式的現代化道路) was put forward by the Party's Central Committee in spring 1979, and has been upheld ever since. For a reference to the relation between independence and aid, see Mao's talk of 30 January 1962, in S. Schram (ed.), *Mao Tse-tung Unrehearsed* (Harmondsworth: Penguin, 1974), p. 178; official version in *Beijing Review*, No. 27, 1978, p. 17.

[56] Dialectical analysis of the contraction between import and export governed by this *fangzhen* in "Nuli zengjia chukou fazhan duiwai maoyi" 努力增加出口發展對外貿易 ("Strive to increase exports and develop foreign trade"), *Renmin ribao*, 15 July 1979.

P.R.C. use foreign capital or not? Concrete contradictions of this kind are governed by the so-called political norms or policies (*zhengce*) of the Party. One Party political norm often invoked at the present time stipulates:

Advanced foreign technology is to be imported and foreign capital to be utilized![57]

This Party political norm has now been given concrete form in statutory law, in particular in the "Law of the P.R.C. concerning joint enterprises with Chinese and foreign investment interests," which came into force on 8 July 1979, and in the "Regulations for the Implementation of the Law" promulgated on 20 September 1983.[58] These texts state how advanced foreign technology and foreign capital may in fact be imported into or utilized in the P.R.C. The duality norms cited above are given expression in a number of legal provisions, aimed at preventing foreign assistance from becoming a dominant factor in the Chinese economy. Thus the formation of a joint venture requires the "approval of the Chinese Government" (Article 1). The joint ventures in the P.R.C. are furthermore subject to "the laws, decrees and pertinent regulations of the P.R.C." (Article 2, Section 2). Accordingly, the joint ventures established in the P.R.C. are corporate bodies (*faren* 法人) subject to the laws of the P.R.C. and not any foreign laws. "Thus the law-abiding partners," writes a Chinese commentator on the law, "who work with us sincerely can be protected, but the lawbreakers who injure our country's interests can be punished forthwith."[59] The chairman of the board of directors of every enterprise is furnished by the Chinese partner (Article 6, Section 1). Under Article 5, Section 2 of the law, the technology or equipment which the foreign partners contribute to capital expenditures must in fact meet modern international standards as well as *China's needs*. A joint venture which does not meet China's needs and which does not bring modern technology and equipment to China is of no use to China. The foreign partner who with outdated technology and outdated installations causes losses as a result of deliberate deception is liable for damages.[60]

---

[57] Jiang Yiguo 蔣一國, Wang Zumin 王祖敏, and Jiang Baoqi 蔣寶祺, "Jiakuai wo guo jingli fazhan sudu de yi xiang zhongda de zhengce—tan tan yinjin xianjin jishu he liyong waizu wenti" 加快我國經濟發展速度的一項重大的政策——談談引進先進技術和利用外資問題 ("An important policy for increasing the speed of our country's economic development—a discussion on importing advanced technology and making use of foreign capital"), *Jingji yanjiu*, No. 10, 1978, pp. 10ff.

[58] *Xin Hua yuebao wenxian ban* 新華月報文獻版, 1979, No. 6, pp. 94-95; *Beijing review* No. 41, 1983.

[59] Wang Baoshu 王保樹, "Tan tan wo guo de Zhong-wai hezi jingying qiye fa" 談談我國的中外合資經營企業法 ("A discussion of our country's law regarding joint ventures with Chinese and foreign capital"), *Nanfang ribao*, 8 August 1979.

[60] *Falü changshi shouce* 法律常識手冊 (*A basic handbook on law*) (Beijing: Zhongguo qingnian chubanshe, 1979), p. 135.

In general, the Chinese commentaries emphasize again and again that the "fundamental economic interests" of the P.R.C. must be protected and that, from a political point of view, the independence and sovereignty of the P.R.C. are inalienable. Hence "all conditions which amount to enslavement"[61] are to be rejected.

Thus the political line and certain Party duality norms and political norms are the point of departure for the P.R.C. laws concerning joint ventures. Foreign technology and foreign capital are to be used as a supplementary means to realize the four modernizations on the basis of reliance upon China's own efforts.

The example of external trade illustrates how the Party political line can ultimately be reflected, by way of the increasingly more concrete stages of the Party duality norms and political norms, in the legal system, in specific governmental regulations, in the formation of state organs, as well as in structural reforms. As is the case with external trade, the enacted laws of the P.R.C. play the role of a vehicle for putting into practice Party norms, and in the final analysis for the enforcement of the prevailing Party political line in all spheres of public life. This state of affairs has been analyzed[62] by Zhang Youyu 張友漁 and Wang Shuwen 王叔文 in their book *Talks Regarding Basic Knowledge of Law*:[63]

> The written law of our state is a vehicle for putting into practice the [Party] political norms (*zhengce*). The written law of our state is promulgated on the basis of the Party political norms. . . . The continuous political and economic development and changes are reflected first of all . . . in the Party political norms. As soon as the political norms change, the legal system has to adjust. [Accordingly,] statutory law [must] be constantly repealed, revised or newly enacted. . . . To be sure, not every change in the Party political norms has to be articulated in statutory law right away. . . . As far as the enforcement of statutory law is concerned, one can comprehend the spirit and nature of the statutory law and use this instrument (*gongju*) correctly only if one understands and has a

---

[61] Li Yangju 李楊舉, "Liyong waizi tong jianchi duli zizhu zili gengsheng fangzhen you maodun ma?" 利用外資同堅持獨立自主自力更生方針有矛盾嗎？ ("Is there a contradiction between using foreign capital, and maintaining the orientation of independence, self-reliance, and developing the country by our own efforts?"), *Gongren ribao*, 11 July 1979; Ru Zhenghu 茹正湖, "Liyong waizi shi fazhan tequ de zhongyao tujing" 利用外資是發展特區的重要途徑 ("Using foreign capital is an important force for developing the special areas"), *Nanfang ribao*, 20 April 1981.

[62] Li Meihua 李美華, "Yi ben faxue rumen shu—jieshao *Faxue jiben zhishi jianghua*" 一本法學入門書——介紹法學基本知識講話 ("An introductory book on law—presenting *Talks Regarding Basic Knowledge of Law*"), *Beijing ribao*, 25 August 1980.

[63] Zhang Youyu and Wang Shuwen, *Faxue jiben zhishi jianghua* 法學基本知識講話 (*Talks regarding basic knowledge of law*), Second Edition (Beijing: Zhongguo qingnian chubanshe, 1980), pp. 74ff.

command of the Party political norms. . . . The spirit of statutory law and political norms is identical. If contradictions between statutory law and political norms arise, then the state shall repeal or revise statutory laws, or promulgate new statutory law.

Zhang Youyu and Wang Shuwen regard statutory law as "one of the most important instruments (*gongju* 工具) for the realization of Party political norms" for the following reasons:

> First of all, statutory law is more concrete in comparison with the [Party] political norms. . . . By promulgating statutory law, the state organs make concrete and articulate Party political norms. . . . In this way, it becomes easier for the masses to comprehend and follow the Party political norms. . . . Furthermore, statutory law is characterized by the fact that the state implements it compulsorily. . . . By using statutory law as an instrument (*gongju*) to suppress enemies and to exercise the dictatorship over them, it serves a useful function in the enforcement of Party political norms with regard to combatting enemies. As far as the relations among the people are concerned, the state organs enact legal promulgations in accordance with the Party political norms and publish a variety of administrative decrees bearing the stamp of compulsion which make it clear to the masses what one is supposed to do and what one is not supposed to do, how one is supposed to do something and how one is not supposed to do something. Hence statutory law is required in this respect also, namely as a means to supplement the methods of persuasion and education. Such administrative decrees serve a useful function in the enforcement of Party political norms, in strengthening leadership and discipline, ensuring regular development of production and life.

To be sure, statutory law is "not the only tool (*gongju*)" to realize the Party political norms:

> To begin with . . . not all Party political norms are necessarily given expression in written law. Whether and at what point in time Party political norms are given expression in statutory law has to be decided according to objective conditions. [For] Party political norms can be expressed in many different ways. Not only statutory law, but also resolutions (*jueding* 决定) and directives (*zhishi* 指示) by the Party, or editorials (*shelun* 社論) in the Party press can express Party political norms. These forms of transmission of Party political norms fulfil the function of appeals and signposts. The methods and forms of the enforcement of Party political norms are also manifold. As far as the masses are concerned, the various Party political norms are implemented primarily by the method of persuasion and education to kindle the enthusiasm and creativity of the masses. Compulsory implementation of Party political norms backed by statutory law is only a supplementary device.

In these translated passages only the relationship of the *zhengce* (political norms or policies) of the Party to statutory law was mentioned. But "*zhengce*" can be taken here as *pars pro toto* for Party norms as such, and in particular the Party political line, for "the political norms are closely linked to the [Party political] line and cannot be separated from it. The political norms serve the line. Only when the Party political norms are resolutely followed can the realization of the Party line be ensured."[64]

An editorial in the *Renmin ribao* of 25 February 1981 entitled "Foreign economy and trade must serve the readjustment of the national economy" emphasizes, in a somewhat condensed translation:

> The political norm that foreign capital is to be utilized in a positive and prudent manner . . . will not be revised during the period of readjustment. But it is necessary to keep a clear head when taking up foreign capital. Borrowed funds must be repaid, and that is why one has to be fully accountable with regard to economic effectiveness and one's ability to repay. If henceforth certain foreign funds are borrowed under the banner of the duality norm "Reliance in our own efforts as the basis!", the amount of the loans will have to be determined by our ability to provide additional infrastructural facilities. We can avail ourselves to a somewhat greater extent of loans granted at favourable terms at medium or low rates of interest. They are to be used especially for setting up an infrastructure in the energy and communications sectors, as well as for technical renovation of existing installations and the expansion of industries which create foreign exchange.

Thus, statutory law cannot develop a separate existence detached from the Party norms. If one asks what is legally possible in the P.R.C. under the current laws, one will only be fully informed if one takes into account the pertinent Party norms. For it is these, and not the public laws, which ultimately determine the course of events in the P.R.C.

IV. RAISING THE STATUS OF THE STATE AND OF STATUTORY LAW?

The legal order has been substantially developed and extended since the end of the Cultural Revolution, particularly since 1979, not only through the promulgation of laws, but also institutionally. During the period from September 1979 to September 1980 alone more than 100,000 new employees took up work in the courts and procuratorates throughout the country. During the same period, notarial offices handled 150,000 material transactions involving foreign countries, and the partly reorganized, partly newly established People's Arbitration Committees settled several million cases of conflict among the people. From September 1980 to August 1982 the number of legal advisory offices throughout the country rose from approximately 300 to over 2,000. Zhang Sizhi 張思之, the Vice-president of the Beijing People's Lawyers' Asso-

---

[64] "Tan tan luoshi nongcun jingji zhengce zhong de ji ge renshi wenti" 談談落實農村經濟政策中的幾個認識問題 ("On some questions regarding the implementation of economic policies for agriculture"), *Renmin ribao*, 29 July 1978.

ciation, restored in August 1979, told me on 26 September 1980 that by 1985 there were expected to be an estimated 1,000 lawyers in Beijing alone. During the half year from September 1980 to March 1981, the number of lawyers in the whole of China rose from about 2,500 to more than 3,000 and by August 1982 to almost 10,000. More than a million people were employed at this time in the politico-legal sector. Jurisprudence has experienced an unexpected boom. Four colleges of political science and law were reopened, and 16 universities established law departments, the number of law students seen as a percentage of the total number of Chinese university students increased during the 1981-82 period from 0.3% to 0.59%—according to Minister of Justice Liu Fuzhi 劉復之 a proportion which will be further increased[65]—and in 1982 a "Chinese Law Society" was founded. The "Legal Publishing Company" (Falü chubanshe 法律出版社) resumed its activities, and in March 1982 among the periodicals of the P.R.C. which were available to the public were eight legal journals and a weekly newspaper.[66] Books on law are already among the bestsellers.[67] In 1981-82 over 50 books with more than 17 million characters were edited for the teaching of law, including at secondary level. Never before had so much material for teaching law been published in the P.R.C. during such a short period of time.[68]

Are these facts indicative of a weakening of the Communist Party of China and a softening of its hitherto total claim to leadership? Are the state organs assuming more and more of the functions hitherto exercised by the Party? Is a gradual transition from the prominent role of Party norms to the "rule of law" taking place?

[65] "Dangqian guonei faxue de yixie dongxiang" 當前國內法學的一些動向 ("Some current legal trends within the country"), *Renmin ribao*, 24 January 1981.

[66] These were the quarterlies *Beijing zhengfa xueyuan xuebao* 北京政法學院學報 (Beijing), *Faxue jikan* 法學季刊 (Chongqing); the Peking journals which appear every two months, *Faxue yanjiu* 法學研究, *Faxue yicong* 法學譯叢, *Faxue zazhi* 法學雜誌, and *Waiguo faxue* 外國法學; the Shanghai monthlies *Minzhu yu fazhi* 民主與法制 and *Faxue* 法學 and the weekly *Zhongguo fazhi bao* 中國法制報. (Information provided by Wu Daying 吳大英, Professor at the Institute of Law, Chinese Academy of Social Sciences at the International Conference on Chinese Law in Vienna, 3-5 March 1982.)

[67] The book *Falü zhishi wenda* 法律知識問答 (*Questions and Answers on Legal Knowledge*) (Beijing: Beijing chubanshe 北京出版社, 1979) was published in an edition of 600,000 copies; see, "Jinkuai bianyin xin neirong xin sixiang xin yuyan de zhengzhi lilun duwu" 盡快編印新內容新思想新語言的政治理論讀物 ("Let us quickly edit theoretical materials on politics with a new content, new thought, and new vocabulary"), *Renmin ribao*, 2 March 1981.

[68] "Falü changshi" 法律常識 ("Basic knowledge of law"), in *Jiaoxue cankao* 教學參考 (*Reference materials on education*) (Beijing, 1982), p. 3; Chen Pixian 陳丕顯, "Zai faxue jiaocai zuotanhui shang de jianghua" 在法學教材座談會上的講話 ("Talk at a forum regarding teaching materials on law"), *Zhongguo fazhi bao* 中國法制報, 24 December 1982.

Indeed, a leading ideologist demanded that the Party ought to confine itself to "controlling the helm" and renounce wanting also to "take hold of the oars."[69] This is an apt characterization of the recent trend of the reorganization of relations between state and Party. These reforms take place under the banner of the "development of socialist democracy and strengthening the socialist legal system" proclaimed by the Third Plenary Session of the Eleventh CCPCC in December 1978 to be an "important aspect of the principal task during the new era."[70] Since the Fifth Plenary Session of the Eleventh CCPCC (23-29 February 1980), the Party Centre calls the "reform of the leadership system of Party and state, which is characterized by the absence of a separation of Party and government and the handling by the Party of all work actually belonging to the government (*yi dang dai zheng* 以黨代政)" "an important problem requiring urgent solution" in view of the "democratization of political life of Party and state."[71] "Improvement of socialist democracy" is regarded as an institutional problem the solution of which necessitates the reform of the political and economic structures as well as of the cadre system. But this reform in particular, like the democratization of political life of the state in general, is "not possible without the leadership of the Party," according to Feng Wenbin, vice-president of CCPCC Party School.[72] Accordingly, it will "be difficult to democratize the state as a whole if the Party is not democratized."[73]

The Statutes of the CCP of 6 September 1982 can be seen as a culmination of the efforts to date for inner-party democratization; amongst the main achievements, according to Hu Qiaomu 胡喬木, a member of the Politburo of the Central Committee of the CCP, are increased protection for the "democratic rights of Party members," the excluding of "unreasonable concentration of power in the hands of one person" and "despotism,"

[69] Li Honglin 李洪林, "Women jianchi shenmayang de dangde lingdao" 我們堅持甚麼樣的黨的領導 ("What kind of Party leadership do we support?"), *Renmin ribao*, 5 October 1979; *Women jianchi shenme?* 我們堅持甚麼? (*What do we support?*) (Beijing: Renmin chubanshe, 1981), p. 4.

[70] Liu Han 劉瀚, "Jianquan fazhi shi fazhan minzhu de baozhang" 建全法制是發展民主的保障 ("To perfect the legal system is a guarantee of democracy"), *Renmin ribao*, 3 February 1981; "Democracy and Political Stability," *Beijing Review*, No. 9, 1981, pp. 20-22.

[71] Song Zhenting, *op. cit.*; Wu Jialin 吳家麟, "Zenyang fahui quanguo Renda zuowei zui gao guojia quanli jiguan de zuoyong" 怎樣發揮全國人大作爲最高國家權力機關的作用 ("How can we develop the role of the National People's Congress as the supreme organ of state power?"), *Guangming ribao*, 30 October 1980.

[72] Feng Wenbin 馮文彬, "Guanyu shehuizhuyi minzhu wenti" 關於社會主義民主問題 ("On the problem of socialist democracy"), *Renmin ribao*, 25 November 1980.

[73] Song Zhenting, *op. cit.*

making secure the "collective leadership," banning "any kind of cult of the individual," and the abolition of party offices held for life. "All these regulations, when compared with the past, offer a better guarantee for the realization of democratic centralism within the Party."[74] This system had always been upheld officially, but evidently usually only in a form which emphasized centralism too much and the development of internal Party democracy too little.[75]

First steps towards internal Party democratization were already undertaken by the Fifth Plenum of the Eleventh CCPCC (23-29 February 1980), which passed "Guiding Principles for Inner-Party Political Life." In his report to the Twelfth Party Congress of the CCP on 1 September 1982 Hu Yaobang 胡耀邦 emphasized their continuing validity under the Party Statutes of 6 September 1982.[76] These principles provide in Section 8 for various regulations which are to ensure that all Party branches regularly hold assemblies of Party members (*dangyuan dahui* 黨員大會) which elect delegates to be sent to Party congresses (*daibiao dahui* 代表大會) which have the duty to elect the respective Party committees. The Party delegates and the members of Party committees are to be selected regularly in secret ballots, in which the number of candidates is to exceed that of the allocated seats.[77] Up to January 1981 Party congresses had been held in more than 700 counties, cities, and administrative regions, which elected new Party committees in accordance with these regulations. On these occasions the plurality of offices and the age of office-holders are said to have been reduced. In Shanghai various Party organizations have established "institutions for democratic life."[78] Different opinions on important questions can also be voiced in the press within the framework of so-called "discussions" (*taolun* 討論), which are, however, supervised by the Party centre.[79] The public self-criticism in the ranks of the Party of its leadership—which had hitherto been taken for granted—can be taken as another sign of nascent democratization inside the Party.

[74] "Hu Qiaomu tongzhi jiu dangzhang xiugai wenti da Xinhuashe jizhe wen" 胡喬木 同志就黨章修改問題答新華社記者問 ("Comrade Hu Qiaomu replies to a Xinhua reporter regarding revision of the Party statutes"), *Renmin ribao*, 14 September 1982.

[75] Feng Wenbin, *op. cit.*; *Dang de jiben zhishi* 黨的基本知識 (*Basic knowledge regarding the Party*) (Beijing: Renmin chubanshe, 1979), pp. 45ff.

[76] Hu Yaobang, *Beijing Review*, No. 37, 1982, p. 27.

[77] "Guanyu dangnei zhengzhi shenghuo de ruogan zhunze" 關於黨內政治生活的若干 準則 ("Some norms regarding inner-Party political life"), *Hongqi*, No. 6, 1980, pp. 2-11.

[78] "Shi jingwei xitong jueda duoshu danwei dang de lingdao banzi jianli le minzhu shenghuo zhidu" 市經委系統絕大多數單位黨的領導班子建立了民主生活制度 ("The leading Party groups in the majority of units in the system of municipal economic committees have established a system of democratic life"), *Jiefang ribao*, 26 March 1981.

[79] See, for example, the norms published in *Gongren ribao*, 15 March 1980.

Thus Teng Wensheng and Jia Chunfeng in the *Renmin ribao* of 14 November 1980, criticize the fact that the "centralization and uniformity" (*jizhong tongyi* 集中統一) to be striven for by the Party, on the one hand, and the struggle against "dispersionism" (*fensanzhuyi* 分散主義) as well as against the insistence on the independence of local, subordinate and state organs, on the other, had often been overemphasized in the past. Adherence to the tendency towards concentration of all power within the pale of the Party, particularly the power in the governmental and economic sphere, is now regarded as outdated and impracticable in view of the new duties which face the Party.[80] Chen Jinyu writes in this respect in the *Jiefang ribao*, the official organ of the CCP Party committee of Shanghai Municipality, on 9 April 1981, *inter alia*:

> The present task of the Party is leading a thousand million people in the construction of the four modernizations. The Party must no longer direct just military undertakings, but also domestic and foreign, economic and cultural affairs. If we continue rigidly to apply the old method of integrated [*yiyuanhua* 一元化 ; see the analysis of this concept in the contribution by Stuart R. Schram] leadership in this situation and concentrate in an incongruous manner all power in the Party committees, and if in addition the powers of the Party committees are combined in the person of one [Party] secretary or two [Party] secretaries, then this leads to a negation of the indispensable social division of labour and to a disregard for and undermining of the powers vested in the Government, the enterprises and the mass organizations. This will in effect inevitably weaken the leadership of the Party. For the Party is not in a position to handle absolutely everything alone.
>
> The system of collective leadership is obviously becoming more and more important. In the wake of the constantly expanding scope of the development of our country's economy, our economic work has become much more complicated than in the 1950s. The knowledge and experience of one single person or a few persons cannot cope with one single important economic decision.[81]

The above-mentioned commentators Teng Wensheng and Jia Chunfeng write on this problem:

> In the past action was rarely taken against the excessive concentration of power in [the hands of] individuals. ... If all power is monopolized by the Party committees, then the lack of division of Party and Government is the inescapable consequence. ... The concentration of all power in the Party committees is the

---

[80] Teng Wensheng 騰文生 , Jia Chunfeng 賈春峰, "Quanli bu neng guofen jizhong" 權力不能過分集中 ("Power cannot be concentrated to excess"), *Renmin ribao*, 14 November 1980.

[81] Chen Jinyu 陳進玉, "Guanyu jianchi dang de lingdao de ji ge wenti" 關於堅持黨的領導的幾個問題 ("On some problems in maintaining Party leadership"), *Jiefang ribao*, 9 April 1981; "Lun dang zheng fengong" 論黨政分工 ("On division of labour between Party and state"), *Renmin ribao*, 18 December 1980. The *yiyuanhua* leadership of the Party is also criticized by Jing Dong 京東, "Bu neng yi dang dai zheng" 不能以黨代政 ("The Party must not replace the state"), *Hongqi*, No. 21, 1980.

basic reason why the Government is neutralized by the Party and the Party committees take charge of everything. The inevitable result is that the Party committees at all levels get mixed up in a tangle of administrative routine work. As a
consequence, the affairs which really need to be tackled by the Party committees
are left unattended to or are entirely neglected. But this represents a weakening of
the leadership of the Party.[82]

As a result of such considerations, Party Centre advocates that the Party
organizations at all levels transfer, if possible, a large part of the administrative
and technical routine work to the governments at all levels and the specialized
organs, and that the most important Party leaders should generally no longer
assume government offices:

> From top to bottom a powerful and efficient government structure must be built
> up and a system of division of labour between Party and government (*dang zheng
> fengong*) introduced so that the functions of the organs of government can fully
> develop.[83]

In future all business falling within government jurisdiction is to be discussed and decided on by the State Council and/or the people's governments
at all levels without having to wait for directives from Party Centre or the
Party committees at the respective levels. The independence of the judiciary
is to be preserved insofar as the courts are to be able to pass judgements
independently.[84] The abolition of the prevailing practice of examination and
approval of court decisions by the competent Party committee was announced
by the President of the Supreme People's Court, Jiang Hua, at the working
conference on the enforcement of punishment in August 1980.[85] (In the
recent campaign against crime of 1983-84, this prohibition was, of course,
scarcely been observed.)

The Party is no longer to give direct orders but only "recommendations"
(*jianyi* 建議) to non-Party organizations, i.e. state and administrative organs,
economic and financial organizations, organizations in the realm of education,
science and culture, as well as mass organizations.[86] "Recommendations"
from Party Centre to the National People's Congress are no longer to be
regarded as "legally binding, as it were" even before their approval by the

[82] Teng Wensheng, Jia Chunfeng, *op. cit.*

[83] Feng Wenbin, *op. cit.*

[84] *Ibid.*

[85] Jiang Hua 江華, "Baozheng renmin fayuan yi fa duli shenpan, quxiao dangwei shen-
pi anjian de xiguan zuofa" 保證人民法院依法獨立審判，取消黨委審批案件的習慣做法
("Guarantee the independent decision of cases by the courts in accordance with the law,
eliminate the usual practice of the Party committee examining and approving [decisions
on] cases"), *Gongren ribao*, 25 August 1980.

[86] Feng Wenbin, *op. cit.*

NPC, as was hitherto the case. On the whole, the National People's Congress, which "in years . . . gone by did not really exercise the function of the highest organ of state power even during the periods of its regular activity," is to be upgraded. Thus it happened for the first time at the Third session of the Fifth NPC (30 August-10 September 1980) that deputies, contrary to the prevailing practice, "openly voiced their opinions," criticized the government report, abstained from voting, put through amendments to certain drafts of bills, and exercised their right to question the state organs.

> This indicates that the National People's Congress is really beginning to exercise the highest power in the state and no longer fulfills merely the function of a "voting machine," as was the case in the past.[87]

But in some respects concrete institutions for the realization of the principle of "socialist democracy" are lacking, and that is why it

> more often than not exists in form only which hides the fact that in deed and truth only a small minority has the say. Although deputies of people's congresses and leading members of governments [at all levels] are nominally elected, in reality the voters cannot sufficiently express their intentions and cannot supervise their representatives and leaders, let alone remove them from office.[88]

A change of the electoral system is, therefore, foremost on the list of proposed reforms of the political structures. Direct elections of deputies to people's congresses from the lowest level to county level have already been introduced. But it will not stop there. On the contrary, the gradual introduction of direct elections is demanded also for the higher levels, with the possibility of choosing from several candidates. The idea of admitting a real opposition party is, however, dismissed.

The role of statutory law is being reconsidered. At the time of the Cultural Revolution its function as an instrument to exercise the "dictatorship over the class enemy" was exclusively stressed. Consequently, everyone associated statutory law with criminal law, and legal proceedings with penal suits, as I discovered in the year before Mao's death. The result was "the misconception that the legal system had not much to do with democracy." Statutory law is to be utilized as an instrument to replace the method of political campaigns or movements (*zhengzhi yundong* 政治運動) which was practised to excess particularly during the Cultural Revolution; however, non-political mass movements, for instance in the area of hygiene and environmental protection, will still be launched. In future, "the class struggle to be waged within definite limits against the activities of counter-revolutionaries and criminals" will also

[87]Wu Jialin, *op. cit.*
[88]Feng Wenbin, *op. cit.*

be carried out with statutory instruments.[89] Constitution and laws are to be binding not only upon the masses, but also upon the Party organizations and their leaders; likewise the resolutions of the "organs of the people's power," i.e., the people's government at all levels.[90] According to the Statutes of the CCP of 6 September 1982: "The Party must conduct its activities within the limits permitted by the Constitution and the laws of the state" (General Programme, last paragraph), and according to the Constitution of the P.R.C. of 4 December 1982, "all political parties," and thus the CCP too, must "take the Constitution as the basic norm of conduct." "They all have the duty to uphold the dignity of the Constitution and ensure its implementation" (Preamble, last sentence), and to "abide by the Constitution and the law" (Article 5, para. 3). The Party "has to learn to exercise leadership in the factories, peasant villages, in science, culture, and education, as well as in all areas of leadership by applying democratic and statutory principles, methods and procedure." In this way "the leadership of the Party will be raised to a new level."[91]

The revaluation of the state and the written laws of the state, initiated by Party Centre itself, is not designed to weaken Party leadership, but on the contrary to strengthen it by concentrating on essentials. But what is the quintessence of Party leadership?

> Certain comrades . . . do not understand what "Party leadership" means. They . . . think that the Party committee has to decide everything, whether important or minute, and that in addition the first, and possibly at most the second man on the Party committee has to nod his head himself.[92]

But in reality, "Party leadership over the state and the undertakings of socialism is political leadership"; at the same time "political leadership" does not mean "administrative, technical, professional or organizational leadership," but "leadership in the line, the duality norms and the [Party] political norms."[93]

The political leadership exercised by the Party means "very strict supervision and control of Party members working in . . . non-Party organizations. The Party committees can issue directives directly to them. Party members are bound by them: their observance is ensured through Party discipline."[94]

---

[89] Wang Guiwu 王桂五 , "Xuehui shiyong falü wuqi" 學會使用法律武器 ("Learn to use the weapon of the law"), *Renmin ribao*, 10 March 1981.

[90] Feng Wenbin, *op. cit.*; Liu Qilin 劉啓林 , "Liyi yu li ji" 利益與利己 ("Interest and self-interest"), *Beijing ribao*, 30 March 1981.

[91] Song Zhenting, *op. cit.*

[92] Chen Jinyu, *op. cit.*

[93] Editorial cited, *Renmin ribao*, 18 December 1980.

[94] Song Zhenting, *op. cit.*

At the end of 1979 there were 1,940,000 Party branches at the basic level alone.[95] Admittedly, the Party organs which exist everywhere must ensure "that the organs of political power, the administrative organs and the judicial organs can fully exercise their [specific] functions and powers."

But this means in effect that all state organs and economic and financial organs, as well as organizations in the sphere of education, science and culture including mass organizations, "carry out their work under the correct leadership of the line, the duality norms and the political norms of the Party in an independent, orderly effective manner, and in co-ordination with one another."[96]

The Party thus does not want to relinquish, but merely refine and rationalize its leadership position. The main force is to be engaged, as it were, to steer the ship. But for the ship's maintenance and operation auxiliary forces are employed. As much as possible of the enforcement work is to be delegated to them. Jiang Hua, the President of the Supreme People's Court of the P.R.C., said to this effect:

> The Party committees must strengthen the leadership over the political and judicial departments. It is primarily a question here of strengthening leadership through implementation of the line, duality and political norms. It is not a question of Party committees examining and ruling on concrete judgements in law suits.[97]

Of course, individual judges, insofar as they are Party members, remain bound by the Party norms and are obliged to expound and administer the laws according to the spirit of these norms when passing judgement. The implementation of Party norms is ensured not only in the courts but in all non-Party organs and organizations so long as Party members hold the key positions. Now as before the Party's aim is that the Party branches and Party members should "unite and guide the masses in the various non-Party organizations."[98]

This is the case not only at the national but at the regional level. Thus Ren Zhongyi, first secretary of the CCP Party Committee of Guangdong Province, stated in his capacity as Deputy to the People's Congress on 4 March 1981 at the final meeting of the Third session of the Fifth People's Congress of Guangdong Province:

[95] *Dang de jiben zhishi*, p. 47.

[96] Feng Wenbin, *op. cit.*; Ma Ye 馬野, Yan Ganwu 鄢淦五, Wei Bingkun 魏炳坤, "Jingji zhongxin, jingji lianheti, qiye—wo guo jingji zuzhi jiegou tantao" 經濟中心、經濟聯合體、企業—我國經濟組織結構探討 ("Economic centre, economic combine, enterprise—an investigation of the organization and structure of China's economy"), *Tianjin ribao*, 7 January 1981.

[97] Article cited, *Gongren ribao*, 25 August 1980.

[98] Feng Wenbin, *op. cit.*

The Provincial Party Committee must not exercise the functions and powers of the [provincial] people's congress in place of the latter, and it must not assume the official functions of the provincial government. The Party organization must expend all its energy on doing a good job in internal Party work, to do a good job in political and ideological work and to ensure the implementation of the Party's line, duality norms and political norms.[99]

Thus the democratization and legalization of life in the P.R.C. remain within the broad limits which in the last resort are set by the political leadership of the CCP.[100] This leadership manifests itself concretely in the promulgation, implementation and continuous adaptation of the political line, the duality norms and the political norms of the Party. The question arises, of course, whether the controlled upgrading of the state and the legal system presently aimed at by the Party might not suddenly slip from its control. By campaigning against bourgeois liberalization[101] as well as against the adoption of Western democracy,[102] castigating "illegal organizations and writings"[103] and "a small minority of persons" who want to overturn the Party leadership,[104] the Chinese press admits that tendencies are afoot which threaten the position of the Party. However, as long as the Party is able to preserve its internal unity and command over the army,[105] its position should be strong enough to check at any time any stirrings of independence by the state and the legal system. To be sure, as long as the statutory laws which the Party wants are in force, the Party will wish to abide by them. But this intention does not undermine the position of Party Centre as the supreme normative body. Whenever deemed necessary, Party Centre has the means and ways to adjust the existing laws. "The [adoption] of

[99] Ren Zhongyi 任仲夷 , "Guangdong sheng wu jie Renda di-san ci huiyi shengli bimu" 廣東省五屆人大第三次會議勝利閉幕 ("The Third Session of the Fifth Guangdong Provincial People's Congress has victoriously drawn to a close"), *Nanfang ribao*, 5 March 1981.

[100] Among many articles, see Man Yu 漫與, "Jianchi si xiang jiben yuanze hui fang'ai jiefang sixiang ma?" 堅持四項基本原則會妨礙解放思想嗎？ ("Can adherence to the four basic principles inhibit the emancipation of thought?"), *Tianjin ribao*, 17 February 1981.

[101] "Guchui zichanjieji ziyouhua jue bu shi jiefang sixiang he jianchi si xiang jiben yuanze" 鼓吹資產階級自由化決不是解放思想和堅持四項基本原則 ("Promoting bourgeois liberalization is assuredly not liberating thought, nor is it adhesion to the four basic principles"), *Beijing ribao*, 27 February 1981.

[102] "Jianchi minzhuhua de shehuizhuyi fangxiang" 堅持民主化的社會主義方向 ("Maintaining the socialist orientation of democratization"), *Gongren ribao*, 30 March 1981.

[103] "Zhuahao ganbu jiaoyu" 抓好幹部教育 ("Grasp well the training of cadres"), *Jiefang ribao*, 21 February 1981.

[104] Liu Han, *op. cit.*

[105] See Yang Dezhi 楊得志 , "Jianding bu yi di jianchi dang dui jundui de juedui lingdao" 堅定不移地堅持黨對軍隊的絕對領導 ("Assert without wavering the absolute leadership of the Party over the army"), *Renmin ribao*, 5 July 1981.

our Constitution and laws is effected in every instance under the leadership of the Party, and is in truth and deed a matter of paragraphing, concretising and making into laws the [line], duality and political norms of the Party."[106]

Nobody prevented the Eleventh CCPCC from voting at its Fifth Plenary Session (23-29 February 1980) on a "suggestion" (*jianyi*) which was directed to the National People's Congress, according to which the "four great conquests" guaranteed in Article 45 of the Constitution of the P.R.C. of 5 March 1978, namely the right of citizens to air views freely, speak out freely, engage in great debates, and affix big-character posters, were to be deleted.[107] The Fifth NPC did, indeed, approve the desired deletion at its Third session of 10 September 1980, and in the final analysis on the grounds that the rejected constitutional provision stood in the way of the unimpeded continuation of "socialist modernization," *inter alia* because it "has given a small number of class enemies and persons with perfidious intentions legal grounds to engineer incidents and oppose the socialist system and the leadership of the Communist Party."[108]

If the relationship between the Party Centre and the National People's Congress, between Party norms and statutory law should ever be reversed, then that would have to be called a basic change in the system, but such does not at all seem to be the intention of Party Centre at the present time. The Party Centre remains the supreme body with the highest normative powers which can be exercised at any time; *de facto* it controls itself, and is beyond institutionalized control by the people as a whole, renewing itself by cooption. It is highly unlikely that serious opposition to this power structure could arise from the masses in the foreseeable future. Even *Renmin ribao*, the official organ of the CCPCC, publishes analyses which rate the P.R.C. as a country that has experienced "several thousand years of feudal despotism" (*fengjian zhuanzhi tongzhi* 封建專制統治), but never an efficiently operating bourgeois-democratic republic,[109] is lacking in democratic traditions and has

[106] "Dang weishenme bixu zai xianfa he falü de fanwei nei huodong?" 黨爲甚麼必須在憲法和法律的範圍內活動?("Why must the Party act within the limits of the Constitution and the laws?"), *Gongren ribao*, 27 October 1982, p. 3.

[107] "Jianchi dang de lingdao, gaishan dang de lingdao, tigao dang de lingdao" 堅持黨的領導，改善黨的領導，提高黨的領導 ("Maintain, improve, and raise the level of leadership by the Party"), *Renmin ribao*, 1 March 1980.

[108] "Guanyu xiugai 'Zhonghua Renmin Gongheguo xianfa' di sishiwu tiao de jueyi" 關於修改'中華人民共和國憲法' 第四十五條的決議 ("Decision regarding the revision of Article 45 of the Constitution of the People's Republic of China"), *Renmin ribao*, 11 September 1980.

[109] Lin Chun 林春, Li Yinhe 李銀河, "Yao da da fayang minzhu he jiaqiang fazhi" 要大大發揚民主和加强法制 ("We must develop democracy and strengthen the rule of law in a big way"), *Renmin ribao*, 13 November 1978.

a poorly developed awareness of the legal system. Indeed, the heritage from the past rests so heavily on modern China that concern is voiced even with regard to the implementation of the official ideal of democracy guided by the Party within the framework of enlightened socialism.[110]

V. ON HISTORICAL CONTINUITY

The most basic decision taken by the Party Centre with regard to the course, that is the definition of the respective principal task during a specific stage of development of Chinese society, is generally expressed by the term "political line," but often simply "line" (*luxian* 路線). But the word "line" appears also in connection with guiding principles such as "ideological line," "organizational line," "general line," "basic line." The Party Centre also determines, for example, the "foreign policy line," the "line for physical education and sport," the "line for literature and art," the "line for work in the area of public safety," the "line for industry and communications," and so forth. An analysis of these various types of lines, which cannot be reconstructed here in detail, reveals that the term line is used not so much as a uniformly understood technical term, but as a label for various kinds of basic guiding principles.

Marcel Granet suggested long ago, with reference to old China, that the Chinese "prefer richly evocative symbols to clearly defined concepts."[111] The expression *luxian*—originally route, way; but later, line[112]—may have such a symbolic value, perhaps because it is instinctively associated with "*dao*" (道) of which the primary meaning is also: way.[113] But *dao* in the sense of a "supremely effective principle of order" was one of the leading concepts in traditional China.[114] The modern combination *daolu* (道路)—"road"— with the character "*dao*"—is in fact used in the P.R.C. to define fundamental orientations such as in the differentiation between the "socialist road" and the "capitalist road." Thus the first of the "four basic principles" laid down by the Party Centre in the spring of 1979 reads: "Hold fast to the socialist road."

Implementation of the present political line of the Party is to be secured

[110] "Dang he guojia lingdao zhidu de yi xiang zhongyao gaige" 黨和國家領導制度的一項重要改革 ("An important reform in the leadership system of the Party and the state"), *Renmin ribao*, 28 October 1980; Liu Han, *op. cit.*

[111] Marcel Granet, *La pensée chinoise* (Paris: La Renaissance du livre, 1934), p. 147.

[112] Morohashi Tetsuji 諸橋轍次, *Dai Kan-Wa jiten* 大漢和辭典 Vol. 10 (Tokyo: Taishūkan 大修館書店 , 1959), p. 11360, character no. 37524, pars. 63 and 64.

[113] Granet, *op. cit.*, p. 303.

[114] Granet, *op. cit.*, p. 301.

largely by statutory law as determined by the Party Centre. This endeavour is probably less an indication of a shift toward the Western concept of the "rule of law" than a swing of the pendulum from "personal rule" (*renzhi* 人治) toward "rule by law" (*fazhi* 法治) in the traditional Chinese sense: "For a long time we have set a high value on personal rule and disregarded rule by law."[115]

"Personal rule" and "rule by law" are two poles between which political thinking moved back and forth during the Spring and Autumn period and during the Warring States period (eighth-third centuries B.C.), and likewise in the P.R.C. during the first thirty years of her existence. In his article "Personal rule and rule by law" in *Renmin ribao* of 26 January 1979, Wang Liming characterizes "personal rule" by way of a quotation from the *Doctrine of the Mean* (*Zhongyong* 中庸), Ch. 20, "So long as a man lives, his policies are maintained, but when he dies, his policies come to an end."[116]

The old Chinese concept of "rule by law" saw the laws merely as an instrument to exercise control and mobilize the people for endeavours of the court. A quotation from the *Guanzi*管子, which has been attributed to the Legalist Guan Zhong 管仲 (died 645 B.C.), may illustrate this point:

> The law must give the court authority. . . .
>
> The law must mobilize the working capacity of the people [for the benefit of the court]. . . . The law must mobilize the talents among the people [for the benefit of the court]. . . . The law must urge the people to give their lives [for the court].[117]

Does this reasoning not resemble the following statements on the significance of the socialist democracy which is to be consolidated through the socialist legal system?

> Only when people's democracy is developed, can the sense of responsibility of the broad masses be strengthened, their enthusiasm and creativeness stimulated and the process of the four modernizations advanced.[118]

In July 1979 Peng Zhen, one of the Vice-Chairmen of the Standing Committee of the NPC, and since the end of September 1979 member of the Politburo of the CCPCC, touched upon the meaning of the concept of the "rule by law": "Are the laws greater or is any leading person greater? The laws are greater!"[119]

---

[115] Feng Wenbin, *op. cit.*

[116] Wang Liming 王禮明 , "Renzhi he fazhi" 人治和法治 ("Personal rule and rule by law"), *Renmin ribao*, 26 January 1979; *The Doctrine of the Mean*, 20.2.

[117] *Guanzi*, I.3.19-20.

[118] "Jianchi minzhuhua de shehuizhuyi fangxiang" 堅持民主化的社會主義方向 ("Grasp firmly the socialist orientation of democratization"), *Gongren ribao*, 20 January 1981.

[119] "Jianquan he jiaqiang fazhi baozhang shehuizhuyi xiandaihua jianshe shunli

The revaluation of statutory law taking place at the present time stems from the awareness of the weakness inherent in the Party norms: they remain all too often rooted in the fundamentally abstract and can be interpreted quite differently in a concrete case, depending on the Party cadre who is applying them. The ambiguity of many a Party norm is illustrated by the example of some political norms drawn up by the Party for the penal system:

> Suppression on the one hand is to be combined with leniency on the other!
> The principal offenders are to be punished, but not the followers!
> Magnanimity towards those admitting guilt, severity towards the obstinate!
> Offset mistakes against merits, give rewards for great merits![120]

That such loosely worded political norms without additional casuistic arrangements in the form of statutory law did not ensure an orderly penal system, has been observed by Gu Chunde:

> Our Party has established a number of political norms for the penal system which fulfill a mighty function. But they are not capable of solving completely certain relatively concrete problems such as the question of guilt, determination of punishment etc. For some time the line between wrongful and non-wrongful behaviour has been vague, the definition of crimes not uniform, abnormally light and abnormally heavy sentences are passed. Persons who ought to be prosecuted are let go, and by the same token others who ought to be protected are roughed up. This is very closely linked to the absence of a relatively comprehensive, reliable criminal law and law of criminal procedure. . . . Many years of judicial practice prove that the Party line, duality and political norms alone without statutory law are not enough.[121]

Wang Liming generalizes these thoughts in his above-mentioned essay on "Personal Rule and Rule by Law":

> What a man can accomplish on the basis of a high degree of consciousness can never be achieved by reliance on laws alone. But the level of human consciousness will always be extremely uneven. This unevenness can be evened out by statutory

jinxing" 健全和加强法制保障社會主義現代化建設順利進行 ("The further elaboration and consolidation of the legal system will guarantee the successful progress of socialist modernization"), *Nanfang ribao*, 29 July 1979.

[120] Jiang Hua 江華, "Shishi xin xianfa shi renmin fayuan de guangrong zhize" 實施新憲法是人民法院的光榮職責 ("To apply the new Constitution is the glorious duty of the courts") *Renmin ribao*, 23 May 1978; *Cihai, Zhengzhi falü* (Shanghai, 1961), p. 73; revised edition (Shanghai, 1978), p. 152.

[121] Gu Chunde 谷春德, "You le zhengce hai bixu you fa" 有了政策還必須有法 ("Even though there is a policy, there must also be a law"), *Renmin ribao*, 7 November 1978; Xu Bing 許炳 puts forward similar thoughts on the relationship between nationality political norms of the Party and nationality laws: "Yingdang zhongshi minzu lifa" 應當重視民族立法 ("We must attach importance to adopting laws about nationalities"), *Minzhu yu fazhi*, No. 11, 1982, p. 9.

law. For it ensures the general dissemination and consolidation of certain correct actions.[122]

The development of the naturally casuistic statutory law in the P.R.C. is thus turning against "personal rule" and is to undermine the tendency toward arbitrariness in pursuance of mere Party norms resulting therefrom. Only in this way can an order based on stability and unity be establised and consolidated, which is in turn indispensable to realize the principal task outlined by the present political line of the Party, "Chinese-style modernization."[123] To be sure, within the framework of the present command structure the Party Centre retains its sovereignty relating to the revision or reformulation of Party norms at all times, which virtually always affects statutory law as well. For it is not a question of bringing Party norms into line with the laws of the state, but with the "objective inherent laws" (*keguan guilü* 客觀規律) operative in the concrete development of all spheres of Chinese society, the recognition of which by the Party Centre is itself a continuous process:

> Certain concrete political norms and provisions of the Party are continuously supplemented, improved, developed in the course of practical experience. The reason why the Party political norms are correct is that they reflect the inherent laws (*guilü* 規律) of the development of things and that they are in keeping with the conditions of objective reality.[124]

With all the emphasis on the concept of "rule by law," there remains nevertheless a trace of the old traditional personal rule at the apex of the Party hierarchy and hence ultimately also of the Chinese state, a fact which the *Spring and Autumn Annals*, attributed to Lü Büwei 呂不韋 (died 235 B.C.), expresses as follows with regard to the old China: "The wise ruler revises the laws in accordance with conditions changing over time."[125]

[122] Wang Liming, *op. cit.*
[123] Liu Guangdi, "Why Is China Striving to Wipe Out Its Deficit?" *Beijing Review*, No. 15, 1981, p. 22.
[124] Liu Peng 劉鵬, " 'Zhengce duo bian' xi" '政策多變' 析 ("An analysis of 'policies changing all the time' "), *Guangming ribao*, 28 March 1981. On the primacy of "objective laws," see Yang Xianzhen 楊獻珍, "Jianchi zhexue genben wenti yuanli, xuehao zhongyang gongzuo huiyi wenjian" 堅持哲學根本問題原理，學好中央工作會議文件 ("Uphold principle regarding the basic questions of philosophy, study well the documents of the Centre's work conference"), *Guangming ribao*, 2 March 1981; Li Honglin 李洪林, "Xinyang weiji' shuoming le shenme?" '信仰危機' 說明了甚麼？ ("What does the 'crisis of faith' signify?"), *Renmin ribao*, 11 November 1980; Yue Yunlong 岳雲龍, "Diaocha yanjiu he zhiding zhengce" 調查研究和制定政策 ("Carry out investigations and research, then establish policies"), *Guangming ribao*, 9 July 1981.
[125] *Lü Shi Chunqiu* 呂氏春秋, 15.3.

It is noticeable in this connection that the abstract norm established by the state or by the Party is evidently not able on its own to appeal to the mass of people in the P.R.C. On the contrary, a person is required who gives an exemplary demonstration of the observance of the abstract norm as a concrete model. The belief in the power of the physical example, likewise an element of "personal rule," is expressed in the Chinese press in sentences such as these:

> The power of the model is unlimited.[126]

> The model has the greatest possible persuasive power.[127]

> Setting an example is better than talking.[128]

Did not Confucius say to his contemporaries:

> If you [addressing Ji Kangzi 季康子, a high official in the state of Lu] begin by setting yourself right, who will dare to deviate from the right?[129]

And:

> The virtue of the gentleman may be compared to the wind and that of the commoner to the weeds. The weeds under the force of the wind cannot but bend.

Of course, today it is no longer the "gentleman" (*junzi* 君子) in the Confucian sense who, from on high, "blows over the weeds," thanks to his inherent virtue. Today this role devolves upon the members of the CCP:

> Stalin coined the famous remark: "We, the members of the Communist Party are people with a special nature, we have been made of a different stamp." Why does the Communist become a special person? Precisely because nothing is special about him, because he remains at all times a member of the working class, a member of the working population, because he keeps in mind at all times the well-being of the working class and the whole people, because he does not claim any privileges and does not pursue his own private interests. When we circulate slogans such as "Completely selfless, committed only to the common good!", "The common good before self-interest!", "First to endure hardships!", then it relates above all to demands directed at Party members and Party cadres. Only when Party mem-

---

[126]Yan Qiuzhi 嚴求實, "Sixiang zhengzhi gongzuo shi yi men kexue" 思想政治工作是一門科學 ("Ideological and political work is a science"), *Guangming ribao*, 11 August 1980.

[127]"Tiaozheng nongye neibu bili, fazhan duozhong jingying" 調整農業內部比例，發展多種經營 ("Adjust the proportions within agriculture, develop a diversified economy"), *Renmin ribao*, 17 July 1979.

[128]"Dakai sixiang zhengzhi gongzuo de xin jumian" 打開思想政治工作的新局面 ("Open the way to a new situation in ideological and political work"), *Renmin ribao*, 24 April 1979.

[129]*Analects*, 12.17.

bers and Party cadres lead the way by their personal example, can the broad masses be united and swept along to put up a hard fight full of hardships.[130]

To be sure, without further action, the Party member is no more a "person with a special nature" than formerly the "gentleman." Just as the "gentleman" had to cultivate himself on the basis of the Rites, certain norms have been drawn up for this purpose especially for Party members: "The state has statutory laws at its disposal, the Party has Party discipline at its disposal."[131]

Since the Fifth Plenary Session of the Eleventh CCPCC (23-29 February 1980) the "Guiding Principles for Inner-Party Political Life" have been added to the rules of Party discipline. This "important law of the Party"[132] is supplemented by the "Regulations concerning the Life-Style of Important Cadres."[133] In a similar fashion, there existed for example during the Tang period (seventh-tenth centuries A.D.) a code of rituals for the emperor and the bureaucracy; it was officially published in A.D. 732 by the same state authority which promulgated state law, in 150 volumes.[134] The question concerning the role of rites in the overall structure of the norms for societal control in traditional China has recently been examined by Karl Bünger.[135] It suffices here to say that the rites, especially from the Tang period, were further developed in the form of ritual codes promulgated by the state, but without having lost any of their spiritual substance grounded in the Confucian books of rites—the *Yili* 儀禮, the *Zhouli* 周禮, and the *Liji* 禮記—which contained the notion that exemplary external behaviour was a manifes-

[130] "Zhenzuo jingshen zhua gongzuo, xiading juexin dang mofan" 振作精神抓工作, 下定決心當模範 ("Raise our spirits, grasp the work, adopt a resolute attitude, and act as models"), *Renmin ribao*, 14 February 1981.
[131] Li Liguang 李黎光, " 'Weihu' jiu shi yi fa banshi" '維護' 就是依法辦事 (" 'To protect' means dealing with matters according to law"), *Gongren ribao*, 8 April 1981.
[132] "Guanyu dangnei zhengzhi shenghuo de ruogan zhunze" 關於黨內政治生活的若干準則 ("Some norms for political life within the Party"), *Gongren ribao*, 15 March 1980.
[133] "Guanyu gaoji ganbu shenghuo daiyu de ruogan guiding" 關於高級幹部生活待遇的若干規定 ("Some regulations for dealing with the lives of high-level cadres"), evoked by Deng Yingqiao 鄧穎超, "Jianding bu yi de gaohao dangfeng" 堅定不移地搞好黨風 ("Improve Party style resolutely and consistently") *Beijing ribao*, 29 March 1981.
[134] *Da Tang Kaiyuan Li* 大唐開元禮 published by Tōkyō Daigaku Tōyō Bunka kenyūsho 東京大學東洋文化研究所, Tokyo, 1972, p. 823. The term "code of rituals," was approved by Professor Shiga Shūzō 滋賀秀三 of the Faculty of Law, Tokyo University, in a discussion with the author in October 1980.
[135] Karl Bünger, "Die normativen Ordnungen in China und ihr Verhältnis zueinander," *Ostasienwissenschaftliche Beiträge zur Sprache, Literatur, Geschichte, Geistesgeschichte, Wirtschaft, Politik und Geographie* (Wiesbaden, 1977), pp. 169-80.

tation of a specific inner moral attitude.[136] This would appear to be a point of contact between the rites and the CCP inner-Party norms imprinted on the mind with the aid of "political-ideological work" (*zhengzhi sixiang gongzuo* 政治思想工作), which in contrast to statutory law do not merely guide external behaviour but in addition want to shape the inner person with his "style of thought and work" (*sixiang gongzuo zuofeng* 思想工作作風):

> To act as a model with a resolute heart means working according to the "Guiding Principles for Inner-Party Political Life," to set right the style of thought and work inside the Party and truly fulfill the function of a pioneering model.[137]

For the following consideration applies:

> The Party now has a correct line, correct duality and political norms. The problem now concerns safeguarding that good [thought-, work-, political and life-] style which ensures the implementation [of these party norms].[138] If the style of work of the Party cadres is not correct, how can they play that exemplary role with which they induce and guide the broad masses to carry out the Party line?[139]

Members of the top strata subject to the rituals were not treated in the same way before the law as the common people.[140] The basis for this was the system of the "Eight Considerations," grounded in the Confucian classic *Zhouli*, which procured to eight groups of members of the social elite a reduction or remission of punishment *inter alia* for great service to the dynasty.[141] Likewise, fallible acts by Party members are often not punished by the state courts, but first of all by inner-Party disciplinary control committees that

---

[136] R. P. Kramers, *Konfuzius—Chinas entthronter Heiliger*? (Bern: Verlag Peter Lang, 1979), p. 71; Li Jiafu 李甲孚 , *Zhongguo fazhi shi* 中國法制史 (*History of Chinese Legal Institutions*) (Taibei: Pan Jingyi 潘靜儀 , 1980), p. 338; Chen Chaobi 陳朝璧 , "Zhongguo faxi tedian chutan" 中國法系特點初談 ("Some preliminary remarks on the peculiarities of China's legal system"), *Faxue yanjiu*, No. 1, 1980, p. 52.

[137] Editorial cited, *Renmin ribao*, 14 February 1981.

[138] According to Huang Kecheng's 黃克誠 definition of the term "*dangfeng*" (黨風 "Party style") in *Renmin ribao*, 28 February 1981.

[139] "Dangfeng wenti shi youguan dang de shengsi cunwang de wenti" 黨風問題是有關黨的生死存亡的問題 ("The problem of Party style is a matter of life and death, survival or oblivion for the Party"), *Renmin ribao* editorial, 9 March 1981.

[140] Shiga Shūzō, *Yakuchu Nihon ritsu-ryo* (5), *To-ritsu sogi* 譯注日本律令、五 · 唐律疏議 (*Annotated Translations of the Japanese Penal and Administrative Codes, Part 5, Tang* (Tokyo: Tōkyōdō shuppan, 1979), 1.65.

[141] "Ba yi" 八議, in *Zhongguo gudai ban'an bai li* 中國古代辦案百例 (*A hundred examples of cases from ancient China*) (Beijing: Zhongguo shehui kexue chubanshe 中國社會科學出版社, 1980), p. 40; Chen Yishi 陳一石 , " 'Li bu xia shuren, xing bu shang daifu' bian" '禮不下庶人，刑不上大夫' 辯 ("The rites do not extent down to the common people; punishments do not reach as far as the officials"), *Faxue yanjiu*, No. 1, 1981, p. 53. (The reference is to the *Liji*.)

impose inner-Party disciplinary punishments.[142] Zhao Wenfu, a delegate to the Fifth National People's Congress, criticizes this special invulnerability to punishment of certain Party officials when he alludes to a passage in the *Book of Rites* (*Liji*):

> In the past there was a formulation which read: "Punishments do not reach as far as the officials" (*xing bu shang daifu* 刑不上大夫); today we can apply to certain districts [the formulation]: "Punishments do not reach as far as the leading [Party] cadres" (*xing bu shang lingdao ganbu* 刑不上領導幹部).[143]

The case against the "Gang of Four" was seen as a turning point in the P.R.C. with regard to equal treatment of all citizens before the law. Never before have such high former Party cadres been called to account by a state court, albeit specially appointed.[144] But it is noteworthy that it was emphasized precisely in connection with this case that the state criminal laws did not apply to mistakes committed exclusively in the sphere of the Party political line or other Party norms.

VI. CONCLUSION

At the apex of this pyramid of norms shaped in the P.R.C. by the Party Centre and the highest national legislator stands the Party political line. It circumscribes the principal task to be achieved by the CCP and the Chinese people under its leadership during the specific stage of development of Chinese society.

"In our state the Party leads everything," emphasizes Zhang Youyu, deputy chairman of the Legal Committee of the Standing Committee of the

---

[142] See for instance, "Wei fuqin ban sangshi da gao mixin, Shen Baoshu shoudao dangji chufen" 爲父親辦喪事大搞迷信，申寶淑受到黨紀處分 ("Flagrant superstition in organizing a funeral for a father; Shen Baoshu is punished according to Party discipline"), *Gongren ribao*, 8 April 1981; "Wuru nü jiaoshi de ren shoudao chufen" 污辱女教師的人受到處分 ("The person who humiliated a female teacher receives punishment"), *Zhongguo qingnian bao* 中國青年報 , 8 January 1981.

[143] "Yi fa ban shi yi fa zhi guo—quanguo Renda daibiao Qiao Xiaoguang, Hu Lijiao, Zhao Wenfu tan xin xianfa" 依法辦事依法治國——全國人大代表喬曉光、胡立教、趙文甫談新憲法 ("Dealing with matters through the law, and running the country through the law— Qiao Xiaoguang, Hu Lijiao, Zhao Wenfu, delegates to the National People's Congress, talk about the new Constitution"), *Renmin ribao*, 4 December 1982, p. 2.

[144] "Shehuizhuyi fazhi de weida shengli" 社會主義法治的偉大勝利 ("A great victory for socialist legality"), *Zhongguo fazhi bao*, editorial, 30 January 1981; "Dui renmin fuze, dui lishi fuze" 對人民負責，對歷史負責 ("We are responsible to the people, and to history"), *Jiefangjun bao*, 12 November 1980, reprinted in *Wen hui bao* 文滙報 , 13 November 1980.

NPC and vice-president of the Chinese Academy of Social Sciences, co-author of the book *Talks Regarding Basic Knowledge of Law*, in an interview granted to the *Chinese Legal Gazette*.[145] According to Xiao Weiyun of the Law Faculty of Beijing University, "The state has to implement without exception the line, the duality norms, and the political norms of the Party in the development of the legal system and in the work in the judicial sector."[146]

In the P.R.C. statutory law thus does not serve the function of an autonomous force for shaping the social order, independent of the CCP Party norms. It serves rather as a vehicle for making casuistic elaborations to Party norms and their translation into guiding principles which are compulsory for all citizens of the P.R.C. The basic orientation and value judgements are made by the Party Centre in the form of Party norms, and not by the national legislator. A substantial change in the paramount importance of the Party norms is not apparent at present, since the contemplated withdrawal of the Party from the domain of executive work, especially in the governmental sphere, is, after all, coupled with renewed stress on the task of the supervision and implementation of Party norms, which has recently been regarded as the Party's essential task. Much as traditional conceptions may continue to operate in the sphere of CCP Party norms as well as in the statutory law of the P.R.C., there is nevertheless no parallel to be found in Chinese history for the duality of two supreme official normative authorities, one of which—the Party Centre—dominates the other—the national legislator.[147]

[145] "Chengji xianzhu, qiantu leguan—Zhang Youyu tongzhi tan fazhi jianshe" 成績顯著，前途樂觀——張友漁同志談法制建設 ("Achievements are primary, and the future gives rise to optimism—Comrade Zhang Youyu talks about building a legal system"), *Zhongguo fazhi bao*, 3 July 1981.

[146] Xiao Weiyun 蕭蔚雲, "Jiaqiang dang dui fazhi gongzuo de lingdao" 加強黨對法制工作的領導 ("Strengthen the Party's leadership of work on the legal system"), in *Jiaqiang shehuizhuyi fazhi jianghua* 加強社會主義法制講話 (*Talks on strengthening the legal system under socialism*) (Guangdong: Guangdong renmin chubanshe, 1979), p. 95.

[147] The author wishes to express his gratitude to the Schweizer Nationalfonds zur Förderung der Wissenschaftlichen Forschung for the support it gave in 1978-1980 for the research embodied in this article.

PART II

The Economic Role of the State

7. The Influence of the "Legalist" Government of Qin on the Economy as Reflected in the Texts Discovered in Yunmeng County

Anthony Hulsewé

I. THE YUNMENG TEXTS

The Yunmeng texts written on bamboo strips were discovered in December 1975 in a tomb situated in the Shuihudi 睡虎地 area in the Xiaogan District 孝感區 of Yunmeng County 雲夢縣, in the central part of Hubei Province, some fifty miles northwest of Hankou. The tomb can be dated in *c.* 217 B.C.; beyond any doubt the texts belong to the third century B.C., if not earlier.

The total number of the strips, sometimes consisting of combined fragments, is 1155. To date they have been published four times:

1. In 1976 in issues 6, 7 and 8 of the archaeological journal *Wenwu*, in transcription in modern, abbreviated characters.
2. In 1977 in a folio volume, Chinese style, consisting of seven stitched fascicles, with full-size photographs of the strips, their transcription in modern characters, and a modest number of notes.
3. In 1978 in a paper-covered octavo edition, without photographs, but in transcription, much fuller notes, and a translation into modern Chinese.

The editions 2 and 3 are both entitled *Shuihudi Qin mu zhu jian* 睡虎地秦墓竹簡, and both were published in Beijing by the Wenwu Press. The three editions contain 727 strips.

Abbreviations:
HFHD H. H. Dubs a. o., *The History of the Former Han Dynasty by Pan Ku*, 3 vols. (Baltimore: Waverly Press, 1938, 1944, 1955).
HHSJJ Wang Xianqian 王先謙, *Hou Han shu jijie* 後漢書集解 (Changsha, 1923; reduced reprint by the Yiwen 藝文 Publishers in Taibei, 1965). In the references, Ann. signifies Annals, Mem. Memoirs and Tr. Treatises.
HSBZ Wang Xianqian, *Han shu bu zhu* 漢書補注 (Changsha, 1900; reduced reprint by the Yiwen Publishers in Taibei, 1965).
Mh Edouard Chavannes, *Les mémoires historiques de Se-ma Ts'ien* (Paris: Leroux, 1895-1905; the original five volumes were republished with a supplementary sixth volume in Paris, by Maisonneuve in 1969).
RCL A.F.P. Hulsewé, *Remnants of Ch'in Law* (Leiden: Brill, 1985).
SJ Takigawa Kametarō 瀧川龜太郎, *Shiki kaichū kōshō* 史記會注考證 (Sima Qian's *Shiji*, with collected commentaries and further notes) (1934; reprinted in Taiwan).

4. The complete collection was published only in 1981, in the Hubei Provincial Museum's report on the excavation of the twelve Qin tombs discovered in the Shuihudi area, the strips being found in the coffin in tomb no. 11. In this report, entitled *Yunmeng Shuihudi Qin mu* (Beijing: Wenwu Press), we find, parallel to the practically illegible photographs of the strips, the transcription in traditional characters, written with the brush. In the following pages, all references are to the pages of the octavo edition of 1978, indicated by SS, followed between brackets by the number adopted in my *Remnants of Ch'in Law*. This annotated translation deals with the 609 strips containing legal material. Here we find 161 articles, often quite long, from 27 administrative statutes, mentioned by title, 190 examples of the application of the penal laws as well as explanations of terms and phrases, and 25 investigation reports concerning criminal cases.[1]

It should be stressed that the legal material from Yunmeng represents only a fraction of the third century Qin code. The whole of the criminal code is absent, only incidental terms and phrases being quoted in the 190 paragraphs which the editors have named "Replies to questions concerning the laws." Many of the administrative statutes are only represented by a few articles, whereas they must have contained many more.[2] It is quite clear that the Yunmeng texts are a selection, consisting for the major part of rules which a subordinate local official needed for his daily work. They mainly concern the management of granaries, the control of agriculture, the work of statute labourers and hard labour convicts, their rations and other issues. Still, although modest in scope, the Yunmeng texts are of inestimable value; it is on the basis of these texts that the following exposition has been compiled. But before starting on this exposition, I would like to make one preliminary remark.[3]

The new material shows that in the third century B.C. the Qin state

---

[1] For a more detailed description of the first three editions and their contents see my "The Ch'in Documents Discovered in Hupei in 1975," in *T'oung Pao*, Vol. LXIV (1978), pp. 175-217 and 338, or the Introduction to *RCL*. The remaining strips, published in the fourth edition, are mantic texts, indicating lucky and unlucky days for all kinds of undertakings.

[2] To give but one example: only two articles are quoted from the Statutes on Aristocratic Rank (SS, pp. 92-94 (A 90 and 91)), whereas the recently discovered fragments of the Han equivalent of this statute provide many detailed rules which must also have existed in the Qin code; see *Wenwu* No. 2, 1981, pp. 21-34.

[3] Here I repeat practically verbatim what I wrote in "The Legalists and the Laws of Ch'in," in W. L. Idema (ed.), *Leyden Studies in Sinology*, papers presented at the conference held in celebration of the fiftieth anniversary of the Sinological Institute of Leyden University, 8-12 December 1980 (Leiden: Brill, 1981), p. 21.

possessed an extensive corpus of administrative and criminal law, handled by a complex hierarchy of officials. Part of these laws may date from the great innovator Shang Yang 商鞅 in the fourth century B.C., some may even be more recent creations, but on the whole I am inclined to believe that a considerable body of laws must have existed before Shang Yang, who, after all, insisted on the rigorous application of the extant codes. It seems only reasonable to suppose that the development of this extensive corpus of written laws had taken several centuries, and not merely the hundred years since Shang Yang's activities. The genesis of these laws will have coincided, I believe, with the creation of the centralizing and increasingly bureaucratic states in the course of the eighth and seventh centuries before our era. This development and this complexity of the code hardly bear witness to the oft-mentioned backwardness or the semi-barbarian condition of the state of Qin, attributed to its position on the edge of the Chinese culture area, with a population that was partly formed by "barbarian" tribes that had been only recently subdued. In this traditional conception it is overlooked that the state of Qin occupied the original homeland of the Zhou, whose early development is now generally recognized. Not to be overlooked either is the fact that these "barbarians" were not racially different from the Chinese, but members of the same stock, who were merely less advanced; they were not alien nomads from the steppe. Although their influence in one way or another cannot be weighed, one cannot attribute to the Qin region a complete lapse into barbarism after the flight of the Zhou king in the eighth century B.C. After all, a millennium later North China remained Chinese in spite of its occupation by alien nomad tribes during the centuries following the year A.D. 317, when part of the cultured upper strata of society fled to the Yangzi region.

II. THE QIN STATE AND ITS ROLE

Before discussing the influence of the Qin state, it is necessary to determine which words were used in these texts for "the state" and its agents. "The state" is unambiguously *bang* 邦 . We find *bang* referring to the state of Qin itself, e.g. *bang guan* 關 , "the border control stations of the state" (SS, p. 211 (D 118)), and *bang wang* 亡 , "to abscond from the state" (SS, pp. 152, 171, 229 (D 4, 93, 160)), as well as referring to other states, e.g. *to* 它 *bang*, "other states" (SS, pp. 227, 240 (D 157, 184)), *chen* 臣 *bang*, "servant states," i.e. "states subordinate to Qin" (SS, pp. 182, 200, 226, 227 (D 58, 94, 156, 157)), and *shu* 屬 *bang*, "dependent states"[4] (SS, p. 110 (A110)).

[4] These dependent states may have been "barbarians who had submitted," in view of the parallel term *shu kuo* 國 of the Han; see *HSBZ* 19A.19b.

Although the term *bang guan* shows that *bang* could be used attributively, the usual word meaning "belonging to the state," or rather "belonging to the public authorities" is *gong* 公. We therefore find *gong ma niu* 馬牛, "government horses and cattle" (SS, pp. 33, 77, 82 (A 9, 64, 75)), *gong qi* 器, "government tools" (SS, pp. 60, 64, 72 (A 39, 47, 57)), and *gong jiabing* 甲兵, "government armour and arms" (SS, p. 71 (A 56)). *Gong* is also found in a different construction: *yi shi* 衣食 *gong*, "clothed and fed by the government" (SS, pp. 48, 87 (A 11, 65)), and *you zhai yu gong* 有責 (for 債) 於公, "having debts towards the government" (SS, p. 60 (A 38)). An ambiguous term is presented by *gong si* 祠, for this may mean "sacrifices presented by the government authorities," or it may refer to "sacrifices performed by the Duke [of Qin]" (SS, p. 161 (D 21)); the latter rendering is quite possible in view of the existence of the term *wang shi* 王室 *si*, "sacrifices performed by the Royal Clan" (SS, p. 163 (D 23)).[5]

A third term is *guan* 官, meaning "office,"[6] in the sense of "agency of the central or the regional government"; it is also used attributively in the expression *guan fu* 府, "official or government storehouse or workshop." In this connection it is to be noted that *guan* is not used as an attribute of concrete objects like tools, arms, animals, carriages or buildings etc., for this kind of government property is always qualified as *gong*.

The ruler is designated by *cheng yu* 乘輿, "[he who] rides in a palanquin" (SS, p. 141 (C 17)), which is also the current Han term for the emperor. In the Chronicle[7] the First Emperor is referred to as *jin* 今 (SS, p. 6), comparable to *jin shang* 上 used in Han times. *Shang* also occurs in the Qin regulations, but there it indicates "superior authorities" (SS, pp. 91, 123 (A 71, B 23)). Orders emanating from the ruler (or from the central government?) are called *ming shu* 命書, "written commands"[8] (SS, pp. 103, 129 (A 95, C 2)).

The Qin state made its influence felt in the economy in several ways, in a similar manner to that of later rulers. We observe this influence in agriculture, in labour—both free and unfree—in trade, and in industry. To this we should add the ubiquitous phenomenon of taxation, and it is here that we find an indication of great interest.

[5] According to Liang Yusheng 梁玉繩 (1745-1819), quoted in *SJ* 5.58, the change in title from duke to king took place in 325 B.C.

[6] During several centuries to come, *guan* never indicated a person, viz. a government official. And even when *guan* had become the word for "an official," it continued to be used attributively with the meaning "belonging to the government," as in *guan bing* 兵, "government troops" (in contrast to local levies).

[7] For this Yunmeng text see p. 182 of my review article in *T'oung Pao*, Vol. LXIV.

[8] Cf. *SJ* 6.22, *Mh* II, p. 126, stating that in 221 B.C. *ming* was changed to *zhi* 制.

Landownership

SS, p. 27 (A 3) reads:

The delivery of hay and straw per *qing*[9] is made according to the number of fields bestowed. Irrespective of whether the fields are cultivated or uncultivated, per *qing* three bushels of hay are delivered and two bushels of straw.... When delivering hay and straw, conversion of the one into the other is permitted.[10]

The interesting point here is that fields, *tian* 田, are said to be "bestowed," *shou* 受 (for 授), and this raises a number of questions.

Because this rule forms part of the *tian lü* 田律, the Statutes on Agriculture, which must have been valid for all agricultural enterprises in the whole of the Qin kingdom, it seems difficult, at first sight, to avoid the conclusion that all land in private hands was "bestowed." However, nothing is known about such bestowals; when the *Hanshu* tells us that in Qin men of merit were given fields with a number of dependent families to work these,[11] it does not provide any information for the bulk of the population, nor do the *Zhou li* or the *Mencius*, which both say that a household received 100 *mu*.[12] Was this a permanent allotment, or was it subject to periodic changes, as Maspero believed, reasoning purely by analogy with the custom prevalent in Vietnam in the early twentieth century?[13] Modern studies on the Qin texts assume

[9] One *qing* 頃 was equal to one hundred *mu* 畝. Now the size of the *mu* changed in the course of time, the old "Zhou" *mu* of 1 × 100 paces being gradually replaced by the new *mu* of 1 × 240 paces; the stages of this development, however, are uncertain. It seems very likely that the Qin used the large *mu*, but its spread over the whole of China seems to have taken until about 100 B.C. (cf. *Yantie lun* 鹽鐵論 15, E. M. Gale, *Discourses on Salt and Iron* [Leiden: Brill, 1931], p. 94). For the author of the dictionary *Shuowen jiezi* 說文解字 of A.D. 100, the Qin created the large *mu*, and his opinion was shared by the Tang monk and mathematician Yixing 一行, based on a lost passage of the *Shiji* 史記, quoted in the encyclopedia *Taiping yulan* 太平御覽 750.4a. With the Qin-Han foot at 23.1 cm. and six feet to the pace, the old *mu* measured about 200 square metres or 0.02 hectare, and the new *mu* about 470 square metres or 0.047 ha, resulting in a *qing* of 4.7 ha. See the discussion in Gao Min 高敏, *Yunmeng Qin jian chutan* 雲夢秦簡初探 (Henan Renmin chubanshe, 1979), pp. 168-70.

[10] A similar conversion is to be observed in Han records of the first half of the second century B.C., discovered upstream from Hankou; see Qiu Xigui 裘錫圭, "Hubei Jiangling Fenghuangshan shi hao Han mu jiandu kaoshi" 湖北江陵鳳凰山十號漢墓簡牘考釋, in *Wenwu* No. 7, 1974, pp. 49-63. From the strips transcribed on pp. 50-51 and discussed on p. 58 we learn that hay was paid in lieu of, *dang* 當, straw at the rate of one to two.

[11] *HSBZ* 23.7b, cf. my *Remnants of Han law* (Leiden: Brill, 1955), p. 327.

[12] *Le Tcheou li ou Rites des Tcheou*, trans. E. Biot (Paris: Imprimerie nationale, 1851), Vol. I, pp. 206 and 340; *Mencius* IA.iii, 4.

[13] Henri Maspero, "Les régimes fonciers en Chine des origines aux temps modernes," originally in *Receuil de la Société Jean Bodin*, Vol. II (Bruxelles, 1937), included in his *Mélanges posthumes*, Vol. III, *Etudes historiques* (Paris, 1950), pp. 159-60, but cf. H. Maspero et E. Balazs, *Histoire et institutions de la Chine ancienne* (Paris, 1967), p. 23.

without further proof that the term *shou tian* was a relic of antiquity, such lands being in actual fact private property,[14] ever since the reforms of Shang Yang in the fourth century B.C. A third author takes a less rigid standpoint.[15] He believes that anciently there had existed a system of bestowal with periodic changes[16] (i.e. Maspero's view), but that in Shang Yang's time, as a result of the increased size of the *mu*,[17] the farmer no longer had to move and could now personally decide on the rotation of cultivated and fallow fields.[18] The author therefore is of the opinion that, under Shang Yang's new dispensation, fields, measured in large *mu* were bestowed with clearly determined boundaries, in this way consolidating the holder's right of usufruct. The author notes that in enlarging the size of the *mu* Shang Yang was only following the example of the eastern states, who had already applied this increase more than a century earlier, as shown by the newly discovered chapter *Wu wen* 吳問 of the *Sunzi bingfa*.[19]

The fact that fields could be "bestowed" leads directly to the problem of land ownership. From the liberty which the authorities had to dispose freely of the land so as to be able to bestow it, one is forced to conclude that there existed a concept of "eminent domain," if not in legal theory, then in actual practice.[20] This is expressed in the famous lines of Ode no. 215, *Bei shan* 北山, *Pu tian zhi xia, mo fei wang tu; shuai tu zhi bin, mo fei wang chen* 溥天之下，莫非王土；率土之濱，莫非王臣, "Under the vast heaven, there is nothing which is not the land of the king; of all the subjects of the earth, there are none who are not the servants of the

---

[14] This is the opinion of Tang Zangong 唐贊功, "Yunmeng Qin jian suosheji tudi suoyouzhi xingshi wenti chutan" 雲夢秦簡所涉及土地所有制形式問題初探, as well as of Xiong Tieji 熊鐵基 and Wang Ruiming 王瑞明, "Qindai de fengjian tudi suoyouzhi" 秦代的封建土地所有制, on pp. 60-61 and pp. 76f. in *Yunmeng Qin jian yanjiu* 雲夢秦簡研究 (Beijing: Zhonghua shuju 中華書局, 1981). This opinion is substantially the same as that of Lin Jianming 林劍鳴, "Qinguo nulizhi shehui xingtai de tedian" 秦國奴隸制社會形態的特點, in *Qin Han shi luncong* 秦漢史論叢, I (Xi'an: Shaanxi Renmin chubanshe, 1981), pp. 9f.

[15] Li Jiemin 李解民, " 'Kai qianmo' bianzheng" 「開阡陌」辨正, in *Wenshi* 文史 No. 11, 1981, pp. 47-60.

[16] *Huan tu yi ju* 換土易居, mentioned by Ho Xiu 何休 (A.D. 129-82) in his commentary to the *Gong Yang zhuan*, Duke Xuan 15 (see *Chunqiu Gong Yang zhuan zhusu* 春秋公羊傳注疏 16.8b (0492) of the Zhonghua shuju edition of the Thirteen Classics).

[17] See n. 9 above.

[18] This is implied by Meng Kang 孟康 (*fl.* A.D. 180-260) in his commentary to *HSBZ* 28Bii.50b.

[19] See *Yinqiaoshan Han mu zhu jian, Sunzi bingfa* 銀雀山漢墓竹簡‧孫子兵法 (Beijing: Wenwu chubanshe, 1976), pp. 94-95 (for the approximate date see p. 144).

[20] See on this point Léon Vandermeersch, "Le statut des terres à l'époque des Han," in L. Lanciotti (ed.), *Il diritto in Cina* (Firenze: Olschki, 1978), pp. 53f.

king."[21] And regardless of the fact whether individual fields were still bestowed or not, the concept persisted, resulting for privately owned land during the Han period in a situation outlined by Hiranaka as follows: "The farmer worked the land he had, and he was free to dispose of it; the state even considered such a deal as the object of a property tax. But he did not possess the land in the modern sense; possession was not a complete material right . . . being an onerous and limited right *in rem* . . . an onerous right, quite close to the right of usufruct and occupation."[22]

A problem directly connected with the bestowal of fields concerns the buying and selling of land. It is well known that according to Han authors it was Shang Yang who, in the middle of the fourth century B.C., had made deals in land possible,[23] but could land granted by the government be disposed of in this way? No solution is provided by the stipulation that the surreptitious shifting of border-marks[24] was a punishable offence,[25] because such marks could be shifted in any type of field, regardless of its origin. Unfortunately, so far no Qin deeds of land sales have been discovered, which might have thrown light on this problem; the few Han deeds are silent on this point.[26]

Finally a negative point. The Qin strips mention that it was a punishable

[21] Bernhard Karlgren, *The Book of Odes* (Göteborg: Elander, 1950), p. 157. For an analysis of these lines see Hiranaka Reiji 平中苓次, *Chūkoku kodai no densei to zeihō* 中國古代の田制と税法 (Kyōto: Tōyōshi kenkyūkai, 1967), pp. 3-20.

[22] Hiranaka, *op. cit.*, p. 104. This view is practically shared by He Changqun 賀昌羣, *Han Tang jian fengjian tudi suoyouzhi xingshi yanjiu* 漢唐間封建土地所有制形式研究 (Shanghai: Renmin chubanshe, 1964), pp. 48 and 53. Gao Min, on pp. 155f. of the work quoted in n. 9 above, disregards the basic assumption that all land remained under the supreme control of the state. He assumes state ownership for government land tilled by "state slaves" and for the land that had been bestowed, but private ownership by "landlords" of estates that had been granted in reward for deeds of military valour since the days of Shang Yang.

[23] *HSBZ* 24A.16b; Nancy Lee Swann, *Food and Money in Ancient China* (Princeton: Princeton University Press, 1950), p. 180; the passage occurs in a memorial submitted sometime after 130 B.C.

[24] *Feng* 封. A recently discovered single article of the Qin Statute on Agriculture, dated 309 B.C., stipulates that these marks were to be four feet high and four feet thick at the base; see the transcription of this strip on p. 11 of *Wenwu* No. 1, 1982, and *RCL*, p. 213.

[25] SS, p. 178 (D 136): *dao xi feng shu nai* 盜徙封贖耐, "surreptitiously to shiff border-marks [is punished by] redemption of [the hard labour punishment called] 'shaving off the beard'." It is to be noted that this type of redemption is not such that, subsequent to condemnation to a certain punishment, redemption was permitted, but that the culprit was directly condemned to redemption! For redemption in Han law see my *Remnants*, pp. 205f., and the abstract of the article by Yaezu Yōhei 八重津洋平, "Kandai shokkei kō" 漢代贖刑考, in *Hōseishi kenkyū* 法制史研究 No. 11, 1960, pp. 254f.

[26] Discussed in my " 'Contracts' of the Han Period," in *Il diritto in Cina* (*op. cit.*), p. 34.

offence when a local functionary *ni tian*匿田, "hid fields," i.e. that he collected the landtax of commoners' fields without reporting to his superior, implying that he pocketed the tax.[27] But the text does not indicate the form of ownership, merely writing *zhu min tian* 者 (for 諸)民田, "fields of commoners." Perhaps this is an indirect indication that such fields were private property, with the restrictions mentioned by Hiranaka.[28] Another indication, likewise an argument from silence, is the lack of any rules for "bestowals" in the present collection, which shows so much concern for the cultivation of the arable; the silence about inheritance is perhaps also telling in this respect. The possibility of selling land may have grown slowly. It is to be noted that Li Jiemin[29] does not think that the sale of land was permitted by Shang Yang as maintained by Dong Zhongshu 董仲舒, writing in the 2nd century B.C.[30] He assumes that eventually an existing situation was formally recognized only in the 31st year of the First Emperor, 216 B.C., when "the black-haired people were made personally to declare their holdings."[31]

Agriculture

The concern of the Qin government for agriculture is clearly shown by the article of the Statutes on Agriculture which the modern editors have placed at the head of the whole collection. SS, p. 34 (A 1) reads:

> Whenever the rain is beneficial and affects the grain in ear, a report in writing is to be made concerning the crop that had been benefited and the grain in ear, as well as the number of *qing* of cultivated fields and areas without crops. Whenever it rains when the crop is already fully grown, also the quantity of the rain and the number of *qing* that had benefited are to be reported in writing. Likewise, in cases of drought and violent wind or rain, floods, hordes of grasshoppers or other creatures which damage the crops, the number of *qing* concerned is always to be reported in writing. Nearby prefectures have light-footed [runners] deliver the letter, distant prefectures have the courier service deliver it. By the end of the eighth month . . . (text defective) it.

The authority to whom these reports were to be sent is not indicated. It might have been the commandery administrators,[32] but, also in view of the

[27] SS, p. 218 (D 135).

[28] See n. 22.

[29] See n. 15.

[30] Li Jiemin, *op. cit.*, p. 59, referring to *HSBZ* 24A.16b (Swann, *op. cit.*, p. 180). Li thinks that Dong Zhongshu's statement reflects the conditions of his own time.

[31] *Zi shi tian* 自實田 . This order is not found in the present text of the *Shiji*, but in the remarks by Xu Guang 徐廣 (352-425) quoted in the *jijie* commentary in *SJ* 6.44 (not in *Mh*). For the explanation of the expression *zi shi tian* see Hiranaka, *op. cit.*, pp. 45-62.

[32] This is not the place to enter into the complicated problem of the commanderies

adjective "distant," I rather expect it to have been an authority in the capital, namely the *nei shi* 內史, the minister for agriculture, or rather finance, and not the governor of the capital area.[33] Such reports were still required under the Han, for we find the rule that "From the Establishment of Spring (*c.* 5th February) to the Establishment of Summer (*c.* 5th May) up to the Establishment of Autumn (*c.* 7th August) the benefits of rain are to be reported. In case this is [too] little, the Offices [of the three excellencies in the capital[34]], the Commanderies and the Prefectures each have the Altar to the Soil and Grain swept and cleaned. In case of drought, the ministers and the chiefs of Offices according to their status perform the rain ceremonies and beg for rain."[35]

The reason for the order to report on the state of the crops was evidently the capital importance which the harvest had for the whole of the population, but it also influenced the state's tax income, as its main source was the land tax, levied in grain. Unfortunately, the Yunmeng texts nowhere mention the rate of this tax. It must have been more than one fifteenth of the harvest, because the first Han emperor is said to have *reduced* it to that amount.[36] It may have been one tenth,[37] but it may have been more.[38] Because the tax on

---

in Qin, discussed by Kamada Shigeo 鎌田重雄, *Shin Kan seiji seido no kenkyū* 秦漢政治 制度の研究 (Tokyo: Gakujutsu shinkōkai, 1962), pp. 3-101. A list of the commanderies established by the Warring States is to be found in Yang Kuan 楊寬, *Zhanguo shi* 戰國史 (Shanghai: Renmin chubanshe, 1955), pp. 121-25. Judging by the list in Kamada, *op. cit.*, pp. 16-17, the establishment of commanderies in Qin only started in the fourth century B.C. In a note in SS, p. 94, the editors remark that twelve commanderies must have been established before 243 B.C.

[33] See pp. 194-95 of my review article mentioned in n. 1.

[34] See H. Bielenstein, *The Bureaucracy of Han Times* (Cambridge: Cambridge University Press, 1980), pp. 7-17.

[35] *HHSJJ* Tr.5.1a (cf. the remarks in the additional notes to this chapter: *jiaobu* 校補 5.1a). For the ceremonies see the forthcoming study by Michael Loewe, "The Cult of the Dragon and the Invocation for Rain," to be published in the Festschrift for Professor Derk Bodde.

[36] *HSBZ* 24A.9b, Swann, *op. cit.*, pp. 149f.; cf. *HSBZ* 2.2b, *HFHD* I, p. 175.

[37] This is said by Deng Zhan 鄧展 (*fl.* A.D. 208) in his commentary to the passage in *HSBZ* 2.2b; cf. *HFHD* I, p. 175, n. 3. This is also the view, based on passages in ancient literature, held by Huang Jinyan 黃今言, "Qindai zufu yaoyi zhidu chutan" 秦代租賦徭 役制度初探, in *Qin Han shi luncong*, I, p. 64.

[38] The *Sunzi bingfa*, chapter *Wu wen* (see n. 19 above), p. 94, reports that in the early fifth century B.C. several states *wu shui* 伍稅, "'fived' the landtax," explained on p. 151 as "they took one fifth of the harvest." The same ratio, expressed as *shi er* 十二, "two out of ten," is mentioned in the *Zhouli, di guan* 地官, *zai shi* 載師 (*Zhouli zhusu* 周禮注疏 13.8b (0476); Sun Yirang 孫詒讓, *Zhouli zhengyi* 周禮正義 7/24.17; Biot, *Le Tcheou-li* I, p. 278). Finally, the same figures are repeated for the time of Duke Zhuang of Lu (traditional dates 692-663 B.C.) in ch. 8 of the *Xin yu* 新語 by Lu Jia 陸賈 of the

hay and straw was calculated per surface unit,[39] it is not impossible that the same procedure was followed for the land tax. This was certainly Han practice, when in theory it was one thirtieth of the harvest (since 156 B.C.);[40] this is clearly apparent from a passage in the 15th chapter of the *Yantie lun*.[41] Figures are both scarce and vague; Hiranaka has calculated that the new *mu*[42] may have produced between three and four bushels of grain, resulting in a tax of perhaps four *dou* 斗, "pecks" or about eight litres.[43]

A strict rule for the use of seed-grain is provided in SS, p. 43 (A 27):

> When sowing rice[44] and hemp,[45] per *mu* use 2 2/3 *dou*;[46] for wheat and barley per *mu* one *dou*; for millet and red beans per *mu* 2/3 *dou*; for soy-beans per *mu* 1/2 *dou*. . . . It is permitted that in some cases these amounts are not fully used. When there are roots, sowing is to be done according to the circumstances.[47]

The records of a local administration, discovered in southern Hubei and to be dated before the middle of the second century B.C., clearly show that this rule was to be followed by managers of grainstores when distributing seed-grain, which was loaned (*dai* 貸) to commoners at the rate of one *dou* per *mu*.[48] That such loans had to be repaid is evident from an amnesty of 178 B.C.,

---

early second century B.C. (p. 14 of the *Zhuzi jicheng* 諸子集成 edition). See also the passages from ancient literature quoted in Yoshida Torao 吉田虎夫, *Ryō Kan sozei no kenkyū* 兩漢租稅の研究 (1st ed. 1942; anastatic reprint Tokyo: Daian, 1966), pp. 7-13. The value of the passage in the diatribe against the First Emperor in *HSBZ* 24A.9a (Swann, *op. cit.*, p. 147), namely that he "collected charges of two thirds" (*shou taiban zhi fu* 收泰半之賦) is difficult to assess, i.a. because the meaning of *fu* is not clear; it seems unlikely that *fu* would exclusively mean "military tax."

[39] SS, p. 34 (A 1).

[40] *HSBZ* 5.3a, *HFHD* I, p. 311.

[41] See Gale, *Discourses*, p. 94.

[42] See n. 9 above.

[43] Hiranaka, *op. cit.*, pp. 147f. and 160f.

[44] In antiquity, rice was mainly cultivated in the Yangzi area; see Yang Kuan, *op. cit.*, p. 22. However, already during the period of the Warring States it was grown in the southern and central parts of North China; see Nishijima Sadao 西嶋定夫, *Chūkoku keizaishi kenkyū* 中國經濟研究史 (Tokyo, 1965), pp. 206f., and Cho-yun Hsu, *Han Agriculture* (Seattle and London: The University of Washington Press, 1980), pp. 84f.

[45] The *Yueling* 月令 chapter of the *Liji* 禮記 prescribes hemp and dog's meat for the first month of autumn.

[46] One *dou* 斗 was almost two litres.

[47] Although the exact meaning of the phrase "*qi you bu jin ci shu zhe*" 其有不盡此數 者 is not clear, it is evident that a certain latitude was allowed. "When there are roots" refers perhaps to the "slash and burn" technique, where nothing would grow around the tree-stumps that had not been removed.

[48] See Qiu Xigui, *op. cit.*; the text of strips 9-34 on pp. 51-52, and the explanation on p. 54.

which expressly remits such debts.[49]

Whereas the stipulations concerning seed-grain were directives for granary managers, it is not immediately evident who were the persons to whom the rule in SS, pp. 44-45 (A 29 and 30) was meant to apply; this rule determines in considerable detail the amounts of the products to be obtained by husking and further refining cereals.[50] But who was to do the actual husking and pounding? If this work was done by the producers, i.e. the farmers, the rule could be used as a normative scale, to be applied when the land tax was paid. This would imply that the farmers had to pay the tax in specified products, and for this a Han strip provides some, but inconclusive evidence.[51] Still, there are indications that the land tax was paid in grain in the ear. A tempting answer to the question to whom the rule concerning husking and refining applied is suggested by the names of two types of hard labour for female convicts, namely *bai can*, traditionally explained as "sifting or sorting white rice" and *chung*, "pounding," i.e. husking.[52] It therefore seems quite likely that it was these women who were made to prepare the grain in the government granaries for distribution as salaries-in-kind and as rations.

It is rather surprising that the Yunmeng texts do not contain any rules for agricultural activities, although the leading authority for such activities is mentioned three times. This was the agricultural overseer (*tian sefu* 田嗇夫). Two of these passages are not directly concerned with agriculture,[53] but the third is, for it provides the first definite textual proof that in the third century B.C. oxen were used for ploughing, thus settling a question that has long been debated.[54] This particular rule[55] shows that the agricultural

---

[49]*HSBZ* 4.10a, *HFHD* I, p. 242: *dai zhong shi wei ru, ru wei bei zhe* 貸種食未入，入未備者. The separate mention of *shi* shows that also grain for food was loaned; this is demonstrated by a similar edict of 48 B.C., which restricts the remission to persons with property of less than 1,000 cash (*HSBZ* 9.2a, *HFHD* II, pp. 302f.).

[50]This rule is translated and discussed in my article "Weights and Measures in Ch'in Law," in *State and Law in East Asia* (Wiesbaden: Harrassowitz, 1981), pp. 20-29.

[51]Qiu Xigui, *op. cit.*, pp. 51 and 57-58.

[52]白餐 and 舂; during the Han period the first was a three year punishment, whereas the term of the second was four or five years; see my *Remnants*, pp. 129-30. It is quite likely that the duration of the hard-labour punishments was the same during both the Qin and the Han, for otherwise the Yunmeng texts would not have expressly mentioned that in some cases convicts were to be detained for six years (SS, p. 202 (D 98)), which presupposes that normally they served for a shorter time. But see *RCL*, pp. 16f.

[53]SS, p. 30 (A 6): the overseer and his subordinates were to prevent commoners living in the countryside from selling wine, and SS, pp. 124-25 (B 25): the overseer was fined for malversations committed by his underlings.

[54]See Sun Kai 孫楷, revised by Xu Fu 徐復, *Qin huiyao ding bu* 秦會要訂補, (Peking: Zhonghua shuju, 1959), pp. 271 and 461-63, referring in particular to the passage—placed in 262 B.C.—in the *Zhanguo ce* 戰國策, ch. 18, *Zhao ce* 趙策 I (*Congshu jicheng*

overseer was rewarded, when on the occasion of the four annual inspections the oxen used in agricultural work[56] were in good condition, and punished if they were thin. Also, other rules show that the physical condition of cattle and horses was controlled regularly.[57]

It goes without saying that the land was tilled by the farmers, but one rule[58] shows that a particular category of hard-labour convicts was occasionally also put to agricultural work; these convicts were the "bond servants" (*li chen* 隸臣), the term of whose punishment was three years.[59] This rule lays down that such bond servants, when engaged in agricultural work,[60] received extra food rations from the second until the end of the ninth month, which shows that they worked in the fields during the whole of the agricultural cycle.

Granaries

The Yunmeng texts contain many regulations for the granaries, but the origin of the grain stored there is nowhere mentioned. In part this must have consisted in cereals delivered as the land tax, but it may also have been produced on government land, worked, perhaps, by the bond servants mentioned above.

The quantities of grain accumulated in the granaries must have been considerable. This can be deduced from the rule that grain had to be stacked in piles of 10,000 bushels (*c.* 200,000 litres or 200 cubic metres) in ordinary granaries, presumably situated at the seat of the prefecture, whereas in the former Qin capital Yueyang 櫟陽 these stacks were each to contain 20,000 bushels (400,000 litres or 400 cubic metres) and those in Xianyang 咸陽

叢書集成 ed., Vol. 2, p. 51; cf. *SJ* 43.86, *Mh* V, p. 117). See also Li Jiannong 李劍農, *Xian Qin liang Han jingji shi gao* 先秦兩漢經濟史稿 (Peking: Zhonghua shuju, 1957), pp. 45f., and Zhang Zhenxin 張振新, "Han dai de niugeng" 漢代的牛耕, in *Wenwu* No. 8, 1977, pp. 57-62.

[55] SS, pp. 30-31 (A 7).

[56] *Tian niu* 田牛 ; *yi niu tian* 以牛田 .

[57] SS, pp. 141-42 (C 17 and 19).

[58] SS, p. 49 (A 12).

[59] See my *Remnants*, p. 130 and cf. p. 336; see also Lin Jianming 林劍鳴, "Li chen qie bian" 隸臣妾辨, in *Zhongguo shi yanjiu* 中國史研究 No. 2, 1980, pp. 91-97.

[60] Their normal tasks are nowhere explained; we only find (SS, p. 53 (A 17)) that they, as well as bond women, were sometimes made to build pisé walls or "to perform tasks of the same difficulty," for which they likewise received extra rations. If they were clever (*qiao* 巧) they could be trained as artisans (*gong* 工), and were not to be employed as servants (*pu* 僕) or cooks. Bond women who were good seamstresses or embroiderers could be made to do this type of work (SS, p. 74 (A 60)), or they could be made to join unspecified artisans, their tasks being rated at one half or a quarter of the artisans' norm (SS, p. 74 (A 59)).

100,000 bushels (two million litres or 2,000 cubic metres).[61] Evidence for the size of small granaries is found in an arithmetical handbook of the first century B.C., which mentions a building of 30 by 45 ft, or *c.* 7 by 11 metres, with a height of 20 ft or *c.* 4.7 m, which could therefore contain 27,000 cubic feet or 10,000 bushels of unhusked grain. The same handbook describes a circular structure, 13½ ft high, or slightly over 3 m, with a circumference of 54 ft (*c.* 12.3 m), containing 2,000 bushels of husked grain.[62] Pottery models of both the square and the round type of granary are frequently found as funerary gifts and they are to be seen in most collections of Far Eastern art.[63] The texts do not mention the circular storage pits for grain, recently discovered in Luoyang 洛陽 .[64]

There exists both textual and archaeological evidence for the size of large granaries. However, the only text to provide indications is both late and disappointing, for when it reports that the Grand Granary (*taicang* 太倉) contained 120 space units (*ying* 楹), it fails to indicate the dimensions of this unit.[65] Sir Aurel Stein discovered the ruins of an enormous granary in the Dunhuang region, divided into three "halls," each measuring *c.* 42 by 14.5 metres, and Chinese archaeologists have recently discovered the remains of the Capital Granary (*jingshi cang* 京師倉) not far from Xi'an, where the surrounding wall measures 1,120 by 700 metres.[66]

Because the grain had to be stacked (*ji* 積 ; the same term is used for stacking the brushwood needed for the signal fires on the watchtowers of the defence lines), it seems likely that the grain entered into the granaries was still in the ear; this is also indicated by the use of the word *he* 禾 , meaning "grain in the ear."[67]

[61] SS, p. 36 (A 19).

[62] This handbook is the *Jiuzhang suanshu* 九章算術 ; the passage is found on p. 82 of the *Zhuzi jicheng* edition, and on p. 54 of the translation by Kurt Vogel, *Neun Bücher arithmetischer Technik*. Ostwalds Klassiker der exakten Wissenschaften, Neue Folge, Band 4 (Braunschweig, 1968).

[63] For illustrations see e.g. Hayashi Minao 林己奈夫, *Kan-dai no bunbutsu* 漢代の文物 (Kyoto, 1976), ills. 4/10-15.

[64] See "Luoyang Zhanguo liangcang shique ji lue" 洛陽戰國糧倉試掘紀略, in *Wenwu* No. 11, 1981, pp. 55-56.

[65] See Zhang Zongxiang 張宗祥 (ed.), *Jiaozheng Sanfu huang tu* 校正三輔黃圖 (Shanghai: Gudian wenxue chubanshe 古典文學出版社, 1958), p. 49; the *Sanfu huang tu* is reputedly a fifth century work.

[66] See Aurel Stein, *On Ancient Central-Asian Tracks* (London: Macmillan, 1933), plate 78; *Zhongguo huabao* 中國畫報 No. 11, 1983, p. 39.

[67] The rule in SS, p. 35 (A 19) reads *ru he cang* 入禾倉 . According to the commentary by Zheng Xuan 鄭玄 (A.D. 127-200) to the chapter *Bin li* 賓禮 of the *Yi li* 儀禮, *he* means "grain with the stalks"; see *Yi li zhu su* 儀禮注疏 (in the *Zhonghua shuju* edition of the Thirteen Classics) 20.3a (0577); John Steele, *The I-Li* (London: Probsthain, 1917), I, p. 198.

As regards the destination of the grain in the granaries, we possess several indications, with one important omission: nothing is said about the salary in kind issued to officials, both high and low, except for one oblique reference.[68] From the positive indications we learn that grain was issued to bearers of credentials which entitled them to such issues,[69] and to hard-labour convicts. For the latter the regulations go into great detail, specifying different rations for men, women, and children according to the type of labour they performed.[70] During the Han period, similar rules existed for the distribution of issues to the personnel on the frontiers and their wives and children.[71]

Rations could also be supplied to a peculiar type of labourers, namely to persons who were unable to pay their debts to the government (these will have included the borrowers of seed-grain, mentioned above), or to pay their fines or redemption fees,[72] and who redeemed these obligations by working them off, in the company of hard-labour convicts.[73] If they received food from outside, they could redeem eight cash per day, but if they received government rations, two cash per day were deducted.[74]

It is rather surprising that the Yunmeng texts lack rules for the issue of food to statute labourers, because the Qin labourers, like those of the Han period, will often have worked at some, occasionally considerable, distance from their homes; one rule mentions food (*shi* 食) but it is silent on its origin and distribution.[75]

The organization of the grain store administration with its detailed rules for checking and for punishment of the officials concerned in case of shortages or malversations, subjects treated in many of the Yunmeng texts, will not be discussed here, because they are not germane to the chief topic. But there are other points which merit attention.

The first is the care bestowed on weights and measures. All storage offices were to have full sets of weights and measures,[76] and these had to be checked

---

[68] SS, p. 82 (A 75). This article allows office chiefs and their personnel to fetch their monthly rations, together with the fodder for government horses and oxen, by means of government carts.

[69] SS, pp. 46 and 101f. (A 31, 92-94); cf. SS, p. 47 (A 33).

[70] SS, pp. 49, 51 (A 12, 15).

[71] See Michael Loewe, *Records of Han Administration* (Cambridge: Cambridge University Press, 1967), Vol. I, pp. 93f.; Vol. II, pp. 64f.

[72] See n. 20.

[73] Shallow graves of such debt-labourers have recently been found west of the First Emperor's tomb; see "Qin Shi-huang ling xice Zhaobeihucun Qin xingtu mu" 秦始皇陵西側趙背戶村秦刑徒墓, in *Wenwu* No. 3, 1982, pp. 6-7.

[74] SS, p. 84 (A 68).

[75] SS, p. 221 (D 144).

[76] SS, p. 108 (A 104).

every year;[77] their loss resulted in punishment.[78] Heavy fines were imposed on overseers when their measures showed deviations from the norm; the tolerance allowed for measures of capacity was not inconsiderable, varying between one twentieth and one eighteenth, but that for weights was much stricter, being about 1/120, or less than one percent.[79] It is impossible to say how this control worked in practice; careful measuring of bronze vessels with inscriptions that record their weight and capacity shows the existence of considerable variations.[80] It is therefore hard to believe that this rule could have been applied effectively, in spite of the existence of standard weights and measures. The availability of such standards is shown by the frequent discoveries of Qin weights, and, although two centuries later, by the standard measure of A.D. 9, of which one hundred copies are supposed to have been distributed.[81]

Another facet of the administration, where the details are unfortunately meagre, concerns accounting and reporting. The granaries had to keep book of the quantities of grain received and issued, and for this purpose they kept store registers (*kuaiji* 會籍).[82] They likewise kept registers of the recipients of grain rations, called "registers of eaters" (*shizhe ji* 食者籍). The grain accounts had to be submitted annually to the minister of agriculture, whereas the "registers of eaters" had to be sent to the Grand Granary, which in Han times,[83] and therefore presumably also under the Qin, was subordinate to the former.[84] The custom persisted under the Later Han, as witnessed by the note in the history of that period, that "in the four seasons the commanderies and kingdoms submit the registers of the cash and the grain in hand" to the minister of agriculture.[85]

Labour

A field of economic importance where the state exercised considerable influence was labour. The labour force at the disposition of the Qin government

[77] SS, p. 70 (A 54).

[78] SS, p. 213 (D 124).

[79] SS, pp. 113, 114 (B 3, 4). This rule is discussed in my article mentioned in n. 50.

[80] See Tianshi 天石, "Xi Han duliangheng lüeshuo" 西漢度量衡略說, in *Wenwu* No. 12, 1975, pp. 79-89.

[81] See Dubs in *HFHD* I, p. 277.

[82] SS, pp. 36, 38, 99, 100 (A 19, 20, 86, 87).

[83] *HSBZ* 19A.14b.

[84] SS, pp. 41-42 (A 25 and 26). For a detailed study of the Han lists found in the Edsin-gol defence lines, see Mori Shikazō 森鹿三, *Tōyōgaku kenkyū, Kyo-en Kan kan hen* 東洋學研究・居延漢簡篇 (Kyōto: Dōhōsha 同朋社, 1975), pp. 95f. and 125f. See also Loewe, *Records of Han Administration*, Vol. II, pp. 64f. and 76f. These Han lists were called *lin ming ji* 廩名籍 and *shi pu* 食簿.

[85] *HHSJJ* Tr. 26.1b.

consisted in principle of two distinct groups of people: statute labourers on the one hand and hard-labour convicts on the other. Among the latter one must include the debt-prisoners discussed above.[86]

Statute labour was performed by all men between the ages of fifteen and sixty; no service was imposed on holders of the higher aristocratic ranks, whereas the possessors of the lower of these ranks no longer served after their 56th year.[87] Their tasks consisted mainly, if not exclusively, of construction work, such as building pisé walls, digging canals, etc.

The men were punished with the bastinado when they did not present themselves at the appointed time and place (*bu hui* 不會 or *bu shi* 逋事), or when they absconded from the work site (*fa yao* 乏徭);[88] the punishment was heavier if they had taken government tools with them.[89] From a report about such a runaway who had given himself up it appears that the length of his absence had been carefully noted,[90] which shows that he had a personal file in the records of the local administration.

The authorities "loaned" tools both to statute labourers and to hard-labour convicts,[91] as well as arms to military conscripts.[92] These tools and weapons had to be marked, by branding, carving or painting,[93] as well as registered, and when they were returned, the marks had to correspond to the register, for otherwise punishment followed;[94] loss and breakage were also punished.[95] When worn out or broken tools were condemned, the marks had to be removed; scrap metal had to be delivered to the Treasury for smelting.[96] In this connection mention should be made of a statute which is occasionally mentioned, but never quoted. This is the Statute on Equipment (*ji lü* 齎律), which, to judge by the references, may have indicated the price or value of articles of equipment.[97]

Nothing was to be wasted, at least in theory. On the one hand there is the rule prescribing the use of condemned tools as firewood or covering (SS, p. 64 (A 47)), and on the other the order to manufacture writing material

---

[86] See p. 224.

[87] For details and sources see my "Some Remarks on Statute Labour during the Ch'in and Han periods," in *Orientalia Veneziana* I (Florence: Olschki, 1984), pp. 195-204.

[88] SS, pp. 220-21 (D 143, 144).

[89] SS, p. 207 (D 109).

[90] SS, p. 278 (E 6).

[91] SS, pp. 32 and 207 (A 8, D 109).

[92] SS, pp. 71 and 134 (A 56, C 8).

[93] SS, pp. 71-72 (A 56, 57).

[94] SS, p. 121 (B 19).

[95] SS, p. 60 (A 39).

[96] SS, p. 64 (A 47).

[97] SS, pp. 71 and 101 (A 56 and 88, the latter being identical with SS, p. 120 = B 15).

from local wood, or from rushes (SS, p. 83 (A 77). This use of rushes is also mentioned in the biography of Lu Wenshu 路溫舒 in *HSBZ* 51.30b (see my *Remnants*, p. 423).

The officials were also tied to strict rules. They were punished when they called up more than one person from the same household at the same time (*tongju wu bing xing* 同居勿並行);[98] they were also punished if they did not register young men of serviceable age,[99] if they did not muster the con-scripts,[100] or if they appointed prospective conscripts as "retainers."[101]

Currency

As regards the economy in general, the widespread use of coined money is striking. Of course, it is nothing new that the period of the Warring States saw the development of a money economy; sixty years ago Kojima Yūba had already demonstrated this,[102] and in recent times Li Jiannong[103] and Yang Kuan[104] have stressed it again. But it is all the same remarkable that the use of money was so general.

The currency consisted of two different types: the round bronze cash (*qian* 錢) and the piece of cloth (*bu* 布) with a standard size of 8 by 2½ feet, or *c*. 185 by 58 cm ;[105] indications concerning the quality of the tissue are lacking.[106] One "cloth" was worth eleven cash; "when cash are disbursed or entered as equivalents of gold or cloth, this is done in accordance with the Statute."[107] Unfortunately, neither this passage nor the rule that certain rewards were given "in cash or gold" (*yi qian ruo jin* 以錢若金)[108] provide

[98] SS, p. 147 (C 25).
[99] SS, p. 143 (C 20).
[100] SS, p. 222 (D 175).
[101] SS, p. 131 (C 5). "Retainers" (*dizi* 弟子) were only to be appointed if the popu-lation records allowed this (SS, p. 130 (C 4)). These *dizi* are assumed to be identical with the *shuzi* 庶子 mentioned by Shang Yang (see J.J.L. Duyvendak, *The Book of Lord Shang* [London: Probsthain, 1928], p. 295); they were assigned to holders of aristo-cratic rank to work for them six days per month and to follow them in war.
[102] Kojima Yūba 小島祐馬, "Shunjū jidai no kahei keizai" 春秋時代の貨幣經濟, in *Shinagaku* No. 1, 1921, p. 638.
[103] Li Jiannong, *op. cit.*, pp. 63f.
[104] Yang Kuan, *op. cit.*, pp. 51f.
[105] SS, p. 56 (A 43).
[106] For the different qualities of hemp cloth, depending on the tightness of the weave, see *SJ* 11.14, *Mh* II, p. 507 (not in *HSBZ* 5.9a), and especially Chen Zhi 陳直, *Liang Han jingji shiliao luncong* 兩漢經濟史料論叢 (Xi'an: Shaanxi Renmin chubanshe, 1958), p. 94.
[107] SS, p. 56 (A. 43).
[108] SS, pp. 173-74 (D 42).

any indication regarding the value of gold expressed in cash.[109]

Although the ratio between gold and cash may not have been of importance to the common people, another factor was, namely the government monopoly of coining. The Yunmeng texts prove the existence of this monopoly, and so they settle a much debated question.[110] They prove this, not by a statutory rule, but by means of an investigation report[111] which mentions the arrest of two men who had "surreptitiously cast cash" (*dao zhu qian* 盜鑄錢), and the discovery of 110 new cash and of two sets of coin moulds. However, this passage does not settle the question of the time when this monopoly was established, because the date when these reports were assembled so as to form the present collection of models is unknown. They may have been collected shortly after the battle of Xingqiu 邢丘 (266 B.C.)[112] which is mentioned in two of these reports,[113] but that does not exclude the possibility that these undated pieces, where moreover all personal names have been replaced by *jia* 甲, *yi* 乙, *bing* 丙 etc.[114] were only assembled several years or even decades later. Hence, the date of the introduction of state-controlled coinage in Qin remains unsolved. Furthermore, the possibility exists that the Qin government granted the privilege of casting coins to certain individuals, for coins have been found bearing the titles of two Qin nobles, datable in the second half of the third century B.C.[115]

Both cash and "cloth" were to be used indiscriminately (*wu gan ze xing* 勿敢擇行),[116] and the same command applied to the bronze cash, "whether good or not good" (*shan bu shan* 善不善), or "beautiful or bad" (*mei o*

---

[109] Usually, the equivalent of one *jin* 斤 or catty of gold is said to be 10,000 cash, but the first century arithmetical handbook *Jiuzhang suanshu* (see n. 62 above) mentions different sums: 6,250 cash on p. 99 (Vogel, p. 63, no. 15) and 9,800 cash on p. 113 (Vogel, p. 72, no. 5). No Qin gold ingots have been found yet, as far as I am aware. They were called *yi* 鎰 and supposedly weighed 20 ounces or about 300 grams; see *HSBZ* 24B.3b (Swann, *op. cit.*, p. 228), and the commentary to this passage by Meng Kang, also in *HFHD* I, p. 111, n. 3. For Han gold "cakes" see An Zhimin 安志敏 , "Jinban yu jinbing" 金版與金餅, in *Kaogu xuebao* 考古學報 No. 2, 1973, pp. 61-88.

[110] See for simplicity's sake Song Xuwu 宋敘五 , *Xi Han huobi shi chu gao* 西漢貨幣 史初稿 (Hong Kong: The Chinese University of Hong Kong, 1971), pp. 6f.

[111] SS, p. 252 (E 9).

[112] See *SJ* 5.75, *Mh* V, p. 90.

[113] SS, pp. 256, 257 (E 13, 14).

[114] See p. 191 of my review article mentioned in n. 1 above.

[115] See *Wenwu* No. 9, 1981, p. 88. Some of these coins bore the words Wenxin 文信, the name of the fief granted to the famous chancellor Lü Buwei 呂不韋 , who committed suicide in 235 B.C. (*SJ* 6.14, *Mh* II, p. 116). Others were marked Changan 長安, the name of the fief of the First Emperor's younger brother Chengjiao 成蟜 , Lord (*jun* 君) of Changan, who rebelled and committed suicide in 239 B.C. (*SJ* 6.6, *Mh* II, p. 106).

[116] SS, p. 57 (A 45).

美惡), which should not be differentiated (*wu gan yi* 勿敢異).[117] Cash were stored in baskets (*ben* 畚) which had to be sealed when they held one thousand pieces,[118] but the texts do not mention the storage of "cloths." Coins received during transactions had to be put in an earthenware money jar (*xiang* 缿).[119]

The ratio between cash and "cloth" of one to eleven appears frequently in the penal cases in the Yunmeng strips, where the value of stolen goods is indicated in multiples of eleven; the figures 110, 220, and 660 cash occur several times.[120] This usage continued in Han times, for a Dunhuang strip of the first century B.C. mentions "illegal profit of fully 220 cash."[121]

Trade

Remarks on trade are scarce. The Yunmeng strips contain only one single article from the *Guan shi lü* 關市律, the Statute on Passes (or control points) and Markets.[122] This article reads: "Whenever in transactions by workshops as well as by government storehouses money is received, it must be entered into the money-jar, making the dealers observe that it has been entered; nonobservance of this order is fined one suit of armour."[123] Other references to markets in the Yunmeng texts are, however, both ambiguous and not very enlightening. The clearest are perhaps those to "dealers who occupy stalls" (*gushi ju lie zhe* 賈市居列者) and to "heads of (the groups of) five stall-keepers" (*lie wu zhang* 列伍長), as well as to officials who made their rounds among them (*li xun zhi* 吏循之).[124] Also to be noted is the rule that all goods for sale, except those worth less than one cash, had to be provided with

---

[117]SS, p. 55 (A 42).

[118]SS, p. 55 (A 42).

[119]SS, p. 68 (A 51).

[120]E.g. SS, pp. 150, 165 (D 1, 27).

[121]See E. Chavannes, *Les documents chinois découverts par Aurel Stein dans les sables du Turkestan oriental* (Oxford: Imprimerie de l'Université, 1913), p. 49, strip no. 175; Wang Guowei 王國維 , *Liu sha zhui jian* 流沙墜簡 , 2.12a, no. 53.

[122]The translation "markets at the borders" is also possible, and under the Han such markets existed on the borders of the state, where the Chinese engaged in trade with the "barbarians." This is shown i.a. by *HSBZ* 94A.15b, 16a-b; Burton Watson, *Records of the Grand Historian of China* (New York and London: Columbia University Press, 1961), II, pp. 176, 178. In the present case this rendering is unsuitable, because the Yunmeng texts refer to markets which were not situated at the passes. It is likewise for the Han period that we know that goods were taxed at the passes in the interior; see *Jiuzhang suanshu* (see n. 62 above), pp. 38, 109; Vogel, *op. cit.*, p. 28, no. 3; p. 63, no. 15; p. 69, nos. 27 and 28. However, for the Qin such data are lacking.

[123]SS, p. 68 (A 51).

[124]SS, p. 57 (A 45).

price-tags.[125] Other references are to commoners, "using cash in their market [deals]" (*shi yong qian* 市用錢),[126] to hard-labour convicts who should not pass through the market (*xing shi zhong* 行市中),[127] to a thief hiding among the day-labourers at the market (*yin shi yong zhong* 陰市庸中),[128] and, of more interest, to "the correct market price (*shi zheng jia* 市正賈 [for 價])" for a slave.[129]

Finally, there is the penal rule: "When a stranger[130] has not yet presented his passport[131] to the officials and trades with them, the fine is one suit of armour" (*ke wei bu li er yu gu zi yi jia*客未布吏而與賈貲一甲).[132] The aim of this rule will have been partly to prevent people from unauthorizedly leaving their place of residence, where they were registered and where they were liable to statute labour and military service. It seems questionable whether the mass of the population had complete freedom to move elsewhere; at least, moving had to be formally announced.[133] And the attempt "to abscond from the state," i.e. escaping from Qin, was heavily punished, with tattooing and hard labour.[134] Another motive for this rule will have been to prevent aliens (potential spies!) from moving uncontrolled through Qin territory. A similar rule points in the same direction; it prescribes a heavy fine for a magistrate who allowed "wandering scholars" to stay in his county without a passport.[135] I do not think that the present rule aimed at protecting the local, let alone the national, market, as has been suggested.

Recent studies of seal impressions and inscriptions on pottery and brief indications on bronze and lacquer objects of the period of the Warring

[125] SS, p. 57 (A 46).
[126] SS, p. 55 (A 42).
[127] SS, p. 90 (A 70).
[128] SS, p. 252 (E 6).
[129] SS, p. 259 (E 15).
[130] *Ke* 客 in the Yunmeng texts indicates a stranger, but not necessarily a foreigner as the editors of SS assume in this case.
[131] For the use of passports in the Han period, most probably based on the Qin system, see Ōba Osamu 大庭脩 , *Shin Kan hōseishi no kenkyū* 秦漢法制史の研究 (Tokyo, 1982), pp. 593-618.
[132] SS, p. 230 (D 163). This is a quotation from an unknown statute. In the second half of the article *bu li* is explained as *yi fu chuan yu li* 詣符傳於吏 , "to take one's passport to the officials." Because in the Yunmeng texts fines in the form of armour or shields are always imposed on officials, it can hardly have been the trader who was fined.
[133] SS, p. 213 (D 125).
[134] SS, p. 171 (D 93).
[135] SS, p. 129 (C 3). So far, no better explanation of *you shi* 游士 has been suggested; the rendering "irregular troops" by the editors of the folio edition of the Yunmeng strips (fascicle 5, p. 86b) is unacceptable.

States[136] show that private workshops and perhaps foundries[137] were connected with the markets; they also show that the organization of the market officials partly agrees with that described in the *Zhouli.*[138]

For the lay-out of a market, the exegetes of the *Zhouli* have furnished a drawing,[139] but Han tomb tiles and a tomb mural painting reproduce more lifelike scenes.[140]

Summarizing this information, we find that there existed coins, that these were used in commercial transactions; that there were markets, where both government organs and private persons engaged in trade; that these markets were inspected by officials; that, like the population in general, traders also were organized in groups of five; that goods had to be provided with price tags; that there existed price norms, mentioned for slaves, but probably also for other goods; that "strangers" (merchants from other states?) came to trade in Qin, provided with passports; that labourers came together in the market, evidently in the expectation of being hired, although in this case the concern of the state is not clear.

Industry

In the Yunmeng texts, the references to industry are as modest as those to trade. In a few strips[141] the term *zuowu* 作務 appears, meaning "workshop."[142] Here we find signs of a "Legalist" attitude with its contempt for

---

[136] Qiu Xigui 裘錫圭, "Zhanguo wenzizhong de 'shi'" 戰國文字中的「市」, in *Kaogu xuebao* No. 3, 1980, pp. 285-96; Yuan Zhongyi 袁仲一, "Qin minying zhitao zuofang de taowen" 秦民營製陶作坊的陶文, and Sun Derun 孫德潤 and Mao Fuyu 毛富玉, "Qin du Xianyang chutu taowen shidu xiaoyi" 秦都咸陽出土陶文釋讀小議, in *Kaogu yu wenwu* 考古與文物 No. 1, 1981, pp. 95-104.

[137] Workshops: Qiu, *op. cit.*, pp. 289, 295; foundries: p. 294. See also Li Xueqin 李學勤, "Qinguo wenwu de xin renshi" 秦國文物的新認識, in *Wenwu* No. 8, 1980, pp. 25-31, esp. pp. 30f.

[138] E. Biot, *Le Tcheou-li* (Paris: Imprimerie national, 1851), I, pp. 321f.

[139] Biot, *op. cit.*, I, facing p. 309.

[140] See the splendid article by Liu Zhiyuan 劉志遠, "Han dai shijing kao" 漢代市井考, in *Wenwu* No. 3, 1973, pp. 52-57 (tomb tiles), and the equally excellent report and studies concerning the wall paintings of the second century A.D., discovered in a tomb *c.* 100 km south of Huhehot in Inner Mongolia, "Helinger faxian yi zuo zhong yao Dong Han mu" 和林格爾發現一座重要東漢墓, in *Wenwu* No. 1, 1974, pp. 8-23, esp. the illustration on p. 16 and the text on p. 17; also the four following articles, pp. 24-50.

[141] SS, pp. 68, 85 (A 51, 68).

[142] To judge by the handbooks, this term occurs only rarely. The thesaurus *Peiwen yunfu* 佩文韻府 and Morohashi Tetsuji's 諸橋轍次 large Sino-Japanese dictionary each provide only one example, where *zuowu* means "work": in ch. 39 of the *Mozi* 墨子 (Sun Yirang 孫詒讓, *Mozi xiangu* 墨子閒詁, p. 180 in the *Zhuzi jicheng* edition) it means "work, task," whereas in *HSBZ* 90.19b it means "to perform work."

the secondary pursuits, for "workshop (owners) as well as traders" were not permitted to have themselves replaced (e.g. by a slave) when redeeming their debts to the government by working (see p. 224), whereas other persons were allowed to do so.[143] This passage implicitly proves that such workshops were private establishments and not government organs, although one author, disregarding the evidence, affirms that *zuowu* were official enterprises, even adding that they may have employed convict labour.[144]

The Yunmeng texts also mention government establishments; a government workshop appears to have been called *gongshi* 工室 ,[145] but other terms are also found, like *xiangong* 縣工 [146] and the frequently mentioned *guanfu* 官府, an ambiguous term. These latter were on the one hand government storehouses, but on the other they seem also to have engaged in manufacture, for instance of tools.[147]

A more difficult problem is posed by the *duguan* 都官 , which are frequently mentioned in the Yunmeng texts. The consensus of modern scholars is that these "General Offices" (and not "offices in the capital") were local branches of those departments of the central government whose tasks were of an economic nature,[148] like the Ministry of Finance and its subordinate organizations, of which the Central Treasury and the Grand Granary are specifically mentioned.[149] Perhaps they were also engaged in the manufacture and/or sale of salt and iron.[150]

The Yunmeng texts show that at least two statutes dealt with the workmen in official establishments, viz. the *gonglü* 工律, the Statute on Artisans, and the *jungong lü* 均工律, the Statute on the Equalization of Artisan Labour. The former contains the rule that when manufacturing objects of the same type, their dimensions should be the same,[151] and a rule concerning accounting.[152] The single rule from the Statute on Equalization concerns the

[143]SS, p. 85 (A 68): *zuowu ji gu . . . bu de dai*作務及賈……不得代.

[144]Wu Rongzeng 吳榮曾 , "Qin de guanfu shougongye"秦的官府手工業, in *Yunmeng Qin jian yanjiu*, p. 43.

[145]SS, p. 74 (A 59). The text only stipulates that these workshops were to be equipped with weights and measures.

[146]SS, p. 137 (C 12).

[147]See Huang Shengzhang 黃盛璋, "Shilun San Jin bingqi de guobie yu niandai ji qi xiangguan wenti"試論三晉兵器的國別與年代及其相關問題,in *Kaogu xuebao* No. 1, 1974, p. 39, and the article by Wu Rongzeng, see n. 144.

[148]See Gao Heng 高恒, "Qin jian zhong yu zhiguan youguan de jige wenti"秦簡中與職官有關的幾個問題, in *Yunmeng Qin jian yanjiu*, p. 222.

[149]See SS, pp. 33, 64, 105 (A 9, 47, 107).

[150]See *Qin huiyao*, p. 220.

[151]SS, p. 69 (A 52).

[152]SS, p. 70 (A 53).

training of artisans, whose chiefs were the masters of the artisans (*gong shi* 工師).[153] Training should be completed in two years and good results should be rewarded.[154] The same rule shows that artisans were expected to fulfil an annual quotum, the "imposed annual work." "Annual work" is also mentioned in a rule from an unnamed statute.[155]

The few indications concerning actual enterprises are perhaps of greater interest. The first is iron mining. The rule mentions the inspection of both the quantity and the quality of the ore; if these were judged to be "poor"[156] the overseer was fined, and if this happened for three consecutive years, he was dismissed.[157] The second is lacquer. The "lacquer gardens" were inspected, and again, if these were "poor," the overseer and his staff were fined, and/or dismissed.[158] Another regulation establishes norms for the quality of the raw lacquer, based on its absorption of water, again imposing fines on the personnel if the quality was below standard.[159] The third is perhaps leather, because two identical rules prescribe regular airing for stored hides and the inevitable fines in case the hides had been damaged by insects.[160] Finally, one rule mentions hard-labour convicts working in workshops, where they made ox-carts.[161] In this case the use of convict labour shows that these workshops were official establishments, as were the brick-works and the stone cutter's yard near the tomb of the First Emperor.[162]

All in all, this is a rather meagre harvest, especially if one considers the rich Han material collected by Chen Zhi and by Satō Takeshige.[163] A reason for this disappointing result may be that government workshops fell outside the sphere of the activities of the local official in whose tomb these rules were discovered.

In this paper I have tried to assemble all references to economic activities in which the Qin state was involved in one way or another, in so far as these references are found in the Yunmeng texts. Although a certain amount of

[153] See p. 39 of the article by Wu Rongzeng, mentioned in note 144.
[154] SS, p. 75 (A 61).
[155] SS, p. 138 (C 14).
[156] *Dian* 殿, as opposed to *zui* 最, "excellent."
[157] SS, p. 138 (C 14).
[158] SS, p. 138 (C 13).
[159] SS, p. 122 (B 22).
[160] SS, pp. 120, 136 (B 18, C 10).
[161] SS, p. 137 (C 12).
[162] See "Lintong Zhengzhuang Qin shiliao jiagongchang izhi diaocha jianbao" 臨潼鄭莊秦石料加工場遺址調查簡報, in *Kaogu yu wenwu* No. 1, 1981, pp. 39-43.
[163] Chen Zhi, *op. cit.* (see n. 106 above), pp. 77-208; Satō Takeshige 佐藤武敏, *Chūgoku kodai kōgyōshi no kenkyū* 中國古代工業史の研究 (Tokyo, 1962).

information has become available, new especially as regards details, there still remain large areas about which we know next to nothing.

To draw conclusions from this fragmentary material is hazardous, particularly conclusions concerning the over-all policy behind the measures described here. It is too easy to argue along the line *post hoc, ergo propter hoc* and to call these measures "Legalist," because they happen to have been recorded in Qin in the third century B.C., i.e. about a hundred years after the father of the School of Law, Shang Yang. If they are "Legalist," then they are so in the widest sense, starting with the *Guanzi* 管子. They may even not be typical for Qin, being measures in general use in the Warring States. For instance, a counterpart of the Qin system of "bestowing" fields[164] appears also to have been practised in the state of Wei 魏 in view of the article from the Wei Statute on Households (*hu lü* 戶律) added to one of the Yunmeng prose texts.[165]

Worse than hazardous is the tendency observed in practically all Chinese and some Japanese studies on the Yunmeng texts, to see in the measures described there conscious attempts of "the newly risen landlord class" to exploit the farmers. This is applying, or rather imposing, dogmatic schemes on the material, often leading to conclusions that are not only premature but demonstrably wrong. However, another view, namely that the Yunmeng texts contained "the laws of Shang Yang" or even those of the First Emperor, proposed with great vigour in the early days of their discovery,[166] is no longer held. In particular, it is now accepted that the prose texts[167] present a strong admixture of "Confucianist" (I would prefer to say typical traditional Chinese) traits. It is even possible to argue that such ideas are found in the laws, as witnessed by the following article from the Statute on Agriculture[168] which agrees closely with passages in the chapters *Wangzhi* 王制 and *Yueling* 月令 of the canonical *Liji*.[169]

> In the second month of spring one should not venture to cut timber in the forests or to build dykes along the watercourses. Except in the months of summer, one should not venture to burn weeds to make ashes, to collect [certain plants], young animals, eggs or fledglings. One should not [lacuna] poison fish or tortoises, or arrange pitfalls and nets; by the seventh month [these prohibitions] are lifted.

---

[164] See pp. 215-17 above.

[165] SS, pp. 292-93 (cf. *RCL*, p. 209). This Wei statute prohibits "giving" (*yu* 與) fields and houses to specified kinds of persons.

[166] See pp. 182-83 of my review article mentioned in n. 1 above.

[167] Not discussed in the present paper; for the main ideas in these texts see pp. 181-86 of my review article mentioned in n. 1.

[168] SS, pp. 26-27 (A 2).

[169] See James Legge, *The Li-ki*, in *The Sacred Books of the East* (Oxford: Clarendon Press, 1885), Vol. 27, pp. 220 and 259-60.

Only when someone has died, felling wood for the inner and outer coffins is not restricted to the seasons. In settlements close to corrals and other forbidden parks one should not venture to take dogs to go hunting during the season of young animals.

It is my impression that, regardless of "Legalist" influence, the Qin laws reflect a system of economy that may well have existed, and which continued to exist, also in other agricultural societies. A typical Chinese feature may have been the importance of the work performed by statute labour conscripts and hard-labour convicts, especially in the domain of public works, like the building of walls and roads, the construction of buildings, and the digging of canals for irrigation and transport, as stressed by Professor L. S. Yang.[170]

Further research may discover typical "Legalist" traits in the Qin economy which I have failed to notice. In other Qin institutions such traits certainly appear. Although mutual responsibility appears to be a general feature of "primitive" law, I am quite ready to believe that its systematization, establishing groups of five for both the civilian population and for the military, was a Legalist invention, perhaps even to be attributed to Shang Yang. It is possible that the relative newness of this idea is reflected in the Yunmeng texts by the necessity that was felt to explain terms like "members of the same household" and "the four neighbouring [households]."[171]

By way of conclusion I would like to quote the remarks made by the famous scholar Gu Yanwu, remarks I also quoted nearly thirty years ago:[172]

From Han times onward there are many cases where Qin law has been in use right up to the present. When Confucian scholars of this time and age mention the laws of Qin, they believe these to be the laws of a vanished dynasty, because they have never deeply investigated this point.[173]

But where Gu Yanwu looked forward, from the Qin to his own day, I think it is legitimate to look also back, and especially around, at the other parts of the contemporary scene, and to suggest that the system and its rules, discussed above, were also applied, with variations and modifications, in the other Warring States. Further research, and particularly new archaeological discoveries, may throw new light on this question.

---

[170] See Lien-sheng Yang, *Les aspects économiques des travaux publiques dans la Chine impériale; quatre conférences* (Paris: Collège de France, 1964), pp. 17f., or "Economic Aspects of Public Works in Imperial China," in the same author's *Excursions in Sinology* (Cambridge, Mass.: Harvard University Press, 1969), pp. 202f. (Harvard-Yenching Institute Studies XXIV)

[171] *Tong ju* 同居 and *si lin* 四鄰 ; SS, pp. 160, 194 (D 19, 82).

[172] *Renmants*, p. 298.

[173] Gu Yanwu 顧炎武 (1613-82), *Ri zhi lu* 日知錄 ; the passage is to be found in *Ri zhi lu ji shi* 日知錄集釋 (*Sibu beiyao* 四部備要 edition) 13.2b.

8. Attempts at Economic Co-ordination during the Western Han Dynasty

Michael Loewe

I. INTRODUCTION

For the empires of Qin and Han and the various régimes set up prior to the re-unification of Sui and Tang, it is probably premature to think in terms of a theoretical "economic role of the state." For such a concept is by no means unsophisticated; it implies that a number of conscious decisions have been taken and that a number of practical conditions have been met.

It must be asked in what sense the terms "state" or "economic role of the state" can properly be applied to these early empires, and whether Qin and

Abbreviations of works cited in footnotes, including important secondary writings on subjects of economic theory and practice:

CFL   *Qianfu lun jian* 潛夫論箋, edited by Peng Duo 彭鐸 (Peking: Zhonghua shuju 中華書局, 1979).

Ch'ü   T'ung-tsu Ch'ü, *Han Social Structure* (Seattle and London: University of Washington Press, 1972).

CICA   A.F.P. Hulsewé and M.A.N. Loewe, *China in Central Asia* (Leiden: Brill, 1979).

Dubs   Homer H. Dubs, "Wang Mang and His Economic Reforms," *T'oung Pao* XXXV (1940), pp. 219-65.

He   He Changqun 賀昌群, *Han Tang jian fengjian tudi suoyouzhi xingshi yanjiu* 漢唐間封建土地所有制形式研究 (*The system of feudal landownership from the Han to the Tang periods*) (Shanghai: Renmin chubanshe, 1964).

HFHD   Pan Ku, *The History of the Former Han Dynasty*, translated by Homer H. Dubs, 3 vols. (Baltimore: Waverly Press, 1938-55).

HHS   *Hou Hanshu jijie* 後漢書集解, edited by Wang Xianqian 王先謙 (Changsha, 1920). References to the punctuated edition of the Zhonghua shuju 1965 follow in parenthesis.

Hiranaka   Hiranaka Reiji 平中苓次, *Chūgoku kodai no densei to zeihō* 中國古代の田制と税法 (*The landownership and tax system of ancient China*) (Kyoto: Kyoto University, 1967).

HS   *Hanshu buzhu* 漢書補注, edited by Wang Xianqian (Changsha, 1900). References to the punctuated edition of the Zhonghua shuju 1962 follow in parenthesis.

Hsu   Cho-yun Hsu, *Han Agriculture* (Seattle and London: University of Washington Press, 1980).

Han possessed the requisite conceptual framework, political aims, and administrative competence. The existence of a "state" must presumably rest on the recognition that the established authority of administration is the sole legitimate instrument of government, backed by acceptable intellectual principles, and, until the nineteenth and twentieth centuries, by religious sanction. Probably there must also be a conscious feeling of membership of that single, legitimate organization; a readiness to obey defined authorities with an acknowledgement of their powers; and a willingness on the part of the population to devote its major effort and life-long support to the maintenance of that authority.

The adoption of an economic role implies a determination of priorities, a conscious decision of the extent to which economic motives should take precedence over other considerations of a moral or religious nature. Such a role would also imply a state's assumption of responsibility for the material well-being of its population and the provision of its necessities; and it would be necessary to formulate criteria for such prosperity that are not contradictory. In China, for example, a conflict could well arise if the general ambition entertained by provincial officials to report an increase in population

Katō	Katō Shigeshi 加藤繁, *Shina keizaishi kōshō* 支那經濟史考證 (*Studies in Chinese economic history*; English summaries by E. G. Pulleyblank), 2 vols. (Tokyo: Tōyō Bunko, 1952-53).
Li	Li Jiannong 李劍農, *Xian Qin liang Han jingji shigao* 先秦兩漢經濟史稿 (*A draft economic history of China for the pre-imperial periods, Qin and Han*) (Peking: Shenghuo Dushu Xinzhi sanlian shudian 生活讀書新知三聯書店, 1957).
Nishijima (1961)	Nishijima Sadao 西嶋定生, *Chūgoku kodai teikoku no keisei to kōzō* 中國古代帝國の形成と構造 (*The formation and structure of early imperial China*) (Tokyo: University of Tokyo, 1961).
Nishijima (1966)	Nishijima Sadao, *Chūgoku keizaishi kenkyū* 中國經濟史研究 (*Studies in the economic history of China*) (Tokyo: University of Tokyo, 1966).
RHA	Michael Loewe, *Records of Han Administration*, 2 vols. (Cambridge: Cambridge University Press, 1967).
SC	*Shiji* 史記; references are to *Shiki kaichū kōshō* 史記會注考證 (Tokyo, 1932-34). References to the punctuated edition of the Zhonghua shuju 1959 follow in parenthesis.
Swann	Nancy Lee Swann, *Food and Money in Ancient China* (Princeton: Princeton University Press, 1950).
Utsunomiya	Utsunomiya Kiyoyoshi 宇都官清吉, *Kan dai shakai keizaishi kenkyū* 漢代社會經濟史研究 (*Researches in the social and economic history of the Han period*) (Tokyo: Kōbundō, 1955).
YTL	*Yantie lun* 鹽鐵論; references are to Wang Liqi 王利器, *Yantie lun jiaozhu* 鹽鐵論校注 (Shanghai: Gudian wenxue chubanshe 古典文學出版社, 1958).
Yü	Ying-shih Yü, *Trade and Expansion in Han China* (Berkeley and Los Angeles: University of California Press, 1967).

coincided with a time when neither their own regions nor the empire as a whole could claim to be self-sufficient. Similarly, on a local level, it would be necessary to determine the relative importance of waterways as a means of transport or as a source of irrigation. In practical terms, an economic role depends on a sense of system sufficient to formulate comprehensive policies, and the ability to impose long-term, and probably unpopular, decisions, and to survive the consequent short-term disadvantages and disaffection. A state must also be able to command sufficient basic information with which to formulate its policies and assess its immediate needs, for instance in the form of an annual budget.

At the outset of the imperial period these conditions had hardly been met, and many had not been attained by the second or third centuries A.D. During the first century of Western Han, statesmen and writers were still seeking to place imperial government within a major cosmic context and to demonstrate the intellectual case for supporting such an authority. Signs of a reaction against the exercise of such authority, and even of a nostalgia for a pre-imperial system, cannot be ignored. According to one writer,[1] it was still necessary for Western Han governments to attempt to engender a sense of participation in imperial polity; and the social unrest of the second century A.D. clearly illustrates that loyalties and service to a single authority of state were easily jettisoned in favour of regional independence.

By no means all Han philosophers would have agreed that the prime responsibility of government lies in the greatest exploitation of natural resources for the benefit of the population, as some argued. Although there are some signs of a sense of system in countering major problems (for example the disruption caused by the Yellow River), it is evident that a sufficient degree of co-ordination could hardly be achieved as yet. While the institutions of Qin, Han, and the later régimes made provision for the regular collection of basic information, by means of an annual census and register of land, it is by no means certain how effectively those tasks could be performed. Nor is it certain that sufficient information was available to alert the central authorities of Xianyang 咸陽, Chang'an 長安 or Luoyang 洛陽 to certain overriding problems, such as the proportion of population to arable land, that cannot be ignored in formulating an "economic role." In alluding to such problems, Cho-yun Hsu assumes that Han governments "were determined to maintain the security and prosperity of the farming population, which was regarded as the foundation of the empire."[2] It would seem to be questionable whether, for Qin and Han, an economic role can be sought in more precise terms.

[1] See Nishijima (1961).
[2] See Hsu, p. 34.

But despite these qualifications, there are two main reasons why the history of Qin and Han has relevance to a study of an economic role of the state in China. In the first instance, in facing the immediate problems of administration, those governments had perforce to take decisions which affected the economic practices of the empire. Such decisions were frequently regarded as precedents that later régimes followed, or taken as the starting point for enquiry by statesmen or philosophers. When theoretical ideas of the state and the economy were formed, the practices of these pioneer dynasties were in the forefront of officials' minds.

Secondly, there is considerable evidence to show that, in their concern with immediate practical problems of government, statesmen enunciated, questioned or rejected a number of principles. Such principles obtrude in the memorials of officials such as Jia Yi 賈誼 (200-168 B.C.), Dong Zhongshu 董仲舒 (c. 179-c. 104 B.C.) or Sang Hongyang 桑弘羊 (152-80 B.C.), when suggesting practical measures to alleviate some of China's problems, promote public enterprises or encourage certain occupations. A number of decisions of a government disclose an attitude towards the economy, such as the employment of two wealthy individuals (Dongguo Xianyang 東郭咸陽 and Kong Jin 孔僅), whose fortunes derived from private enterprise, to manage projects on behalf of the empire. Towards the end of the Western Han period it is possible to cite views expressed by leading statesmen on matters of principle, such as Gong Yu 貢禹 (fl. c. 40 B.C.) or Wang Mang 王莽 (r. A.D. 9-23).

Moreover, the governments of the early empires took a whole host of measures that were directly concerned with individual aspects of the economy. In addition to the offices and commissions designed to raise revenue and manage finance, institutions were found to operate sponsored agricultural settlements at the periphery of the empire. Some attempts were made to control the size of land-holdings and to organize imperial monopolies for the salt and iron industries and for some other types of production. There were statesmen who initiated steps to control the minting of coin and the circulation of gold; to standardize weights and measures or to supervise markets. Experiments were made to render stable the prices of certain staple goods or to establish a balanced means of distribution. Han imperial governments also concerned themselves with trade with peoples living outside China; officials were certainly concerned with the erection, maintenance, and repair of communications lines.

Some of these subjects are open to study in theoretical as well as in practical terms. In addition to the positive proposals whose texts are given in the standard histories, there is also the highly valuable evidence of critics. This may be found in documents such as the *Yantie lun* 鹽鐵論 compiled c. 50 B.C., or the *Qianfu lun* 潛夫論 of Wang Fu 王符 (A.D. 90-165) as discussed below. For the end of the Han period, the histories include the criticism voiced in theoretical terms by men such as Zhongchang Tong 仲長統 (b. 180), Xun Yue 荀悅 (148-209) or Cui Shi 崔寔 (b. *c.* 110). In terms of practical achievements, the consistency, success or weakness of the government's enterprises may be studied in the records of the standard histories. It need hardly be stressed that those records are likely to be unsatisfactory and incomplete, and that they often record events or conditions to illustrate abnormal rather than normal circumstances.[3]

II. BASIC ATTITUDES AND THEIR APPLICATION

Decisions that concerned the operation of the economy derived from one of two basic attitudes to the role and duty of the government. At times those attitudes may be seen to be at complete variance, on grounds of principle; at times they vary in respect of degree or priorities only, as the protagonists of the two sides shared considerable ground in common. The two attitudes stand revealed in respect of ideology, domestic policy, and foreign policy alike.

In political terms, the difference lay between those who saw dynastic power as that of a dictator and those who saw it as an instrument of protection; between those who admired the achievements and the ruthlessness ascribed to Qin, or those who espoused the ideals claimed on behalf of Zhou 周. In religious practice, the choice lay between worshipping the five *di* 帝 or *tian* 天. In matters of domestic policies, the principal question at issue was whether officials should be entitled to control and organize individuals in the interests of the governing power, without concern for individual circumstances, or whether they should recognize that individuals had a right to enjoy their private interests and exploit their own occupations. It was asked how far the government would be justified in coercing individuals so as to

---

[3] The principal sources of information in the standard histories will be found in *SC* 30 and *HS* 24 (translated in Swann, and partly in *HFHD*, Vol. III, pp. 476-505); *SC* 129 and *HS* 91 (translated in Swann). See also Rhea C. Blue, "The Argumentation of the *Shih-huo chih* Chapters of the Han, Wei and Sui Dynastic Histories," *Harvard Journal of Asiatic Studies*, Vol. 11 (1948), pp. 1-118. For the Han government's concern with irrigation and transport, see *SC* 29 and *HS* 29. For partial translations of the *Yantie lun*, see Esson M. Gale, *Discourses on Salt and Iron* (Leyden: Brill, 1931) and Esson M. Gale, Peter A. Boodberg and T. C. Lin, "Discourses on Salt and Iron," *Journal of the North China Branch of the Royal Asiatic Society*, Vol. LXV (1934), pp. 73-110. Both items have been reprinted, in one volume, by Ch'eng-wen Publishing Company, Taipei, 1967. For a summary of the arguments presented in *YTL*, See Michael Loewe, *Crisis and Conflict in Han China* (London: George Allen and Unwin, 1974) hereafter *Crisis and Conflict*, Chapter 3.

build up its own strength and wealth. In foreign affairs the difference lay between expansionist ventures on the one hand and retrenchment on the other. Should the dynasty be ready to extend its power by means of aggression, annexation and a display of force, or should it renounce positive attempts to expand its sphere of influence by means of armed strength, and rest content with a display of moral example?

As identification of these two attitudes with a "Legalist" and a "Confucian" category is somewhat imprecise and misleading; they have been described under the terms "modernist" and "reformist."[4] It is highly fortunate that the account of an important debate on these principles refers to specific questions that were raised just at a moment of transition in Han history when they had become subject to criticism and review. In chronological terms it is possible to trace four stages whereby these attitudes developed and changed during the four centuries of the Qin and Han periods.

1. From 221 to *c.* 90 B.C. This period was characterized by a modernist approach, as may be seen in the attempts of the Qin government to impose a discipline throughout China. Even when due allowance is made for the exaggerations of later critics, of Han, it must be accepted that Qin's style of government comprised a new measure of purposeful organization. The attitude was inherited by the rulers of Han, who introduced some measure of modification during the first seven decades of the dynasty, when the emphasis lay on internal consolidation rather than expansion. But for a period of some fifty years, beginning *c.* 130 B.C., a new forward-looking approach may be identified, both in domestic matters and foreign policies. In so far as the economy was concerned, it was these decades which witnessed the reorganization of the offices of imperial finance; the final measures to standardize and control the minting of coin; the establishment of monopolies for the mines; the introduction of measures to stabilize prices and ease distribution; attention to the control of water, for the purposes both of transport and irrigation; and the sponsorship of agricultural colonies at China's perimeter. The highest point of achievement and pride of the modernist statesmen was marked in symbolic terms by the religious innovations and introduction of a new regnal title in 105 B.C.

2. From *c.* 90 B.C. to Wang Mang's dynasty (A.D. 9-23). A change set in with the realization that the expansionist foreign policies of earlier years were beginning to take their toll of the government's resources and to breed hardship, despair, and popular bitterness. Statesmen were arguing that moderation was now necessary together with retrenchment, and that human suffering could be ignored only at the cost of potential rebellion. In practical

[4] See Loewe, *Crisis and Conflict.*

242

terms the change may be noticed in the reduction of public expenditure, the relaxation of some controls and the mitigation of punishments; abortive attempts were made to control the size of land-holdings. An aggressive foreign policy gave way to attempts at peaceful colonization and, later, to accommodation with foreign leaders. Ideological change was conspicuous in the new forms and objectives of imperial worship introduced in the first instance in 31 B.C. At least one statesman questioned the value of a monetary economy. Amidst a host of measures designed to identify his régime with the glorious past, Wang Mang tried to circulate new forms of currency that were alleged to derive from ancient practice.

3. From *c.* A.D. 25 to 150. Of all times in Qin and Han, this period is the most difficult to characterize. The attention of historians has focussed mainly on the dynastic developments and intrigues, and considerable research is still needed to establish what issues were dominant. With the restoration of the Han dynasty, there developed a renewal of self-confidence and strength, as may be seen in the expansionist foreign policies. At the same time it was the ideals of the kings of Zhou rather than the house of Qin that were in favour. Possibly it was a lack of strict disciplined government which permitted the growth of some of the excesses and abuses of the final stage. For example, it was at this time that the great landed families were exerting considerable strength and practising local autonomy at the expense of the authority of the central and provincial organs of government.[5]

4. From *c.* 150 to 220. These decades were characterized by unstable dynastic conditions, with subsequent social and political abuse. A few men or women occupied dominant positions whence they could exercise arbitrary powers. Decisions depended partly on personal jealousies or intrigues in high places, with an attendant loosening of the structure and fabric of government. Economic imbalances and social unrest gave rise to a re-assessment of the ideals of government. A few critics called for a re-introduction of controls and effective legal sanctions, so as to repair the damage of a "permissive" society. It was realized that the ideals of the house of Zhou or a "Confucian" way of life were insufficient by themselves to govern an empire; there was a call for some of the measures associated with the "Legalist" régime of Qin.[6]

[5] See Lien-sheng Yang, "Great Families of Eastern Han," in E-tu Zen Sun and John de Francis (eds.), *Chinese Social History* (Washington: American Council of Learned Societies, 1956), pp. 103-34. Original Chinese text in *The Tsing Hua Journal*, Vol. XI, No. 4 (1936), pp. 1007-63. I am indebted to Professor Hulsewé for pointing out (in a private communication) that the growth of these families and their influence can be traced back to the first century B.C. or even earlier.

[6] For a study of some of the writers of this period, see Etienne Balazs, "Political Philosophy and Social Crisis at the End of the Han Dynasty," in his *Chinese Civilization*

In the following pages we shall first consider four basic principles and distinctions that concern (1) primary and secondary occupations; (2) public and private profits; (3) the proper use of conscripted labour; and (4) the advantages of thrift or consumption. We shall then observe how these principles applied in practical terms to landownership, the mines, taxation and labour, commerce and the distribution of goods, coinage and the role of money, and foreign policies.

III. PRINCIPLES AND DISTINCTIONS

A. Primary and Secondary Occupations

The terms *ben* and *mo* 本末 (the root and the tip) are used in contradistinction in the *Guanzi* 管子 and in many texts of the Han period. To Han writers, *ben* signified agriculture and sericulture; *mo* signified mining, manufacture, and commerce. At first sight it might appear that the distinction lay, in theoretical terms, between occupations which depended on gathering the products of nature; and those which involved the employment of intermediate labour, the collection of benefits that resulted from such persons' work and the use of a medium of exchange. But the distinction is by no means so clear, for several reasons. First, there were some types of livelihood, such as forestry or fisheries, which depended on the direct gathering of natural products but which were not included in the category of *ben* or primary occupations; secondly, sericulture was a highly complex process, far removed from the simple collection of nature's gifts, and requiring skills, training, and intermediate labour; thirdly, by the time of Mengzi 孟子 at least it was being recognized that the various occupations of mankind cannot be worked in isolation.[7] It was accepted that efficient agriculture depended on the provision of iron-made tools, and that this derived from the product of the mines and distribution by merchants. Similarly, conscript or hired workers

---

and Bureaucracy, translated by H. M. Wright, edited by Arthur F. Wright (New Haven and London: Yale University Press, 1964), pp. 187-225. For special studies of Xun Yue, see Chi-yun Chen, *Hsün Yüeh (A.D. 148-209)* (Cambridge: Cambridge University Press, 1975); and Ch'en Ch'i-yün, *Hsün Yüeh and the Mind of Late Han China* (Princeton: Princeton University Press, 1980). For specialist studies of Cui Shi, see Patricia Ebrey, "Estate and Family Management in Later Han, as Seen in the *Monthly Instructions for the Four Classes of People*," *Journal of the Economic and Social History of the Orient*, Vol. XVII, 1974, pp. 173-205, and Patricia Buckley Ebrey, *The Aristocratic Families of Early Imperial China* (Cambridge: Cambridge University Press, 1978).

[7] See, e.g., James Legge, *The Chinese Classics*, Vol. II (Oxford: Clarendon Press, 1895), pp. 246f.

244

in the mines required and deserved the products of the farm; and merchants must be able to concentrate their energies on the distribution of goods, without needing to expend effort on the work of the fields. A forceful reiteration of the point that all three types of occupation, those of farmer, artisan and merchant, are necessary for a nation is to be found in the *Shiji*.[8]

The question that was always to the forefront of Chinese minds at this time, and indeed later, was that of the proportionate effort suitable for these different occupations. As those who were engaged in industry or commerce handled money and had greater opportunities to benefit thereby, there was a constant fear that too many persons would flee the countryside in preference for the towns, in the hope of acquiring wealth more quickly than by the drudgery of the fields; and that as a result, while private fortunes might accumulate, the real wealth of the nation would dwindle. Expressions of this fear recur in many passages of Han writing, whatever the persuasion of the author might be.[9] In discussing suggestions that concerned China's economy, Han officials did not question the principle that *ben* should take priority over *mo*; they argued about the changes in priorities for the two types of work that might ensue from any major decisions that were taken.

B. Public and Private Profits

Closely associated with the distinction that was drawn between *ben* and *mo* was the further distinction between profits which could be said to accrue to the community at large and those that benefited a private individual. The distinction lies behind the conflicting claims made on behalf of private and public ownership of land and it is manifest in the arguments raised concerning the work of the mines. It appears very clearly, in connection with *ben* and *mo*, in a passage of the *Qianfu lun*, which was written towards the end of the Eastern Han period.[10] "Of all the principles of setting a country in order," the chapter starts, "none is more commendable than restraining secondary occupations and concentrating on basic enterprises; none is less commendable than the abandonment of primary tasks and the cultivation of secondary work." While this view re-echoes ideas that had been expressed much earlier, the argument continues by exposing the fallacy inherent in an excessive pursuit of immediate short-term profits. Public wealth is of much greater

---

[8]*SC*, 129.4f (3254f.), Swann, 420f.; *YTL*, 1 (2f.) (Gale's translation, p. 6).

[9] For the distinction between *ben* and *mo* in Western Han writings and the stress laid upon the prior claims of *ben*, see *HS*, 4.11a and 14a (118 and 124), *HFHD*, Vol. I, pp. 245 and 253; *HS*, 24A.9b (1127f.), for a memorial by Jia Yi (Swann, pp. 153f.); and *YTL*, 1.1 (Gale's translation, pp. 1-2).

[10]*CFL*, 2.14f.

importance than private wealth. Certain occupations, in industry and commerce, which are categorised as "inessential" (*youye* 游業) are criticized on the grounds that they lead simply to private gain at the expense of the people and to the detriment of the commonwealth:

> By adopting the order of heaven and distributing the benefits of the earth, the six types of domestic animal are born in their due season and the manifold creations of nature are stored up in the fields; this is the basic way (*ben*) of enriching a country. The secondary work (*moshi* 末事) of inessential occupations (*youye*) is a means of collecting the profits of the population, and therein lies the basic cause of impoverishing the country (*bang* 邦).

Wang Fu was writing at a time when social and political instability had seen the growth of the semi-independent estates and the consequent loss of revenue to the central government. It is hardly surprising that he places responsibility firmly with the ruler for maintaining the right balance between *ben* and *mo*. He expounds his argument with some subtlety and adds a point that might not have been accepted by all. This is that a distinction between primary and secondary priorities should be drawn not only between those who work for the common good in the fields, or the silkfarms, and those who follow exotic and inessential occupations for their own private benefit. There is a similar distinction between the proper and improper work of two other types of individual, the artisan and the merchant. The proper objectives of artisans and merchants are respectively to make utilities and to circulate goods; their objectives are to be deprecated, as being of a secondary nature, if they are engaged in the work of embellishment or in trafficking in exotics.

C. Conscript Labour

By the Qin and Han period it was a well-established tradition that, while the proper and natural work of the great majority of the population lay in producing cereal crops from the soil, officials of kings and emperors were entitled to require the services of able-bodied men for certain tasks that devolved on the government. Men were liable to be called up both to serve in the armed forces, in the interests of security, and also as labourers to work on civil projects. Some of the Zhanguo 戰國 philosophers, notably Mengzi, were accustomed to warn their sovereigns that the excessive use of conscript labour would be self-defeating in view of the harm wrought to agriculture; for not only does a lengthy period of call-up remove men from the productive work of the fields at just the time when they are required; it imposes on those who are left there the burden of providing the necessities of life for those serving in the forces or the labour gangs.

Conscript labour may have been employed by the kings of Shang in the casting of bronze, but there is no certain evidence to prove this supposition.

246

It was probably needed from a comparatively early period to transport staple goods, or to build roads, cut canals and erect lines of fortifications; and with the growth of the larger and prouder political units of the Zhanguo period such labour could well have been directed to the construction of palaces or mausolea or to supply other forms of royal requirements.

By the time of the empires metal working had long been organized as a private enterprise by commercial or industrial magnates.[11] Able-bodied men owed statutory periods of service, both for military and for civil purposes, and it was part of the responsibility of provincial and local officials to call up and organize this labour. Probably much of it was used for the transport of grain and textiles (i.e. tax dues) from the farms, and for their delivery to the armed forces, although the services of merchants were sometimes recruited for this arduous work. Conscript servicemen may also have been used to maintain waterways and roads; we know, for example, how they took part sometimes in repairing the breaches of the Yellow River. Some conscript labour, known as *tianzu* 田卒 was employed in working the officially sponsored farms at the northwestern frontiers. In addition, it is possible that some of these men were put to work by offices such as the *Shangfang* 尚方, whose duty lay in manufacturing objects of beauty, or utility, for the imperial palace and elsewhere (e.g., bronze mirrors and lacquer vessels).[12] It will be seen below how at one stage conscript labour was put to work in the mines at the behest of the state.

D. Thrift or Consumption

It is a general and well-worn theme of Han statesman and philosophers that the emperor and his officials bear the prime duty of restricting public expenditure to a minimum, so as to avoid the imposition of unduly heavy taxation on the population. In this connection Wendi 文帝 (r. 180-157 B.C.)[13] is usually cited as a paragon, whose choice of thrift formed a stark contrast with the practices of certain other monarchs. In practical terms, some of the measures of the reformist statesmen who served Yuandi 元帝 (r. 49-33 B.C.) and Chengdi 成帝 (r. 33-7 B.C.) were deliberately designed to reduce the expenses of the palace in order to relieve the population.

The view that indulgence in extravagant luxury is a mark of poor

---

[11] *HS*, 91.8b (3690f.); Swann, pp. 425f.

[12] For the use of conscript labour to repair breaches in the dykes, see *HS*, 29.9a, 11a (1680, 1684), *Crisis and Conflict*, pp. 191-92; for the *tianzu*, see *RHA*, Vol. I, pp. 56, 70, 81; for the *Shangfang*, see Michael Loewe, *Ways to Paradise: The Chinese Quest for Immortality* (London: George Allen and Unwin, 1979), p. 175, note 33.

[13] For praise of Wendi's parsimony, see *HS*, 36.20a (1951) and *CFL*, 12.130.

government and social imbalance is brought out forcefully in the *Yantie lun* and in at least one of Wang Fu's essays.[14] Not only do we hear the complaint that there was a grave difference between contemporary practice and the ideals of the past; it was also claimed that the differences in the standards of living enjoyed or suffered by different classes of society were deplorable. As an example, Wang Fu writes about the useless expenditure of labour and materials for the sake of embellishing Luoyang's buildings with splendidly carved rare timber, brought from the difficult terrain of the deep south or the west. He points out the cost of these habits in terms of the production of staple goods; and he claims that the extravagant habits of Luoyang's pampered inhabitants were being aped in other classes of society and practised as far afield as Lelang 樂浪 and Dunhuang 敦煌 in the extreme northeastern and northwestern parts of the empire.

As against this point of view there is some evidence of the opposite opinion, that the consumption of goods is to be encouraged as a means of distributing wealth and keeping the economy active rather than sluggish. In discussing this question, Lien-sheng Yang cites evidence from the *Guanzi* to show how this principle was sometimes expressed and put forward. The passage favours the consumption of luxury articles, the brisk circulation of goods and the custom of extravagant funerals, in the interests of inducing fuller employment; the luxurious fashions of life of the rich will, it is hoped, provide work and a livelihood for the poor. Lien-shang Yang adds that a justification for spending, on similar grounds, may be found in a few passages of the *Xunzi* 荀子 and the *Yantie lun*, and that it is promoted somewhat conspicuously much later, by Fan Zhongyan 范仲淹 (989-1052).[15]

The passages cited by Yang for the Han period apply to the consumption of material resources rather than to the expenditure of money. It has also been suggested that the main passage that is cited, from the *Guanzi*, was written as late as *c.* 190 B.C., but this suggestion remains to be proved. It should perhaps be stressed that the view that consumption of goods would be likely to benefit the economy rather than to impoverish the empire or individuals was exceptional at this time, when policies of thrift were usually being praised.

---

[14] *YTL*, 29 (201f.) and *CFL*, 12 (120f.).

[15] See Lien-sheng Yang, "Economic Justification for Spending—An Uncommon Idea in Traditional China," originally published in the *Harvard Journal of Asiatic Studies*, Vol. 20 (1957), pp. 36-52; reprinted in Lien-sheng Yang, *Studies in Chinese Institutional History* (Cambridge, Mass.: Harvard University Press, 1961), pp. 58-74.

IV. PRACTICE AND PROBLEMS

A. Landownership

Although there is insufficient evidence to define conditions of land-tenure accurately, or in full, it is both possible and necessary to draw certain basic distinctions, as between land vested in the imperial family, estates made over to noblemen, privately owned land, and land disposed by officials.

Lands such as the imperial pleasure grounds were regarded as being the property of the emperor and guarded somewhat jealously from a threat of take-over. It is not possible to determine the size of such lands or to estimate how they grew or diminished over the years. They seem to have been situated mostly within the metropolitan area itself.

Further afield, and scattered throughout the empire, were the lands over which named individuals held certain rights. These were the *guo* 國 that were made over to the *liehou* 列侯 (nobles or marquises), in the sense that they were entitled to levy taxation from a specified number of households and to retain part of those dues as their personal emoluments. This right was bestowed on the nobles in hereditary form, and to holders of some of the lower orders of aristocratic rank (*jue* 爵) on a personal basis and on a much smaller scale. Part of the value of the genealogical tables incorporated in the *Hanshu* as chapters 16 to 18 lies in their specification of the extent of these entitlements.

It should be stressed that the bestowal of a nobility did not imply a grant of land to the holder. The institution, which had both a political and an administrative function, had been established at the outset of the Han period, before the system of commanderies and prefectures had been put into full operation under officials appointed for personal tenure. Nobilities were bestowed directly in return for meritorious service, and the history of the institution shows how they could be used to reward an emperor's loyal followers or to settle potential dissident elements. While political or dynastic considerations could thus influence the administration of the land, they did not concern the ownership of the land in this connection.

Individual owners stood possessed of land on which they paid the *zu* 租 or land-tax. There is some difference of opinion regarding the legal basis upon which such land was held, some scholars regarding it as being held in perpetuity, others as being held on lease from the sovereign or the officials.[16] However this may be, the land in question had probably been acquired in the first instance by purchase or through inheritance from an ancestor. It remains

[16] For the nature of landownership, see Li, Hiranaka, Ch. I-V, and A.F.P. Hulsewé, Chapter 7 of this volume.

an open question whether the use of the different terms *mingtian* 名田 in Western Han and *zhantian* 佔田 in Eastern Han signifies a change in the character or legal basis of land-tenure.

That land was disposable by other means is shown by the instances in which it was officially bestowed by authorities of the government or by imperial decree. The principle was enunciated shortly after Liu Bang's 劉邦 victory over his rivals[17] and was exemplified on a number of occasions later. By the time of Wudi's 武帝 reign (141-87 B.C.) it is possible to assume the existence of a category of *gongtian* 公田 [18] which included not only arable land but also parkland and lakeland. Some of the *gongtian* had come into the hands of official authorities as a result of confiscation from criminals; some had been simply taken over by servicemen or colonists during the campaigns of expansion and imperial advance.

To statesmen of a modernist frame of mind, land was primarily to be regarded as a source of revenue which was usually collected, at least in part, in kind. So long as there was still more land potentially available than the labour that could work it, those who wished to increase the wealth and strength of the empire would see no reason why a limit should be imposed on the extent of an individual's holdings; for the wider the extent of the land that individual owners possessed and worked, the greater the revenue that would acrue to the imperial treasury.

By contrast, those who believed that the duty of the emperor and his officials lay principally in alleviating popular hardship could scarcely avoid observing the growing disparity between the rich landowners with their large properties and the living conditions of the very poor peasantry. Possibly the sources tend to overplay this disparity which may be mentioned for purposes of special pleading; there is no means available with which to estimate the proportion of large landowners or small holders. The principal and earliest protests against the disparity were voiced by Dong Zhongshu (*c.* 179-104 B.C.), whose plea for restricting the size of landholdings has frequently been quoted.[19]

Dong Zhongshu was arguing in terms of the conditions that had emerged while modernist policies were being promoted to their most intense degree; he did not fall into the trap of appealing for a re-institution of the communal *jingtian* 井田 system in the circumstances then prevailing. We also hear of a further complaint in regard to the development of conditions of land-tenure. It would seem that from Wudi's time onwards the authorities had been

[17] *HS*, 1B.5a (54), *HFHD*, Vol. I, p. 105.
[18] See He, pp. 158f.
[19] *HS*, 24A.16a (1137f.), Swann, pp. 179f.

making over plots of *gongtian* to privileged individuals who were thereupon leasing it out to farmers or peasantry for rent. A spokesman in the *Yantie lun* complains that this practice had reduced the actual output of the fields and appeals for such lands to be made over directly to those who were working them, in return for payment of tax rather than rent.[20]

It is hardly surprising that Dong Zhongshu's advice lay unheeded at the time. But changes are noticeable in the succeeding decades, as modernist politicians were losing ground to reformist officials. In the reigns of Zhaodi 昭帝 (87-74 B.C.) and particularly Yuandi (49-33 B.C.) definite steps were taken to redistribute some of the *gongtian*, perhaps to allay criticism of the type that is incorporated in the *Yantie lun*. Moreover, towards the end of the Western Han dynasty more definite attempts were made to implement Dong Zhongshu's principles. In 7 B.C. an official named Shi Dan 師丹 suggested that the extent of landholdings, together with the number of slaves that an inidividual could possess, should be limited by law, according to a scale which corresponded with the status of the owner. It has been suggested that this proposal was directed against the ever increasing landholdings of certain prominent families; it is related that although the proposal was accepted, it was owing to the opposition of such families that it was not put into effect.[21]

More drastic measures were actually attempted by Wang Mang, shortly after his accession in A.D. 9. These were no less than a compulsory division of property by the rich and a ban on the sale and purchase of land and slaves; in this instance support was sought from the supposition that China had enjoyed prosperity in the golden past, thanks to the *jingtian* system. By coining the new term *wangtian* 王田, Wang Mang was perhaps attempting to introduce recognition of the principle of state ownership, on the basis of a famous line in the *Odes*.[22] Like Dong Zhongshu, Wang Mang pointed to the tragic disparity between the living standards of the rich and the poor, and sought to remedy injustice; like Shi Dan he was unable to put his scheme into practice. A number of judicial processes followed the institution of his ban and the consequent disruption was such that in A.D. 12 Wang Mang was reluctantly forced to abandon his order and to recognize exchanges of land by sale and purchase.[23] In the later part of Eastern Han, such a scheme would have been even less likely to succeed, in view of the growth of the large

[20] *YTL*, 13 (95f.) (Gale's translation, pp. 81f.).

[21] *HS*, 11.2b (336f.), *HFHD*, Vol. III, p. 21; *HS*, 24A.20a (1142), Swann, p. 200; *HS*, 86.16a (3503); He, pp. 159f.; Loewe, *Crisis and Conflict*, pp. 267-69. For the value of land as an investment, see Hsu, pp. 36-57.

[22] *HS*, 24A.21a (1143f.), Swann, pp. 208f.; *Crisis and Conflict*, p. 294.

[23] *HS*, 24A.21b (1144), Swann, p. 211.

semi-independent estates.[24]

Officials of government were also concerned with landownership when administering the frontier areas of the northwest. Permanent defences and communication lines had been erected in those remote regions, and the normal provincial organs of commandery and prefecture could hardly operate in the same way as in central China. As a means of supporting the garrisons on duty and in order to preclude or reduce the need for the transport of grain over long distances, attempts were made to establish sponsored farms, or military colonies, organized by officials with the help of conscript labour. The work involved a considerable amount of engineering and irrigation before the land could be rendered fertile, and the history of these projects shows that considerable initiative, and sometimes inducement, was necessary.

During Wendi's reign (180-157 B.C.) a statesman with a modernist outlook named Chao Cuo 鼂錯 urged that, rather than depend on conscript servicemen for the settlement of these regions, it would be better to call for volunteers. Families should be invited to proceed to the frontiers, as yet far less deeply advanced into Central Asia than they were later, and to establish themselves as colonists; the government should provide material support and inducement.[25] Later, as a result of the territorial advances of Wudi's reign (141-87 B.C.), the problem of effectively occupying and working the frontier areas had been aggravated. Longer distances were involved and farming conditions were less attractive; it became regular practice to detail some of the servicemen for duty in the newly established fields, and they are appropriately described in documents as *tianzu* 田卒.

In addition, new institutions set up to administer the lands of the advanced frontier included imperial commissioners who were responsible for organizing agricultural work (i.e. the *nong duwei* 農都尉 and the *tianguan* 田官);[26] in such enterprises it is to be presumed that the land was effectively possessed and controlled by officials rather than being vested in private ownership. However, there is some evidence to show that there were also private landholdings in these areas. Fragments found from the sites of Juyan 居延 suggest the presence of civilians who were liable to land-tax, and there are a few assessments of property belonging to officers of the forces which included dwellings and arable land. Recently found documents from the northwest that are said to concern taxation may possibly reveal more about the nature of landholdings in these parts.[27]

[24] See Lien-sheng Yang as cited in n. 5 above.

[25] *HS* 49.14a (2286f.).

[26] For the *nong duwei, tianguan,* and *tianzu,* see *RHA,* Vol. I, pp. 56, 70, 81.

[27] For fragments found at Juyan and already published, see *RHA,* Vol. III, pp. 288f., 295f.; for valuation of property held by individuals, see *RHA,* Vol. I, pp. 71-72.

One final incident may be quoted to illustrate how changes in economic activities could follow major changes of policy. Shortly after 92 B.C. a leading modernist statesman, Sang Hongyang, suggested the establishment of forward colonies at Luntai 輪臺, which lay to the north of the Taklamakan desert. They were to be staffed by conscript servicemen, whose duties would include the construction of irrigation channels and the organization of agriculture. Sang Hongyang hoped to establish a source of supply for the forces guarding the defence lines. But his proposal was made just at the time when the expansionist foreign policies of Wudi's reign were drawing to their close; it was being realized that further advances would be too expensive, and that the strength of China had already been overtaxed in the campaigns of Central Asia. The refusal of Sang Hongyang's proposal marks a turning point from modernist to reformist policies.[28]

B. The Mines

The attitude towards the products of the iron and salt mines stood in direct contrast to those that concerned the ownership of land. Modernists, who saw no reason to limit private landholdings, suggested control of the mines by official authorities; reformists, who objected to the growth of private wealth from large landholdings, wished to leave the mines free for individuals to work at their own profit. Modernists believed that the government was entitled to organize human labour and use the profits of such work to promote its own schemes and increase its strength; reformists reacted sharply against restrictions which would prevent individuals from engaging in private enterprise. The difference between these two points of view formed the initial point at issue in the discussions of 81 B.C., of which we possess a written record.

The tradition of an official monopoly of these enterprises was traced back to Guan Zhong 管仲 of the kingdom of Qi 齊, in the seventh century. Whether or not such monopolies were imposed or to what extent they were successful may never be known; it is the existence of the precedent as envisaged in the third century B.C. that was of importance towards the close of the second century B.C.[29] It may certainly be supposed that at that time officials were well aware that very large fortunes had been made and were continuing to be made by individual families which owned or worked the iron and salt industries. This may be inferred from the biographical accounts of

---

Recently found material (as mentioned in *Wenwu* No. 1, 1978) has yet to be published. For fragments of taxation documents from central China (*c.* 153 B.C.), see *Wenwu* No. 6, 1974, pp. 41f.

[28] For Luntai, see *RHA*, Vol. I, p. 57, and *CICA*, pp. 165f.

[29] See Utsunomiya, p. 122.

the magnates that are included in the *Shiji* and *Hanshu*.[30] In addition there was the well-known case of the king of Wu 吳 in east China. The copper mines that he owned provided sufficient wealth to tempt him to make a bid for independence and threaten the integrity of the empire (154 B.C.).[31]

Major changes, of *c.* 119 B.C., should be regarded as an attempt to remove the operation of the mines from private hands and vest it in the government as a monopoly. The changes were introduced just at the time when modernist statesmen were initiating a number of intensive measures to strengthen China, and the inspiration of these measures may well have come from Sang Hong-yang. That statesman eventually rose to hold the office of imperial counsellor (*yushi dafu* 御史大夫) from 87 B.C., until his implication in a plot of treason, and his execution in 80 B.C. From the historian's point of view it is highly unfortunate that his final venture cost him the right to a biography in the histories, as there are indications that he was one of the most forward-thinking statesmen of his day. From the treatises on economics we learn that he came from a mercantile family of Luoyang and that as an infant he had shown a prodigious ability at mathematics.[32] The *dafu* 大夫 whose views are expressed in the *Yantie lun* has sometimes been identified as Sang Hongyang.

Prior to 119 B.C. taxation had been raised on the products of the mines at the time of sale. Thereafter monopolies were introduced in two stages. First, in *c.* 119 B.C., the dues that were raised from these products were diverted from the *shaofu* 少府 (superintendent of the lesser treasury) to the *dasinong* 大司農 (superintendent of agriculture). The difference was considerably more than a formal removal of a source of income from one chest to another. The *shaofu*, as the name implies, was responsible for less important items of state business that the *dasinong*; his office had collected dues from ancillary projects such as the lakes and the forests; and it had been responsible for matters such as the upkeep of the palace and the provision of its services. The *dasinong* on the other hand had been in receipt of the main source of revenue, the land-tax, and had been responsible for providing for major items of imperial expenditure.[33] Transfer of the dues on salt and iron to the *dasinong* showed immediately that these enterprises were to be treated as major projects in which the government was actively concerned.

The second and final step in establishing the monopolies was the institution

---

[30] *SC*, 129.14 (3259), Swann, p. 430; *HS*, 91.8b (3690), Swann, pp. 452f.

[31] *SC*, 106.4 (2822); *HS*, 24B.6b (1157), Swann, p. 240.

[32] *HS*, 24B.12a (1164), Swann, p. 272. For Sang Hongyang, see J. L. Kroll, "Toward a Study of the Economic Views of Sang Hung-yang," *Early China* No. 4 (1978-79), pp. 11-18.

[33] For the organization of financial responsibilities under the Han governments, see Katō, Chapter 4.

of agencies which were responsible for the operation of the mines in the area of production; in A.D. 1-2, 34 had been set up for salt and 48 for iron.[34] Two leading industrialists, Dongguo Xienyang and Kong Jin, took a leading part in organizing the venture on an imperial scale, but as yet there was probably no fully effective authority at the centre that would co-ordinate the effort of each locality. It was intended that the commissioners should operate the mines with the use of conscript labour and some convict labour, in place of the hired labour that had been employed by private mine-owners. In this way it was hoped that the standard of production would be improved and that distribution would be more efficient. In place of the profits which accrued to private hands from salt and iron, the commissioners would sell these products for the benefit of the government and raise revenue in the process.[35]

When the policies of the modernists were beginning to show signs of weakness and their expenses were becoming only too apparent (*c.* 90 B.C.) it was only natural that the success and efficacy of the monopolies should be brought into question. If we may believe the assertions made by critics in the *Yantie lun*, the quality of the iron goods produced by the agencies was poor and uneven; distribution was unreliable; and the prices were high. Some decades later (*c.* 44 B.C.) an official named Gong Yu added the bitter complaint that an excessive amount of the conscript manpower was being employed in keeping the mines operating.[36] Objections had also been raised on principle against both the monopolies and the institutions that were set up to stabilize prices (see p. 259 below); it was felt that it would be improper for the government to compete with members of the public for monetary profit.[37]

According to the *Yantie lun* the attacks of the critics on modernist policies were sometimes so strong that they reduced the defendants of the monopolies and other measures to abject silence. But as, notwithstanding these onslaughts, the monopolies remained mainly in force after the debate of 81 B.C., it could well be that the tone of the *Yantie lun*'s account is somewhat anachronistic. In 44 B.C., when reformist policies were being introduced in several respects (for instance the reduction of government expenditure, mitigation of punishments, withdrawal of commanderies from remote regions), the monopolies of salt and iron were abolished; it could well be that the arguments recited in

[34] The sites of these agencies are given in the notes appended to prefectures and other administrative divisions in *HS*, 28.

[35] For the history of the monopolies, see Li, p. 249, Katō, pp. 41-50, Swann, pp. 62f.

[36] See *YTL*, 36 (252-53); for Gong Yu, see *HS*, 72.10a (3070f.).

[37] For objections on principle, see *HS*, 24A.20a (1142) and *HS*, 24B.20b (1176), Swann, pp. 197, 320.

Yantie lun, which was probably compiled *c.* 50 B.C., drew on opinion that was being voiced at that time rather than forty years previously. Be this as it may, the abolition of 44 B.C. was short-lived; for reasons which are not stated the monopolies were restored after a mere three years, probably because they had become an indispensable source of revenue.

Wang Mang retained the monopolies within a major scheme whose organs were ascribed to the precedents set by the kings of Zhou. The monopolies continued in Eastern Han, but probably with less degree of rigour, in so far as they were even less subject to control from the centre. In A.D. 88 they were abolished, and their subsequent history is somewhat uncertain.[38]

C. Taxation and Labour

The methods and degree of taxation form the most obvious and pervasive way in which the economic policies of a government affected individuals. During the Han period, tax was levied in kind, cash, and labour.

The land-tax (*zu* 租) was in principle paid in kind, as grain or possibly as textiles; exceptionally, where local conditions were suitable, payment could be rendered in other products, including valuables. When the land-tax was raised or assessed in terms of grain, it was fixed at a proportion of the yield, first at one fifteenth and later at one thirtieth part. There were occasions when this was remitted, either in whole or in part, for instance in time of poor harvests, as a reward for special services rendered or public expenses involved, or as a recompense for exceptional hardships.[39]

The principal source of raising revenue in cash was the poll-tax, which was levied on a *per capita* basis, with the rate varying according to age and sex. The dues collected by the nobles and the kings, which were calculated according to the number of households registered, were rendered in gold or

---

[38] For the suspension of the iron agencies in the metropolitan area, in 81 B.C., see *YTL*, 41 (276); for the withdrawal of the orders for a monopoly in liquor (established in 98 B.C.), also in 81 B.C., see *HS*, 7.5a (224), *HFHD*, Vol. II, p. 161; *HS*, 24B.20b (1176), Swann, p. 321. For the monopolies under Wang Mang and in Eastern Han, see Dubs, pp. 219f.; Yü, pp. 19f.; Li p. 180; and *HHS*, 43 (biog. 33).3b (1460). The system initially adopted in Eastern Han was on a localized basis, rather than by control exercised from an authority in the centre; it is possible that Zhang Lin's 張林 plea (A.D. 84-86; see p. 259) was for a re-institution of a more rigorous type of control, such as had been envisaged in Western Han.

[39] For the terms used in taxation, see Swann, pp. 366f. That the land-tax became payable in coin is evident from Gong Yu's remarks (see pp. 263-64). For examples of the remission or reduction of tax, see *HS*, 4.14b (125), *HFHD*, Vol. I, p. 255; *HS*, 6.30a (196), *HFHD*, Vol. II, p. 96; and *HS*, 9.5b (285), *HFHD*, Vol. II, p. 313. These are dated in 167, 106 and 45 B.C. respectively.

other valuables, such as rhinoceros horn, tortoise shell or ivory.[40] A tax in cash was also raised on ancillary products, such as those of the hills, forests and lakes, and, as has been seen, at first from the mines. It was also raised on sites used for purposes of trade in the officially controlled markets.[41]

The third principal source of taxation, to which reference has been made above, was that of statutory labour, rendered annually for one month at the behest of local officials. Except for those who were distinguished by the receipt of the higher orders of honour, able-bodied males were subject to this service between the years of twenty-three (at times twenty) and fifty-six. Arrangements for commuting this service into payment for substitutes may have existed, but full information is not available.[42]

The effective collection of these dues and the conscription of men for service depended on maintaining up-to-date records of the population and the extent of arable land and other resources. There was statutory provision for drawing up an annual register of the population throughout the empire together with a register of land, but the only surviving near-complete examples of these counts are for A.D. 1-2 and 140. It is particularly unfortunate that the figures given for the extent of the land have so far defied satisfactory interpretation.[43]

These three forms of tax were inextricably related. Grain and textiles were recognized as being the most useful forms of material wealth and were used directly by the government, partly for the payment of official stipends, and for distribution to the armed forces as rations.[44] Conscript labour was essential for the purpose of collecting and distributing these bulky and perishable goods, and it is only exceptionally that merchants undertook such tasks. Cash was essential to the government as a medium of exchange and as part of the payment due to officials. There does not appear to have been a major dispute regarding these principles, other than the question of the use of cash for the collection of tax, as will be seen below. Repeated protests were

---

[40] See Katō, p. 74 and *HFHD*, Vol. II, pp. 126f.

[41] For the markets, see Li, pp. 205f.; Katō, p. 57; and Swann, p. 233, n. 401.

[42] For the payment for substitute servicemen, see *RHA*, Vol. I, pp. 81, 162f.

[43] Figures for the numbers of registered individuals and households are given for each of the major administrative units (*jun* 郡 and *guo* 國) in *HS*, 28. For figures for the registered land, and a total for the population, see *HS*, 28B2.48b (1639f.) and *HHS*, 23B.31b (3533) (corrected by Hans Bielenstein, "The Census of China during the Period 2-742 A.D.," *Bulletin of the Museum of Far Eastern Antiquities*, No. 19 (1947), p. 128). Figures for other years are given in the notes to *HHS*, but the sources are not always specified.

[44] For the question of the proportionate use of coin and kind in the payment of stipends, see Nunome Chōfū 布目潮渢, "Hanzen hankoku ron" 半錢半穀論 , *Ritsumeikan bungaku*, No. 148 (1957), pp. 633-53.

voiced at raising excessive amounts of revenue or imposing harsh burdens on the population for purposes such as aggressive military campaigns, which were not always to be commended.

D. Commerce and the Distribution of Goods

Both modernist and reformist statesmen regarded commerce as one of the secondary occupations, to be classified as *mo*, but it should not be assumed that Han governments set out to discourage trade as much as has sometimes been suggested. It is possible that the subject has been treated anachronistically by Chinese theorists, who may themselves have been unaware of the whole situation. In addition it is necessary to discriminate between different shades of opinion. Some felt that the growth of mercantile fortunes detracted from the wealth of the empire; some stressed that trade had a specific part to play in the economy, provided that it was the organs of government that took the profits. Sang Hongyang took the view that trade and the circulation of goods formed an integral part of the universal order; and for this reason it was a recognizable duty of a sovereign to promote the distribution of goods over different parts of the empire. Possibly Sang Hongyang's personal background had allowed him to see that the merchant had a distinct part to play in the welfare of the empire and the operation of the economy.[45]

Both in the Zhanguo period and in the empires it had been possible for merchants to accumulate considerable fortunes, as may be seen in the examples that are given in the *Shiji* and *Hanshu*.[46] These men dealt in processed foodstuffs or timber; in vehicles or utensils of lacquer, bronze, iron or wood; they sold furs and textiles; and they dealt in horses and other domestic animals. It would appear that the *shang* 商 or large-scale traders and the *gu* 賈 or smaller men did not usually deal in staples. Their stock-in-trade consisted of the goods turned out by the cottage crafts, and, until the monopolies were imposed, by the mines. They dealt in utilities, luxuries, and valuables; only exceptionally, in return for the gift of legal and social privileges (*jue* 爵 or orders of aristocratic rank) did they trade in grain.

It is hardly surprising that fortunes made in this way excited envy. Criticism of the wealthy merchants may have arisen on the part of officials or law-abiding farmers, who felt it unjust that some could make large profits thanks to the labour of others and invest such profits in land. A reaction may be noted in a number of measures that were apparently designed to discourage or even prevent merchants from enjoying some of the highest benefits of a civilized life, such as wearing silk, riding in horse-drawn vehicles,

[45] For Sang Hongyang, see Kroll as cited in n. 32 above.
[46] For the evidence contained in *SC*, 129 and *HS*, 91, see Swann, pp. 405f.

owning land or serving as officials. Some of these measures were only temporary, and it remains questionable how effective they were or ever could have been.[47] In addition, not only was the conduct of trade in Chinese towns of the interior bound by regulations, for instance, for the concentration of shops or the official supervision of markets; restrictions were also imposed on the free export of certain wares, during the time of the empress Lü 呂 (effective ruler 188-80 B.C.), for instance, agricultural tools of iron and female stock animals.[48] At the northwest frontier a sharp watch was maintained to prevent the export of contraband goods, and specially controlled markets were established for dealings with foreign traders.

The clearest evidence for a government's intention to control or take part in trade is seen in the institutions set up by modernist governments *c.* 115-110 B.C. to stabilize prices and ease distribution, the *junshu* 均輸 and *pingzhun* 平準. These were designed to eliminate the imbalance that followed from poor harvests and to promote distribution.[49] A similar idea lay behind the establishment of the *changpingcang* 常平倉 (54-44 B.C.).[50] As in the case of the monopolies, so here Wang Mang tried to compromise, by retaining some measures of co-ordination while ascribing them to precedents of the Zhou period (i.e. the *liu guan* 六筦 which included the *wujun* 五均).[51]

However, these ideas and institutions came under criticism in Eastern Han. During the years A.D. 84-86, when the central government was acutely short of money, the price of grain had risen to a very high point.[52] It was suggested by Zhang Lin 張林 that, as these conditions were due to the low value of the coinage, it would be best to stop dealings in cash, levying all land-tax in textiles; and these could be distributed for the general benefit of the population. He also suggested the re-institution of the government's controls for salt and added that the government would do well to make a profit out of a trade in valuables and exotica; this would be little different from the so-called *junshu* of Wudi's period. Discussions were ordered to examine these proposals, which were contested by Zhu Hui 朱暉; as a result they were dropped, only to be approved shortly afterwards. Zhu Hui had tried to argue that arrangements for the *junshu* were no different from government trading;

---

[47] For anti-mercantile measures, see Swann, p. 24. For Chao Cuo's criticism and observation that such measures were ineffective, see *HS*, 24A.13b (1132f.), Swann, pp. 164f., and Yü, pp. 17, 18, n. 30. For the ban on merchants' use of silk and carriages, and ownership of land, see *HS*, 24B.4a and 13b (1153 and 1167), Swann, pp. 231, 282. For attempts to prevent officials from engaging in trade, see *HS*, 72.14a (3077).

[48] This ban was imposed on certain exports to the south; see *HS*, 95.10b (3851).

[49] For the *junshu* and *pingzhun*, see Swann, p. 64 and Kroll, as cited in n. 32 above.

[50] For the *changpingcang*, see *HS*, 24A.19a (1141f.), Swann, pp. 25, 191f.

[51] For these institutions, see Dubs, p. 251 and Swann, p. 67.

[52] *HHS*, 43 (biog. 33).3a (1460).

that a monopoly of salt would breed poverty and bitterness; and that the collection of the land-tax in the form of textiles would transform a large number of officials into robbers.

E. Coinage and the Role of Money

The development of a Chinese coinage may be traced in a number of stages, beginning with the use of cowrie shells in the Shang-Yin period. These rare and valuable objects were followed by replica shells, of bronze; by the use of spades and knives in barter; by replica spades and knives, cast in gradually smaller and smaller styles; and finally by the circular bronze coin, cast with a hole left in the centre. As might be expected, archaeology discloses how these coins and items were circulated over long distances, and how different types of coin from different parts of China came to be used in one and the same area. It was probably not until the fifth century B.C. that a coinage proper became the regular medium of exchange.

Han officials needed a coinage for a number of purposes. The poll-tax was assessed and usually collected in coin, and assessment in other terms could not have been sufficiently flexible to meet all variations in respect of age or sex. Similarly coin was needed for the payment of officials' stipends. These were graded, notionally, in terms of measures of grain, and it is likely that some of the payments was made in grain and some in cash.[53] From the remnants of records found at Juyan, it can be shown that whereas officers sometimes received part of their pay in textiles, coin formed the regular item.[54]

Coins were required for the payment of fines. Some of the recently found documents of the Qin period show how fines had originally been assessed in payments of suits of armour, but by the Han period it seems that payments were being made in coin. Purchase of office was also effected by coin at times during Eastern Han.[55] Other transactions in which officials were concerned and which required the use of coin included the gift of imperial bounties, and the contributions made by subordinate officials, protegés or clients towards the memorial shrines of their superiors. Cash coins were also needed at the close of life, when they were buried as payment to the authorities of the next world, possibly as a purchase price for the burial plot, possibly for the needs

[53] See n. 44 above.

[54] See RHA, Vol. II, pp. 100f., 282f.

[55] For assessments of payments in terms of suits of armour, see A.F.P. Hulsewé, "The Ch'in Documents Discovered in Hupei in 1975," T'oung Pao, Vol. LXIV, Nos. 4-5 (1978), pp. 208-209, and Chapter 7 of this volume, pp. 229-30. For the payment of money as redemption from punishments, see Hulsewé, Remnants of Han Law (Leiden: Brill, 1955), pp. 205f. For the sale of orders of aristocratic rank and of offices, for ready money, in A.D. 109, 161, and 178, see HHS, 5.6b (213), 7.10b (309), and 8.8a (342).

of the deceased in the world to come.

The coins raised four main issues that were subject to controversy. There were the two questions of whether minting should be subject to a monopoly and control of the government, and whether the currency should be single or multi-denominational. It was also necessary to determine the place, if any, of gold in a system of exchange; and there was the fundamental question of the use of coinage in the system of taxation.

(1) In the first days of the Han period the minting of coin was left free and uncontrolled; as a result considerable varieties of coin were produced, doubtless with considerable confusion. After early experiments to bring minting under centralized control, the government was finally able to introduce a monopoly; it is hardly surprising to find that this occurred at the time when modernist ideas of government were being promoted, such as those of monopolies for salt and iron, or means of balancing prices and equalizing distribution (*c.* 115 B.C.).[56] In addition, practical measures were taken to discourage those who wished to circumvent the monopoly. The monopoly was criticized by the reformist Gong Yu, shortly after 44 B.C., on the grounds that, like those of the salt and iron industries, it involved the use of too much conscript manpower. Further attention will be paid to Gong Yu below, in connection with the whole question of the place of a monetary economy. It would seem that no other arguments were put forward, either by Gong Yu or in the time of Wang Mang, for restoring the right of minting to the public.

(2) It was a tradition that in the dim pre-imperial past, China had used a multi-denominational currency, which incorporated valuables of gold, silver, jade or tortoise-shell, each with their own place on a scale.[57] To what extent this supposition could be verified in historical terms is questionable. For whereas the Chunqiu 春秋 and Zhanguo periods had witnessed the growth of different types of media and currency in different parts of the continent (e.g., spades in the west and centre, knives in the east), so far as may be told there is no material evidence for a multi-denominational system, apart from the use of small gold ingots in the state of Chu 楚. Nor was any such system tried, except temporarily and abortively from 119-113 B.C., until the days of Wang Mang. As in other respects, that statesman may have been inspired to make the experiment so as to demonstrate his continuity from the kings of the glorious past. Between A.D. 7 and 14, Wang Mang made four attempts to introduce coins of different values, ranging from the use of different units in bronze to that of valuable objects or rare substances such as gold, silver or

[56] For the changes effected in the coinage, see Swann, pp. 377f., and the table on pp. 382-83.
[57] See the opening passage of *HS*, 24B.1a (1149), Swann, pp. 219f.; Lien-sheng Yang, *Money and Credit in China* (Cambridge, Mass.: Harvard University Press, 1952), pp. 11f.

turtle-shells. None of these attempts attracted sufficient confidence to make them successful.[58]

The opportunity should perhaps be taken to clear up one possible misconception. In 120 B.C. orders were given that nobles should render their annual payments to the throne in the form of strips of the rare and valuable skin of white deer. It was specified that each piece of skin, measuring one foot square, should be valued at 400,000 cash. The order has been interpreted as an early experiment in the use of paper money. That it should not be so judged is clear from the consideration that, as a rarity, the white deerskin was in no way replaceable without limit; nor was it intrinsically valueless, as is the manufactured currency of paper. In addition there is nothing to show that deerskin was ever used as a unit in general circulation.[59]

Finally, it may be remarked that the style of the regular bronze *wu shu* 五銖 coin of Han was simple and unadorned. Variations of design were sometimes introduced in a minor way to discourage clipping, but there was no endeavour to use the coinage, in an embellished form, as an instrument of propaganda. When Chinese explorers to the west encountered coins of Greek provenance of gold or silver, which proudly displayed the human head of a monarch or the figure of a mounted rider, they thought the matter worthy of report, as may be seen in the passages of the standard histories.[60]

(3) The major disadvantage of the single denominational system of the copper cash lay in the difficulty of handling large sums of money. It was customary to string coins together with the use of a hempen or leather throng; but when these fastenings perished, transport and accountancy became correspondingly awkward, as a famous passage of the *Hanshu* testifies.[61]

A precedent for the use of small gold ingots as units of exchange could be found in the pre-imperial state of Chu. For Han, gold was used in the specified weight of one catty (*jin* 斤), whose value was set at 10,000 cash. In view of the prevailing prices of goods and the scale of stipends, it is unlikely that gold would have been handled other than exceptionally or by the very rich.[62]

[58] For Wang Mang's experiments, see Dubs, pp. 233f., Swann, p. 66; *HFHD*, Vol. III, pp. 507f. For attempts during Wudi's reign, see *HS*, 24B.11a, 15b (1164, 1169), Swann, pp. 270, 292.

[59] This view is taken despite the statement in *HS*, 24B.11b (1163), Swann, p. 269 that each piece of deerskin was valued at cash 400,000 and that the pieces were intended to constitute a currency. See Lien-sheng Yang, *Money and Credit*, p. 51.

[60] *HS*, 96A.24a, 29a, 30a (*CICA*, pp. 106, 115, 116).

[61] *HS*, 24A.15b (1135), Swann, pp. 174-75.

[62] For the payments made by nobles and kings, in gold, see p. 256 above. For officials' stipends, see Swann, p. 47, *RHA*, Vol. I, p. 95; for the value of gold as against copper, see Swann, pp. 383-84. The mathematical textbook *Jiu chang suan shu* 九章算術 includes in its problems some hypothetical examples in which the rate of the gold unit

The use of gold raises a number of problems. In the absence of further evidence, it is to be presumed that the sources of this metal lay entirely within China, but little is known about its provenance. The record of Wang Mang's collection of gold from the empire implies that it was in circulation to some extent, or at least present in private hoards, but we do not know how far. The reasons for Wang Mang's actions have yet to be fully explained.[63]

(4) The critics whose views are reported in the *Yantie lun* had made the point that the coinage did not necessarily make for a just and happy society. They preferred to raise taxation in local produce, and to prevent exploitation by officials and merchants thanks to disparities of prices. In reply the spokesman for the government defended the use of money as a means of circulating goods and relieving distress; he argued that private minting, if allowed, could lead to the growth of considerable private fortunes, while minting by the government would prevent the growth of disparities of wealth.[64]

The next voice to be raised in protest at the use of coins was that of Gong Yu who became imperial counsellor (*yushi dafu*) in 44 B.C. In a memorial submitted immediately after his appointment he began by questioning the value of the part played by the poll-tax in the economy.[65] The rate had been increased at the time of Wudi's military campaigns, when decisions of government were in the hands of the modernists. Gong Yu alleged that its demands were so severe that it drove parents to infanticide, and he urged the abolition of the tax for those under seven years of age.

Gong Yu then referred to the past when there was no monetary economy, and when failure to work productively in the fields laid the malingerers open to the risk of starvation. He contrasted such a state of affairs with the contemporary situation of a centrally minted coinage, in which over 100,000 conscripts and convicts were employed annually for this purpose and to mine copper and iron. As a result of their consequent absence from the productive work of the farms, some 700,000 persons were liable to suffer starvation. He also deplored the spoliation of the natural resources of the earth that was involved in mining for these metals. He continued:

> Over seventy years have passed since the introduction of the *wu shu* cash, and large numbers of persons have been brought up on charges of illicit minting and punished accordingly. Rich persons have hoarded coin in sufficient quantity to fill their houses and are still not satisfied, to the general consternation of the

varied from 6,250 to 12,000 cash (*Congshu jicheng* 叢書集成 ed., pp. 99, 113, 132). This may possibly suggest that the rate of 1:10,000 was notional and that the actual value fluctuated.

[63] See Dubs, pp. 233f.; *HFHD*, Vol. III, pp. 507f.

[64] *YTL*, 1 (4) and 2 (11); Gale's translation, pp. 10-12; *Crisis and Conflict*, p. 100.

[65] *HS*, 72.13a (3075f.)

general population. Eager for their profits, merchants operate in all directions, putting their skills to good use; with their fine clothes and excellent table they make an annual profit of 20% on their capital, on which they are not taxed.

It is with such persons that Gong Yu contrasts the families where father and son toil in the fields, exposed to all conditions of climate, and suffering chapped hands and callous feet as a result of their labours. Such families are subject to payment not only of tax in grain but also of dues on straw; and they are also open to the insatiable demands of local officials.

> This is why the people abandon primary production and chase after secondary occupations; those who till the fields cannot [earn half as much as others?]; and even though land were to be given to the impoverished persons, they would still sell it, at a low price, and take to trade with the proceeds; and then, when they fall into abject penury, they rise up as robbers and thieves. Why? Because of the considerable profits in secondary occupations they are deceived by the thought of cash coins. This is why the reason that corruption cannot be prevented lies basically in the cash coin.

Gong Yu urges the abolition of all those agencies of the government which were responsible for the collection of pearls, jade, gold and silver, and for minting coin. He preferred that in the future these items should not be regarded as valuables; and he expressed the hope that the growth of private monopolies in certain goods could be thwarted. He suggested the repeal of the statute that provided for payment of the land-tax in coin, and that taxation, stipends and bounties should all be rendered in textiles and grain. This would be the way to turn the population back to the land.

Gong Yu's views bear some resemblance to those advocated later by Zhang Lin (see p. 256 above) and by Gu Yanwu 顧炎武 at a far more advanced stage of the Chinese economy.[66] It may be noted that, following the end of the Han dynasty (A.D. 220) and in the prevalent political and social uncertainty, grain, silk and hemp cloth tended to take the place of the cash and of gold.[67]

F. Foreign Policies

In a recent study,[68] a scholar of the western world has argued cogently, on

[66] *Qian liang lun*, *shang* 錢糧論上, reprinted in *Gu Tinglin shiwenji* 顧亭林詩文集 (Peking: Zhonghua shuju, 1959), pp. 18f.

[67] Lien-sheng Yang, *Money and Credit*, p. 16. Even in the first century A.D., fees required for redemption from punishment were expressed in terms of bolts of cloth; see Hulsewé, *Remnants of Han Law*, pp. 213, 214.

[68] Manfred G. Rashke, "New Studies in Roman Commerce with the East," in *Aufstieg und Niedergang der Römischen Welt: Geschichte und Kultur Roms im Spiegel der neueren Forschung*, Principat IX (2) (Berlin and New York: Walter de Gruyter, 1978), pp. 604-1361.

the basis of a variety of types of evidence from both east and west, that during the Han period the initiative for silk to travel to Central Asia came from the Asiatic confederacies, rather than from a positive Chinese desire to export produce; and that China's supply of silk to these areas was no more than a response to demands which could not be refused. Rashke adds that he can find no evidence to show that China grew more wealthy thanks to the promotion of an export trade. While there may be a general agreement with this thesis, it should perhaps be modified by the consideration that there was no single, constant Chinese foreign policy during the period, and that due allowance should be made for the different stages that may be discerned in the Han attitude to foreign peoples.

During the first decades of the Han dynasty, China was certainly in no position to refuse the demands made by a powerful and potentially hostile neighbour. However, it was in such circumstances that one statesman (Jia Yi) put forward the view that advantage could be taken of this situation; for the provision of certain goods to the Xiongnu 匈奴 would encourage a softening of their way of life and thus reduce their strength. This was the well-known policy of the "Five baits." A warning that is reported to have been given by a Chinese deserter to his Xiongnu masters suggests that such a policy would not have been entirely unsuccessful. In the event it was not pursued for a sufficiently long and sustained period to demonstrate its efficacy.[69]

The defensive and negative attitude of Han governments to foreigners during the early decades changed conspicuously shortly after Wudi's accession (141 B.C.), as may be seen in the military undertakings that were started.[70] Moreover it was just at this time that there seems to have arisen a surplus of raw products, mainly of grain, in central China, to the extent that the stock was beginning to rot.[71] Very shortly Zhang Qian 張騫 was to report on the possibilities of trading in far-flung areas to the west; and it was being realized that if military campaigns were to be successful, China needed a better and regular supply of horses.[72]

By 110 B.C., when Han armies had been able to free China from the active threats of incursion, measures were being taken to encourage the export of some goods in exchange for certain imports; but it is still perhaps too early to regard this as a systematic exercise in an import-export trade. According to the standard histories, several caravans set out annually from Chang'an to the

[69] See Yü, pp. 36f.
[70] See the initial statement in *HS*, 96A.1a (3871), *CICA*, p. 71; and Michael Loewe, "The Campaigns of Han Wu-ti," in Frank A. Kierman, Jr. and John K. Fairbank (eds.), *Chinese Ways in Warfare* (Cambridge, Mass.: Harvard University Press, 1974), pp. 67f.
[71] *HS*, 24A.15b (1135), Swann, pp. 174-75.
[72] For Zhang Qian, see *HS*, 61.3a *et seq.*, *CICA*, pp. 211f., and Yü, pp. 111f.

west, each one being manned by up to several hundred persons;[73] and it was partly for the protection of these travellers that the line of earth-work defences was extended, until eventually it reached Dunhuang. These ventures were in the hands of official missions. The caravans proceeded along routes that enjoyed Han military and official protection; their visits to the west formed the basis upon which diplomatic relations were built between the Han court and the peoples of the "Silk Roads"; and trading at the frontiers was controlled by Chinese officials. That the frequency of the trading varied considerably from decade to decade, rising and falling with the changes of Han policy, hardly needs stress.

The *Yantie lun* shows that some statesmen actively believed in the value of these commercial ventures.[74] In a famous passage the defendant of the modernist policies describes the variety of products that may be obtained and his vision of the caravans. China would receive live-stock, furs and woollens; China would part with surplus silk; China would gain materially at the expense of her neighbours. It is not surprising that this view was countered by the reformist critic, just at the time when retrenchment was taking the place of expansionist policies. It was argued that, so far from really enriching China, these commercial exercises simply brought exotic luxuries into the country, and that their value was grossly overrated.

Three points should perhaps be mentioned in conclusion.

1. The acquisition of horses was one of the motives for the establishment of diplomatic relations between Han and Wu-sun 烏孫, and for the highly expensive campaigns undertaken by Li Guangli 李廣利 against Da Yuan 大宛 from 104 to 100 B.C. After an abortive and wasteful start that campaign was eventually brought to a conclusion, and under the terms of the agreement for peace China received a large number of horses of various grades.[75]

2. During the reign of Chengdi 成帝 (perhaps in 25 B.C.) a statesman named Du Qin 杜欽, who was contending against Han involvement with Jibin 罽賓,[76] successfully argued that trading transactions were not to China's advantage and that relations should not be encouraged.

3. From the *Hanshu*[77] we learn that there were some who appreciated that

---

[73] *SC*, 123.24 (3170). See A.F.P. Hulsewé, "Quelque considérations sur le commerce de la soie au temps de la dynastie des Han," in *Mélanges de sinologie offerts à Monsieur P. Demiéville*, Vol. II (Paris, 1974), pp. 117-36.

[74] *YTL*, 2 (12) (Gale's translation, p. 14).

[75] For this campaign, see *HS*, 61.9a, *CICA*, pp. 228f.; see also *HS*, 96B.3b, *CICA*, p. 147 for the agreement with Wu-sun for the exchange of a princess for 1,000 head of horse.

[76] Sometimes identified with Kashmir; *HS*, 96A.25b, *CICA*, p. 109.

[77] See the appreciation in *HS*, 96B.37a, *CICA*, pp. 198f.

the material wealth, extravagant living habits and sophisticated way of life of Changan could form a valuable means of impressing visitors from beyond the pale with the value, dignity, and strength of Han China, and thus securing their friendship and loyalty; such displays could involve the Han economy in considerable expenditure.

V. SUMMARY

By way of summary it may be asked in what way the economic practices of Western Han may be construed as signs of a state's adoption of an economic role or as precedents upon which later governments could draw. Attention would focus here on two experiments that concerned land-holding, the one designed to limit their extent and the other to establish sponsored farms or settlements. From such beginnings it is possible to look forward to the more sophisticated and complex institutions or policies of Cao Cao 曹操 and the Tang governments. Similarly, the Han governments' recognition of responsibilities for the mines or their desire to profit therefrom constituted a precedent that was set early in the imperial era, to which allusion could be made at the later and more advanced stages of Chinese history, when a government could exercise greater influence over the economy. The government's monopoly of the production of coin was an achievement of the Han governments that affected fiscal practice permanently. Attempts to regulate the prices of staple goods and to introduce an equable means of distribution, coupled with the use of conscript labour, were subject to considerable variation in later imperial days; their efficacy was questionable during the Han period.

9. The Imperial Factories of Suzhou: Limits and Characteristics of State Intervention during the Ming and Qing Dynasties

Paolo Santangelo

The factories of Suzhou[1] are part of the system of offices assigned to the supply of goods necessary to the life of the imperial court, and in particular of the section for the supplies of textiles and ceremonial dresses. This system goes back to the Qin and perpetuated itself under various names during the whole imperial period.[2]

Suzhou is one of the major prefectures of southern China, renowned since ancient times for textile production. The importance of the prefecture grew in the Ming and Qing era, during which agriculture was increasingly commercialized in the region of Jiangnan. The city of Suzhou was also caught up

[1] The theme of the role of the state in the textile factories during the Ming and Qing periods has up to now only been treated occasionally, if at all. I found useful information in Jonathan Spence, *Ts'ao Yin and the K'ang-hsi Emperor: Bondservant and Master* (New York: Columbia University Press, 1966); Preston Torbert, *The Ch'ing Imperial Household Department. A Study of Its Organization and Principal Function: 1662-1796* (Cambridge, Mass.: Harvard University Press, 1977); Shi Mingxiong 施敏雄, *Qingdai sizhigongye de fazhan* 清代絲織工業的發展 (Taibei, 1968); and the abridged translation of Sun E-tu Zen, *The Silk Industry in Ch'ing China* (Ann Arbor: Center for Chinese Studies, 1976). Finally, on the conditions of the textile industry *vis-à-vis* the state, see Saeki Yuichi 佐伯有一, "Minzen hanki no kiko" 明前半期の機戸, in *Toyo bunka kenkyusho kiyo*, No. 8 (1956), pp. 167-210. On the textile factories of Suzhou we have no specific studies. I am, none the less, indebted to Nakayama Hachiro 中山八郎 for his article "Mindai no shokusenkyoku" 明代の織染局 in *Hitotsubashi ronso*, Vol. 9, No. 5 (1948), pp. 479-502, and to Peng Zeyi 彭澤益, "Cong Mingdai guanying zhizao de jingyingfangshi kan Jiangnan sizhiye shengchan de xingzhi" 從明代官營織造的經營方式看江南絲織業生產的性質, *Lishi yanjiu*, No. 2, 1963 (reprinted in *Mingdai shehuijingji shi lunji* 明代社會經濟史論集, Vol. III, Hong Kong, 1975), pp. 46-69, and "Qingdai qianqi Jiangnan zhizao de yanjiu" 清代前期江南織造的研究, *Lishi yanjiu*, No. 4, 1963, pp. 91-116. (From now on quotations from these last two articles will be labelled by the author's name followed by I or II.) However, despite the richness of the data, we lack an investigation on the nature of such textile factories. In particular, in Peng Zeyi, the analysis centres on production relations, in the context of the great debate that took place in the People's Republic of China in the late 1950s and early 1960s, concerning the issue of "the sprouts of capitalism" and the "transition from feudalism to capitalism."

[2] For the Han period, see *Han shu* (Beijing: Zhonghua shuju, 1962), 19A.731-32; *Hou Han shu* (Hong Kong: Zhonghua shuju, 1971), zhi 26.3592-3601; *Jiu Tang shu* (Beijing, 1975), 44.1893; Cf. also *Shi ji* (Beijing, 1973), 122.3138; *Han shu*, 59.2638,

in these changes, and, from being a centre of consumption, it became more and more a centre of production; thus, especially during the Qing era, apart from the traditional shops engaged in the working of silk, there was a noticeable development in shops engaged in the weaving, spinning and dyeing of cotton.

Apart from being linked to the imperial household, the textile factories were also deeply rooted in society and in the local economy. Hence, an analysis of them is useful for an understanding of the "role of the state" at various levels of the economy. Much has, of course, already been written on this vast topic, and many hypotheses have been formulated on the dimensions of state intervention. None the less, to deepen our understanding of this topic, I think it appropriate to start from the analysis of specific cases, during periods of time appropriately limited, seeking to avoid as much as possible a terminology that already at the outset might condition in some way the conclusions of the research. An example of the inherent risks in the uncritical use of terms and distinctions such as "private," "public" or "state sectors" is given by the ambiguity of the nature of the so-called *jihu* 機戶, families involved in textile production. These, if set against the imperial factories, can be considered shops or "pre-modern private businesses"; none the less, they were often invested by the factories with duties and powers that resembled more "public functions." In turn, these same factories can occasionally be seen as mere "private" businesses of the "crown."

Historical sources on the Suzhou factories are numerous, scattered in various official, semi-official and private compilations. The richest and most detailed source dealing specifically with this topic is the *Treatise on the Manufactories of Suzhou* (*Suzhou zhizaoju zhi* 蘇州織造局志) by Sun Pei 孫珮. It consists of a private document, written in 1686, which groups in chronological order and divides under different headings information regarding the evolution of the offices, of the plants, the labour force, production and the internal organization of the factories,[3] and thus offers a broad framework for the study of their structure and activities. Another more recent

---

and 86.3501. For the Tang period, cf. *Xin Tang shu* (Beijing, 1975), 48.1268; *Jiu Tang shu*, 44.1894; also Des Rotours, *Traité des fonctionnaires et traité de l'armée, traduits de la Nouvelle Histoire des T'ang*, (Leiden: Brill, 1947-48), pp. 458, 470-72; Takahashi Yasuo 高橋泰郎, "Tōdai orimono kōgyō zakkō"唐代織物工業雜考, in *Tōaronsō* V (1941). For the Song period, see *Song shi* (Beijing, 1977), 175.4321-40.

[3] Henceforth Sun Pei. (Reprinted in 1959 by the Jiangsu renmin chubanshe.) A selection of the most significant passages has been published in the anthology of historical materials on modern Chinese arts and crafts, *Zhongguo jindai shougongyeshi ziliao* 中國近代手工業史資料 (Beijing: Sanlian shudian, 1962), Vol. I, pp. 78-82, 87-98, 100-103 (henceforth *ZJS*).

compilation is *Notes on Silk* (*Sixiu biji* 絲繡筆記) by Zhu Qiqian 朱啟鈐 .[4]

Other material is found in the official collections of laws and regulations: the *Da Ming huidian* 大明會典[5] for the Ming period; the *Da Qing huidian* 大清 會典[6] for the following dynasty, in various editions; the *Da Qing huidian zeli* 大清會典則例;[7] the *Da Qing huidian shili* 大清會典事例,[8] and the *Qingchao* (or *Huangchao*) *wenxian tongkao* 清朝(皇朝) 文獻通考.[9] Other documents are found in the encyclopaedic collection *Gujin tushu jicheng* 古今圖書集成,[10] and naturally in the *Shilu* 實錄 both of the Ming and of the Qing, in the official histories[11] and in the local chronicles, such as the *Jiangnan tongzhi* 江南通志,[12] the *Suzhou fu zhi* 蘇州府志,[13] and the chronicles of the various counties of Suzhou.[14]

There are also some primary, semi-official sources of great value, among them the correspondence between officials of the factories and the emperor or other bureaucrats, which supply important data on the internal running and the management of the factories. Particularly interesting are the "vermilion" decrees of approval by the emperor Yongzheng, *Yongzheng zhupi yuzhi*

---

[4] The *Sixiu biji*, compiled in 1928, has been reprinted in Taibei in 1970 (henceforth *SXBJ*).

[5] Henceforth *DMHD*. Generally, I have referred to the Wanli edition (1585) published in Shanghai in 1936, and reprinted in Taibei in 1963.

[6] Henceforth *DQHD*. For the present work I have used mainly the Guangxu edition (1899), reprinted in Taibei in 1963. See *juan* 24 (*hubu*), in which are defined the functions of the three supervisors of the imperial textile factories, the quantity and quality of the quotas allotted to each one of the textile factories, and the relations between buyers and suppliers.

[7] Henceforth *DQHDZL*, Qianlong edition (1748).

[8] Henceforth *DQHDSL*, Guanxu edition (1899), reprinted in Taibei in 1963. On the imperial textile factories cf. Chs. 940 and 1190.

[9] *Qingchao wenxian tongkao* (henceforth *QCWXTK*) includes the Qing period up to 1785. Reprinted in Taibei in 1958.

[10] Henceforth *GJTSJC*, work of 1725, reprinted in Taibei in 1964. Cf. the section on the Suzhou prefecture, *Suzhou fu bu huikao* 蘇州府部會考, *juan* 674, and the section on the economy, *jingji huibian shihuodian* 經濟彙編食貨典, *juan* 310.

[11] See the economic and financial section of *Ming shi* and of *Qing shi gao* 清史稿 . Also cf. the non-official edition of *Qing shi*, published in 1927, and reprinted in Taibei in 1961. For the *Ming shi* and the *Qing shi gao*, *The Collective Index of the Fifteen Economic Treaties* (*Shihuozhi shiwu zhong zonghe yinde* 食貨志十五種綜合引得), No. 32 of the Harvard-Yenching Institute Sinological Index Series (reprinted in 1966) is useful. See also the *Qing shilu jingji ziliao jiyao* 清實錄經濟資料輯要, by the Department of History, Nankai University (Beijing: Zhonghua shuju, 1959).

[12] Henceforth *JNTZ*, compiled in 1736.

[13] Edition of the 9th year of Guangxu (1883), reprint of the publisher Chengwen (Taibei, 1960).

[14] See, for example, the history of Wujiang, *Wujiang xian zhi* 吳江縣志 (1747), and that of Wu, *Wu xian zhi* 吳縣志 (1933), published in Taibei in 1970.

271

雍正硃批諭旨[15] and the collection of documents of the imperial palaces, *Wenxian congbian* 文獻叢編.[16]

Finally, the documents discovered some years ago in Jiangnan and published in Beijing in 1959 in *Jiangsu sheng Ming-Qing yi lai beike ziliao xuanji* 江蘇省明清以來碑刻資料選集 are of great utility for understanding official objectives which the governmental organs set themselves for the factories; they are a collection of Ming and Qing inscriptions of Jiangnan province.

In Suzhou imperial factories had already been in operation at the time of the Tang and of the Song, but only temporarily.[17] Only under the Yuan was a factory established there permanently.[18] The Ming took over in part the organization of the Yuan, both for the factory and more generally for the system of corvée of the textile artisans.[19] None the less, the system became more complex. In Nanjing, some special centres were established, such as the *neizhiranju* 內織染局 (the internal factory, part of the offices of the imperial household, as opposed to the *waizhiranju* 外織染局, the external factory in Beijing, directly responsible to the *gongbu* 工部), while in almost every province one or more peripheral factories were created. The most numerous were in (Nan) Zhili, including those of Suzhou, and in Zhejiang, where the traditional centres of Chinese silk production are found.[20]

---

[15] Compilation of various volumes of the 1923-35 period, published in Shanghai in 1887 and reprinted in Taibei in 1965. Henceforth *YZZPYZ*.

[16] Henceforth *WXCB*, reprinted in Taibei in 1964. In particular, in the second volume are published the memorials of Li Xu, imperial supervisor of the textile factories of Suzhou during the Kangxi period, *Suzhou zhizao Li Xu zouzhe* 蘇州織造李煦奏摺. There is another shorter collection, entitled *Li Xu zouzhe*, covering the 1693-1722 period, i.e., from the 32nd to the 61st year of Kangxi, and again it is taken from *WXCB*. Relevant to some memorials of the supervisor of the textile factories of Nanjing during the reigns of Kangxi, Yongzheng and Qianlong, is the *Guanyu Jiangning zhizao Caojia dangan shiliao* 關於江寧織造曹家檔案史料 (henceforth *Guanyu* ...) (Beijing: Zhonghua shuju, 1975).

[17] Sun Pei, 3.1.

[18] *Ibid.*

[19] Saeki Yuichi, *op. cit.*, pp. 169-70.

[20] According to the *DMHD*, the textile production for the state was split up as follows. In the following list the quotas allotted after 1528 are in brackets; the additional figures for the bissextile months and the relative variations are not shown. Cf. *DMHD*, 201.7-9, 11.

Zhejiang	12,817 (12,662) *pi* 匹	Hubei-Hunan	1,919 *pi* (7,526 taels)
Jiangxi	2,803 (from 1528, following the bad quality of the products, their quota was changed into money: 10,561 taels)	Fujian	3,292 (2,258) *pi*
		Shanxi	1,000 *pi*
		Sichuan	4,516 *pi*
		Zhili: Suzhou *fu*	1,534 *pi*
		Songjiang *fu*	1,167 *pi*
Henan	800 *pi* (3,169 taels)	Changzhou *fu*	200 *pi*
Shandong	720 *pi* (2,170 taels)	Zhenjiang *fu*	1,440 *pi*

These were managed from the centre by eunuchs, one *dashi* 大使 and two *fushi* 副使, under whom were placed the *sili* 司吏 and *dianli* 典吏. The responsibility of the *dashi* and of the *fushi* consisted in supervising the work carried out within the factories and in checking that the quality and quantity of the production assigned annually were respected and delivered within the deadline. Their rank, which in 1384 had been respectively 9a and 9b, was raised in 1395 to 5a and 5b.[21] They were assisted in running the factories by officials of the prefectures, and the factories were also controlled by the regional censors, *xun'an yushi* 巡按御史.[22] None the less, the system of administration was rather complex and unstable, and it even seems that initially officials of the *gongbu* were sent there. In fact, the Board of Works, which had authority over all the public works undertaken in the country through its Directorate of Waterworks (*dushui qingli si* 都水清吏司) carried out the management and co-ordination of the textile production,[23] bringing it thus in some way within the ambit of the state machine. Thus, the *gongbu*, while supervising directly the activities of the *waizhiranju*,[24] was also involved in the activities of the local factories, and of all the offices of the imperial household concerned with the supply of textiles, particularly as regarded the special orders.[25]

To this one must add that in the fifteenth century the practice was instituted of sending a eunuch supervisor with a 4a rank,[26] who also had fiscal functions, the *taijian* 太監. They came mostly from the *silijian* 司禮監, the ceremonial office of the imperial household. With the growing power of the eunuchs, the *taijian* became, in fact, the top-ranking official of the factory.

The necessary labour force was requisitioned by means of the corvée, the latter being governed by the *lijia* 里甲 system through the so-called "yellow registers" (*huangce* 黃冊) in which the artisans had to be listed. They had to give their services periodically as an obligation to the state, and sometimes— legally and illegally—even to the officials and eunuchs of the factory.[27]

Zhili (*cont.*):

Huizhou *fu*	721 *pi*	Anqing *fu*	608 *pi*
Ningguo *fu*	796 *pi*	Yangzhou *fu*	1,132 *pi* (931 *pi* and
Chizhou *fu*	211 *pi*		701 taels)
Taiping *fu*	500 *pi*		

[21] *Ming shi*, 74.1824-25; cf. also Wada Sei 和田清, *Minshi shokka shi yakuchū* 明史食貨志譯註 (Tokyo: Tōyō Bunko, 1957), p. 512.

[22] Cf. Peng Zeyi, I, p. 51.

[23] Cf. *DMHD*, 181.1; cf. also *Ming shi*, 72.1759-60.

[24] Cf. *Ming shi*, 72.1760.

[25] *Ibid.*, p. 1761.

[26] *Ibid.*, 74.1822.

[27] Cf. *Da Ming lü* 大明律 in Saeki Yuichi, *op. cit.*, pp. 187, 206.

Although their registration was the task of the *hubu*, different boards were responsible for the arrangements in the factory, depending on their status: thus the artisans were divided into *zhuzuo* 住坐 residents, listed in the local registers of the factory, at least since the Yongle reign,[28] and *lunban* 輪班 , seasonal labour, responsible to the *gongbu*; soldiers were listed in the military registers, and were responsible to the local military district, *duzhihuisi* 都指揮司.

On the financial side, the factory was responsible to the *hubu* and the *gongbu*,[29] but mainly to the *hubu*, since it was dependent on the ordinary tax revenue both for expenses and for the purchase of raw materials, such as yarn. The factory was also responsible to the *hubu* as regarded the sale by the *taijian* of salt certificates.[31] The overall situation can be represented by the following diagram:

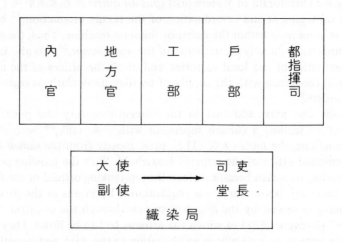

The factories, called *zhiranju*, had the task, as their name implies, of weaving and dyeing the cloth ordered from them. The work did not, however, always take place within the factory, and at various periods they faced reduced activity, slackening of the organization or even closure.[32] For example within

[28] Cf. *DMHD*, 188.1, and 189.11-38. Also see Chen Shiqi 陳詩啟 , "Mingdai de gongjiang zhidu" 明代的工匠制度 , in *Mingdai shehuijingji shi lunji*, Vol. III, p. 33.

[29] Cf. *Ming shi*, 82.1998.

[30] Cf. *Ming shilu*, Shizong, Jiajing, 14th year, 2nd lunar month, 乙巳 , Ch. 172.

[31] Cf. *Ming shilu*, Xiaozong, Hongzhi, 12th year, 4th lunar month, 己酉 , Ch. 149, also 108.7; 125.2, and 147.8; Shenzong, Wanli, 12th year, 8th lunar month, 甲辰 , 152.1; *Ming shi*, 82.1997 and 80.1939, 1957.

[32] Cf. *Ming shi*, 82.1998.

the scope of their organization, the *tangzhang* 堂長 not only had the task of controlling the work of the manufacturing plants, but also were often obliged to contribute to the cost of the supplies of yarn from their own funds, or to advance money for expenses. Therefore they were generally rich producers. In times of low activity in the factories, they had the task of seeing that various products were ordered and delivered, through a kind of government contract called *qianpai* 僉派.

The factories of Suzhou were founded in 1368,[33] and were situated in the central part of town, to the east of the Tianxin 天心 bridge, in the *xian* of Changzhou 長洲.[34] Under the next dynasty, this location was attributed to the so-called *beiju* 北局, *bei zhizaoju* 北織造局.[35] Then, at the beginning of the Hongxi period (1425-26), the premises were expanded, and probably included even looms and artisans from Hangzhou.[36]

From the second half of the fifteenth century, the minor factories of Jiangxi, Henan, Shandong, Hunan and Hubei resorted to buying more and more finished products instead of relying on their own production.[37] This was the result of their inferior technical level, in comparison with the factories of Suzhou and Nanjing,[38] as well as of their inability to satisfy the requirements of the state.[39] In turn this phenomenon provoked, apart from a rise in the price of silk, the birth of more efficient and advanced factories, such as those of Suzhou, to which the others turned for the supply of their prescribed quotas, on top of the supplies provided by the private producers. Nevertheless, towards the end of the Ming, even the factories of Suzhou suffered progressive neglect and decline, and the output that was assigned to them was virtually all produced by the very same artisans working at home and no longer on the factory premises,[40] but still under the system of corvée.

The annual quota for Suzhou amounted to 1,534 *pi* 匹 of silk, with an extra 139 *pi* for years in which there was an extra month.[41] This burden was greater than that of the other centres in Zhili, and it was equal to roughly five

---

[33] Cf. *Changzhou xian zhi* 長洲縣志 (Longjing), *juan* 5, in Nakayama, *op. cit.*, p. 491.
[34] Cf. *Suzhou fu zhi* (Daoguang), 21.30; (Guangxu) 22.41; *Wu xian zhi*, 29B.13.
[35] Cf. *Suzhou fu zhi* (Daoguang), 21.31.
[36] Cf. *Changzhou xian zhi* (Longjing), *juan* 5, in Nakayama, *op. cit.*, p. 491.
[37] For example, in the second half of the fifteenth century, the textile factories of Jiangxi, Huguang and Fujian began to purchase processed cloth from the textile factories of Suzhou (cf. *Ming shilu*, Xianzong, Chenghua, 12th year, 7th lunar month, 戊申, 155.3).
[38] Cf. *DMHD*, 201.11.
[39] Cf. Peng Zeyi, I, pp. 55-56.
[40] Cf. Sun Pei, 3.5.
[41] Cf. *GJTSJC*, Vol. 87, p. 340, and *DMHD*, Ch. 201.

per cent of the total demanded of all the peripheral factories. While the production of the latter factories was generally destined for the gifts and rewards that the emperor granted periodically to the tributary states, and as a reward (*zengci* 贈賜) to worthy officials, that of Suzhou (and of Hangzhou) was partly destined for the imperial court.[42] But as time went by, this allocation became a small part of the total amount of silken cloth demanded from the prefecture of Suzhou. Beginning in the second half of the sixteenth century, the requests made by the central authorities grew year by year until they reached huge sums. Special orders, called *zuopai* 坐派, became the rule, and even the dimensions of the cloth were increased.[43] From the Wanli period onwards, according to the *Ming shi*, the authorities asked for up to 150,000 *pi* in one year from the two factories of Suzhou and Hangzhou.[44]

With the increase in the power of the eunuchs, and the appointment of the *taijian*, a double series of contradictions developed. On the one hand, there was the resistance of the producers and textile merchants, on whom fell an ever-increasing burden of taxes and corvée; on the other hand, there was opposition to the *taijian* by officials of the central bureaucracy. The first kind of opposition, whose leading figures were the rich textile producers, the *jihu*, resulted in a series of revolts in Suzhou between the end of the sixteenth and the beginning of the seventeenth century. The revolts of 1601 against the *taijian* Sun Long 孫隆 and those of 1602 directed against the *taijian* Liu Cheng 劉成[45] are particularly well known.

The second type of opposition is embodied in a series of petitions such as those of the officials of the *gongbu* Weng Shizi 翁世資 (around 1460)[46] and Xu Ke 徐恪,[47] or the censor Zhai Fengchong 翟鳳翀 in 1616.[48] Their aim was on the one hand to diminish the influence of the eunuchs over the factories and bring about the withdrawal of the *taijian*, and on the other to reduce the burden on the population, until the quotas were brought down to their original level, or even to bring about the closure of

[42] Cf. Sun Pei, 4.1.

[43] Compare the standard measures of one *pi* of silk as in *DMHD*, 201.1, with those demanded in 1587 (*Ming shilu*, Shenzong, Wanli, 15th year, 6th lunar month, 己巳, 187.6).

[44] According to *Ming shi*, 82.1998, and *Ming shi gao, zhi* 64.19 (Taibei, 1962, p. 300); however according to *Ming shilu*, Shenzong, Wanli, 15th year, 6th lunar month, 丙寅, 187.3, 120,000 *pi* were never exceeded.

[45] Cf. *Ming shilu*, Shenzong, Wanli, 26th year, 6th lunar month, 壬申, 360.2, and 30th year, 5th lunar month, 戊辰, 372.3.

[46] It is the first case mentioned in *Ming shi*, 82.1997, and 157.3400.

[47] Cf. *Ming shi*, 185.4904; *Chunming mengyu lu* 春明夢餘錄 in *Guxiangzhai xiuzhen shizhong* 古香齋袖珍十種, 46.55.

[48] Cf. Wen Bing 文秉, *Dingling zhulue* 定陵註略 (Taibei, 1976), p. 349.

the factories.[49] The *taijian*, for their part, were interested solely in obtaining as much as possible without caring either about the producers' reactions, or even about the organization and production of the factories. Thus it is clear that their attitude was one of the major reasons for the decline of the Suzhou factories, the flight of the artisans and the neglect of the plants. Chen You-ming 陳有明, the official sent by the Qing at the beginning of the new dynasty to restore the activity of the imperial factories at Suzhou, deplored the extreme state of deterioration in which he found the factories because of the neglect they had suffered. This neglect had gone so far that the premises and the buildings which had gone without repairs for a long time were reduced to ruins, or converted into stables, the activities were paralysed and the production scattered.[50] Further, according to the same official, this situation was not limited to the internal organization of the factories, but was directly responsible for negative effects on all the silk production of the region, if, as confirmed by the inscription of 1648, "The artisans were dispersed and the shop shut down" (*jigong xingsan jihu diaoling* 機工星散機戶雕零).[51] This should remind us that the importance of the factories went beyond their institutional functions and that they had a notable function of stimulus for the local system of production and trade. At the same time, bearing in mind what I said previously regarding the criticism of the *taijian*, and bearing in mind also the disproportion between the number of looms and of artisans employed in the factories on the one hand, and the "private" plants on the other,[52] one should note that the closure of the factories would have given greater breathing space to the producers and thus indirectly helped local production rather than the reverse.

With the establishment of the Qing dynasty, the process started half-way through the Ming era was accelerated, and a noticeable contraction took place both in the number of centres assigned to the imperial factories and in the amount of material commissioned. Furthermore, the peripheral factories were reduced to three, among which was the one at Suzhou.[53]

Thus, a national reduction of the factories as a whole corresponded to the

[49] Cf. *Ming shilu*, Shenzong, Wanli, 7th year, 11th lunar month, 丁巳, 93.2; 7th year, 7th lunar month. 乙丑, 89.5-6; 9th year, 9th lunar month, 戊寅, 116.3.

[50] Cf. Sun Pei, 3.7.

[51] Cf. *Zhizao jingzhi ji* 織造經制記, in *Ming-Qing Suzhou gongshangye beike ji* 明清蘇州工商業碑刻集 (n.p.: Jiangsu renmin chubanshe, 1981), p. 5.

[52] Cf. *Ming shilu*, Shenzong, Wanli, 29th year, 7th lunar month, 丁未, *juan* 361, p. 5. See also Ji Yong 紀庸, "Mingdai Suzhou de zhiranju" 明代蘇州的織染局, in *Guangming ribao*, 5 July 1956. Thus one has to presume that the departure of the artisans was not caused by the closure of the textile factories, but by the extortions of the *taijian*.

[53] Cf. *DQHD* (Yongzheng), 201.3: 在京有內織染局，在外江甯蘇州杭州有織造局.

277

strengthening of the southern factories and in particular of Suzhou. This was the first change from the previous period. But this also implied the concentration of the silk production in the Jiangnan province, thus making this sector more and more specialized. Secondly, the concentration of the imperial orders meant greater influence of the state upon the local economy. Moreover, the factories of Suzhou began to function regularly once more, and re-established themselves as a well-co-ordinated centre of production. Lastly, the general denomination was changed from *zhiranju* to *zhizaoju*.

In 1644 (the third year of Shunzhi), two officials of the imperial household, Chen Youming and the Manchu Shang Zhi 尚志, were sent as special commissioners to reorganize the southern factories.[54] The Suzhou factories were now divided into the two branches of *zongzhiju* 總織局 and of *zhiranju*. Chen was posted as head of the former, and Shang as head of the latter.[55] Subsequently, these branches were also called respectively *nanju* 南局 and *beiju* 北局. Chen had to content himself with living temporarily in the *bingbeidaoshu* 兵備道署. Since the place was too small, he moved into the palace that had been the residence of the *bo* 伯 of Jiading, Zhou Kui 周奎.[56] He decided to expand and restore the three factories, and in Suzhou 196 *jihu* were installed, in these and many other premises.[57] However, one should note that not all the methods of the previous dynasty were changed, and, with the system of "contracts," both the extraordinary commissioners designated the richest families of the three prefectures of Suzhou, Songjiang and Changzhan, to assume the role of *jihu* with regard to the factories.[58] This caused further discontent among the population of the *jihu*, which the authorities tried to placate with seemingly unsuccessful measures, as proved by the protests of the *tangzhang* and *guanshi* 管事 who, under a different name, were forced to perform the same tasks as the *jihu*.[59] So those who were called up[60] were no different from the old *tangzhang* of the Ming era; they were genuine contractors who dealt with the purchase of raw materials and with the organization of labour so as to deliver the goods requested. The only difference was that the majority of the work was no longer divided among the various private shops,[61] but now took place within the plants of the factories. What is more, it happened from time to time, as in the summer of 1655, that the

[54] Cf. *SXBJ*, I, p. 16.
[55] Cf. Sun Pei, 1.3.
[56] *Ibid.*, 3.2.
[57] Cf. *Suzhou fu zhi* (Daoguang), 21.30; (Guangxu), 22.41-42.
[58] Cf. Sun Pei, 1.3.
[59] Cf. Peng Zeyi, II, p. 95.
[60] *Ibid.*, pp. 93-94.
[61] *Ibid.*, p. 94.

factories did not have the raw silk to process nor the rice with which to pay the artisans, and as a consequence the latter fled and dispersed.[62]

Apart from these similarities with the situation of the late Ming era, the general principle that governed the factories during the Qing era was that of "buying the silk first and then employing the artisans" (*maisizhaojiang* 買絲招匠).

In 1647, in the two branches of the Suzhou factories, there existed more than one thousand artisans and workers, at the head of whom were three officials (*suoguan* 所官), twelve masters (*gaoshou* 高手), twenty-two foremen (*guangong* 管工) and twelve supervisors (*guanshi* 管事).[63] In 1654, in the various departments there were in all four hundred looms (*huasuji* 花素機) and 1,170 artisans. These received a total of 468 *dan* 石 of rice each month, exactly four *dou* 斗 each. Moreover, another 140 employees and attendants were working in the offices and received a total of 77.2 *dan*, i.e., about 5.5 *dou* each.[64] Another class of workers was employed for a limited time, such as the employees working the "spinning-wheel" (*chejiang* 車匠) and thus were excluded from the distribution of rice. These workers were not considered as being part of the body of "permanent" artisans that made up the majority of the workforce.[65] Apart from the precise assignment of responsibility for each duty including the fixing of processing time and delivery dates, other important aspects of the new regulations were the system of incentives[66] and sanctions, involving controls during and after work, daily shifts, and a body of managers and checkers.[67] Afterwards the factories sent the finished goods to be controlled in the capital, and on discovering any defect sanctions would be imposed.[68]

Another phenomenon that grew stronger during the Qing era was the increasing personal dependence of the managers of the factories on the emperor. This was made possible by sending slaves of the imperial court to the factories. These were men of proven loyalty and competence, and had the status of *baoyi* 包衣. This phenomenon can be equated to a kind of "personal bureaucracy" and proved itself more efficient than the use of eunuchs.

In 1653, Chen Youming was replaced by the *baoyi* Zhou Tiancheng 周天成 who had the same task as Chen in the *neigongbu* (one of the offices of the

[62] Quoted from *Qingdai chaodang* 清代鈔檔, in *ZJS*, p. 93.

[63] According to the inscription on stone by Chen Youming in 1648, *Zhizao jingzhi ji*, there were 12 foremen and 11 guards (*Ming-Qing Suzhou gongshangye beike ji*, p. 6).

[64] Sun Pei, *juan* 6, pp. 1, 3.

[65] Cf. *SXBJ*, I, p. 16.

[66] Silver medals were given as prizes for particularly refined works (織挽精美者立賞銀牌一面) (cf. *Ming-Qing Suzhou gongshangye beike ji*, p. 6).

[67] *Ibid.*

[68] Cf. *DQHDSL*, 1190.19.

imperial household)[69] before managing the factories, and was replaced the following year by another *baoyi*, the Manchu Ma Piane 馬偏俄 .[70]

This situation was officially defined by the edict of 1663, which established the origin of the supervisors (chosen from among the officials of the *neiwufu* 內務府)[71] and the elimination of any limit to the length of the office.[72] This enhanced the powers of the supervisors and the arbitrary powers of the ruling emperor.

Thus, as a consequence of the simplified organization of the factories, there were only two levels, the *neizhiranju* in Beijing and the *zhizaoju* in Suzhou, Nanjing and Hangzhou, all of which were responsible to the *neiwufu*.[73] Among the various officials and employees, the managers of the southern factories (*guanyuan* 官員) were selected from among the managers (*langzhong* 郎中) and vice-managers (*yuanwailang* 員外郎) of the *neiwufu*, whereas the treasurers of the *neiwufu*, the *siku* 司庫, were chosen from the secretaries (*bitieshi* 筆帖式) and the storekeepers (*kushi* 庫使) of the three factories, and of the one in Beijing. Lastly, the secretaries and the storekeepers of the three southern factories were picked from among the corresponding employees at the factories of the capital.[74]

Despite the attempts of the new dynasty to control directly the production of the cloth necessary to the court, what really happened was that, generally speaking, the concentration of the labour force in the workshops of the factories, and the direct responsibility of the artisans to the officials, prevailed only for part of the textile production required. For the rest, recourse was had to the *jihu* and the contractors as intermediaries.[75] In

[69] Cf. Sun Pei, 1.3. On the internal organization of the *neiwufu*, see *Qing shi gao* (Beijing, 1976), 118.3421-25; cf. also Cao Zongru 曹宗儒 , *Zhongguan neiwufu kaolue* 總管內務府考略, in *Wenxian luncong* 文獻論叢 (1936), p. 96, and Zhang Deze 張德澤 , *Qingdai guojia jiguan kaolue* 清代國家機關考略 (Beijing: Zhongguo renmin daxue chubanshe, 1981), pp. 169-97.

[70] Cf. Sun Pei, 1.4, and 9.2-3.

[71] Cf. *DQHDSL*, 1190.13. The *neiwufu* was divided into seven sections and three departments. Among the sections, the most important was the one concerned with supplies, among which was silk. Cf. Chang Te-ch'ang, "The Economic Role of the Imperial Household in the Ch'ing Dynasty," *The Journal of Asian Studies*, Vol. XXXI, No. 2 (1972), p. 249. The tendency in keeping these ties can be seen in the successive appointments of the supervisor. In 1676 at the head of the textile factory another *shilang* 侍郎 of the *neigongbu*, Lei Xiansheng 雷先聲 , was appointed, followed by officials of the *neiwufu*, many of whom were *baoyi*.

[72] The edicts of 1644 and of 1661 limited its duration to three and one year respectively. Cf. Spence, *op. cit.*, p. 87.

[73] Cf. *SXBJ*, I, p. 16.

[74] Cf. *DQHDSL*, 1190.13.

[75] Cf. *Suzhou fu zhi* (Daoguang), 17.33; *Qing shilu*, Shizu, Shunzhi, 8th year, 2nd lunar month, 54.9.

contrast, for the precious cloth required for the emperor, such as the imperial dresses, brocades, satins, muslins and other precious silks, the officials bought all the necessary material and the processing took place within the factories.[76] As for the other cloth, the officials of the factories bought the raw silk and commissioned the weaving and dyeing from the *jihu*, and these processes were carried out in private shops; afterwards the finished product was sent back to the factories.

Thus the *jihu* were private shops, which none the less had a particular status arising from their registration.[77] Apart from their "private activities" these factories received payments and raw materials from the officials in charge of the factories for delivering the required products, or even for supplying the artisans who should have worked in the factories.[78] But this dual "public and private" nature concerned only the richest shops that could guarantee to bear part of the financial burden.[79] This gave rise to repeated protests on the part of the *jihu*, sometimes resulting in arrangements in their favour, though generally these were of little effect.[80] But we still have to investigate fully the nature and depth of the dependence of the *jihu* on the factories.

In this historical overview, we have seen how the textile factories were dependent on the state apparatus, and how they were positioned halfway between the official bureaucracy and the special administration of the court. This peculiar situation is illustrated also by two other aspects, the location and the financing of the factories.

Regarding location, decisions on size, displacement, and various modifications to the plants were naturally made by the emperor or his representatives.[81]

As for the second aspect, since the factories were not a profit-seeking

[76] Cf. *Suzhou fu zhi* (Daoguang), 17.33.

[77] For the eighteenth century, see the passage of the *Yuanhe xian zhi* 元和縣志, cited in *ZJS*, pp. 214-15.

[78] Cf. Peng Zeyi, II, pp. 212-14.

[79] Cf. Spence, *op. cit.*, p. 88.

[80] For example, according to the Annals of the Qing dynasty, in 1651 an official taking the side of the rich local textile producers, complained that in Jiangnan and Zhejiang, "falsely using the name of *jihu*, they entered in the registers the most well-off families, . . . thus provoking the ruin and flight of many" (江南浙江等處，巧立機戶名色，僉報富家承充……民多破產求股) (*Qing shilu*, Shizu, Shunzhi, 8th year, 2nd lunar month, 己未). See also the inscription of 1648, note 43, in which is stressed the function of the *jihu*.

[81] In Suzhou, the *zhizaoju*, as we have seen, was divided into the *zhiranju* or *beiju*, and the *zongzhiju* or *nanju*. The *zongzhiju* was already open in the Tang and Song periods, but had its own fixed location in Suzhou beginning with the Yuan dynasty, south of the Ping 平 bridge. In the same location was the *zhiranju*. During the Ming dynasty, the *zhizaoju* was placed to the west of the *shuilifensi* 水利分司 whereas the

activity, they normally could not be self-financing, and thus had to rely on external finances, which came from the revenues of the state. Usually, during the Ming period, they made use of local tax revenue, in addition to allocations from the central ministries. During the Qing dynasty, the amount and source of finance varied with time, and in addition to the sums from the *gongbu* and from the *hubu*,[82] they had incomes of different kinds. But there were variations, too, in the share of the two ministries in these contributions.[83]

At the beginning of the dynasty, the *hubu* was in charge of all matters relating to production, expenditure and to supplies of textiles.[84] In 1651, financial responsibility was handed over instead to the *gongbu*, and in the following year it was established that this board would provide 247,244 taels, to be distributed among the three southern factories.[85] But the arrangement was not definitive, since in 1664, these responsibilities were divided between the two boards so as to fall predominantly on the *gongbu*, especially in the case of Suzhou.[86] Out of a total of 156,655 taels, roughly 142,123 came from the *gongbu*, whereas the remaining 12,832 had to come from the *hubu*. The ratio for the other factories was different. However, these figures varied according to the financial condition of the state.[87]

Furthermore, it was decided that three ships would be placed at the disposal of the factories for the transport of textile products from Suzhou to the capital.[88]

Additional sources of finance were derived from commercial activities managed by the supervisors, and usually handled by other suppliers and entrepreneurs, such as the supervisor of the Nanjing factory[89] for the purchase of copper.

"A statute of 1699 had given the rights of copper purchasing to the

zhiranju was initially to the east of Tianxin bridge. It was rebuilt and extended several times under Yongle, Hongxi, Tianshun, Jiajing, Wanli and Tianqi, and in 1628 was closed down. During the reign of Jiajing, the *zhongzhiju* was transferred to the location of the *cuiduneishi* 催督內使, and under Wanli the *Taijian* Sun Long built an East wing, adding other rooms. The *zhizaoguan*, located to the west of the Nüguanzi 女冠子 bridge, was transformed into the military inspector's office, *Qingjunchayuan* 清軍察院, in 1461 and restored in 1525 and at the end of the sixteenth century. During the Qing era, the *zongzhiju* was to the east of the Daicheng 帶城 bridge.

[82] Cf. *Ming-Qing shiliao* 明清史料, *bingbian* 丙編, III, p. 294.

[83] Cf. *SZBJ*, I, p. 16 and *DQHD* (Yongzheng), 201.4.

[84] *Ibid.*

[85] *Ibid.*

[86] Cf. *DQHD* (Yongzheng), 201.4.

[87] As, for example, in 1670. Cf. Sun Pei, 1.4 and 9.2-3.

[88] Another three ships were given to the textile factories of Hangzhou, and two or three to Nanking (*DQHD*, 201.4).

[89] Cf. *Guanyu* . . . , pp. 64, 68, 69, 71-73.

merchants from the Imperial Household, instead of leaving these rights in the hands of private merchants, and it has been rightly said that this was 'apparently for the purpose of putting the copper procurements under closer government control'. But the surprising thing is that these purchasing rights were not just granted to merchants under the control of the Imperial Household; they were granted also to the textile commissioner of Nanking who was one of the emperor's trusted bondservants."[90] This means that the textile factories were not only a case of direct state control in their specific field of activity, but that, at least during the Qing period, the state could control other sectors of the economy through them. Thus, the supervisors were given the control of other profitable activities, in the shape of state monopolies, such as the trade in salt, the customs, or the trade in ginseng. In return, the sums derived from the income from salt grew larger, until from 1708 the whole of the income derived from these monopolies came from salt.[91]

Therefore we can conclude from the above analysis that all the funding came from the "public" sector. Nevertheless, the specific activities of the factories and the problems of an economic nature meant that they had to make use, for their financial support, of different channels and sources; only one part came from the treasury, i.e., through the boards. This situation derived essentially from the financial problems that prevented the central administration from bearing the total cost, but at the same time it also meant a great independence of the textile factories, and a widening of their functions through the activities of their supervisors.

Thus the expanding responsibilities of the supervisors were first of all due to financial reasons. But there were other factors involved. Even though detailed norms governed the activities of the factories, in practice these were often in conflict with each other and not always applicable.[92] Furthermore, as I have mentioned before, the supervisor was often selected from the most

[90] Spence, *op. cit.*, p. 109.

[91] *Ibid.*, p. 95, From a memorial of Chen Youming we learn that the funds for the financing of the textile factories came not only from the government and the province but also as a contribution (53,000 taels) from seven prefectures of the Jiangsu. But these contributions were difficult to collect because of local resistance. (Cf. *Ming-Qing shiliao*, *bingbian*, III, p. 294.) Other income also came from balances under other headings, from the selling of certain shares and the product of some taxes, such as the tax on boats and salt.

[92] For example, in 1651 regulations were issued specifying the exact quantity of cloth of the type called *gaoming* 誥命 to be sent periodically to the capital; but subsequently this production was reduced or stopped because it was surplus to needs. This led to a series of problems regarding the use both of the plants and of the artisans skilled in this work. In the same year the abolition of the selection system of *jihu* and *tangzhang* was ordered, but these arrangements did not have the desired effect, for in successive periods this problem was repeatedly raised.

trusted men of the emperor. Usually he did not come from the official bureaucracy nor had he taken the path of the official's career; he was a kind of "personal bureaucrat" of the ruling house.[93] In this respect the Qing dynasty did not depart very much from the practice of the preceding dynasty, merely replacing the eunuchs with the category of those servants or slaves called *baoyi*. This condition made the supervisors particularly suited to perform confidential and classified duties, such as the sending of secret information. This information was of various kinds, and sometimes fell within the competence of the censors.[94]

The most frequent information concerned fluctuations in the price of rice,[95] the climate and the harvest in the surrounding area.[96] These economic issues led immediately to matters of a more political character; in fact we often find the combined term *mijia minqing* 米價民情 (the price of rice and popular sentiments).[97]

The very wide range of types of information to be reported to the emperor was sometimes stressed.[98] In this way the behaviour of the population was reported, both when it was calm[99] and when scandals or unrest had occurred. On this subject we find of particular interest the memorials on the attitude of "public opinion" (*zhonglun* 衆論) requested by the emperor himself,[100] and on certain rebellions[101] and epidemics.[102] Other communications referred to the uprising of Galdan[103] and the raids of pirates and their causes.[104]

More closely linked to the functions of the factories was the information

[93] Cf. *Suzhou zhizao Li Xu zouzhe*, in *WXCB*, II, p. 854.

[94] Among the offices which Li Xu, the supervisor of the textile factory of Suzhou, obtained was also an appointment as censor, *jianchayushi* 監察御史 (cf. *Guanyu . . .*, pp. 56, 59; *WXCB*, II, p. 859).

[95] Cf. *Li Xu zouzhe*, pp. 1, 10, 11, 22, 30, 34, 39, 48-49, 55-56, 60-63, 67, 69, 72-77, 80, 82-85, 88, 92, 94-95, 99-100, 107-108, 116, 128, 131-33, 135, 147, 149-50, 152-53, 167-68, 174, 177-78, 180-81, 183, 189, 191, 193-95, 198, 203, 210, 221-23, 230, 236, 239-40, 242-45, 254, 268-93, *passim*.

[96] *Ibid.*, pp. 17, 19-20, 22, 25, 29, 33-34, 53-54, 61-63, 67-69, 70, 71, 73-75, 90, 92, 95, 105, 128, 144, 152-53, 162, 174, 175, 177, 180-81, 183, 186, 189, 191, 193-95, 204-205, 210, 233, 246-50, 256-61.

[97] *Ibid.*, p. 77.

[98] 所奏事多關地方政務，不盡屬職權內事……殆亦爲耳目計 (*WXCB*, II, p. 854).

[99] 各處地方皆安靜無事 (*Li Xu zouzhe*, pp. 64, 88).

[100] In fact the emperor asked for an immediate report on the investigation so as to clarify the attitude of public opinion (明白衆論如何) toward a case of contested state examinations in Yangzhou in 1711. (*Li Xu zonzhe*, pp. 100-28, *passim*. See also Spence, *op. cit.*, pp. 240-54.)

[101] *Li Xu zouzhe*, pp. 40, 66, 68, 88.

[102] *Ibid.*, pp. 69-70.

[103] *Ibid.*, pp. 6-7.

[104] *Ibid.*, pp. 117, 121-22.

on the price of silk,[105] on the activities and expenditure[106] of the factories, and on their most successful commercial operations.[107]

Further reports dealt with the running of certain services, such as transport[108] and the activities of the bureaucracy in general.[109] In particular one should note the control over the activities of highly-placed officials, as in the case of a scandal concerning the examinations[110] or the denunciation of cases of embezzlement.[111]

Many of these reports should be seen as part of the development, during the Qing era, of the system of secret memorials, *zouzhe* 奏摺, especially under the emperors Kangxi and Yongzheng.[112] For example, at the beginning of 1710, the emperor Kangxi wrote to Li Xu, the supervisor of the Suzhou factories: "I have learnt that at present in the south there is a good deal of gossip and fabrication concerning both important and minor matters. I cannot just commission someone to make inquiries; you have received many major favours from me, so whenever you hear something, send me a memorial about it, written out in your own hand, and that will be satisfactory. You must let absolutely no one learn of this arrangement; if anyone finds out, it will be disastrous for you."[113]

The two supervisors of Nanjing and Suzhou often sent detailed confidential information concerning various occurrences, such as raids by pirates, smuggling,[114] cases of corruption and of illicit appropriation, judicial cases, the control of the waterworks, the transport of rice, etc.,[115] and generally on the condition of the population and of social control.

Therefore we can state that the task of sending more-or-less confidential information had become a second activity of the supervisors of the imperial

[105] *Ibid.*, pp. 110, 214, 266, 281-82.

[106] For example, see *ibid.*, pp. 57-59.

[107] *Ibid.*, pp. 5-6. (Cf. also Spence, *op. cit.*, p. 101.)

[108] For example, *Li Xu zouzhe*, pp. 108-10, 115.

[109] For example, *ibid.*, pp. 96-97, 163-64, 199.

[110] Apart from the works already quoted, see on this point the translation by Silas H. L. Wu, in *Communication and Imperial Control in China: Evolution of the Palace Memorial System, 1693-1735* (Cambridge, Mass., 1970), pp. 142-48.

[111] Cf. *Li Xu zouzhe*, pp. 194-95.

[112] Cf. Silas H. L. Wu, "The Memorial Systems of the Ch'ing Dynasty (1644-1911)," *Harvard Journal of Asiatic Studies*, 27 (1967), pp. 7-75, and Huang Pei 黄培, "Yong-zheng shidai de mizou zhidu" 雍正時代的密奏制度, *Qinghua xuebao* 清華學報, III (1962), pp. 17-52. See also Spence, *op. cit.*, who show how the two supervisors Cao and Li were "the first two men known to have used this system" (p. 241).

[113] Cf. Spence, *op. cit.*, p. 227, and *Li Xu zouzhe*, pp. 77-78.

[114] According to Cao, the supervisors were temporary and were not sufficient to remove the rebels from their bases in the mountains (*Guanyu . . .* , pp. 47-48).

[115] Spence, *op. cit.*, pp. 238, 240-54, 228.

textile factories. Such tasks were not institutionally limited to the management of the factories, as explicitly stated by Cao Yin 曹寅 in 1710: "My office is involved with silk and salt, I do not dare report on such things. Now I have received the emperor's orders I dare not but report as carefully as possible."[116]

As a consequence of the nature of the task, the status of the *baoyi* and relevant financial involvements, the different functions became closely linked. On the other hand, the supervisors themselves considered strictly inherent to their duties all the tasks that they managed to acquire in order to improve the financial situation of the factories, such as that of "inspection of the salt trade" ([巡視兩淮] 鹽 [課] 差).[117] The office of inspector for the administration of salt of the Liang Huai bore great responsibility. It consisted in delivering certificates, *yin* 引 , to the salt merchants, a kind of concession that authorized them to sell a certain quantity of salt in a particular area, in exchange for the payment of a tax.[118] The Liang Huai was one of the most important areas for revenue from salt, with average annual yields of taxes and surtaxes on salt of 2,500,000 taels at the beginning of the eighteenth century.[119] Between 1704 and 1720 this office was held mainly by the supervisors of Nanjing and Suzhou. Cao realized the delicacy of the office when writing to the emperor: "The office of inspector of salt, although it is of a fiscal nature, involves at the top level state policy, and at the lower level the life of the people" (*yen zheng sui xi shui cha, dan shang guan guo ji, xia ji min sheng* 鹽政雖係稅差，但上關國計，下濟民生).[120] Another important responsibility entrusted to the supervisors was the fixing of the official prices of rice, *pingtiao* 平糶 .[121] These operations, not always controllable by the central offices, had a decisive role in the local economy, and could generate further invisible sources of finance. Further revenue was possible from other tasks, such as the supplying of ginseng to the court.[122]

[116]*Ibid.*, p. 235.

[117]Cf. *WXCB*, II, pp. 859, 865.

[118]Cf. Ho Ping-ti, "The Salt Merchants of Yang-chou: A Study of Commercial Capitalism in Eighteenth-century China," *Harvard Journal of Asiatic Studies*, No. 17 (1954), pp. 130-68; Essen M. Gale and Ch'en Sung-ch'iao, "China's Salt Administration: Excerpts from Native Sources," *Asea yon'gu*, I, Nos. 1 and 2, II, No. 1 (1958-59) (in particular the final section, pp. 273-316).

[119]Cf. Spence, *op. cit.*, p. 168.

[120]*Guanyu* . . . , p. 23. In his answer the emperor ordered that that he be kept *secretly* informed of any problem that might arise, and recommended him time and time again to be on guard. As to the responsibilities of the supervisor of Suzhou, Li Xu, see *Li Xu zouzhe*, pp. 26-28, 30-31, 33, 45, 52, 59-60, 74, 89, 119-20, 125-26, 127, 129, 140, 142-43, 148, 153, 159-60, 164, 166, 168, 185, 206-209, 213-15, 217-18, 219-20, 225-28, 234-35, 250-53, 260, 263.

[121]*Guanyu* . . . , pp. 59-60.

[122]*Ibid.*, pp. 66, 148, 150-51, 155-56, 159-62.

The delivery of particular goods—at times ordered, at times given spontaneously as gifts—constituted a further activity of the supervisors: so we learn of the delivery of perfumes, and other precious objects,[123] of fruits and bamboo seeds.[124] Furthermore, the supervisor was involved with the restoration of temples and monuments,[125] and could take autonomous initiatives, as in the case of the repairing of dams.[126] At other times he was even in charge of finding the right persons for certain tasks and missions, as when he had to choose a technician to be sent to Japan disguised as a merchant so that he could gather information on Japanese commercial and naval activities.[127] Finally, he took care of the preparations for the reception of the emperor when he visited the town where the supervisor resided, as in the case of Kangxi in April 1705.[128]

The expansion of imperial power in various sectors through the officials of the factories is testified to by the multiplicity of all those ordinary and special duties often not connected to the primary functions of the supervisor. But it does not appear to demonstrate an authentic and proper expansion of state intervention in economic activities, even in the Qing period. If it is true, as I have said, that the factories were an instrument of state control over the various sectors of the economy, in reality we must not forget that these sectors were not taken out of "private" hands, but simply passed from the control of the bureaucracy to the direct control of the emperor.

The establishment of the imperial textile factories showed, from the outset, the interest of the state in controlling at least part of the textile sector.

Under the empire, state intervention in the economic field was determined by different motivations, depending on the sector, such as the control of those activities considered particularly dangerous for social order, the control of certain products of particular importance, the possibility of obtaining considerable fiscal income, and the importance of certain interventions in terms of "public" affairs.

In the specific case of the textile factories, however, state intervention was limited to the production of cloth to be sent to the emperor or to the court.

---

[123]*Li Xu zouzhe*, pp. 2-3, 8, 10-11, 32, 88, 152-53; *Guanyu* . . . , pp. 44-45.

[124]*Li Xu zouzhe*, pp. 29, 85, 164.

[125]For Li Xu at Suzhou, see *Li Xu zouzhe*, pp. 86-87, 284. For Cao Yin at Nanking, see *Guanyu* . . . , p. 153. For the reparations of the Ming tombs, cf. *Guanyu* . . . , p. 13.

[126]Cf. *Li Xu zouzhe*, pp. 139-42.

[127]The person involved was an employee of the textile factory of Hangzhou, whom the Franciscan monks described as a "shrewd explorer" (*Sinica francescana, V, Relationes et epistolas ill.mi D.Fr. Bernardini della Chiesa O.F.M.*, ed. PP. Anastasius van den Wyngaert et Georgius Mensaert O.F.M., Roma, 1954, p. 441). Cf. also Spence, *op. cit.*, pp. 117-18, and *Li Xu zouzhe*, pp. 15, 18.

[128]Cf. Spence, *op. cit.*, pp. 144-51.

This cloth was used directly by them or sent to worthy officials as a token of appreciation by the sovereign, or as a means of exchange in the ceremonials connected with the "Sinocentric" system of "international" relations. Thus we can consider as fundamental to the monopoly exerted by the state over this production the "destination of the product," to the extent that this gave it a certain significance.

The interest of the state in this sector of economic activity cannot be compared with state intervention in mining and metalwork, or to the salt monopoly. In each of these cases the motivations were different. In the first instance, it was a question of controlling the production of especially important goods, for military and financial reasons, as well as for meeting the needs of the local population, offering them, as a lesser evil, an alternative to hunger, emigration and revolt. The second case lay much more in the fiscal domain, and thus had a more clearly marked economic nature. As for the textile factories, on the contrary, the state did not control the free market, apart from the distribution of licences and the imposition of taxes on production and trade. Apart from this, the weavers and textile merchants were free to go about their business, under the tutelage and control of the guilds. Not only this, but the factories, when they had to purchase silk to process it, paid the market price. The price limits fixed by imperial decrees did not concern the suppliers or the merchants, but only the persons in charge of the textile factories.[129] On the other hand, we can find some analogies between the textile factories and the porcelain factories, even though the latter lacked an equivalent structure for direct control by the state, as well as being less organically linked to the offices of the imperial household. The above-mentioned principle of the destination of the product, according to which the Board of Works issued annual orders as well as special ones that could subsequently be reduced or suspended, was applied also in the case of porcelain. Thus even in this sector, there existed particular legislation, but always for those products in which the state had an interest. Above all, during the latter half of the Ming era, we encounter a similar controversy over the sending of eunuchs, involving attitudes and consequences similar to those witnessed at the same time in the textile factories. I shall return to this matter in the conclusion.

Before proceeding further, it should be stressed once more that in the period under consideration the distinction between private and public sectors was not as clear-cut as in today's Western world. Usually even the managing personnel of the textile factories was not chosen from the official bureaucracy, but was made up mainly of eunuchs in the Ming era, and of *baoyi* in

[129] Cf. *Qingdai chaodang*, reported in *ZJS*, pp. 97-98.

288

the Qing era, belonging in both cases mainly to the organization of the imperial household. In fact, we can consider the textile factories as being part of the emperor's personal domain; but at the same time they had, in modern terms, a public function in as much as the production was for the use of the head of state and for official ceremonies. The distinction is made more difficult by the ambigious nature of the *baoyi*, who were both private servants of the emperor and instruments of his despotism, as were the eunuchs who preceded them as supervisors of the textile factories. To this must be added the fact that at least a part of the *jihu*, the "private" textile producers who worked within the textile factories, had a "public" function, with duties and powers derived from the fact that they were "the families of the [textile] machines." And they were also public tax collectors, or contractors on behalf of the state, or again, privileged merchant entrepreneurs.

However, although we can say that the personnel of the textile factories with managerial functions had a specific but not continuous link with the imperial household through the so-called "personal bureaucracy" made up of the eunuchs (in the Ming era) or the *baoyi* (in the Qing era), on the other hand the ambiguity of the situation is confirmed in the historic compilations and in the administrative registers, where these officials were classified now as responsible to the *gongbu*, now as responsible to the *neiwufu*, or again as eunuchs. Even for the labour-force, the distinction was unclear, because only one class of artisans, the *zhuzuo*, was directly employed by the officials of the imperial household, whereas the remainder were employed by the Boards of Works, Finance and War, i.e., the conventional state structure. Although the distinction between the treasury of the imperial household and public finance is very old in China, the question becomes extremely complex if examined from the aspect of financing the textile factories. In fact the funds came mainly from the state and not from the imperial household, as one would expect. Briefly we can conclude that the textile factories were considered part of the state machine, although they were connected with the imperial household.

Another problem linked with state intervention in the role of the textile factories is the production of the textile sector. From the reading of the sources one has the impression that the role played by the state factories was extremely important, and that a large part of the merchants' production resulted directly or indirectly from their activity. It seems that their function of promoting production and trade went far beyond the quotas of silk demanded each year, as it would appear from the negative influence of the declining textile factories of Suzhou on the local textile production towards the end of the Ming period. But even this fact can be interpreted in different ways and has to be examined carefully. The official reports had a vested interest and stressed the positive role of the textile factories. Moreover, quantitative data that could prove or disprove such reports are lacking, and so are the production rates for the market.

But if we compare the approximate but still considerable figures of the looms, of other textile machinery and of the "private" artisans with these relatively small figures of the textile factories, one sees the disproportion between "state" production and the global production of Suzhou. Thus, if nothing else, we can note the existence of a political power far superior to the economic importance of the factories, resulting from their privileged position in the market, and their control over many producers and textile plants.

The benefits derived from the availability of manpower and of production structures already in existence in the area, which had been a well-known centre of silk production for centuries, are symptomatic of the reasons for the choice of Suzhou.[130] On the other hand, we cannot prove that the choice of Suzhou was aimed directly at the promotion of the handicraft trade as well as increasing exports. For various reasons these aspects could fall within the competence of local officials, merchants or the supervisors of the textile factories. But these aspects were not considered duties of the state, at least until half-way through the Qing period. Indeed, an excessive growth of these sectors would result, as actually happened towards the end of the dynasty, in disequilibria considered damaging to public order and social control, which were the principal aims of the state. As a consequence prices rose, both of food—due to the growth and concentration of the population—and of silk —due to increasing exports. Consequently, major problems arose in controlling the masses of workers, especially in the cases of unemployment and of conflict of interests. Solving these problems was the duty partly of the local authorities, partly of the various semi-private, semi-official organizations, such as the guilds of the artisans, and the various "private entrepreneurs" who were held co-responsible for possible disorders.

It is difficult to construct a general argument capable of embracing such a vast historical period rich in political and economic changes which affected also the context in which the textile factories operated. In any case, the textile factories displayed, at least up to the high point of the Qing dynasty, a noticeable evolution in the course of Chinese history, marked by the expansion of their functions and by the concentration of their activity. Indeed, during the Qing era they became great centres of state and economic power thanks to the assumption by the supervisors of numerous responsibilities that rendered the textile factories an efficient tool of imperial authority and control.

[130]Cf., for example, the inscribed tablet of the textile factory of Suzhou in 1547, *Chongxiu Suzhou zhiranju ji* 重修蘇州織染局記, in *Ming-Qing Suzhou gongshangye beike ji*, pp. 1-2, 131.

The degree of capital and labour concentration in the textile factories varied from period to period. In some instances, mainly during the early periods of the Ming and Qing dynasties, the textile factories were a productive organization, reflecting the needs of the state, in which a concentration of plants and skilled manpower corresponded to an articulated division of labour under the strict control of imperial and state officials. They also had the function of buying certain textile products that could not be produced by them, although this activity took second place. At other times, on the contrary, internal discipline was weakened and the organization was virtually reduced to appointing a few textile producers responsible for the output. Thus the importance of the fiscal aspect was accentuated, and their function was limited to supplying the required quantity and quality of goods. The producers to whom in turn responsibility was assigned, did not possess the productive apparatus of the textile factories; hence, they had to commission other smaller producers to undertake much of the required textile production, advancing money or raw materials, and contributing with their own capital as a duty towards the state.

All this shows that the state was not interested in the control of textile production *per se*, nor in its development as a purely economic activity. There were two principal objectives of the textile factories. The first and most pressing was of a fiscal nature; the second and more general concerned political and ethical matters.

The fiscal aspect consisted in finding the products required by the state organizations at the highest level, in this case cloth and costumes. These were primarily for the personal use of the emperor and his court, since he was head of state. In addition, they had the function of distinguishing between the various offices and ranks given by the emperor to the officials. Another part was for "international relations"; they were used as gifts that the emperor deigned to give to the sovereigns, courts and diplomatic envoys of the tributary states, or at least considered as such according to the Sinocentric Confucian system.[131]

In the Qing period, the orders for cloth for sale in Xinjiang were limited to predetermined quantities, and there is no evidence of any desire to expand production indiscriminately, not even for exports. These quantities were delivered to the offices administering the patrimony of the imperial household, and the cloth was used for barter.

Even where monetary advantage was to be gained, as in the case of direct relations with the West before the Opium War, considerations of social and

[131] Cf. *Chongxiu Suzhou zhizao gongshu beiji* 重修蘇州織造公署碑記, in *Ming-Qing Suzhou gongshangye beike ji*, pp. 10-11.

public order prevailed.

The orders were always spelled out in detail, and limited to the real requirements of the state. They never considered the idea of using the textile factories as an economic tool for the development of local production, still less for state exports.

Productivity and competitiveness of the textile factories were also disregarded, since utility came second to political objectives, and they were instead looked upon not so much as economic enterprises, but rather as political and organizational centres. Whereas in Europe the *Manufactures Royales* had as primary function the production in large textile factories of certain goods required by the Crown, or simply their production under the patronage of the latter, in China we can say, on the contrary, that the significant aspect was that of a bureaucratic organization aiming at delivering the goods required by the state independent of the fact that these goods were produced within the organization, or required as taxes in kind, or put out on contract to external artisans.

The second objective consisted in running the plants in such a way as to contribute to social equilibrium. The organization of these offices was designed as a means to achieve the aims just stated. Thus, they contributed to the goal of maintaining social order, while avoiding inequalities and speculations which would have negative consequences on social harmony.

The exorbitant requests of the eunuchs in the second half of the Ming period provided negative proof of this trend. The *taijian*, being also tax inspectors, represented in an extreme form the tendency to give priority to the fiscal aspect, to the point of damaging local productive resources. The negative consequences of their actions are part of the pathological involution of which the *taijian* were the expression. At an institutional level this regression was manifested in the disproportionate expansion of their powers; at an economic level it led to the financial crisis of the state that required an ever greater income; at a political level it led to the birth of an opposition of scholar-officials (*donglin* 東林) and the outbreak of popular uprising (as in 1601 in Suzhou).

The activity of the supervisors, when performed with shrewd economic ability, was justified both as a manifestation of loyalty to the emperor, and because it favoured the welfare of the population and social peace.[132] This does not mean that the authorities ignored or displayed contempt for wealth

---

[132] It is in this sense, I believe, that we can interpret the promotion, on the part of the literate and officials, of the textile production. See for example, Tang Zhen 唐甄, *Jiao can* 教蠶, in *Qian shu* 潛書 (Beijing: Zhonghua shuju, 1963), pp. 157-58; Gu Yanwu 顧炎武, *Rizhilu* 日知錄 (Taibei, 1974), 10.243, and also *Huangchao jingshi wenbian* 皇朝經世文編, 37 (*huzheng* 戶政).1-12.

as such. It appears from many historical sources, especially the more official ones, that the merchants were not as despised as one is led to believe, nor held to ransom provided they did not alter the established social order. Thus we find many examples of economic measures taken for the welfare of the people and thus for the prosperity of the country. If one looks at the intellectual movement that developed at the end of the Ming and beginning of the Qing periods (what we can describe as "practical science," *shixue* 實學) we see that in it the priority of socio-economic problems is given theoretical expression. But even this instance falls into the category of the ethical-political function, i.e., the ideal of harmony in which *si li* 私利 (private advantage) coincides with *gong li* 公利 (public advantage).

Finally, conclusive demonstration of what I have argued here can be drawn from some memorials of the Ming era. Regarding the controversy over the sending of eunuchs as supervisors of the textile factories and as fiscal inspectors in the latter half of the Ming dynasty, there exists a relatively abundant documentation, both in the *Shilu* and in private compilations. This material implicitly discloses the attitude of numerous officials of the ministries and of local administrations, as well as of the censors, regarding the functions of the textile factories. We can deduce from these materials, in particular, the concern that the textile factories should be administered by the state bureaucracy so that they would serve the ends already noted, and conform to the interests of the state. It is not a question of a general polemic against the excessive power of the eunuchs nor a simple defence of the textile producers and distributors, still less of a concern with production alone. From time to time the memorialists even criticized the emperor in more or less veiled fashion for excessive demands and luxuries; they attacked the *taijian* for illicit enrichment at the expense of the population. But the heart of the matter was related above all to the fiscal problem, in the broad sense, and more generally to the security of the state. The production and the use of precious cloth in excess of the quantity allowed by the state finances had two consequences: either it diverted funds meant for primary requirements, such as national defence, or it fell on the tax-payers, worsening their tax burden and corvée. Neither of the two options would have been advantageous to the stability of the state. In the first case the defence of the borders would have been weakened, and in the second case disorder and rebellion would have resulted.

With such clear arguments, the memorialists indeed took up the defence of the population and the textile producers, but their main concern was once again the smooth running of the whole state machine, and the resulting social peace.

In this respect, the textile factories represented an example of the interaction between imperial power and bureaucratic powers in fiscal matters; at the same time they showed the dual nature, with different shades according to the moment in time, of being an instrument for the supply of certain luxury goods to the state, and a body relying heavily on public funds. In any case, this means that the activity of the textile factories took place wholly in the economic field, either in the guise of the state as a tax collector, or of the state as a consumer, and that it changed its methods depending on which of these aspects prevailed. Therefore the history of the textile factories of Suzhou followed the course of the political and economic history of the empire. With the coming of the Ming era it probably became the most important of the numerous centres catering for specific textiles. Then with the decline of the dynasty, the textile factories, too, fell into decay, even if the volume of the products required from the factories was increasing.

Since the factories were part of the state organization, a weakening of state controls and of the efficacy of the state inevitably affected them. Moreover, factors not linked to the dynastic cycle also contributed to their decay since, because they were based on the corvée, the decline of the latter as a fiscal device could not fail to affect their activity. With the rise of a new dynasty, even the textile factories readjusted themselves and began to function with improved efficiency and greater scope, but only after a few decades. Among the many causes were the spirit of initiative of the new administration, a greater rationalization of the inner organization, and a more up-to-date use of the labour-force and the greater availability of funds through direct and indirect backing.

But in any case, the aim of the authorities was to intervene directly as little as possible, to control the textile factories through the intermediary of private and semi-private entities, and to confine themselves to controlling the production of a few goods.

10. State Intervention in the Administration of a Hydraulic Infrastructure: The Example of Hubei Province in Late Imperial Times*

Pierre-Etienne Will

As anybody knows, the role of the state apparatus in the construction and administration of the hydraulic installations conditioning agricultural and demographic development in the delta plains of southern and eastern Asia is generally considered crucial, to such an extent that certain well-known theories hold that both state and society in most Asian countries may justi-fiably be described as "hydraulic." However, it is by no means certain that such a generalization is tenable in the case of a geographic entity as vast, diverse and compartmentalized as China. Moreover, the centralized Chinese state, both in its origins and in its final stages of development, may be defined by many functions and plans other than administering the various irrigation and hydraulic protection works, even if these are essential in most areas. And finally, even if this sole function is considered, the state and its bureaucracy are not the only factors in question, the only decision makers and the only executants. As will be seen in this paper, matters occur on several levels, which are not necessarily integrated and which represent options and interests often contradictory to each other.

In actual fact, to theorize on the state and hydraulics in China can only be done by taking fully into account the contrast between the homogeneity, standardization and centralization of the bureaucratic apparatus, on the one hand, and, on the other, the extreme diversity of topographic, climatic, hydrographic and even social conditions between the different regions and macroregions (to use Skinnerian terms) of the empire. How does the state organization adapt to the variety of conditions both regional and local? To what extent is the state committed? Are there institutions or regulations particular to such and such region and, if this is the case, how are they integrated into the global system of the centralized state? Detailed regional studies are clearly a necessary prerequisite of any attempt to elaborate

*Previous drafts of this paper have benefited from remarks by Marianne Bastid, Yves Chevrier, Mark Elvin, Jacques Gernet, Pierre Gourou, Stuart Schram and Eduard Vermeer. The shortcomings in the final product are, of course, my own responsibility.

Note: In local gazetteer citations *XZ* stands for *xianzhi* 縣志, *ZZ* for *Zhouzhi* 州志 and *FZ* for *fuzhi* 府志.

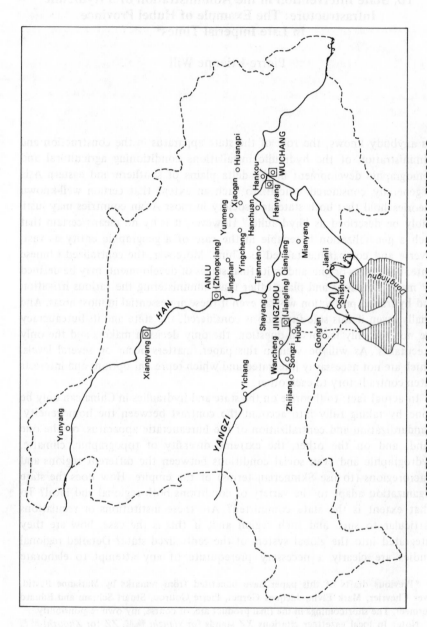

HUBEI PROVINCE DURING THE MING AND QING PERIODS

theories on a general level.

The specific hydraulic problems of the middle Yangzi and, more particularly, of the northern half of the Huguang plain, to be dealt with here, have already been approached, at times in some detail, by such authors as E. L. Oxenham, Sun Fushi, Zhong Xin, Wang Yiya, Kōno Michihiro, Morita Akira, Liu Ts'ui-jung, and more recently Peter Perdue.[1] Before modern times, the hydraulic history of the basin had already been considered in relation to the acute ecological problems due to economic and demographic growth, notably by Gu Yanwu 顧炎武 (1613-82) in a much quoted passage from his *Tianxia junguo libing shu* 天下郡國利病書, and in the nineteenth century by the historian and statecraft scholar Wei Yuan (1794-1856) in two short texts which show how certain representatives of the so-called "hydraulic state" had a clear view of problems which they could no longer overcome—but I shall come back to this.[2] I have, for my part, made a study of this history taking particular interest in the interior delta formed by the Yangzi and its main tributary, the Han, in the central Hubei basin.[3] In this study I sought to take into account hydrographical as well as political factors, the latter including not only the part played by the state in the development and maintenance of the hydraulic infrastructures, but also the negative effect of the wars and rebellions, most of which, in the case of Hubei, originated

[1] See E. L. Oxenham, "On the Inundations of the Yang-tse-kiang," *Journal of the Royal Geographical Society*, Vol. 45 (1875), pp. 1-14; Sun Fushi 孫輔世, *Yangzijiang zhi shuili* 揚子江之水利 (Chongqing, 1938; Taibei, 1973); Zhong Xin 鍾歆, *Yangzijiang shuili kao* 揚子江水利考 (Shanghai, 1936); Wang Yiya 王益厓, *Changjiang* 長江 (Taibei, 1957) (these three works devote particular chapters to the problems of the middle Yangzi); Kōno Michihiro 河野通博, "Shindai ni okeru Kohoku shō no kōzui" 清代にお ける湖北省の洪水, *Jimbun chiri*, Vol. I, No. 2 (1948), pp. 35-45, and "Keikō bunkō oboegaki" 荊江分洪覺書, *Okayama shigaku*, 10 (1961), pp. 242-66; Morita Akira 森田明, *Shindai suiri shi kenkyū* 清代水利史研究 (Tokyo, 1974), Chaps. I-III (resuming studies published between 1960 and 1972); Liu Ts'ui-jung, "Dike Construction in Ching-chou: A Study Based on the 'T'i-fang chih' Section of the *Ching-chou fu-chih*," *Papers on China*, Vol. 23 (1970), pp. 1-28 (largely duplicates Morita's chapter II, originally published in 1961, which she does not seem to have used); Peter Perdue, "Official Goals and Local Interests: Water Control in the Dongting Lake Region during the Ming and Qing Periods," *Journal of Asian Studies*, Vol. XLI, No. 4 (1982), pp. 747-65.

[2] Wei Yuan 魏源, "Huguang shuili lun" 湖廣水利論 and "Hubei tifang yi" 湖北堤防 議, in *Guweitang waiji* 古微堂外集, 6.4a-7b and 11a-13b. (Also in *Wei Yuan ji* 魏源集, Beijing, 1976, pp. 388-93.)

[3] On the slow development of this delta in the course of the centuries and its advance from west to east at the expense of the vast marshes which occupied all the central plain, see the ingenious historical reconstruction by Zhang Xiugui 張修桂, "Yunmeng ze de yanbian yu xia Jingjiang hequ de xingcheng" 雲夢澤的演變與下荊江河曲的形成, *Fudan daxue xuebao* 復旦大學學報, No. 2, 1980, pp. 40-48. (This reference was pointed out to me by James Lee.)

outside the area. I have thus been led to propose a cyclical pattern: development—(crisis)—recession, or phase A—phase B. This pattern was reproduced
in a striking way, even though not identically, under the Ming and Qing
dynasties.[4]

Without returning in detail to this pattern, which provides the general
historical framework of the present essay, I shall simply recall that in the
central plain of Hubei, the major hydraulic problem is one of self-protection
from the seasonal floods (in summer and autumn) by systems of dykes
allowing permanent farming zones to be preserved. Were the basin left in its
"natural" state, these areas would be flooded annually. At the same time, the
drainage of flood waters towards the lower part of the province (to the east)
must be ensured with maximal efficiency and speed. This represents a
difficulty, because the flow of these high waters is naturally delayed by the
narrowness of the gullies downstream from the junction of the Han and the
Yangzi (in the case of the Han, upstream from this junction as well). This
difficulty is compounded by the flatness of the plain and the very gentle
incline of both rivers between the western accesses to the basin and its eastern
outlet. The often very fast flowing flood waters must, therefore, be kept for
a time in the multitude of lakes, marshes and floodable moorland which are
scattered over the central basin *outside* the main courses of the rivers. The
development of a system of dykes risks precisely to run counter to this
natural storage function.

In Hubei, actually, the dyke-system is a dual one. On the one hand are the
long dykes designed to contain the Yangzi and the Han within their main
beds and to limit the number of lateral outflows during the time of high
waters; on the other hand are circular dykes, called *yuan* 垸 in Hubei, for
which I suggest the term *enclosure* and which could also be defined as
"caissons." These surrounded the fields and villages and protected them from
the seasonal floods. The proliferation of such enclosures at the expense of
the marshes and lakes, creeks and fluvial banks, progressively hindered the
drainage of the basin and resulted in a state of overconcentration of human
settlements and permanent agricultural land. The consequence, when waters
rose to exceptionally high levels in the Yangzi, Han and Dongting Lake, was

---

[4] Pierre-Etienne Will, "Un cycle hydraulique en Chine: la province du Hubei du XVIe
au XIXe siecles," *Bulletin de l'Ecole Française d'Extrême-Orient*, Vol. 68 (1980), pp. 261-
87. (This study had been presented as a paper in June 1976.) The parallelism of the cycle
development-crisis-recession in the 16th-17th and 18th-19th centuries, and of the
factors which determined it, was not noticed by the authors cited in note 1, except for
Perdue concerning the construction of "polders" in the area surrounding Dongting Lake
in Hunan. "Phase A" of the first of the two cycles began in fact as early as the beginning
of the 15th century.

catastrophic flooding which broke the long dykes, submerged the enclosures and took months to drain away.

This process culminated in the 1560s and again in the 1780s. From that point on began "phase B," referred to earlier, during which the inhabitants of the basin were on the defensive regarding water, while measures to ensure hydraulic protection only became less effective and less profitable.

Such are, in outline, the natural context of the central Hubei plain and the problems of ecological balance arising from it.[5] Although the above-mentioned authors have extensively referred to the role played by state and bureaucracy in the administration of river-control, a key link in the analysis —namely the question of how state power fitted into the set of ecological, social and economic factors which went to make up the history of the basin —has been most of the time overlooked. Without being in a position to offer any general conclusion on the subject, I shall present in the following pages facts and ideas which, I believe, are worth incorporating in the already copious literature dealing with the relations between state and hydraulics in China.

I. STAGE ONE: LARGE-SCALE STATE INTERVENTION

Clearly, the Hubei plain is a good example of those complex and extensive hydrographic systems discharging a quantity of water at once enormous and highly variable, presenting a landscape which is constantly being reshaped by floods and alluviation, and involving in the process of domestication heavy initial investment and the construction of basic facilities which are both on a large scale and, often, very far from the communities deriving benefit from them. In other words, the systematic development and dense populating of such regions can only be effected with the impetus and means provided by a state apparatus, whatever form that may take. (I understand by this that the impetus does not come necessarily from the highly centralized bureaucracy characteristic of phases of imperial unification, but may be in the way of a power merely regional in its scale and ambitions.)

In this section, after dealing with the historical beginnings of large-scale state intervention in the Hubei plain, I shall consider the efforts at restoration carried out at the beginning of "phase A" of the cycle mentioned above, in this case at the beginning of the Ming and Qing dynasties. As will be seen, these efforts very quickly gave rise to the autonomous growth of a private sector, the interests of which were expressed on a local scale and caused problems of co-ordination. These, again, could only be solved by a state

[5] For further details, see Will, "Un cycle hydraulique . . ."

organization. Actually, matters evolved in such a way that, at a certain point, the state was no longer able to solve them. These developments will be the subject of later sections.

It is quite difficult to know when exactly the first important embankments were built in the central Yangzi basin. The oldest seem to have been constructed at strategic places (i.e. from a hydraulic point of view) allowing the region of the ancient prefecture of Jiangling 江陵 (later Jingzhou *fu* 荊州府) to be sheltered from floods. The first sections of the dyke later called Jinti 金堤, then Wanchengti 萬城堤, possibly go back to the Jin 晉 dynasty.[6] As for the first long dykes on the southern bank of the Han, stretching between Jingmen 荊門 and Qianjiang 潛江, they are supposed to date from the Five Dynasties period.[7] However, it was only during the Song period that the long dykes of Jiangling, protecting the area north of the Yangzi in the section where the river flows in successive bends, were the target of a first series of systematic works relating to a deliberate effort of economic development.[8]

This effort, it must be made clear, essentially dates from the Southern Song, and it is interesting to see that it was coupled with a strategic aim, namely, creating a *glacis* against the Jin, then the Mongols, in order to protect the empire from attacks using this classical invasion route. *Glacis* here should be understood in two different senses: human and natural. We shall see that a different attitude regarding local hydraulic problems corresponded to each of these meanings.

The idea of a natural rampart protecting Jiangling against attacks coming from the north by using both the river Ju 沮 (or Zhang 漳), which normally flows in upstream from the city, and the network of lakes stretching parallel to the left bank of the Yangzi, seems old. According to some sources, it had been put into operation as early as the Three Kingdoms period, by a certain Lu Kang 陸抗 who sought to defend the kingdom of Wu, and later by Gao Baorong 高保融, a regional potentate of the Five Dynasties

---

[6] See *Jiangling XZ* (1877), 8.2b-3a, quoting from the *Shuijingzhu* 水經注 .

[7] According to *ibid.*, 54.16a, these dykes had been constructed by Gao Jixing 高季興 (d. 928), a warlord appointed governor of Jingnan 荊南 under the Later Liang and Later Tang, who in a more or less independent way occupied and rehabilitated this region which had been laid waste at the end of the Tang (see his biography in *Jiu Wudai shi* 舊五代史, 133). See also *Mianyang ZZ* 沔陽州志 (1894), 3.11a, and a text quoted in *Xia Jingnan daozhi* 下荊南道志 (1740), 24.58b, pointing out that Gao Jixing had had this hundred *li* of dykes built on the southern bank of the Han in order to protect his Jiangling fief. Some thousand years later the local people were still calling this dyke, situated downstream from the town of Shayang, "Mr. Gao's dyke" 高氏堤 .

[8] *Jiangling XZ* (1877), 8.5a, tells us for instance that the long dyke near Shashi 沙市, downstream from Jiangling, is said to date from the Xining era (1068-77).

period.[9] However, the high-ranking officials of the Southern Song were the men who eventually succeeded in creating an uninterrupted stretch of water capable of halting the foraying barbarian horsemen, placed just behind the first defensive line (that one author[10] does not hesitate to call the "Maginot Line of Xiangyang"). Li Shikui 李師夔 in 1160, Wu Lie 吳獵 in 1165-73, and Liu Jia 劉甲 in 1207 had reconstruction work done on the site, called the "Two," later "Three Seas" (上中下三海). But the one to take the problem in hand in a comprehensive fashion was Meng Gong 孟珙 (1195-1246) who, in 1244, diverted the Ju River and made it skirt Jiangling by the north and flow into the Han. He then organized the Three Seas into a succession of eight "caissons" (*bagui* 八櫃) in tiers, stretching over 300 *li* and connected by nine "separations" (*jiuge* 九隔) allowing, probably by a system of sluice gates, the "storage and release" of water.[11]

The human *glacis*, on the other hand, consisted of the armies to be stationed in the area and the people who had to feed them. Here again the hydraulic installations came into play, and problems began. As we saw, agricultural development in the lowlands partially took place by encroaching on the flood-prone areas and by taking over the exceptionally fertile beds of alluvial lakes. Moreover, it is clear that the attempt at "military colonization of Jingnan" (*Jingnan tunliu* 荆南屯留) led by the Southern Song brought in its wake an important civil immigration. We know, for instance, that in 1228 Meng Gong—who was by no means the first one to do so—had had a huge reservoir (*yan* 堰) constructed in order to reinforce the economic potential of the anti-Jin base for which he was responsible at Zaoyang 棗陽 in the north of the province. This reservoir allowed 100,000 *qing* of land to be irrigated, which produced from the start some 150,000 *shi* of grain. The operation had been given partly to civilians and partly to the military. In 1239,

[9] See *Jiangling XZ* (1794), 3.25a; *id.* (1877), 50.6b. For Lu Kang, see *Sanguozhi* 三國志, Zhonghua shuju 中華書局 ed., 58.1356. Gao Baorong (d. 960) was the grandson of Gao Jixing.

[10] Chikusa Masaaki 竺沙雅章, in Saeki Tomi 佐伯富 (ed.), *Sō no shin bunka* 宋の新文化 (Tokyo, 1967), pp. 297-300. ("*Tōyō no rekishi*, 6"). In the same vein we might mention the network of "mountain forts" (*shanzhai* 山寨) developed in Western Anhui and Eastern Hubei by Wu Yuan 吳淵, a contemporary of Meng Gong, in the 1240s. The "hydraulic *glacis*" discussed here was but one element amongst the numerous lines of defence erected to protect the central basin of the Yangzi from the invaders based in North China. See Tao Jinsheng 陶晉生, "Nan Song liyong shanshuizhai de fangshou zhanlüe" 南宋利用山水寨的防守戰略, *Shihuo yuekan* 食貨月刊, Vol. VII, No.1/2 (1977), esp. p. 7.

[11] See *Jiangling XZ* (1794), 3.25a-b; *id.* (1877), 50.6b-7a; *Songshi*, 412 (biography of Meng Gong). One of these sources notes that, "if the Jin have often raided Jingmen department, they always withdrew without coming within 100 *li* of Jiangling: they knew they would be stopped by the Three Seas." See also Meng's biography in H. Franke (ed.), *Sung biographies* (Wiesbaden: Franz Steiner, 1976), pp. 779-86.

still engaged in supplying the armies and having been appointed "high commissioner for colonization" (*tuntian dashi* 屯田大使), he apparently had other reservoirs built, taking on peasants to whom the means for making a start were given. This is said to have resulted in the creation of 170 "domains" (*zhuang* 莊) and 20 "colonies" (*tun* 屯) totalling some 188,280 *qing*.[12]

The immigration movement set in motion, or speeded up, by such measures, was also favoured by the pursuit of dyke construction along the Yangzi, which had the effect of putting new areas out of the path of the floods. One source tells us that as early as 1158 the important Huangtan dyke 黃潭堤 at Jiangling was subjected to major repair work.[13] The Jinti dyke, already mentioned, was reportedly built in 1189.[14] We also know that in 1236 the same Meng Gong had dyked the right bank of the Yangzi in the Gong'an 公安 sector, downstream from Jiangling.[15] These are but a few examples from among many others. Now this development, which as a side effect was favouring the expansion of big landowning, seems to have worked against the concept of what we called a natural *glacis*, since, we are told, the water areas which were part of the device were steadily reduced by the encroachment of the "powerful" (*haoyou* 豪右): the latter caused them to be filled in and then built small dyke systems in order to protect the reclaimed paddy-fields.[16] This, actually, is one of the reasons why Meng Gong was obliged to reorganize the whole system of the Three Seas in 1244. Thus, during that time when Hubei found itself in the front line facing the barbarian empires, there was an ironic contradiction between one of the important functions assigned to the "hydraulic state" by its theoreticians, namely the implementing of large defence systems[17]—in this case involving

[12] See *Songshi*, 412. It is interesting to note that, in a similar way, the development of the lower Yangzi delta before the end of the Tang period, thanks to the construction of polders (comparable to the *yuan* in Hubei) and to the setting up of a network of irrigation and drainage canals, had been stimulated by a development programme of military colonies: the Tang army thus played the role of a catalyst in the mostly alluvial lower Yangzi plain. See Mira Mihelich, "Polders and the Politics of Land Reclamation in Southeast China during the Northern Sung Dynasty (960-1126)" (Unpublished Ph.D. dissertation, Cornell University, 1979), p. 10.

[13] *Jiangling XZ* (1877), 8.5b, quoting from the "Treatise on water courses" (*hequzhi* 河渠志) of the *Songshi*.

[14] By Zhang Xiaoxiang 張孝祥, then "Commissioner for the pacification of Jingnan and Hubei" (*Jingnan Hubei lu anfushi* 荊南湖北路安撫使), at least according to Shen Baixian 沈百先 and Zhang Guangcai 張光彩, *Zhonghua shuili shi* 中華水利史 (Taibei, 1979), p. 144, but as Zhang died in 1170 the information may be inaccurate.

[15] See *Jingzhou FZ* (1880), 19.6b.

[16] See e.g. *ibid.*, 20.5b.

[17] See for example Karl Wittfogel, *Oriental Despotism: A Comparative Study of Total Power* (New Haven: Yale University Press, 1957), pp. 34-37.

the preservation of vast expanses of water—and the very function defining such a state, i.e. promoting land reclamation and agricultural development through water conservancy.

However, it must be stressed from the start that the situation just described illustrates another type of difficulty, more generally observed in China, one that we shall come across continually in the rest of this paper and which also tends to find fault with the Wittfogelian model. I am alluding to the fact that the state's efforts at developing large mechanisms for water control, far from leading to a stricter control on local society and on the disposition of land resources, favoured on the contrary the hold of private interests over these resources and furthered the development of private property at the expense of what was originally communal or state land. By way of consequence, they rendered the centralized and rational administration of the hydraulic system more and more problematic.[18] A further type of contradiction, evidenced as early as the Song, was the fact that the development of new lands made possible by the multiplication of hydraulic works eventually undermined the safety of the whole system.

*   *   *

I shall, however, elaborate on these consequences below. What is in consideration here is the kind of situation where the initiative was mostly retained by one form or another of the centralized bureaucracy. In this respect, the process of economic reconstruction at the beginning of a dynasty (and at the start of a cycle in the case of the Hubei interior delta) indisputably suggests the archetypal "hydraulic state" as instigator, co-ordinator and realizer of those large public works on which the whole economy depended.

The achievements of the early Ming régime in rehabilitating the country after several decades of governmental impotence, natural calamities and civil war, are well known. It goes without saying that great attention was paid to the provision of irrigation and hydraulic protection works. As early as 1358 Zhu Yuanzhang 朱元璋, aware of the need for securing a solid economic base for his ambitions, had appointed Kang Maocai 康茂才 (1314-70), one of his generals, "commissioner in charge of supervising irrigation and organizing agricultural colonization" (*dushui yingtian shi* 督水營田使). Zhu's edict insisted emphatically on the dilapidated state of dyke-works and the crisis in agricultural production. It assigned to the new commissioner the primary task of restoring water-control with the aim of avoiding droughts

---

[18] This theme is abundantly illustrated in Mira Mihelich's aforementioned study of the lower Yangzi during the Northern Song. Note particularly her conclusion, and esp. pp. 276-79.

and floods.[19]

After the dynasty had been finally established and until the middle of the fifteenth century, the central government kept stirring its bureaucracy into putting back into working order the damaged installations, drawing suggestions from local people, and applying them. Specialized posts were on occasion created. One of the most interesting measures was the sending, in 1394, of students from the Imperial College (*Guozijian* 國子監) and "people of talent" (*rencai* 人才) throughout the empire to supervise the building or repairing of ponds, reservoirs, dams, lakes etc., for storage or drainage of water. This they were to do by taking advantage of the slack season, and, needless to say, they were urged not to undertake useless projects or to indulge in extortion. This original way of dealing with the perennial problem of an insufficient "bureaucratic density," so to speak, in the Chinese field administration (whose members were also accused by Zhu Yuanzhang of being too slow in carrying out his orders in the matter) is to my knowledge unique in the history of the imperial administration. It was undoubtedly made possible by the still very flexible conditions for recruiting public servants which prevailed during the Hongwu period. The lack of regular staff (i.e. passed through the examination system) and Zhu Yuanzhang's preference for the "new men" recruited through the *Guozijian* led the emperor to draw on this source of personnel much more than his successors were to do.[20] In this case the step seems to have borne fruit. We are told that during the following winter a total of 40,987 reservoirs and dams (*tang-yan* 塘堰), 4,162 canals (*he* 河) and 5,418 dykes and embankments (*beiqu*

[19] See Shimizu Taiji 清水泰次, "Eiden kō" 營田考, in Shimizu, *Mindai tochi seido shi kenkyū* 明代土地制度史研究 (Tokyo, 1968), esp. the passage from *Taizu shilu* 太祖實錄 cited on p. 360. In this text the title conferred on Kang is simply *yingtian shi*, while the words *dushui* are added in other sources (e.g. Kang's biography in the *Mingshi*, 130). Shimizu clearly establishes that the mission entrusted to Kang Maocai concerned hydraulic rehabilitation *in general* (in the zone then controlled by Zhu Yuanzhang), and not simply, as suggested by other sources, the settlement of military colonies to be cultivated by the soldiery (*juntian* 軍田). For Zhu Yuanzhang's interventionist attitude regarding agricultural economy (including irrigation, famine relief, and the like), see generally Edward Dreyer, *Early Ming China: A Political History 1355-1435* (Stanford: Stanford University Press, 1982), esp. p. 153; likewise Wu Han 吳晗, "Mingchu shehui shengchanli de fazhan" 明初社會生產力的發展, *Lishi yanjiu* 歷史研究, No. 3, 1955, pp. 53-83, who offers an extensive and impressive view of the steps taken by the founder of the Ming towards economic reconstruction.

[20] See Lin Liyue 林麗月, *Mingdai de guozijiansheng* 明代的國子監生 (Taibei, 1978), e.g. p. 50. The students of the Imperial College were also engaged in registering the land of the empire: see the order of 1387 cited by Wu Han in his aforementioned article, p. 79.

ti'an 陂渠堤岸) were created in this way.[21] Subsequently a number of other projects were realized by conscripting the local populace or even that of neighbouring counties, by opening up work sites in the dead season, by sending high-ranking officials especially charged with directing operations, by ordering the administration to supply the materials, etc. The Hongwu emperor's order to collect the proposals formulated by the local inhabitants, and more generally to speed up all construction and maintenance work (*zhuxiu* 築修) was repeated several times, notably in 1423, 1428, and 1440, each time together with threats against the magistrates who would manifest neglectfulness in the matter.[22]

As far as Hubei province is concerned, we know that it was from this same period, and more particularly during the three opening decades of the fifteenth century, that rehabilitation and construction work was carried out section by section on several groups of dykes along the Han and Yangzi rivers.[23] In some cases the effort was also concentrated on the second line of protection offered by the enclosures, as well as on the dredging of the channels essential to the drainage of the areas most exposed to flooding.[24]

[21] See e.g. *Mingshi*, 88; *Ming Taizu shilu* (Academia Sinica ed., Taibei, 1961), 234.1a-b and 243.5a.

[22] See for instance *Xu wenxian tongkao* 續文獻通考 (Shitong ed.), 3.2802ff.; *Ming huiyao* 明會要 , 53; *Mingshi*, 88. An edict of 1428 cited in this last source maintains that "the field of hydraulics is an urgent case for concern. If the local inhabitants are obliged to claim by themselves at court, this proves that bad magistrates have been appointed."

[23] In 1403 the "collapsed riverbanks" (*ta'an* 塌岸) of the Han were strengthened at Anlu and Jingshan. In 1406 the Wanshi dyke 萬石堤 at Shishou 石首 , on the Yangzi, was reconstructed; this dyke was 370 *zhang* 丈 long and protected also Huarong and Anxiang in Hunan. In 1409 further work was effected at Anlu. In 1411 the Cheshui dyke 車水堤 was repaired over more than 4,400 *zhang* at Jianli 監利 , downstream from Jiangling. In 1429 the residents of Qianjiang successfully demanded the mobilization of civilian and military labourers to dyke up lakes which were regularly submerged by the waters of the Han, the latter engulfing "innumerable" lands, as much military as civilian or belonging to the state, at Qianjiang, Jingmen and Jiangling. In 1431, at Shishou, the "Three dykes along the Yangzi" (*lin Jiang san ti* 臨江三堤) were repaired, and three years later the same was done for the Yangzi dykes on the territories of Jiangling and Zhijiang 支江. At Zhongxiang 鍾祥, the "dyke protecting the town" (*huchengti* 護城堤) was built by the local magistrate during the Xuande reign (1426-33). In 1437, following serious flooding, all the destroyed parts of the long dykes at Jiangling, Songzi 松滋 , Gong'an, Shishou, Qianjiang and Jianli were rebuilt, and so was the Old Dragon dyke (*Laolongti* 老龍堤) at Xiangyang on the Han. At Jiangling, the Huangtan dyke was reinforced and enlarged during the Zhengtong reign (1436-49), then again in 1465, with the prefects of Jingzhou being in charge. These are but selected examples. See *Mingshi*, 88; *Shishou XZ* (1866), 1, *tifang* 堤防 ; *Jiangling XZ* (1794), 8.3b; *Zhongxiang XZ* (1937), 1.7a; *Zhonghua shuili shi*, pp. 144-45.

[24] Dating from 1404, an edict to the Board of Works ordered that local officials should direct rebuilding of the small dykes demarcating the "caissons" (*yu'an* 圩岸) in

This activity, which was carried out with corvée labour (as had been the case with the Southern Song, although at that time the military work force seems to have played the leading part) and under the aegis of the local bureaucracy, continued well into the sixteenth century. By then, however, although the state kept investing its authority, if not always great financial support, in an active dyking policy along the Yangzi and the Han, its motivations no longer appeared the same as during the initial century of reconstruction. Two new factors intervened, at first sight unconnected with each other, but in fact mutually supportive. On the one hand were the growing obstacles opposed to flood storage and run-off by the interior dykeworks that were constructed (i.e. the enclosures) and encroached on the lakes and creeks—a secular phenomenon; on the other were the indirect consequences of the Jiajing emperor's enthronement in 1521—a wholly contingent fact.

The first factor resulted naturally from the policy of encouraging land reclamation, immigration and the development of irrigation systems which had been followed at the beginning of the dynasty. This policy had led to the construction, under the aegis of the administration, of an increasing number of enclosures. The sustained wave of immigration which resulted from these efforts also meant (as under the Song, but on a much more important scale) the non-controlled development of "private" installations which were not always known to and/or authorized by the officials. From that time on, which can be regarded as the end of "phase A" in the cyclical pattern suggested above, the increasing density of "second line" dykes made the storage and free flow of the highest seasonal waters more difficult and forced the administration to bring most effort to bear on the long dykes which would hopefully prevent the Yangzi and the Han from leaving their main beds, although they appeared at the same time increasingly fragile and threatened.[25]

---

the lowest lying areas and along the lakes in the various Yangzi provinces. In 1411 work of this nature was mentioned at Anlu, Jingshan 京山 and Jingling 景陵 (i.e. Tianmen). In 1442 dredging work was mentioned in the area between the Han and the Yangzi at Jiangling, Jingmen and Qianjiang. See *Mingshi, loc. cit.*

[25] Among many sources I shall quote as an example a memorial by one Chu Xun 儲洵 (then Mianyang magistrate), entitled "On river conservancy" (*Hefang shu* 河防疏). This text, which dates from the beginning of the Jiajing era, is to be found in *Xia Jingnan daozhi* (1740), 24.1a-2b. The author described the considerable difficulties encountered in the region of Mianyang since the great floods of 1517, which had opened long-lasting breaches in the dykes of the Yangzi (to the south) and of the Han (to the north), with resulting destruction of numerous enclosures and silting up of lakes and watercourses. The only solution in his eyes (but was he heeded?) would have consisted, in line with what had already been done in the Suzhou-Songjiang area, of entrusting the bureaucracy of the province with the job of making a comprehensive enquiry into the current situation and deciding on the steps to be taken (which dykes had to be reinforced or moved, or left in their present state). He suggested, in addition, various

The second factor alluded to only heightened the negative consequences of this policy (to which there were few alternatives). As is well known, the Jiajing emperor (r. 1522-66) did not descend in a direct line from his immediate predecessors, and from the beginning of his reign he had insisted emphatically that his father, prince Xing 興王 (d. 1519), should posthumously receive the titles and honours due to an emperor. Now prince Xing had been enfeoffed at Anlu 安陸, Hubei, in 1491, where the new emperor had resided until his accession to the throne, and there he was buried.[26] It was in order to "protect" his tomb (known as the Xianling 顯陵 tomb) that from 1522 the eunuchs who were in charge of it, putting forward pretexts of geomancy, had the left bank of the Han hermetically sealed by building a continuous series of long dykes and by suppressing all the exits which served as overflow channels (the texts speak of "nine mouths," *jiukou* 九口).[27] This had grave consequences for the group of counties situated along the Han. In the following decades the hydraulic risk grew rapidly as the river bed rose higher while its course became much more violent.[28] As the phrase goes, "when the dykes did not give way, they were submerged. . . ." The ground liable to flooding that had been freed by the dyking of the left bank was quickly squatted and converted into enclosures, notably by the "powerful eunuchs" who took opportunity to enlarge their own domains (or possibly those of the

---

financial steps aiming to keep in the area an increased share of the land tax, or to obtain advances on the funds from the provincial government (*siku guanyin* 司庫官銀).

[26] See for further details Goodrich and Fang, *A Dictionary of Ming Biography*, pp. 316-17.

[27] See for instance *Zhongxiang XZ* (1937), 3.13aff., or *Jingshan XZ* (1882), 4 (introduction to the hydraulics chapter), which specifies that the "eunuch-captain of the princely palace of Anlu" 郢邸守備太監 (*not* Wuchang, as it is erroneously written in "Un cycle hydraulique . . . ," p. 272, n. 1), in order to do this, had imposed on the people of Qianjiang the building of 100 *li* of dykes through the Jingshan boundary, to that of Jingshan 90 *li* through the Zhongxiang boundary, while the inhabitants of Zhongxiang had to build 180 *li* for their part. Where the "nine mouths" are concerned the chronology is not absolutely clear. Certain texts (notably Gu Yanwu, cited in several gazetteers) maintain that some of them remained in service after 1522, and then became progressively silted up.

[28] The raising of the Han bed by alluviation is a fact established by the sources of the time. This should, however, not be seen as a direct and necessary consequence of the continuous dyking just discussed. Matters are indeed more complex. Contrary to current belief, a carefully contained river does not rise if the "major bed" determined by the dykes is correctly calculated taking into account both discharge and gradient. In the case of the Han in the 16th century and after, there probably was an interaction of various factors: closing and reopening of outlets, resulting in changes of discharge inside the principal bed, narrowing and widening of the "major bed" causing acceleration and slowing down of the flow, hence eroding of the dykes or alluviation, etc. (Pierre Gourou, personal communication).

imperial establishment of Anlu, renamed Chengtian 承天 in 1531); but it was also subject to much more brutal and destructive flooding than before. The dyking of the north (or left) bank of the Han at the beginning of Jiajing, often considered the source of all the hydraulic misfortunes of the region,[29] was to be maintained in spite of serious accidents such as the series of breaks which occurred in 1549. In 1569 again the eunuch in charge of the Chengtian tomb duly proceeded to have the dykes rebuilt.[30] More generally, the power of the "eunuch party" during the Longqing and Wanli reigns may explain the efforts engaged in by local representatives of this group in continuing to dyke up their domains.[31] These efforts, it must be said, did not fail to meet with opposition and arouse problems. Thus, since the reconstruction of the Shayang 沙洋 dyke on the southern bank of the Han in 1567, which will be dealt with shortly, greatly compromised the security of the northern dykes, in 1574 it was requested successfully that certain breaks be left as they were and that several outlets be reopened and cleared.[32] Yet these outflows apparently became quickly blocked again[33] and, in fact, the filling in process was irreversible. This might be seen at the beginning of the Qing dynasty when there was for a time talk of returning to an "easy flow" policy: the sites of former drainage outlets were lost and the whole region was covered with villages.

There are under the Ming further examples of the same sort. As we have just seen, the northern dyke of the Han was under serious threat after the very important Shayang dyke had been rebuilt in 1567-68 (this dyke was located on the south bank of the Han at the point where the latter turns east and enters the territory of Qianjiang county; it had been destroyed by a flood

[29] See the texts mentioned below, n. 72.

[30] See *Qianjiang XZ* (1879), 2.

[31] See *Zhongxiang XZ* (1937), 21.19a; for this text, and others which take up the arguments, see the note below.

[32] See *Qianjiang XZ* (1694, rep. 1879), 10.2b. These measures were put forward by Zhao Xian 趙賢, then governor (*xunfu* 巡撫) of Huguang and formerly prefect of Jingzhou and responsible for rebuilding the Shayang dyke. In particular, a northern branch of the Han called Sigang 泗港, which crossed the territories of Tianmen and Hanchuan, was to be reopened. Other waterways were apparently cleared at the same time, both to the north and south, thanks to an advance of 8,650 taels taken from the funds of the De'an 德安 granaries and from various other sources—a much smaller amount than the 15,000 *liang* 兩 it would have taken to seal up the breaches in the dykes once again. See *Xingshui jinjian* 行水金鑒 (Shanghai, 1937), 79.1167.

[33] According to *Qianjiang XZ xu* (1879), 10.1a-b, this happened in spite of repeated demands on the part of the local administration, during the Wanli reign, to keep them open. Subsequently the site of the former drainage channels was transformed into fields. A further obstacle to reopening was opposition from the minister Zhou Jiamo (see below).

twenty years earlier).[34] This decision, heavy as it was in consequences for the hydraulic structure of the whole region, was an initiative of the then dominant man in the Grand Secretariat, Zhang Juzheng 張居正 (1525-82). Zhang, who had come to power in 1567, was a native of Jiangling and wanted to "protect" his father's tomb.[35] Indeed the same preoccupation with geomancy caused him to organize other sealings on the dykes of the Yangzi, in Jianli and Mianyang counties.[36] Then in 1610 and again in 1613 it was on the northern bank of the Han, on the territory of Qianjiang county, that certain outlets, among them that of Sigang, were to be closed at the express demand of Zhou Jiamo 周家謨 (1546-1629), then governor of Sichuan and a future minister. Zhou was a native of Hanchuan 漢川 (downstream of the system) and had this done against the advice of the magistrate and elite of Qianjiang.[37]

I have dwelt on these examples because they show how the so-called "hydraulic state," or its representatives, could also operate a system in an apparently arbitrary way, and, for reasons in fact alien to hydraulics, impose irrational, even nonsensical decisions, as was the case with the dyking up of the Han in 1522—or decisions which at the very least were not unanimously accepted.[38] In such instances, hydraulic decisions became almost a stake in political rivalries at the heart of the state apparatus and central government. It is interesting to note that a similar situation developed in the nineteenth century, between 1830 and 1850 and again in 1886-87, although this time the region concerned was the lower basin of the Yellow

[34] For the problems involving the Shayang dyke, see below. A new outlet of the Han had opened up as a result of the breakdown in 1547, by which a large part of the water continued southwards instead of using the main channel towards the east, and crossed the territories situated between Jiangling and Mianyang.

[35] See *Hanchuan XZ* (1873), 14 (list of natural disasters), year 1567. The biographies of Zhang Juzheng say nothing about this episode, but for the sake of curiosity it is worth pointing out a dream his father reportedly had the night before his birth—of a flood engulfing his own house. (See Zhu Dongrun 朱東潤, *Zhang Juzheng dazhuan* 張居正大傳, 1947, p. 6.)

[36] See *Jingmen ZZ* (1808), 12, "Hubei shuili pian" 湖北水利篇, by Wang Zhiyi 汪志伊, 6a-b (this important text also appears in *Hubei shuili tifang jiyao* 湖北水利堤防紀要, comp. Yu Changlie 俞昌烈 [1865, preface of 1840]).

[37] See *Qianjiang XZ xu* (1879), 2.1b; a similar case was reported in 1565 (2b).

[38] Thus, how is the action of Zhang Juzheng to be judged in the field of hydraulics in Hubei? Wang Boxin 王柏心 (1799-1873), a native of Jianli and one of the most competent writers on the hydraulic problems of the province, deemed this action to be quite impartial and effective, although it is often denounced in other texts. Yet Wang was more in favour of measures facilitating drainage (see below, section III), while Zhang Juzheng is known to have been a consistent "dyke-sealer," if I may say, to such an extent that Wang Boxin says he heard the "elders" of Jingzhou impute to his "reign" the closing of the outlets on the Yangzi, which in fact goes back to the Song, if not earlier. See *Jiangling XZ* (1877), 8.44a-b.

and Huai rivers.[39] In both cases the hydraulic context at the centre of the debates was in crisis, with no coherent policy which might be imposed in an indisputable way. For this reason the way was open to theoretical confrontations as well as to conflicts of interests. The important point here is that these confrontations found an echo and served interests at central level in the bureaucracy, and that as a result the regions concerned did not necessarily benefit from the debates which were pursued. Perhaps it is neessary in this respect to contrast the link between centralized state and regional management of hydraulics in its effects at the beginning and at the end of a cycle—i.e. during (re)construction and during management of a system already developed. In the first case the priority seemed to go to a coherent policy regarding the basin, in the interest of economic reconstruction and fiscal profitability. In the second case, local and private interests tended to gain the upper hand, favoured as they were by the essentially defensive position where the state apparatus stood facing the internal contradictions in the working of the hydrographic system. Besides, as we have just seen, some people within the state apparatus took advantage of this situation to further their personal or political interests.[40]

It is also certain that the link between centralized state and regional management of hydraulics changed according to the way in which the economic and organizational capabilities of the state and bureaucracy evolved. In this respect the contrast is striking between the late Ming period and what happened during the beginning of "phase A" of the second cycle in Hubei—that of the Qing—when the state once more took in hand the global reconstruction of the system. This phase, which in spite of serious efforts as early as the 1650s began in earnest from about 1680, was characterized, like that of the early Ming, by an exceptional effort to mobilize and motivate the bureaucracy, both local and provincial. But to this was added a much more evident willingness to supervise the entire system of hydraulic installations in the basin than had been the case during the preceding dynasty. Also added to this was a much greater and obviously crucial capacity for financial

[39] Marianne Bastid, personal communication.

[40] However, this pattern was not applied always and everywhere. In her study referred to above, M. Mihelich shows that it was *at the outset*, when the task immediately at hand was putting back into working order the remarkably integrated irrigation system installed by the Wu-Yue state, that the Northern Song opted for a partial withdrawal of the administration: "Faced with the task of governing a region whose irrigation and drainage network truly required coordinated maintenance, the Northern Sung government refrained from supplying such administrative coordination until it was too late" (*op. cit.*, p. 276). An explanation put forward by Mihelich could be the priority given by the Northern Song, in terms of allocation of resources and personnel, to the problems which confronted them on the northern frontier.

314

intervention, and this was a definite boon.

I have elsewhere described this action in broad outline.[41] It included an increase in the hydraulic responsibilities conferred on local officials;[42] extension of the control exercised over the maintenance of hydraulic works, including private ones;[43] mobility of staff to ensure an administrative presence

[41] "Un cycle hydraulique . . . ," pp. 280ff.

[42] Very quickly, in most counties, sub-prefects, assistant magistrates and other subordinate officials were given specific responsibility for the hydraulic problems in their sector (from 1674: see Morita, *op. cit.*, p. 59). In 1729—in the batch of measures taken in the wake of the 1726-27 floods—were added to the functions of the Wuchang, Jingzhou and Xiangyang circuit intendants that of being "in charge of hydraulic matters" (but no special officials were added, as I mistakenly wrote in "Un cycle . . . ," p. 280): see *Xu xingshui jinjian* 續行水金鑒 (Shanghai, 1937), 152.3553. Besides, a system of sanctions, first modelled on that of the Yellow River administration, then reduced in severity, was set up to punish the officials (governors included) on whose territories breaches occurred in the dykes: see the 1700 and 1715 entries from *Da Qing huidian shili* cited in *Huangchao zhengdian leizuan* 皇朝政典類纂 (1903), 47.1a.

[43] However, in the case of private enclosures it is often difficult to tell whether the control exercised by the administration was imposed by regulation or simply came from the eagerness of certain activist magistrates not to leave things going on their own in their jurisdictions. Let me mention here the example of a cluster of enclosures called Qingcun tiyuan 青村堤垸, situated to the southwest of the town (and of the dyke) of Shayang in Jingmen Department, near the borders of Jiangling and Qianjiang. We are told that traditionally it was for the landlords living directly along the enclosure dykes to take charge, obeying the "enclosure chiefs" (*yuanzhang* 垸長), of the maintenance in proportion to the length of dyke bordering on their fields (*an tiantou* 按田頭). The consequence was inadequate repair work in the case of landlords lacking in sufficient means, and frequent breaches which flooded the entire enclosure. It was only after magistrate Shu Chenglong 舒成龍 had personally visited the area, in 1744, and made a careful inquiry into the situation, that it could be decided, "in accordance with the insistent demand of the educated and the common people," to finance the upkeep in proportion to the area owned by *every* resident in the enclosure (*an tian tongyuan hexiu* 按田通垸合修). The operation of this system, which gave excellent results, was checked regularly on the spot by the magistrate or his deputy, who took the opportunity to remind the inhabitants of the new regulation. It is difficult to say in such a case how far the community represented by the enclosure functioned autonomously (on rules decreed by the administration), and to what extent administrative presence was a *sine qua non* of the working of the system (see *Jingmen ZZ* [1808], 12.14a-b). Let me also mention a memorial sent in 1754 by the Hubei provincial treasurer, Shen Shifeng 沈世楓, where the latter announced to the emperor his intention to take advantage of a dry winter following a year without flooding to order the officials with hydraulic responsibilities to go and inspect the numerous privately owned dykes and enclosures (particularly in Mianyang, Qianjiang, Tianmen, Jingshan and Jianli) and to encourage local people to make them higher and thicker in anticipation of the next high waters. Shen maintained that it was incumbent on the officials to combat the natural inertia of the people who thought above all of taking advantage of the immediate (a favourite line with the bureaucracy). See Shen's memorial, *Gongzhongdang* 宮中檔 archives, Taibei, Old Palace Museum, Qianlong reign, no. 008243.

315

in strategic spots;[44] vigilance demanded from the highest ranks of the provincial bureaucracy, which were urged to keep themselves informed of everything down to local dyking, to send reports, to keep the magistrates on their toes, etc.[45] Last but not least, constant and multifarious financial aid was granted, either through direct funding of important repair works by the treasury,[46] or through reimbursable advances, both regular and exceptional,[47] or with the interests on public capital "deposited with the merchants,"[48] or

[44] Thus, in 1737, the task of supervising dyke works in the very exposed department of Mianyang was shared between the first class assistant department magistrate in charge of river conservancy (*shuili zhoutong* 水利州同) for the southern, eastern and western sectors, and the second class assistant department magistrate (*zhoupan* 州判) for the northern sector, where he was to reside permanently, transferring his offices to the town of Xiantao 仙桃鎮, on the southern bank of the Han. In 1746, a whole series of subordinate officials were moved to ensure a tighter control over the dykes presenting a risk. The territories involved were Anlu *fu* (whose sub-prefect was sent to Shayang, near the famous dyke), Qianjiang, Tianmen, Zhongxiang, and once again Mianyang. See the *Huidian shili* entries corresponding to these two dates in *Huangchao zhengdian leizuan*, 47.1b-2a.

[45] The activism of the provincial officials at *dufu* 督撫 level and their concern with being informed of all details appear on every page of the texts from the Yongzheng and Qianlong eras collected in *Xu xingshui jinjian*, 152-54, as well as in other memorials, which seem generally to have had some effect. Several mention their inspections on the spot, such as Emida 鄂彌達 in a memorial of 1744 (in *Huang Qing zouyi* 皇清奏議, 39) which concerns various sites in the province, or again his predecessors Sun Jiagan 孫嘉淦 (in 1742) and Aersai 阿爾賽 (in 1743), who visited the site of the Shayang dyke. The repair of the latter was long debated by the whole hierarchy from governor general down to magistrate, then effected under the direction of the concerned authorities (see details in *Jingmen ZZ* [1808], 12.8b-10b). Examples of this type are legion.

[46] The extreme case is the two million taels spent by the Board of Revenue in the wake of the 1788 flood, but there are numerous examples of a more modest nature, e.g. the 60,000 taels worth of aid granted for dyke works in Hubei and Hunan in 1716, and again in 1728: see the edict quoted in *Xu xingshui jinjian*, 152.3548-49.

[47] This is the system which was adopted in 1789 for annual repairs on the Wancheng dyke, at Jiangling, but it existed long before. The expenses were advanced by the administration and recuperated the following year according to the area of protected land owned by each taxpayer—a system called *tanzheng* 攤徵 (see *Jiangling XZ* [1877], 8.44bff.). The reimbursement of these advances was sometimes exempted: see an example in *Qing Gaozong shilu* 清高宗實錄, 721.10b-11a, related to a flood in 1764.

[48] In this system the interest yielded on the capital advanced by the government served in part to maintain a given installation annually and in part to repay the capital itself. The interest demanded of the merchants—one memorial speaks of the "firms and shops" (*hangpu* 行鋪) in Hanyang and Wuchang—ranged from 1 to 1.5% per month, which left them with a large margin of profit. This means of financing appears to have been quite common as early as the 1740s: see for example Emida's memorial mentioned above, note 45; similarly, Shen Shifeng's memorial cited in note 43 mentions four "strategic dykes" (*xianyao dagong* 險要大工) whose maintenance was financed by yield from capital. There is an important discussion on the recourse to interest-yielding

by using yet other procedures.[49] A feature of paramount importance, such financial involvement decisively distinguished the Qing from the Ming state, as the latter relied almost exclusively on unpaid corvée labour (at the beginning of the dynasty) and on financing by the people benefiting directly from the works, a formula which displayed fatal shortcomings at times of hydraulic disaster.[50]

It must be made clear, on the other hand, that the hydraulic policies evolved at the end of the seventeenth and in the course of the eighteenth century did not aim to install a "state only" system of some kind, that is to say, entirely run by the bureaucracy and financed by the public treasury (and thus working on an exclusively fiscal basis). Such a system would have been impracticable in any case within the framework of the traditional Chinese bureaucracy and tax system, which the Qing had no reasons to change. What surfaced on the contrary was an infinite variety of ways of sharing or cooperating between administration and local communities (or individual landlords), for both management and financing—or in other words, a set of compromises which were endlessly adjusted and put under review. The basic fact, concerning the central Hubei basin, is that, although faced with a natural environment where hydraulic problems dominated everything and required large scale operations for water control, the state sought out of principle not to be involved beyond defining the rules, taking the decisions and overseeing their application. This well fitted an ideal of minimal intervention to which I shall return later. In contrast with what happened with the Yellow River, there was no autonomous "Yangzi administration" directly responsible to the throne.[51] In the same way there was, apart from a few exceptions, no regular,

---

deposits by the state in the 18th century in Helen Dunstan's forthcoming work on the *Huangchao jingshi wenbian* 皇朝經世文編.

[49] Thus, Emida's memorial proposed, and apparently had adopted, an original measure of which I can find no other mention: reserving 100,000 *shi* of grain from the "imperial student contributions" (*juanjian* 捐監) intended for the state granaries, and storing them in the ever-normal granaries of the various counties. If a break occurred in a dyke, this "grain for hydraulic protection" (*jiangfang canggu* 江防倉穀) would be loaned to the poor peasants called to work on the rebuilding sites.

[50] On the weakness of the hydraulic "service" provided by the Ming state in the 16th century, see Ray Huang, *Taxation and Governmental Finance in 16th Century China* (Cambridge: Cambridge University Press, 1974), p. 186; also pp. 279ff., from which it emerges that the only significant efforts were brought to bear on the maintenance of the Grand Canal and the protection works on the Yellow River. The reading of sources on Hubei in the 16th and 17th centuries goes along the same lines. Local initiative and proposals were not lacking, but, except for extraordinary cases, they came up against the inadequacy of financing and the absence of a coherent policy.

[51] The contrast between the Yellow River and Yangzi is put in an interesting way in an edict of 1715, asserting that "the dykes of the Yangzi and the dykes of the Yellow

autonomous source of funding for the maintenance of hydraulic works. To be sure, organizational as well as financial state involvement was constantly requested, and until the turn of the nineteenth century the state did not apparently hesitate to respond favourably, in so far as its means allowed; but this could only be on an *ad hoc* basis.

Still, the problem of the desirable degree of commitment on the part of the bureaucratic apparatus in the management and financing of hydraulics in Hubei was raised several times by high-ranking officials for whom the current system of "maintenance provided by the population under the supervision of the officials" (*guandu minxiu* 官督民修) was not always satisfactory. At the time of the great floods of 1726-27, which caused serious damage on the long dykes of the Yangzi and provoked an important effort on the part of the central government,[52] governor general Fumin 傅敏 asked in vain that the control and maintenance of the Yangzi dykes be undertaken from then on by the administration and [regularly] financed by the tax surpluses (*haoxian* 耗羨) levied locally. In his reply, the Yongzheng emperor estimated that, if it was normal for the public treasury to send funds for individual operations, then on the other hand, the institution of a regular financing and of a purely administrative system would cause the local people to neglect the maintenance and overseeing of the dykes protecting their fields. These had to remain "civilian dykes" (*minti* 民堤) after the completion of special works financed by the government.[53]

River are not the same thing. The course of the Yellow River is not fixed and changes constantly, and this is why 'river officials' (*heguan* 河官) have been appointed to keep watch on it (*kanshou* 看守). The waters of the Yangzi never change course, and for this reason it is enough to entrust their control to the field administration." The edict concluded on the need to reduce the sanctions promised to officials if breaches occurred in the dykes (the cause being automatically deemed to be insufficient maintenance work); as we have seen, these sanctions had been brought into line with those applicable to the Yellow River bureaucracy by a decision of 1700. See *Huangchao zhengdian leizuan*, 47.1a. In fact, if the course of the Yangzi proper was more or less stabilized at the time of the Ming and Qing dynasties, the Hubei basin, when considered as a whole, offered an extremely unstable hydrography (as illustrated by the often brutal changes which occurred in the division of the Han course between its different branches, to which this study makes several references) and would most certainly have justified the institution of an autonomous administrative hierarchy for river conservancy.

[52] In order to ensure the rapid completion of building work, important funds were sent and the supervision of the Huguang governor general was requested. In the sector of Mianyang, reportedly, the repairs were carried out successfully within three months, thanks to the expenditure of more than 350,000 man-days (see *Mianyang ZZ* [1894] 3.21b-23a).

[53] See the edict of 5th month, 1727, cited in *Jingzhou FZ* (1880), 17.1a-b, and *Xu xingshui jinjian*, 152.3545-46.

We know also of a long memorial addressed to the throne in 1763 by governor Fude 輔德, apparently approved by the emperor, which recommended a tightening of bureaucratic control over the maintenance of the enclosures.[54] It was, however, only a question of improving the performance of the existing structures, where the final responsibility for the works remained with the local inhabitants, and not of involving the state further in the overall management and financing of the system. We may also mention the limited change which occurred after the disaster of 1788 for the most exposed sections of the Wancheng dyke at Jiangling: these sections were thence designated "official sections" (*guangong* 官工) and directly administered and financed by the administration. At the same time, a certain number of steps were taken to reaffirm control over the maintenance of the dykes by the bureaucratic hierarchy.[55]

The author who apparently went the farthest in his criticism of the state's lack of commitment was a censor named Huang Juezi 黃爵滋 . In a memorial of 1833, Huang expressed the opinion that the *guandu minxiu* system indeed had disastrous consequences because of the abuses to which it gave rise and the disaffection of the people which resulted from it. Rather than leave the effective responsibility of maintaining the dykes to "elders" exposed to the extortion of the administrative underlings and who in any case were not judged on the results obtained, he suggested a drastic bureaucratization of the system: "It seems that the best thing would be to switch over to a system of 'maintenance by the administration' (*guanxiu* 官修) for the responsibilities to be clearly set out." He moreover noted that the "official sections" instituted after 1788 held good because responsible officials did not hesitate to go to the area and take their duties seriously. Indeed, they had to "guarantee the reliability [of the works they had directed] for ten years" (*shinian baogu* 十年保固)—in other words, they pledged both career and personal fortune. It was, therefore, a system of maintenance expressly modelled on that of the

---

[54]The steps proposed included a close supervision by the magistrates of the nomination of the "enclosure chiefs" and of the way in which they organized and distributed maintenance work; regular monitoring by the intendants and prefects of the dykes which were a danger and must be destroyed; an increase in the responsibilities of all officials in charge of hydraulics—and therefore a working system of rewards and punishments and more efficient hierarchical control and guaranteeing; greater job stability for subordinate officials (*zuoza* 佐雜) in charge of high risk dyke sections. This last point is interesting because it emphasized the need to make officials more familiar with the sites and people they had to administer. See *Gaozong shilu*, 693.13b-16a.

[55]See for instance Perdue, p. 760. It may be noted that, symmetrically, it was after the hydraulic catastrophe of 1560-66 that the system of dyke tithes (*tijiafa* 堤甲法) was instituted to improve the upkeep of those same dykes.

Yellow River of which Huang demanded the institution.[56] But this was only to a limited extent, and his suggestions remained within the traditional framework of field administration without trying to make the control of the Yangzi a state matter in the same way as that of the Yellow River or the Grand Canal. In any event, his memorial does not seem to have been paid heed to.

In sum, in spite of the efforts at global intervention described above and characteristic of the beginning of a cycle—repairing of large-scale works of key interest to the entire basin, definition of maintenance regulations, and the like—the administration, in the long run, was not able to master the hydraulic, ecological and social problems of the area. On the contrary, these problems quickly became very acute again, owing to population growth (encouraged from the onset by official aid in clearing new land, redistributing abandoned property, etc.) and to the connected resumption of private dyking beyond official control. From then on the role of the bureaucracy was rather to maintain a minimum level of balance and security by manoeuvring between contradictory forces and demands, to smooth rivalries between different regions of the basin whose hydraulic interests were opposed, and to counteract tendencies to unauthorized dyking and tax evasion which were developing at the very time when demand for public aid rose and security was more costly. This type of relationship between state and hydraulics—what may be defined as the state's *arbitral function*—will be the central topic of our next section.

II. STAGE TWO: THE STATE AS AN ARBITRATOR AMIDST THE CONTRADICTIONS OF THE BASIN

One of the major aspects of the regulating role of the state after a phase of restoration and reconstruction stemmed from the conflicts of hydraulic interests which officials had to mediate in order to enforce decisions conforming in principle with the general interest. It is probably through this aspect that we may gain the most concrete understanding of how state power fitted into a hydraulic context such as the one in Hubei. For this reason I shall dwell at some length on this topic in the following pages.

Broadly speaking, the problem was that, given the density of settlement in the central plain from the middle of the Ming and even more after restoration work was completed at the beginning of the Qing, it was most of the

---

[56] See *Huangchao zhengdian leizuan*, 42.6b–8a.

time impossible to satisfy everyone at once. Better still, one might say that the organization of hydraulics in Hubei was by its very nature a source of conflict and rivalry on a local scale as well as throughout the whole basin.

Disagreements were essentially due to two problems, often linked. First, how was the managerial and financial responsibility for dyke maintenance to be allotted, socially as well as geographically? Second, how was the excess water to be disposed of, when the space where unrestricted flooding was possible kept diminishing? What could be called "hydraulic rivalries" left upstream and downstream, or else north and south (to keep to the usual appellation of the opposite banks of the Yangzi and Han), confronting each other. Upstream communities wanted to allow the water to pass, while downstream people wanted to be protected from it. Reinforcing the northern dykes resulted in an overloading of the southern dykes and vice versa. Besides, there was an opposition between those who were directly protected by a structure and those who only benefited at a distance from it, and therefore balked at taking part in its maintenance. In most cases, grievances were voiced through the channel of the local gentry and richest landowners. At least this may be safely assumed whenever the sources quote "public opinion" (*yulun* 輿論), since these were the people who had access to local officials, or even, in the case of very influential individuals, to the provincial or metropolitan bureaucracy. Common peasants and tenant farmers, on the other hand, seem to have been used as rank and file for purposes of intimidation or when it was intended to create a *fait accompli*.[57]

Local hydraulic claims, too, often contradicted the overall balance of the whole basin. The role of the government, therefore, was to evaluate the situations fairly by dispatching its representatives to the area, and to impose solutions, whether by conciliatory means or by wielding its authority. For this reason, its capacity for control and decision making appeared to be fundamental, although it was not the only factor, in the destiny of a hydraulic system which was both integrated and threatened by a diversity of local interests.

There are innumerable cases of disputes between up- and downstream communities in the matter of sharing costs on installations of interest to both parties. Hubei had quite a few dykes of strategic importance, such as the

---

[57] See the example given below, p. 329. On the other hand, we do not find before the middle of the 19th century such episodes as those of the "monk" Cai Fulong 蔡福隆 (in 1844) or of the ex-officer Yan Shilian 嚴士連 (in 1863-64), who took the lead of the poor peasants of the interior delta in contesting the prevailing "hydraulic order" (related in Morita, *op. cit.*, pp. 120ff.). To my knowledge such large-scale movements, apparently not controlled and not manipulated by the gentry, did not have any precedent in the region.

Wancheng dyke in Jiangling, the Shayang dyke in Jingmen or the Zhongxiang dyke, all of which protected (or flooded in the event of breaks) territories sometimes very far from their immediate hinterland.[58] If logic dictated that all communities, however remote, should participate in their upkeep, especially when the importance of the work to be done exceeded the capacities of the people living directly in the vicinity, short-term interest led those communities located farthest away to do everything in their power to shirk the responsibility.

Reliance on the administrative boundaries which served as a basic framework in the allocation of responsibilities was a frequent argument. The tendency in the counties downstream was to ignore the overlapping of hydraulic interests above *xian*, possibly prefectural level, by advocating the principle of "every man for himself," or more literally, "each community builds its own dykes" (*ge zhu ge ti* 各築各堤). Those upstream—on whose territories were the dykes in question—naturally favoured the principle of "co-operation" (*xiangxie* 相協). The role of the representatives of the local gentry was to circumvent the magistrates in such a way as to make them adopt and support local claims. Indeed, the parochial aspect of the opposing interests is illustrated, as will be seen, in the sometimes very polemic texts collected in the local gazetteers. It should be emphasized that administrative boundaries obviously were a potential obstacle in the path of effective management of macro-hydraulic problems. Local administrations tended to offload the responsibilities onto each other, and the problem became still more complicated when the military garrisons (*wei* 衞), which could control certain important sections of the dykes, intervened, or even (under the Ming) the princely domains.[59] There was, however, a distinct contrast between the

[58] See "Un cycle hydraulique . . . ," pp. 266-67, and Morita, chaps. II and III (devoted respectively to the Wancheng dyke and to the long dykes of the Han).
[59] The last mentioned held a considerable place in Hubei from the middle of the Ming period onwards, notably in the Han valley: see for instance, in *Zhongxiang XZ* (1936), 1.7b, the very long list of domains conceded after 1495 to prince Xing, future father of the future Jiajing emperor, who was enfeoffed that year at Anlu; the toponymy, which includes many "lakes" (*hu* 湖), "ponds" (*chi* 池) and "rivers" (*he* 河), suggests that a notable part of these domains consisted of floodable lands. Hence the interest of the eunuchs from the princely establishment in encouraging a policy of systematic dyking of the Han, which permitted development of this kind of terrain. Similarly, mention should be made of the hesitation aroused by a Qianjiang magistrate's plan for dredging the alluvial strips of land in order to lessen the risk of flooding: because "all along the (Yangzi or Han?) river, the entirety of alluvial islands are imperial domains" (*yanjiang yidai, yuzhou jin shu huangzhuang* 沿江一帶淤洲盡屬皇莊), nobody dared to launch into dredging-work on his own responsibility. The Board of Revenue noted, however, that the income from these stretches of alluvial land was very low and that their levelling was a possibility if it turned out that their presence indeed threatened the security of the population in the concerned county. See *Xingshui jinjian*, 78.1157.

Ming and the Qing, as the provincial bureaucracy's ability to arbitrate and the will of the central power to impose a coherent policy appear clearly greater under the latter dynasty.

The upstream-downstream problem is illustrated particularly well by relations between the two groups of counties centred respectively on the Han and the Yangzi, which broadly corresponded to the prefectures of Anlu and Jingzhou.[60] Hydrographically, these two groups communicated through a whole series of creeks, channels and lakes, which made them mutually dependant as far as water-control was concerned. Some outlets of the Han, in particular, were liable to flood the territories of Jiangling and Jianli (located along the Yangzi), whereas Mianyang department, sandwiched as it was between the two rivers, depended for its security on the northern dykes of Jingzhou as well as on the southern dykes of Anlu. It was above all around the famed Shayang dyke—administratively dependant on Jingmen department, therefore on Anlu prefecture—that the difficulties built up.[61] In 1547 the collapse of the dyke had opened a new outlet to the Han, which essentially flooded Jiangling, the leading county of Jingzhou prefecture, as well as Jianli (attached to that same prefecture), Qianjiang and Mianyang (attached to Anlu prefecture). This did not prevent the inhabitants of Jingzhou, after this episode, from regularly rising up against the demands for co-operation formulated by upstream communities and officials for the maintenance or reconstruction of the dyke.

For the authors of the hydraulics chapter of the Jingmen gazetteer,[62] on the contrary, the necessity of mutual aid between the inhabitants of the five counties concerned with the Shayang dyke should be self-evident; besides, they claimed, "it was done thus in the past." Indeed, the reconstruction of the dyke in 1567, demanded by the prefect of Jingzhou, had been the result of a common effort in the two prefectures.[63] Ninety years later, after the Ming-Qing transition, when the then very damaged dyke had been once more

[60] The first at its maximum extension, controlling the two departments of Jingmen (from Jiajing through 1791) and Mianyang (from 1531 to 1763).

[61] Let it be recalled that the Shayang dyke, about 10 km long, was located on the right bank of the Han at the place where the latter, having followed a general north-south direction, bends towards the east and enters the territories of Tianmen (to the north) and Qianjiang (to the south).

[62] See *Jingmen ZZ* (1818), 12.1b-3a, 8bff.

[63] We saw, however, that the man behind the project was grand secretary Zhang Juzheng (above, p. 313). According to one text, Zhang "had mobilized the resources of the whole province (*he quansheng zhi wuli* 合全省之物力) and allocated treasury funds": see Li Zanyuan 李贊元, "Memorial asking that the counties of Jingzhou and Anlu give each other mutual aid in dyke works" (*Qing Jing An ge shu ticheng bici xiexiu shu* 請荆安各屬堤塍彼此協修疏), *Xia Jingnan daozhi*, 24.22b-25b.

securely rebuilt,[64] the administrations of the five counties concerned had again worked in co-operation under the direction of the highest authorities of the province.[65] Therefore the Jingmen authors deplored that since 1674 help from Jingzhou had been refused to Anlu (in retaliation against a parallel refusal by the Jingmen administration) and that, consequently, the responsibility for the Shayang dyke fell entirely on the inhabitants of Anlu, and worse still, on the sole population of Jingmen, since in 1680 a former magistrate of Qianjiang, promoted to president of the Board of Works, had put an end to the aid from Qianjiang and Mianyang by arguing that the dyke was not on their territory.

If the texts relating to this problem in the Jiangling gazetteer are to be believed, non co-operation should be, on the contrary, the rule, and it seems that after a relatively experimental period at the beginning of the dynasty, the Qing government finally stood by this opinion in order to stop the disputes aroused each time mutual aid between different prefectures was attempted.[66] In 1660, a sub-prefect of Anlu, pretexting help that had been

[64] During the 1650s the dyke was reported to be half-destroyed and in danger of breaking down completely, which could entail consequences comparable to those of 1547. Apart from normal wear and tear, the havoc wrought by the events of the Ming-Qing transition and by the last episodes of the Manchu conquest also played a part in creating these conditions. The last factor, in particular, had deterred the local bureaucracy (whose primary task was to mobilize corvée labourers as carriers for the army, to levy food rations, etc.) from dealing with dyke reconstruction: see, among various sources, the text referred to in the previous note, as well as the text by Wu Zhiji cited in the following note.

[65] See Li Zanyuan's text quoted above, note 63, esp. on p. 24b, where decisions made after 1654 are mentioned which defined a whole set of rules for co-operation: the sharing out of the responsibility for the Shayang dyke among five counties was but one aspect. For the restoration of the dyke in 1655-56, see the stela by Wu Zhiji 吳之紀 (then Jingxi circuit intendant), "Chongxiu Shayangti bei" 重修沙洋堤碑, in *Xia Jingnan daozhi*, 24.56b-57b, as well as another one by the same title, due to Ma Fenggao 馬逢皋 (then sub-prefect of Anlu in charge of hydraulic work), *ibid.*, 57b-58b. The reinforcement of the dyke, which included the building of two crescent-shaped breakwaters in the most exposed places, as well as a jetty made of stone situated upstream in order to divert the force of the current, reportedly cost 340,870 man-days and more than 34,000 taels. It was decided to share out the costs in the following way: 40% from Jingmen, 15% from Jiangling, Jianli, Qianjiang and Mianyang respectively.

[66] Based on a passage from the biography of Zhang Huacheng 張化成, a member of the Jiangling gentry who lived at the end of the Ming and the beginning of the Qing: see *Jiangling XZ* (1877), 54.11b-12a. This biography is due to Hu Zaike 胡在恪, a 1655 *jinshi* to whom we owe several texts on the hydraulic problems of the Jingzhou area. See also the text of a stela entitled "Dyke works on the Yangzi and the Han will be carried out by the respective [riparian communities] without their ever being able to ask for co-operation" (*Jiang Han liangti ge zhu yong bu xiangxie* 江漢兩堤各築永不相協), written in 1695 by Zhang Keqian 張可前, Huacheng's son (*ibid.*). One of these texts rather mythically

granted by Mianyang to Jianli—and, it is said, circumvented by a citizen of the prefecture—had obtained by way of "reciprocity" (*huxie* 互協) that Jingzhou should participate (regularly, it seems) in the repairs on the Shayang dyke. In view of the extortions of which the people of Jingzhou complained on the part of the minor officials who had been sent to collect the contributions making up its share, Zhang Huacheng—a member of the Jiangling elite whose biography reports the episode—had taken the lead in a delegation of the Jiangling gentry to protest to the provincial government. He succeeded in having the system of reciprocity abolished after a general negotiation involving the provincial authorities, local officials and gentry of the two prefectures had been organized. In 1670, however, it was Jingzhou which managed to obtain aid from Anlu, the officials and inhabitants of both prefectures having been invited to the Yangzi dykes to ascertain with their own eyes how much their maintenance affected the safety of the counties on the Han, of which the secondary courses flowed lower than the Yangzi. But in 1672, the provincial government called everything into question after a native of Jiangling had vociferously claimed more consistent aid. In 1694, again, a resident of Jingmen prevailed upon a circuit intendant to summon corvée labourers immediately from the five concerned counties to go and work on the Shayang dyke. It took the intervention of the Jingzhou prefect to stop the undertaking, which was in the process of bringing the affected population to boiling point, and to impose the principle of "non co-operation" on a permanent basis.

In this case, the formula "let everyone look to his own dykes" was finally accepted because of the difficulty in co-ordinating the efforts of two large prefectures, each one covering a river system with its own problems. But within each of these systems, several cases occurred where the administration imposed percentages of regular participation on the counties protected by installations outside their territories, and this in spite of occasional resistance. On the left bank of the Han for instance, during the Ming dynasty dyke breaks in the upstream section—i.e. the so-called Zhongxiang dyke—were to be repaired by a division of labour (*fengong hezhu* 分工合築) between the four counties and three garrisons coming under the prefecture of Anlu (Chengtian *fu* at that time).[67] In 1663, the year when the *tijia* 堤甲 system

___

evokes the situation prevailing under the Ming, when "each [county] worked on its own dykes and the administration and population each assumed its own responsibilities and people did not need to lament for calamities."

[67] See the chronology provided by the hydraulics chapter in *Zhongxiang XZ* (1867), 3, *tifang* 堤防. Not only did this dyke, called *Zhongti* 鍾堤, ensure the safety of at least seven counties, but in Zhongxiang itself it served only a reduced area: in case of breaching 10% of the damage involved Zhongxiang, 90% the counties downstream (see for instance *Zhongxiang XZ* [1937], 3.15b).

was put back into operation for regular maintenance of the long dykes, permanent rates on the sharing of costs were fixed. These were applicable each time the Zhongxiang dyke broke and downstream flooding occurred. Three years earlier the downstream counties had suddenly refused to respond to demands for funds and workers.[68]

The fact is that this type of arrangement remained permanently threatened by local rivalries, even on a much more reduced scale. This was particularly true when, within one county, the inhabitants of districts which were not directly protected were made to contribute to the very burdensome upkeep of the long dykes. In Qianjiang, for example, in the 1690s the totality of the enclosures had been registered and regrouped into "districts" (qu 區) sharing the burden of the maintenance of the Han dykes; but as early as the following decade the landlords of three "interior" enclosures (that is, not situated along the Han), including one metropolitan official, succeeded in withdrawing (lit. "making off," jiaotuo 狡脫) by making the magistrate admit to the principle "each man to his own dykes." Disputes and lawsuits then followed one another, and it was not until 1717 that a circuit intendant commissioned by the provincial government, while admitting that the enclosures in question had no immediate interest in the maintenance of the main dyke, brought back the former distribution of costs into effect. His report compared the enclosure dykes and the long dykes, respectively, to the walls of a private house and the wall of a town: would it not be inconceivable that town residents should remain unconcerned with the condition of the latter? The economic argument, too, is interesting and displays a constant preoccupation on the part of the administration: to leave the upkeep of the long dykes to the riparian communities alone amounted to introducing a factor of disparity which only worsened because the inhabitants of the enclosures that were not involved took the opportunity to grow richer, while the riparians were less and less in a position to take on the expense of the dykes. There was danger of a vicious circle arising at the expense, in the last resort, of the public purse.[69]

[68] See ibid. From 1663 the burden of repair work on the Zhongxiang dyke was shared as follows: Zhongxiang 40%, Jingshan 25%, Tianmen 25%, Qianjiang 3%, garrisons 7%. A document cited by Morita, p. 89, apparently dating from the Xianfeng period (1851-61), mentions a different division, where the largest share (50%) was to be borne by Tianmen (this county was indeed the most exposed to floods resulting from breaches in the Zhongxiang dyke), the rest being shared by Zhongxiang (30%) and Jingshan (20%).

[69] See Qianjiang XZ xu (1879), 10.13a-15b. This is but one example among many. In the last Qianlong years there was, still in Qianjiang, a similar problem regarding an important dyke whose function was to bear the brunt of the shock of the Han as it entered the county (during peak flood periods it contained water one zhang above the level of the fields). One of the five districts (qu) responsible for its upkeep appealed

The same type of problem is to be found at the most elementary level, that of the enclosures themselves. I have mentioned (see note 43 above) the circumstances in which, in a group of enclosures in Jingmen county, a system for maintenance of the dykes had been eventually established on a pro rata basis involving all the protected fields, not just those contiguous to the dykes. But even where this system was applied, that is in the vast majority of cases, the temptation was great for "those far away and residing in elevated places" to refuse to work on the dykes. This is one of the various "abuses" which are mentioned concerning the large cluster of enclosures called Xiangheti 襄河堤, to the north-east of Jiangling.[70] There are good reasons to think it was wide-spread in other areas as well.

These few examples should suffice to set in context the problem faced by the bureaucracy, namely to guarantee the upkeep of costly infrastructures by struggling against the centrifugal effects of local selfishness compounded by arguments which sometimes emphasized, by way of excuse, the existence of administrative boundaries ill suited to the needs of hydraulic control. It is certain that the coercive aspect which characterized hydraulic management almost everywhere, at all levels,[71] is to be linked with this kind of contradiction.

Such contradictions play a still more active role when considering the second type of problems mentioned above, namely that of disposing of

---

directly (*yuekong* 越控) to the provincial authorities and obtained exemption from joining in, on the grounds that it "did not border on the river" (*ge he* 隔河). Another followed this example, so that as a result the dyke found itself in a critical state. The sub-prefect who, with difficulty and interminable discussion, eventually managed to set the situation to rights, referred in so doing to an allegory from the *Huainanzi* 准南子 which was often cited in similar circumstances: just as "passengers who have embarked on the same boat to cross a river" (*tongzhou gongji* 同舟共濟) will not escape drowning in the event of a storm if they do not help each other, so those people who only think of their personal interest and refuse to help in dyke repair should know that in the end their own safety will be at stake. See *ibid.*, 20B.5a-6b, "Stela on the construction of a crescent-shaped [dyke] to strengthen the Qima dyke" (*Qimati wan yue bei ji* 騎馬堤挽月碑記) (1798). The problem was more delicate when trying to make districts contribute whose safety was in no way involved, for instance those located on high ground: thus in Jingmen, where 20% of the cultivated lands were classified as "lake-fields" (*hutian* 湖田), as against 80% of "hill-fields" (*shantian* 山田), the owners of the latter stopped contributing to the upkeep of the Shayang dyke in 1714. As we saw, a few years earlier all the weight of the burden had fallen onto Jingmen county alone, so that from that time on all important work had to be financed by the province (*Jingmen ZZ* [1808], 12.8bff.).

[70] See *Jiangling XZ* (1877), 8.13a, *Xiangti lun* 襄堤論 (likewise in *Jingzhou FZ* [1880], 20.2a, with a few variants).

[71] Noted by Mark Elvin, "On Water Control and Management during the Ming and Ch'ing Periods," *Ch'ing-shih wen-t'i*, Vol. III, No. 3 (1975), p. 92.

excess water. Here, obviously, the opposition between up- and downstream is revealed in its most concrete form, and once more at every level. A typical example, of fairly important dimensions, is provided by the conflict which set Zhongxiang against the counties located downstream on the left bank of the Han. We saw above how at the beginning of the Jiajing reign, in the Ming dynasty, the construction of a continuous dyke from the prefectural city of Zhongxiang/Anlu had led to a rapid filling up and reclaiming of the outlets and storage lakes, while it narrowed at the same time the main channel of the river. Subsequently Zhongxiang, which until then had benefited from a relatively "natural" hydraulic system, had found itself exposed to the classical consequences of excessively tight dyking and of the sealing up of outlets, namely a speeding up and rise in the current, and violent and devastating flooding at the slightest breach. For this reason, the texts dealing with the question in the various editions of the Zhongxiang local gazetteer are, more than two centuries later, unanimous in denouncing the initiatives attributed to the eunuchs of the princely establishment where the Jiajing emperor had been born.[72]

But if the reopening of former outlets was repeatedly advocated,[73] and even, after certain disasters, the non-rehabilitation of the destroyed dykes,[74] opposition was each time too strong. It came not only from the inhabitants of Zhongxiang established sometimes for generations on the sites formerly occupied by lakes and creeks, but also and above all from the downstream counties: the interest of the latter was to benefit from the protection of the dyking situated upstream, since the results of possible breaks did not strike them with full force, rather than to allow the overflows to pass permanently through their territory. During the first years of the eighteenth century, when the Huguang governor general, who was in favour of dredging the

[72] See *juan* 3, *tifang*, *passim*, in the 1867 and 1937 editions of *Zhongxiang XZ*. Also, in the 1937 ed., 21.18a-19a, biography of Jiang Fengqian 蔣鳳騫, a 1727 *jinshi* who renounced his career in public life for personal reasons and became actively involved in defending local interests in the Zhongxiang area. This biography quotes from one of his texts, where in a dramatic fashion he stresses the brutal and destructive nature of the floods since the Han was dyked up in the Jiajing era. Likewise *Zhongxiang wenzheng* 鐘祥文徵 (1937), 1.9a-10a (memorial by Governor General Depei 德沛, 1738); *ibid.*, 30a-31b (an extremely plaintive and vindictive text on the hydraulic misfortunes of Zhongxiang, attributed to "public opinion" (*yulun*), partly inspired by Jiang's text mentioned above, dating probably from the middle of the Qianlong period); *ibid.*, 31b-33a (a text relating repeated and fruitless attempts, from late Ming through 1738, to re-establish an outlet of the Han diverted by the eunuchs in the Jiajing period).

[73] See most of the texts mentioned in the preceding note.

[74] Notably at the beginning of the Qing period and in the Republican era after the floods of 1919-21 and especially of 1935: see respectively *Zhongxiang XZ* (1937), 3.13a; 3.24b-25b; 3.14a, 29a.

Zhongxiang outlets, had sent to the site a commission of enquiry, "the powerful families and big clans of Tianmen, Mianyang and Qianjiang had incited their tenants to mobilize in their hundreds and thousands, surrounding the investigators and preventing them from advancing, so that the undertaking was abandoned."[75] The extreme frustration and hostility that such machinations could arouse upstream may be gauged from the vehemence with which some of the texts emanating from the inhabitants of Zhongxiang denounced the effects of a hydraulic order which was unfavourable to them, stressing, for instance, the rage and despair of the families unable to identify the remains of the victims swept away by the waves, or even worse, to trace the site of their ancestral tombs.[76]

Illegal actions carried out by force by those who considered themselves victims of an unjust distribution of water, or simply sought to improve their immediate situation,[77] were in fact common. It was most often the downstream people who sought to dam up outlets by which they were flooded. I have mentioned above the quasi rebellions on the part of Mianyang residents in the middle of the nineteenth century, even though apparently this was an extreme example. On the other hand, disagreements and incidents of local importance seemed unavoidable in the areas where enclosure-settlement reached a certain density.

Although the problem was a dual one, involving both irrigation and drainage, the second aspect was of greater importance in the interior delta of

---

[75] See *Zhongxiang wenzheng*, 1.13a; Chen Shen 陳詵, the governor general in question, was in office from 1708 to 1711.

[76] See note 72 above, texts by Jiang Fengqian and "public opinion."

[77] A good example is the deliberate closing, at the beginning of the Qing, of an important southern outlet of the Han called the Lufu mouth 蘆洑口, at Qianjiang, due to a few "wicked bullies" (*jianhao* 姦豪) who did not bother about consulting local opinion or asking authorization from the officials. This action, which benefited only one part of the territory of Qianjiang, was tantamount to "transferring the disaster onto one's neighbours" and had aroused intense discontent in the rest of the county. Furthermore, it was only worsening the problems of the counties downstream by increasing the velocity and volume of the flow of the Han. On this, see a petition written by one Gu Ruhua 顧如華, entitled *Zhu he shu* 築河疏, in *Xia Jingnan daozhi*, 24.26a-28a. This resident of Qianjiang demanded the immediate opening of the outlet in question and the rapid arrest of the people responsible. Like many others at the same time (right at the beginning of the Qing), he sought to move the authorities by playing on the financial and military aspects. Such action, he said, increased the risk of flooding and therefore of fiscal loss for the government, which was then supporting important troops in the Jingzhou area. Besides, the Lufu river, which had just been blocked off, was an important access route to the Jingzhou garrisons. In conclusion, Gu considered that, rather than close useful watercourses in this way, it was for everyone to protect himself by building enclosures (*zhi xu ge xiu tiyuan yi yu shuihuan* 止許各修堤垸以禦水患).

Hubei. As the channels branching off from the Han at "mouths" like the one at Dazekou 大澤口[78] and evacuating excess water towards the Yangzi silted up and grew rarer, their excess load became a permanent danger for the enclosures they crossed or skirted. And whereas the inhabitants living upstream opened their locks wide, those downstream opposed, with all possible means, the digging of new channels and went as far as secretely erecting dams (*dang* 塆) to divert floods in other directions. From that moment the problem facing the local bureaucracy was doubled, since public as well as hydraulic order was threatened.[79] Such illegal behaviour was even more dangerous when it involved the long dykes. The Jingmen gazetteer states, for instance, that since the reconstruction of the Shayang dyke in 1567-68, "whenever there is a flood the people protected by the Hongmiao dyke 紅廟堤 [on the opposite bank of the Han] are numerous who want to go and fraudulently open (*daojue* 盗決) the Shayang dyke for the water to pour out [onto the right bank]. Therefore there is no question of lifting the prohibition against acting in this way."[80]

When faced with those tensions and contradictions, the role of the state was to act as a mediator and to impose its own solutions. This implied a certain number of conditions which were generally fulfilled, albeit to varying degrees, during the course of the eighteenth century: the provincial government should have an overall view of the problems in the basin, as well as the willingness and the means to keep itself informed and to act on a local level; the state should be politically prepared to sanction illegal practices contrary to the general balance of the system, even when they were the actions of influential people;[81] and finally, the public budgets should be sufficient to finance necessary operations or to grant advances.

*   *   *

Other types of contradictions existed as well: first, between the interests pertaining to the state and those pertaining to the residents of the basin, and second, between the interests of the residents and the conservation of a

---

[78] Also called Yecha 夜汊 , situated downstream from the Shayang dyke, opened when the latter was rebuilt in 1567.

[79] See for instance, on the situation in Qianjiang, *Qianjiang XZ xu* (1879), 10.6bff. This text relates the local officials' efforts, right through the Qianlong reign and during the first half of the 19th century, to prevent fraudulent manoeuvres aiming at obstructing watercourses and to conciliate the interests of downstream and upstream residents. *Ibid.*, 11b-12a, shows how the problem became complicated when the people responsible for these manoeuvres lived outside the county boundaries, in Tianmen or Mianyang.

[80] See *Jingmen ZZ* (1808), 12.3a.

[81] See below on this subject.

general hydraulic balance. The first type basically concerns problems related to land registration and the fiscal system. The two types, however, are closely interwoven.

The dyking and cultivation of new land reclaimed from floodable moorland or lakes without the administration being aware was a permanent feature in the delta zones of the middle and lower Yangzi.[82] It was impossible to keep land registers regularly up to date as the regulations would have it.[83] In Hubei and Hunan especially, one can see the development of a vast untaxed sector, or undertaxed in the case of former lakes and marshes which remained subject to a very light taxation for a long time after they had been converted into ricefields.[84]

This sector comprised two aspects: on the one hand were the floodable shores (*tandi* 灘地) or lake-bottoms (*hudi* 湖地) given over to the seasonal cultivation of late cereals or winter wheat or even rice in the years when this was possible;[85] on the other hand were to be found the "guest" (*keti* 客堤,

---

[82] For Hubei, see "Un cycle hydraulique . . .," *passim*. For the Yangzi delta during the late Ming period, the problem is pointed out by Ray Huang, *op. cit.*, pp. 98-99; this author also mentions (p. 165) the uncertain topography, from a fiscal point of view, of Huguang province: although the shores of Dongting Lake are more specifically referred to, the same problems are apparent along the lakes and creeks of the Hubei interior delta.

[83] Under the Qing the unstable zones situated along the coasts and the watercourses were supposed to be surveyed and registered by the administration every five years: see Wang Yeh-chien, *Land Taxation in Imperial China, 1750-1911* (Cambridge, Mass.: Harvard University Press, 1973), p. 27. This rule dated from 1727 (in 1723 the period had been fixed at ten years): see *Qingchao wenxian tongkao*, 3.4871, 4876. The difficulties raised by its application are mentioned more than once by this source in the chapters devoted to the land tax. The corruption of the magistrates, who continued to tax eroded lands or took bribes for not taxing lands which had been recently cleared, is sometimes denounced.

[84] These banks, supposed to yield only reeds or aquatic products, were very lightly taxed and not included in the overall quota of arable land. They are the subject of a special entry in the *Huangzheng zheyao* 荒政摘要, an official handbook on famine-relief published in 1833, in this case referring to the Huai and Yellow River area (see on p. 18b). The lands inside the dykes, which were free of water for only part of the time, could not, in principle, be declared a "disaster area" when flooded. However they could be declared on a special register when the calamity spread to "normal" lands as well. Possibly, there existed a similar difference in the way of treating floodable and normal land in Hubei and Hunan. Land which had been dyked up in an area classified as "floodable" ran a greater risk of escaping official attention in case of climatic difficulties, but this was compensated for by exceptionally low or even non-existent taxation.

[85] For the term *hutian* 湖田 as used in Hunan, indicating reclaimed undyked lakeshores given over to rice cultivation, with the chances of a good, untaxed harvest one season out of three, see Wang Yiya, *Changjiang*, p. 70, quoting from *Hubei tongzhi*. It should be noted, however, that the term is used as well—and currently—to refer to dyked lands reclaimed from the lakes (i.e. permanently), in which case it is equivalent to

keyuan 客垸) or "private" (*siyuan* 私垸) enclosures, as opposed to the "official enclosures" (*guanyuan* 官垸) built on the initiative of and/or with financial aid from the state, and to the "people's enclosures" (*minyuan* 民垸), built by private landlords but with the authorization of the state.[86] In local gazetteers providing lists of enclosures, it can be seen that most of the time only the "official" ones are given with their name and incidentally their site and dimensions; otherwise, when private works are mentioned, the reason is generally that they have been the subject of disputes or bans (hence some degree of administrative involvement).

Indeed, the "private enclosures" were very often dangerous installations. Those built on the floodable river banks beyond the long dykes (*tiwai* 堤外), or on alluvial strips directly in the bed of the Yangzi, were subjected to repeated prohibitions, although, it seems, without much effect. The *siyuan* which are listed for the Jiangling territory in the Jingzhou prefectural gazetteer were of this type, as their names, moreover, bear witness: "Enclosure of White Sands Island" (Baishazhou yuan 白沙洲垸), "Young alluvion enclosure" (Xinyu yuan 新淤垸), "Fresh silt enclosure" (Xinni yuan 新泥垸), and the like. And yet they existed and appear on all the maps.[87] These

---

yuantian 垸田 (or *weitian* 圍田 in Hunan). The use of *yutian* 圩田, *weitian* and *hutian* as near synonyms is to be found in the lower Yangzi basin during the Song period: see Mihelich's interesting discussion of the problems posed by the coexistence of these terms (*op. cit.*, pp. 25ff.).

[86] The nomenclature sometimes varies, but generally these three statutes are to be found: see for instance Morita, p. 36, and Perdue, p. 754, concerning the enclosures (or polders) in the area surrounding Lake Dongting (where they are called *wei* 圍). A memorial by the Hunan governor Qiao Guanglie 喬光烈 , dating from late 1763, defines "official enclosures" as "having been built with public funds (*dongtang zhuti* 動帑築堤), the annual upkeep being assured by the population"; "civilian enclosures" as "protecting lands cleared and reported by the people (*baoken zhuti* 報墾築堤), without hampering the water flow"; that is precisely what most of the "private enclosures" (70 out of 77) do, and so their destruction has been ordered. See *Qing Gaozong shilu*, 699.21b-22a. For Hubei, see Morita, p. 37, regarding the situation in Hanchuan county; and Fude's memorial cited above, note 54, also of 1763, which makes a distinction between the "Board's enclosures" (*buyuan* 部垸) long ago reported to the Board of Revenue and managed by the administration (*guan wei jingli* 官爲經理), and the "civilian enclosures" (*minyuan* 民垸). The latter, which were closely imbricated with the "Board's enclosures," had not been reported to the Board but were subjected to the same rate of taxation: according to Fude, their management should be similarly entrusted to the authorities. As for the "private enclosures" (*siyuan*), they had to be prohibited and destroyed whenever they hindered the water flow. The distinction between "native" and "guest" dykes (e.g. in *Mianyang ZZ* [1894], 3.12a, in a text relating to the Ming period) apparently corresponds to that between declared and undeclared dykes. Perhaps there was also a distinction between dykes built by local people and by immigrants.

[87] See *Jingzhou FZ* (1880), 20.4b-5a.

structures, which were easily 5 to 10 *li* long, made the surface of the river narrower; during high-discharge periods they considerably hampered the current. Of course the most prejudicial of these (partly) artificial islands was to be the Jiaojinzhou island 窖金洲, illegally enlarged over the decades just in front of the Jiangling main dyke, towards which it diverted the force of the current. This island was one of the causes of the 1788 disaster.[88]

As for the dyking on the edges of the lakes, creeks and floodable marshes, there too the contrast was frequently emphasized between "native" and "guest" enclosures, the latter often higher and more solid, and therefore even threatening the security of the former, which in addition bore the heavier tax burden. Regarding safety, though, the distinction between authorized and private dykes seems to have become obscure in the long run. Wei Yuan 魏源, writing in the Daoguang period (1821-50), noticed that the illegal dykes (*siyuan*) were in their thousands, by far outnumbering the authorized dykes, often higher and more solid than the latter. He noted however, that in many cases, far from threatening the older "official enclosures," they protected them on the contrary (being situated on their periphery), and sometimes even reinforced the dykes directly protecting the cities (*chengti* 城堤). Because of numerous changes in the hydrography since "earlier times" (i.e. the beginning of the Qing probably), old authorized *yuan* now found themselves hampering the current, unlike others which were illegal ones. Therefore, said Wei, it was not on these differences of status, going back over the decades, that one should rely in order to elaborate a policy.[89]

However, when during the eighteenth century "phase A" the signs of a growing contradiction between the people's demands for still more dykes to be raised and the overall hydraulic security of the basin became more and more clear, it was essentially to a struggle against the proliferation of "private" dykes and to a reinforcement of the others that administrations considered resorting. In a memorial of 1748, written in response to an edict demanding that a policy be studied to "forbid encroachment on the floodable banks of the lakes and rivers," the recently appointed governor of Hubei, Peng Shukui 彭樹葵, advocated that the number of *yuan* should be frozen at the present level by forbidding all new construction.[90] In his text of 1763[91] Governor

[88] On this, see *ibid.*, 17.2b-5b; *Xu xingshui jinjian*, 154.3600ff.; and Perdue, pp. 758-60.

[89] See Wei Yuan, *Guweitang waiji*, 6.6a-7b.

[90] "Chen Hubei shuidao qingxing shu" 陳湖北水道情形疏, in *Huang Qing zouyi*, 45.12a-13b. It was practically at the same time, in 1747, that Hunan governor Yang Xifu 楊錫紱 tried to ban the building of new dykes around Lake Dongting: see Perdue, p. 754.

[91] See above, note 54.

Fude again proposed the banning of "private dykes" erected on the alluvial strips of land which had recently emerged, and suggested that the intendants and prefects proceed to annual inspections in the area and have all the enclosures which would hamper the water flow razed (*ping-hui* 平毀), "whether the fields [they protected] be fertile or not." However, the seasonal cultivation of these fields was to remain permitted in order to avoid people "losing their jobs" (*shi ye* 失業).

But it is obvious that such policies posed considerable problems regarding authority and control. If the repeated bans on building "private dykes" were not respected, it was, according to Peng Shukui, because "when the people's interests are involved, they do not hesitate to resort to all available means to obtain what they want, whereas the officials are lacking in foresight and breadth of vision: the immediate consequence of their relaxing, however little, their vigilance, is an impossibility to avoid the abusive construction of enclosures." Besides, in order to block the growth in the number of *yuan*, it would first be necessary to have a clear idea of the existing situation, which apparently was far from being always the case. Peng therefore asked that the magistrates be ordered to take advantage of the winter and spring slack season to survey their districts thoroughly and do the exact inventory of the enclosures. This was neither the first nor the last appeal in this direction, and the mere fact that it was deemed necessary as an extraordinary step shows how little the current regulations for updating the land registers were enforced.[92]

The reasons for engaging in an undertaking which was tantamount to a general re-registration would have been as much fiscal (to increase state revenue and improve the basis of assessment) as hydraulic. The two aspects were most closely interwoven. The constant increase in state hydraulic expenses could not be endlessly financed on the same basis of taxation. Besides, the "official" sector of the enclosures, which was yielding the largest share of taxes, often tended to suffer from the proliferation of private dykes and thus to become poorer, while private enclosures became richer without contributing their fair share of tax.

But Qing officials never attempted to update land-registration comprehensively, taking into account the profound transformations in the basin's settlement pattern after the end of the Ming dynasty.[93] We do know, however, of a few isolated attempts. As early as 1691, the magistrate of Qianjiang is said to have divided his county into eleven "districts" (*qu*) comprising 156 *yuan* duly surveyed and measured in order to facilitate an equitable distribution of

[92] On this, see above, note 83.

[93] As is well known, the last nationwide cadastral survey in China before the modern era goes back to the late 16th century: see Wang Yeh-chien, *op. cit.*, pp. 21-26.

costs for maintaining the dykes on the Han.[94] Furthermore, although the Mianyang gazetteer states that "in 1736 the ricefields in 'every' (*ge* 各) county were measured and divided into the categories superior, medium, and inferior (*shang zhong xia shuixiang* 上中下水鄉)," the beneficial effects of the enterprise are only mentioned for Mianyang itself, where the same tax scales were applied to all the enclosures whether public or private,[95] and we do not hear elsewhere of such an operation; it is therefore doubtful that it was carried out successfully in many places. On the other hand, mention is made of a detailed land enquiry conducted in 1795-96, still in Mianyang. Indeed, "if [this county] is difficult to administer, it is because the land distribution is not clear (*tianmu bu qing* 田畝不清); as a result, the taxes are not fairly allocated, there are arrears as well as resistance to payment, the dykes are badly maintained and collapse. The troubles of the administration and people come from no other source!"[96]

In addition, there are indications that during the Jiaqing reign (1796-1820) a serious attempt was made to incorporate the recently cultivated alluvial lands into the registers. A note to a poem by a certain Song Xiangfeng 宋翔鳳 (a 1800 *juren* 舉人) entitled "The River Waters" (*Jiang zhi shui* 江之水) says: "In Hubei during the Jiaqing years, they searched the lands cleared on a private basis (i.e. undeclared) by the people in order to survey them and submit them to taxation. Besides, they sought to levy about 400,000 taels [of arrears] in taxes on foreshore land.[97] But it did not take long for a part of these newly taxed lands to be covered again by the water, and although tax-exemption was demanded as it occurred, they kept insisting upon repayment of the arrears. Only sounds of cries and whipping could be heard—the life of the people was no longer bearable. [Deng],[98] who was in charge of the seals of provincial treasurer, made an issue of this problem. President Chen Wangpo 陳望波[99] petitioned for the remission of these arrears, which was

[94] See *Qianjiang XZ xu* (1879), 10.14a, and above, p. 326.

[95] See *Mianyang ZZ* (1894), 3.23b. Mianyang, situated between the Han and the Yangzi, is probably the most flood-prone county in Hubei and the one where the amount of land protected by enclosures is the greatest—nearly all of it, in fact.

[96] See *ibid.*, 24b: the decision to register the land anew, after petitioning the central government, is dated *jiayin* 甲寅, which must be 1794 according to the place of the entry.

[97] *Huaxi* 花息. I have found this term (in this sense) only in the Giles dictionary, where *huaxiyin* 花息銀 is defined: "The tax on crops raised on foreshore land," which fits here perfectly.

[98] Deng Tingzhen 鄧廷楨 (1776-1846), Hubei provincial judge from 1820-21, whose qualities as an official are celebrated in four poems under the collective title *Deng Jieyun zhongcheng shance* 登嶰筠中丞善策.

[99] Chen Ruolin 陳若霖 , for a long time president of the Board of Punishments, and then Huguang governor general.

335

granted to him by imperial rescript."[100] The poem itself, moreover, exemplifies this official will to prevent newly emerged and cultivated land from evading taxation any further: "The water of the river now overflows, now recedes; it is not to be foreseen. . . . Sometimes, when it is becalmed, strips of land appear. People clear and cultivate them for just one season. On the riverside, there is unoccupied ground which has not been demarcated. This they cultivate stealthily and make bear harvest for several years; gradually drainage ditches and channels form a continuous network. Then along come the officials measuring every inch of land. From that time onwards there is no question of delay in paying the tax. . . ."

Perhaps this zeal in keeping the register up to date, with all the abuses and vexations it brought with it, is to be linked with the efforts to resume control over hydraulic problems in Hubei on the part of Governor General Wang Zhiyi 汪志伊 (1743-1818) from 1807 onwards[101] —a presumption which, at least, is worth closer investigation. In any case, it contrasts with the relative indifference which characterized almost the whole dynasty and resulted in a worsening of land under-registration, "especially in the recently developed regions"[102] —of which the alluvial lowlands of Hubei and Hunan may be considered a typical example.

Viewed as a whole, within such a complex web of contradictions between state interests, those of local society, and the hydraulic balance, the position of the state seems undoubtedly to have been defensive, sometimes ambiguous, and its potential for action quite limited. This soon becomes evident when we leave the period of active reconstruction at the beginning of "phase A." At the outset, as we have seen, the state unhesitatingly encouraged private enterprise and sought to create conditions for demographic and land development by favouring immigration and the bringing into use of new lands, for which easy terms for tax payment were granted on a temporary basis. But the profitability of this development, as much from the point of view of hydraulic security as from the financial and political interests of the state, after a time underwent an overall decline; it could even cancel itself out, as it were, at least in the areas where the cost of administering the environment and its inhabitants (repair of dykes and other river-control works, settling of conflicts, famine relief . . .) came to equal or exceed the tax revenue. We have no means of approaching the latter situation in quantitative terms, but it is clearly suggested in certain crucial areas during "phase B."

[100] See *Qing shiduo* 清詩鐸 (1857) (Peking, 1960), p. 29.
[101] See "Un cycle hydraulique . . . ," pp. 283-84.
[102] See Wang Yeh-chien, *op. cit.*, p. 27.

Still, the uncontrolled development of land reclamation and the multiplication of "private" dykes, which forged ahead, remained profitable for many,
even if it meant, from the point of view of overall hydraulic balance, congesting
the outlet channels and an increased danger of flooding, and from the point of
view of the administration, conspicuous tax evasion, or even social imbalance.
Thus there was a conflict of interests and a danger for the basin taken as a
whole, a danger which was recognized as such by many an official belonging to
the provincial hierarchy, and which had obviously to be coped with. And yet it
was never possible to succeed in doing so. Should this be regarded as a consequence of the impotence of the state apparatus, or of its lack of commitment?
Was it the effect of local rivalries that the magistrates were more or less
forced to espouse? Or rather, as some authors suggest, was it due to collusion
between "feudal landowners" and bureaucrats all from the same social class?[103]

It is true that practically since the Song, the active element in privately
developing hydraulic facilities always had been composed of those "influential
people" (*haoyou* 豪右), "powerful people" (*youlizhe* 有力者) and other
"large clans" (*daxing* 大姓) which had, at the same time, the economic means
to invest in these installations to which they subsequently attracted tenant
farmers, and the necessary connections to ensure that they would escape
punishment when diverting water courses, building dykes in forbidden places,
omitting to declare them to the administration, and contriving to pay little or
no tax. If such facts are often exposed in general, specific cases of collusion
or abuse of influence are met only rarely in the sources.[104] But it is certain
that everywhere the clans who were influential locally had the means to
secure for themselves the neutrality of the magistrates and lesser officials in
charge of hydraulics—if only by obliging them in various ways or by contributing to social undertakings such as relief to the poor, building bridges and
the like.[105] It may be added that, in bureaucratic speech, the problem is

---

[103] See for instance Kōno, "Keikō bunkō," p. 252. It must also be said that the collusion (*niu* 狃) between magistrates on the one hand, "evil gentry"(*liejin* 劣衿) and "wicked
bullies" (*jiangun* 奸棍) on the other—the latter arranging for the authorities to turn a
blind eye to their deeds and to champion their claims—is a frequent theme in the
sources. See for example Ma Fenggao 馬逢皋, sub-prefect of Anlu from 1654, quoted in
Xia Jingnan daozhi, 24.23a-24a, on the resistance and quarelling encountered in Tianmen (then Jingling) when he wanted to repair the numerous breaches which remained in
the dykes of the Han.

[104] It must be possible to gather more material by turning to archival sources, as
Perdue's study demonstrates. The aforementioned Jiaojinzhou island affair, however,
which had dramatic consequences and brought to light the collusion of the incriminated
clan with officials up to provincial level, is fully treated in the printed sources.

[105] See the example of the Jiang 蔣 clan at Xiangyin 湘陰 (Hunan), as treated by
Perdue, p. 756.

obscured by the ritualistic reference to extortion and dealings on the part of clerks, runners and *yamen* secretaries (the *lishu* 吏書, *xuyi* 胥役, etc.), on whom the officials flung all ills past, present and to come.

Here we find again the problem of too weak a commitment on the part of the regular bureaucracy in the direct management of hydraulics, from which there ensued insufficient motivation to control the schemings of the under-lings.[106] As we saw, the proposals tending to maximal administrative control on the regular upkeep of the dykes hardly had any consequences, with the exception of a few ultra-sensitive sections along the dykes of the Yangzi and Han. More particularly, the major part of the huge sector of "second-line" dykes—the enclosure dykes, the equivalent of which did not exist in the Yellow River plain—had always remained outside the pale of direct control by the regular bureaucracy. For this reason, it was impossible to prevent this sector from developing with a minimum of autonomy.

I am tempted to see here a normal consequence of the very nature of the Chinese state during late imperial times, and of its relation to economic problems. With the exception of the efforts at civil and, above all, military colonization (the so-called *mintun* 民屯 and *juntun* 軍屯) which were, at best, of peripheral importance in Ming and especially Qing Hubei, the centralized state did not embark on programmes of agricultural development directly run by its own officials, of which it would therefore keep complete control. (In the same way, the state limited its direct transport undertakings to a few specific cases, such as the grain tribute or transportation to famine-stricken areas, and the same again was true with regard to industrial production, etc.) On the contrary, its option, particularly during the Qing, tended in most areas to be one of minimal intervention.

Or to be more precise—as this is not simply a question of some sort of ultra-liberal *laisser-faire*—it seems to me that the state and those who repre-sented it, or reflected on its nature and functions, were permanently seeking the ideal way of intervening or place for intervention which would allow for maximal control of both society and economy—with an ultimate view to economic stability and public order, as is more or less subsumed by the concept of *taiping* 太平—at the least cost. In other words, what was to be done was maintaining the field of direct intervention and the expenses of the bureaucratic apparatus within the strictest possible limits, making an effort to indoctrinate and organize the local communities to themselves be responsible for their well-being and safety, in short, formulating the rules and seeking to make the population concerned take on their enforcement with all the costs

---

[106] See above, p. 319. For a typical example of the accusations levelled against clerks and runners, see Wei Yuan's text cited above.

involved. The ideal state is not a non-active (*wuwei* 無爲) one, but rather one of minimal action together with maximal effect.[107]

Such was at least the ideal view, as I see it, to which certain well-known facts bear witness, such as the reluctance, during the eighteenth and nineteenth centuries, to allow the field administration to grow (in number of employees or budget) in proportion to the demographic growth of the empire and the development of new settlements.[108] On the other hand, it is clear that the late imperial Chinese state, if it wanted the peace and wealth on which its existence depended to be maintained, could not but intervene to a varied and some-times, in fact, considerable extent. Such was the case when it was necessary to take on responsibilities on too vast a scale for the local communities to be able to face them (e.g. construction of long dykes, maintenance of an inte-grated system of grain storage, famine relief on a large scale), or to compensate for inadequacies or ill-will on the part of the private sector (of equally frequent occurrence in the fields of famine relief and grain storage), or again to remedy malfunctioning due to community or private rivalries (of which we have seen a score of examples in this section).

To develop this line of reasoning and to put it to the test in the various possible areas of state intervention would take us too far, but we can come back to our Hubei enclosures: there we find all the consequences of this fundamental ambiguity in the role of the state—an ideal of minimal inter-vention, a necessity to complement, but also to check or even contain private enterprise. The position of the local magistrates faced with the proliferation of private dykes and the dangers it brought was, fundamentally, uncom-fortable, and their means of action very limited. Some of the landlords infringing orders against the construction of new enclosures and neglecting to fulfill their obligations in maintaining the dykes were not readily accessible because they lived in other counties and only left tenant farmers on the land:[109] here again is an example of the way in which the compartmentalized and hierarchical nature of the administrative framework left the way open for those who sought to bend the rules and ignore prohibitions. Besides, it was most of the time difficult to challenge a *fait accompli*. As Perdue has shown

[107]Here I understand "minimum action" in a broad sense , which by no means con-tradicts the ideal of "strenuous effort" imposed on the infinitesimal proportion of the Chinese population constituting the civil service.

[108]To be sure, new *xian* or new posts of assistant magistrate were on occasion created, but it is obvious that the number of creations was far from keeping up with the actual expansion of the Chinese people within and outside the borders of China proper.

[109]See for example the text of 1755 quoted by Morita, p. 47, and translated by Elvin, *op. cit.*, p. 96. There are numerous other examples.

for the area surrounding Dongting Lake,[110] where from 1747 the provincial government had forbidden the building of new polders, governors did not hesitate in ordering the destruction of illegal works, but local officials rather tended to protect them. Besides belonging to people powerful in the locality, these unauthorized polders fed and gave employment to a considerable number of people. The destruction of installations which, while dangerous for the environment, were highly productive, posed economic and social problems of which the members of the bureaucracy living directly in the area could scarcely be ignorant.

III. STAGE THREE: THE STATE OVERCOME BY THE DIFFICULTIES OF THE BASIN

This may suggest yet another type of contradiction, namely the contradiction opposing the local bureaucracy and those responsible for the region as a whole, or else, those living in daily contact with the claims of local society and those supposed to have a global view of the problems. Many examples may be found as early as the first half of the eighteenth century, but things evolved as the intensification of the diverse forms of competition between land-reclamation and hydraulic safety led to the opportunity for manoeuvre and negotiation being reduced. I shall attempt in this section to show briefly how, as the nineteenth century advanced, the hydraulic debate among those responsible for the basin, or rather the most lucid "experts" who sought to advise them, became both more radical and more utopian, at a time when the financial capacity to intervene on the part of the state was dramatically diminished.

The overall evolution may be summed up as follows: whereas in the middle of the eighteenth century there still appeared to be a choice between a policy of resolutely dyking the rivers and a policy of improvement of the outflows, even if the latter involved sacrificing certain local interests, from the early nineteenth century on the contrary, the failure of the "dyking only" policy, due to the growing pressure of a more and more constricted river system, clashed with the demographic, political and financial impossibility of switching over to the alternative option. A few texts underlying this evolution may be quoted here.

The debate between partisans of dyking at all costs and partisans of improving the outflows was an ancient one, but it began to gain in intensity in the upper echelons of the bureaucracy at the beginning of the Qianlong

[110]Perdue, op. cit., p. 756.

340

reign, that is, when the demographic consequences of the recuperation phase began to be strongly felt. Thus, in 1744, a controversy opposed a censor by the name of Zhang Han 張漢, who had sent a memorial to the throne regarding the hydraulic problems in Hubei, and the Huguang governor general Emida 鄂彌達, whom the emperor asked to take account of Zhang's memorial and hold an investigation.[111] Zhang Han noted that a certain number of important diversions of the Han were out of use, thus making the current extremely dangerous, and proposed a comprehensive programme of dredging and reopening of the old drainage channels of the Yangzi as well as of the Han, beginning downstream and going steadily upstream. This would avoid the "dyking race" resulting from perseverance in existing policy. Emida, for his part, contended straight away that "a dredging and drainage flow policy would be difficult to put into effect, while the building and repair [of dykes] could in no way be delayed." And so his memorial only spoke of dykes to be reinforced.

In fact, the only policy for conserving the drainage channels and storage lakes that the higher officials in charge of the basin could, at that time, consider, consisted in freezing the number of dykes at the present level and authorizing farming on un-dyked riverbanks or lake shores only. This is what several governors ordered, as we saw. Yet we also saw that the essential condition for enforcement—to know exactly the number and position of all the enclosures—was almost never fulfilled and that, on the other hand, the destruction of installations erected in spite of bans was by no means an easy matter.

The next stage[112] was when, rather than re-establish former drainage channels whose courses had been lost, it was suggested to leave as they were the breaches that floods had opened in the dykes, which in a way amounted to shifting the responsibility for opening up new drainage routes on to the rivers themselves. This was advocated by Wei Yuan, among others (probably *circa* 1830): he suggested not to repair the enclosures smashed down by the water —because they hampered drainage—to destroy only the private enclosures which represented a real danger, to prevent new constructions,[113] to leave open the breaches in the dykes when there was really nothing else to be done, and even to "transform a defeat into victory" by dredging the water channels opened up by the flooding, in such a way as to re-establish outflows

---

[111] Zhang Han's text is quoted in Song Xishang 宋希尙, *Lidai zhishui wenxian* 歷代 治水文獻 (Taibei, 1954), pp. 150-51; Emida's memorial is in *Huang Qing zouyi*, 39.

[112] Next in the line of thinking, but not necessarily in the chronology: certain radical proposals for returning to the "natural" state of things were put forward very early, at least in some problem-ridden areas.

[113] See *Hubei shuili lun, passim.*

comparable to those of former times.[114]

It must be recalled that between the mid-eighteenth century writers and Wei Yuan the disastrous flood of 1788 had taken place, a momentous event whose consequences—dykes broken in numerous places, hundreds of enclosures almost permanently flooded[115]—lasted through 1808 and showed the futility of a policy centred only on the maintenance and reinforcement of the dykes. In point of fact Wang Zhiyi was the last governor general of Huguang (from 1807 onwards) to have the means, as much political as, apparently, financial, to run an overall hydraulic programme of reconstruction and development—a programme which seems to have laid great stress on the drainage of water channels and the control of flow by sluice gates, but whose effects cannot have lasted for much more than a decade. Therefore the texts dating from the Daoguang reign (1821-50) where defining a general policy for the basin was, once more, attempted, admitted more and more that a few dykes, a few enclosures and their inhabitants should be sacrificed in the public interest, which was quite obviously, at least on the theoretical level where these texts stood, to re-establish as much drainage as possible. I have already quoted from Wei Yuan,[116] and it is worth pointing out with regard to him that one of his Hubei texts, the *Hubei tifang yi* 湖北堤防議, was in actual fact a preface (written for Tao Zhu 陶澍) to a work by Wang Fengsheng 王鳳生 (1756-1834), the *Chu you jilue* 楚輶紀略 (*Memoir of a tour across Hubei*), which combined two texts on the hydraulic problems of the Yangzi and the Han. Now these texts, Wei Yuan tells us, had been composed in a state of dejection: Wang Fengsheng, called to Hubei by the governor general of the province to supervise dyke reconstruction after the great floods of 1832, had asked to resign pleading illness once he had persuaded himself of the impossible nature of the task (*ji er zhi qi shi bu ke cheng* 既而知其事不可成)! Such an attitude, coming from an official who was known as an activist and a practician much in demand, illustrates the depth of the problem posed at the time by the fragility of the "first line" of defence against floods in Hubei.[117]

---

[114] See *Hubei tifang yi*.

[115] See Wang Zhiyi, *Hubei shuili pian*, 1b-3a, and "Un cycle hydraulique . . . ," pp. 283-84.

[116] Wei said (*Hubei shuili lun*, 7b) that the vagrants (*liuli* 流離) from a few enclosures mattered less than those of four entire provinces (referring to the successive rungs of the Hunan-Hubei-Jiangxi-Jiangnan "ladder" which had to bear the consequences of what went on upstream).

[117] Wang Fengsheng was an expert in local government, much in demand from senior officials as an adviser or as "acting official," whose highest post had been salt controller for the Liang-Huai region. See John R. Watt, *The District Magistrate in Late Imperial China* (New York, 1972), p. 257. Wei's preface locates the affair in 1829, but that is

These inextricable difficulties and the illusory nature of a policy based first and for all on "protection" (*fang* 防) are again illustrated in a fairly contemporary memorial (dated 1833) due to a censor by the name of Zhu Kuiji 朱逵吉. While mentioning the works completed by Wang Zhiyi twenty-five years earlier in glowing terms, Zhu noted that the drainage channels cleared at that time were again silting up. In his turn he defended a programme of dredging of the southern outlets of the Yangzi (he mentioned five of them flowing into Lake Dongting) and northern outlets of the Han. In the latter case he made it clear that the former lakes north of the Han had to be restored to their first function of storing excess water.[118]

One last writer I shall mention in connection with this is Wang Boxin 王柏心, to whom I referred above as one of the best experts on hydraulic problems in Hubei.[119] Wang had, even more than his predecessors, the opportunity to ascertain the vulnerability of the basin in the face of ever increasingly disastrous floods, since he wrote about it after the great inundations of 1848 and 1849 which reached heights and violence never before witnessed. The three texts, meticulously argued, in which he proposed a plan to "help the River flow,"[120] are typical of the time in the praise given to the "old," "natural" anti-dyke technique at the very time when the proliferation of dykes built for a century and a half were undergoing the effects of unprecedented floods. Wang suggested redeveloping the southern branch of the Yangzi (leading to Lake Dongting) at the cost of abandoning a few hundred *li* of land which in any case (he said) was always under flood water. As Wei Yuan did, but in a much more drastic fashion, he proposed returning to the natural hydrography of the river—or something approaching it—by allowing the breakage points to remain, among which, according to him, some were close to those quasi mythical "outlet mouths" (*xuekou* 穴口) dating from before the Song and long disappeared.

Wang points out clearly that his proposals were "opposed by public opinion" (*zu yu zhonglun* 阻于眾論), obviously because they involved sacrificing important areas. Once again, the old debate on the respective advantages of a policy of consistently embanking the main rivers and a policy

---

obviously an error, as is clear from Wang's biography in *Qingshi*, 385.4618, and from his epitaph (again due to Wei Yuan) in *Xu beizhuan ji* 續碑傳集, 34.11b-13a; indeed, 1832 was a year of repeated flooding in Hubei. These sources show that Wang Fengsheng, who had spent six months travelling across the province to investigate the situation and carry out reconstruction work, was disheartened when the autumn floods (in 1833?) opened up fresh breaches, bringing about a situation for which he felt responsible.

[118] See *Hubei tongzhi*, quoted in Zhong Yin, *Yangzijiang shuili kao*, p. 134.

[119] See above, note 38.

[120] See *Dao Jiang san yi* 導江三議, quoted in Song Xishang, *Lidai zhishui wenxian*, pp. 56-64 (also to be found in *Hubei congshu* 湖北叢書 [1891], Vol. 73).

more respectful of the natural forces at work was never closed.[121] As far as nineteenth-century Hubei is concerned, we sometimes gain the impression that this debate was each time revived by the occurrence of yet another large flood. Witnesses to this were the contrasting memorials sent in by Governor General Lin Zexu 林則徐 (in 1838) and his successor Zhou Tianjue 周天爵 (in 1840). One only spoke of reinforcing the dykes and of making preparations which were to be based on the highest water levels observed. The other recognized that, while he had been able to ascertain with his own eyes that work had been "sincerely" carried out on the dykes downstream from Jing-zhou, still the most exposed points were as much threatened by accidents with far-reaching consequences as before; he consequently proposed a plan which laid emphasis on drainage and on an increased discharge of water in the lateral outlets. The explanation, possibly, is that in the meantime the great floods of 1839 had occurred.[122] Whatever the case, it is certain that during "phase B" in the wake of the 1788 disaster, the state and bureaucracy stood more than ever on the defensive, being confronted not only with the contradictions between the basin and the society living in it, which have been dealt with at length above, but also with the ever more dangerous evolution of the environment itself.

CONCLUSION

These considerations lead us once more to put the question of the relations between state and hydraulics in China. More specifically, to what extent is the situation observed in the Hubei interior delta typical of the centralized Chinese state's nature and capabilities? Where and when does the state's inter-vention appear decisive or even essential?

At the beginning of this essay I stressed the diversity of natural conditions within China. Inasmuch as the problems of hydraulic protection and irrigation varied from region to region, so the degree of commitment and intervention on

[121] In this regard it may be noted that E. L. Oxenham, who lived in Hankow for three years and witnessed the great floods of 1869 and 1870, as well as the much less severe one of 1872, expressed his disquietude at the dyking policy and its excesses in the following terms: "In some places the system of raising embankments to defend the low lands from the floods has been resorted to, and has resulted in making the bed of the river far above the surrounding country. The expense and trouble of keeping these banks in repair is very great, and increases in magnitude every year; while some frightful calamity would appear to be inevitable should they ever give way. *It is therefore far better to allow the forces of Nature to work their own cure unimpeded by artificial restraints.*" See "On the Inundations of the Yang-tse-kiang," p. 13 (italics mine).
[122] Both texts are reproduced in *Huangchao zhengdian leizuan*, 42.8a-10b.

the part of the state apparatus differed too. The central Hubei plain could, for instance, be contrasted with the polder zones on the edges of Lake Dongting in Hunan or Lake Tai in Jiangnan, where the local communities (whatever their social definition and internal hierarchy) did not depend on protection from large scale installations extending over tens or hundreds of kilometres in order to develop their own settlements and dyking systems, where the dispersal of the properties, communities and basic administrative units (below *xian* level) did not pose any major technical problems in hydraulic matters, in any case not as immediately as elsewhere, and where consequently the need for an organizational macrostructure appeared less evident than in more imposing hydraulic landscapes. It is regions such as these, let it be noted, which led economic development in premodern China and were comparatively the most generous in their contribution to imperial and state revenue (although in this respect the lower Yangzi and Hunan did play different parts). Yet in such contexts too, the initial impetus from an administrative apparatus capable of mobilizing means superior to those of the local communities and of defining a global policy of water-conservancy appeared decisive, whereas administrative decadence had a decidedly negative impact on irrigation and water-control. Thus, the drainage of the lower Yangzi delta, vital for the agriculture of the polder lands, apparently experienced a double cycle development-recession which in its timing does not fail to recall the cyclical history of Hubei, even if the hydraulic problem presented itself in different terms and if other causes were at work.[123]

Yet, the contrast remained great with the necessity for a permanent, specific and high-ranking administrative presence in complex large-scale hydraulic systems such as the Yellow River or the Grand Canal. In this respect the Hubei basin may be regarded as a mixed example, with both a vast, integrated structure of hydraulic protection, and a multiplicity of installations of local importance, the development of which was to a great extent due to private enterprise. The insertion of state intervention into this context appears both fluctuating and ambiguous. As has been seen, the state apparatus intervened on a large scale and on central government initiative during the initial phase of construction. At this point it only had to face a weak concentration, so to speak, of contradictory interests, while the limited

---

[123] On this see for example Miyazaki Ichisada 宮崎市定, "Min Shin jidai no Soshū to seikōgyō no hattatsu" 明清時代の蘇州と輕工業の發達, in Miyazaki, *Ajia shi kenkyū*, Vol. 4 (Kyoto, 1975), especially pp. 313-18. See also Pierre-Etienne Will, "The occurrences of, and responses to, catastrophes and economic change in the lower and middle Yangtze, 1500-1850," paper prepared for the International Conference on Spatial and Temporal Trends and Cycles in Chinese Economic History, 980-1980, Bellagio (Italy), August 1984.

pressure exerted on the ecological framework secured the maintenance of the recent investments at minimal financial and organizational costs. In the following phase of intensive development, the state sought to keep to a role of limited intervention against certain dangerous developments, or to impose certain measures which it judged to be vital (such as reconstructing dykes or dredging outflow channels after a flood). On the other hand, it strictly limited its intervention in the field of daily maintenance—even if the latter posed more and more problems—which it in fact handed over to a whole series of more or less autonomous intermediate bodies: heads of dyke tithes, enclosure chiefs, groups of prominent people, not to mention the infra-bureaucracy comprising the subordinate officials in charge of hydraulics (*shuili zuoza* 水利佐雜) and the clerks and runners whose authority, where it existed, stemmed above all from their connections with local society.[124]

Thus the responsibilities seem to have been diluted even at the level of the large networks of dykes along the Yangzi and the Han, increasing the rift between the administrative macrostructure and the local organizations on which the former relied, in the last resort, to maintain and to develop the hydraulic installations.[125] This led to an increasing facility for short-term local or individual interests—which might be nothing but a consequence of demographic pressure—to slip through the net of regulations and policies which the bureaucracy continued to promote. One would be tempted to say, to reverse and paraphrase the title of a chapter of *Oriental Despotism*, that hydraulic society was stronger than the hydraulic state (if this concept still makes sense).

In the last stage (which was reached at varying times according to locality), both state and society appeared to be impotent in the face of increasing dangers, and recession set in as the returns of building dykes and enclosures were drastically diminished or even gave way to losses. It may be that there was something inevitable and quasi Malthusian about this evolution. Could the outcome have been different had the state been "more hydraulic," that is to say, more interventionist, more represented at all levels and benefiting

---

[124] The precise history of the roles played by these different "intermediate bodies," with their ups and downs—they did not necessarily coexist—remains to be written. This would no longer be a regional history, but a local one. The excessive powers left to the lower rungs of the bureaucratic apparatus, such as yamen underlings, upon whom the magistrates discharged themselves of their role of "leading" (*du shuai* 督率) the local workforce, and the resulting abuses, are mentioned in several memorials. See, for example, Governor Kaitai's 開泰 memorial of 1754, *gongzhongdang* archives, Taibei, Old Palace Museum, Qianlong reign, no. 007166.

[125] As we have seen, this prompted criticism of the so-called *guandu minxiu* system by some authors.

from a greater administrative density? The current problems in this same Hubei basin suggest not. The contradictory interests or options of central (or provincial) power and local communities have simply been transferred to the interior of a much more integrated, "totalitarian" and omnipresent structure than the traditional imperial state was, in the sense that the impulsion of land-hungry communities to encroach on the lakes and increase by every possible means the area devoted to rice-growing, has been taken over by people's communes and brigades which are, more than ever, bound by the demands of productivity.[126] In this respect the continuities between late imperial and modern times would deserve closer study.

[126] Of course, I am not speaking here of a state (or of an administration) intervening *in the wrong direction*, as the Republican government appears to have done after 1911 in encouraging precisely the pursuit of land reclamation at the expense of reservoir space with the aim of increasing fiscal revenue: "As concerns the encroachment on [floodable] lands," wrote an author of the 1930s, "and the clearing and enclosing of lake-fields, the former Qing dynasty had misgivings [about its growing occurrence] and promulgated strict prohibitions against it. Now since the beginning of the Republic, as [the administration] wished to increase fiscal income, Bureaux for the reclamation of alluvial lands (*shadi kenfang ju* 沙地墾放局) and Offices for checking up lake-fields (*Hutian qingli chu* 湖田清理處) were established. People were empowered to enclose and reclaim the alluvial land arising from silting in the rivers and lakes and to report it, in exchange for which they received certificates [of ownership] and were subjected to taxation. Although the income from land tax increased, the vacant space left [to the water] of the rivers and lakes was reduced by the day, and each day the floods became more serious. This is what is called a gain which does not make up for a loss." See Zhong Yin, *Yangzijiang shuili kao*, p. 153. For the dramatic drive toward lake reclamation in Hubei (and other regions) during the past few decades, and its far-reaching consequences in terms of decreased production of fish, reeds and the like, and of increased flooding, see Vaclav Smil, *The Bad Earth: Environmental Degradation in China* (Armonk, N. Y.: M. E. Sharpe, 1984), pp. 62-66.

List of Contributors

MARIANNE BASTID is Directeur de recherche at the Centre National de la Recherche Scientifique in Paris. Her research interests lie in late Qing political and social history, and in the history of education and cultural contacts in the nineteenth and twentieth centuries. She has published *Aspects de la réforme de l'enseignement en Chine au début du XXe siècle* (Paris: Mouton, 1971), *L'évolution de la société chinoise à la fin de la dynastie des Qing, 1873-1911* (Paris: Centre de recherches et de documentation sur la Chine contemporaine de l'Ecole des Hautes Etudes en Sciences Sociales, 1979), and various articles on political and educational developments in the late Qing and in the People's Republic of China.

JEAN-FRANÇOIS BILLETER is Maître d'enseignement et de recherche and Head of the Department of Chinese Studies of the Faculty of Letters, University of Geneva. His main research fields are the history of Chinese thought, comparative philosophy, and comparative sociology. Among his publications are *Li Zhi, philosophe maudit (1527-1602)* (Geneva: Librairie Droz, 1979), and "Pensée occidentale et pensée chinoise: l'acte et le regard," in *Différences, valeurs, hiérarchies*. Textes offerts à Louis Dumont (ed. Jean-Pierre Galey) (Paris: Ecole des Hautes Etudes en Sciences Sociales, 1984).

KARL BÜNGER is Emeritus Professor of Law in the University of Bonn. His main field of research has been the history of Chinese law. Among his publications are *Das Zivil- und Handelsgesetzbuch Chinas* (Marburg, 1934), *Quellen zur Rechtsgeschichte der T'ang-Zeit* (Beiping, 1946), and numerous articles on law, bureaucracy, and the state in China.

JACQUES GERNET is Professor at the Collège de France, Paris. He was formerly Professor of History at the Sorbonne. His research interests lie in the history of relations between society and thought in the evolution of China. His main publications are *Les aspects économiques du bouddhisme dans la société chinoise du Ve au Xe siècle* (Saigon: Ecole française d'Extrême-Orient, 1956); *La vie quotidienne en Chine à la veille de l'invasion mongole* (Paris:

349

Hachette, 1959) [English translation, London: Allen and Unwin, 1962, reprinted Stanford: Stanford University Press, 1977]; *Le monde chinois* (Paris: Armand Colin, 1972) [English translation, *A History of Chinese Civilization*, Cambridge: Cambridge University Press, 1982]; and *Chine et Christianisme, Action et réaction* (Paris: Gallimard, 1982) [English translation, *China and the Christian Impact: a Conflict of Cultures*, Cambridge: Cambridge University Press, 1985].

TILEMANN GRIMM is Professor at the University of Tübingen. His main research interests lie in the intellectual and institutional history of China, especially during the Ming period. His publications include *Erziehung und Politik im konfuzianischen China der Ming-Zeit (1368-1644)* (Hamburg: Gesellschaft für Natur- und Völkerkunde Ostasiens, 1960), *Meister Kung. zur Geschichte der Wirkungen des Konfuzius* (Opladen: Westdeutscher Verlag, 1976), and *Chinas Traditionen im Umbruch der Zeit* (Opladen: Westdeutscher Verlag, 1971).

ANTHONY HULSEWÉ is Emeritus Professor for Chinese at the University of Leiden. His principal research interest is in the history of the Qin and Han dynasties. His publications include *China in Central Asia; the Early Stage: 125 B.C.-A.D. 23.* An annotated translation of chapters 61 and 96 of the *History of the Former Han Dynasty* (Leiden: Brill, 1979), *Remnants of Han Law* (Leiden: Brill, 1955), and *Remnants of Ch'in Law* (Leiden: Brill, 1985).

MICHAEL LOEWE is Lecturer in Chinese Studies in Cambridge. From 1956 to 1963 he was Lecturer in the History of the Far East in the University of London. His principal research interests are concerned with the history, archeology, and intellectual and religious developments of the early Chinese empires. His publications include *Records of Han Administration* (Cambridge: Cambridge University Press, 1967, 2 vols.), *Crisis and Conflict in Han China* (London: Allen and Unwin, 1974), *Ways to Paradise: the Chinese Quest for Immortality* (London: Allen and Unwin, 1979), and *Chinese Ideas of Life and Death: Faith, Myth and Reason in the Han Period (202 B.C.-A.D. 220)* (London: Allen and Unwin, 1982).

PAOLO SANTANGELO is Associate Professor of Chinese History at the Istituto Universitario Orientale in Naples. He was formerly at the University of Bologna. His field of research is the economic, social and intellectual history of China in the Ming and Qing periods, and related developments in other Far Eastern countries, especially Korea. He has published *La Vita e l'Opera di Yu Suwŏn, Pensatore Coreano del XVIII Secolo* (Naples: Istituto Universitario Orientale,

1981), "Gu Yanwu's contribution to history: the historian's method and tasks," *East and West* No. 32, 1982, pp. 145-185, and *Le manifatture tessili imperiali durante le dinastie Ming e Qing con particolare attenzione a quelle di Suzhou* (Naples: Istituto Universitario Orientale, 1984).

STUART R. SCHRAM is Professor of Politics with reference to China in the University of London, School of Oriental and African Studies. From 1968 to 1972 he was concurrently Head of the Contemporary China Institute. Prior to 1968 he was Maître de recherche at the Fondation Nationale des Sciences Politiques in Paris. His research has focussed on the role of ideology in politics, especially in Communist countries, with particular attention to the history of the Chinese Communist Party, and to the thought and leadership role of Mao Zedong. His writings include *Mao Tse-tung* (Harmondsworth: Penguin, 1966), *The Political Thought of Mao Tse-tung* (Revised edition, New York: Praeger, 1969), *Marxism and Asia* (in collaboration with Hélène Carrère d'Encausse) (London: Allen Lane The Penguin Press, 1969), and *Ideology and Policy in China since the Third Plenum* (London: S.O.A.S., 1984).

HARRO VON SENGER is Privatdozent für Sinologie in the Philosophy Faculty of the University of Zürich. His research interests include the history of Chinese and Japanese political and legal philosophy and institutions, systems for guiding society in the People's Republic and in ancient China, and problems of war and strategy in China. His publications include "Der Staatsgeheimnisschutz in der Volksrepublik China," in *Schweizer Asiatische Studien, Studienhefte*, Vol. 3 (Bern: Verlag Peter Lang, 1979), *Partei, Ideologie und Gesetz in der Volksrepublik China* (Bern: Verlag Peter Lang, 1982), and *Chinesische Bodeninstitutionen im Taihō-Verwaltungskodex*. Niida Noborus Beitrag zur Rekonstruktion der Bodeninstitutionen der Tang-Zeit (Wiesbaden: Verlag Otto Harrassowitz, 1983).

LÉON VANDERMEERSCH is Directeur d'études at the Ecole des Hautes Etudes, 5ème Section, Paris. He has carried out research on political thought and institutions in ancient China, with particular reference to the history of Confucianism. His publications include *La formation du Légisme* (Paris: Publications de l'Ecole Française d'Extrême Orient, 1965), and *Wangdao ou La Voie Royale*, Tome I, Structures cultuelles et structures familiales, and Tome II, Structures politiques, Les Rites (Paris: Publications de l'Ecole Française d'Extrême Orient, 1977 and 1980).

PIERRE-ETIENNE WILL is Maître de conférences at the Ecole des Hautes Etudes en Sciences Sociales, Paris. His research is devoted to the social and economic history of Ming and Qing China. He has published *Bureaucratie et famine en Chine au 18e siècle* (Paris: Mouton, 1980), and has co-edited and co-authored a book on granaries and food redistribution during the Qing dynasty (Ann Arbor: University of Michigan Center for Chinese Studies, in the press).

Index

absolutism, continuing influence on state in West, xiv

administration: as sole legitimate instrument of government a condition for the existence of a state, 238

administrative apparatus: importance in defining global water-conservancy policy, 345

administrative boundaries: ill-suited to hydraulic control, 327

administrative decadence: negative impact on water control, 345

administrative division into districts, in third century B.C. in China, xxxii

administrative function of law, 19

administrative regulations, statutes merely, 16

admiralty (*haijun yamen* 海軍衙門), 65

agrarian reform, 131, 145

agricultural development: state not directly involved under Ming and Qing, 338

agricultural overseer (*tian sefu* 田嗇夫), 221

agricultural workers, 128

agriculture: Qin law on, 218-222

alchemy, 41

America, xiii

Analects, 84

anarchy: created by Cultural Revolution, 115; Mao's hostility to in 1943, 86; Mao repudiates in February 1967, 110

Anlu 安陸 (Hubei), 311, 312, 323, 324

"Anti-rightist" campaign (1957), 107

anti-Confucius campaign of 1970s, 164

appointments: Party's control over, 124

aristocratic ranks: exemption from labour under Qin, 226

armed force: decisive in foundation of empires, xxxiii

armies: stationing in Hubei as defence against Mongols in Southern Song, 301

army: Ming, 48

autocracy, people's democratic: identical with people's democratic dictatorship, 91

autonomous intermediate bodies (heads of dyke tithes, groups of prominent people): responsibility for dyke maintenance, 346

bad elements, 135, 152, 166

Balazs, Etienne, xvi

bang 邦 : use as term for state in Yunmeng materials, 213

Banners, 54, 56, 58

bao 褒 and *bian* 貶 in Chinese historiography, 27

baoyi 包衣: as personal bureaucracy of emperor, 279; status and role of, 286

Bastid, Marianne, 113, 177

bei zhizaoju 北織造局 , 275

Beidaihe meeting (August 1958), 105

beidangfang 北檔房 , 54, 63, 67; control by Manchus, 63

Beijing 北京 , 53, 272, 280

Beijing Training Divisions: controlled by Liu Jin, 43

ben 本 and *mo* 末 : as categories of occupations under Han, 244

bi 比, 17

bianfa 變法 : Liu Jin's reforms called, 45

birth: as criterion for distribution, 147

Bloch, Marc, xvii

Board: *see also* Ministry

Board of Academicians, 34

353

cosmic nature of the Chinese state, xxxiii
counter-revolutionaries, 135, 151, 152, 155, 166, 173
coup d'Etat of 1457, 30
Court of Imperial Sacrifices: magician Li Zisheng as chief of, 42
craftsmen, 44, 129, 163; access to Ming bureaucracy, 44
credentials (*fu* 符), 11
"crisis of the state", xxiv
criteria for distribution: qualification, birth and virtue most important, 147
cruel officials, 15
Cui Shi 崔寔, 241
Cultural Revolution, 83, 85, 107-115, 166, 172, 173, 179, 188, 194; attacks on regional secretaries, 109; class struggle principal task during, 183; human nature repudiated during, 159
currency: Qin law on, 227-229
customs houses, 57
customs intendants (*haiguandao* 海關道), 52, 57
cyclical model in Chinese historiography, 27
cyclical pattern: in hydraulic infrastructure, 298

Da Ming huidian 大明會典, 19, 271
Da Qing huidian 大清會典, 8, 19, 61, 69, 271
Da Qing huidian shili 大清會典事例, 271
Da Qing lüli 大清律例, 19
Da Tang liu dian 大唐六典, 23
da xueshi 大學士, 36
dang tongyi lingdao 黨統一領導, 113
dangxing 黨性, 103
dangyuechu 當月處, 54
dao 道 (intendants), 56
Daoguang 道光 period, 333, 342
daotai 道台, 65; Shanghai, 66
daquan dulan 大權獨攬, 102
dashi 大使, 273
dasinong 大司農, 254
dated decrees (*fa (ri) chi* 發 (日) 敕), 10
daxing 大姓: and private hydraulic facilities, 337
Dazekou 大澤口, 330
"deceitful adventure hunters" (*ning xing* 佞倖), 39

decentralization: in a unitary state, 81-125; limits in Mao's view, 100; Schurmann's distinction between I and II, 101
Decision: of 1 June 1943, 88; of Third Plenum of October 1984 on Reform of the Economic Structure, 123
decision-making power: giving enterprises, 123; resided in emperor, 31
decree in sections (*tiaozhi* 條旨), 32
"decree prison" (*zhao yu* 詔獄), 37, 38
decrees (*chi* 敕), 11, 18
decrees (*chishu* 敕書), 10
decrees of mandate (*chiming* 敕命), 11
decrees of nomination (*zuomingchi* 坐名敕), 11
decretal bills (*chibang* 敕牓), 10
decretal edicts (*chiyu* 敕諭), 11
decretal instructions (*chizhi* 敕旨), 10
decretal missives (*chidie* 敕牒), 10
democracy and centralism, 114
democratic centralism, 81, 84, 85, 92, 106
democratization: Deng Xiaoping calls for, 117; of Party and state interdependent, 190; promoted by Fifth Plenum of February 1980, 191; to remain within limits set by Party, 197
Deng Xiaoping 鄧小平 , 119; campaign of 1976 against, 114; opts for competence criterion, 166; speech of 18 August 1980, 117, 123; states at Eighth Party Congress that class status system has lost its importance, 131
Department of Granaries (*cangchang yamen*), 54
Department of State Affairs (*shangshuling* 尚書令), 9
Department of State Affairs (*shangshusheng* 尚書省), 5
Department of the Masters of Documents, 5
Depot for Conduct and Ways in the Internal Apartments (*neixing chang* 內行廠), 44
despotism: horizontal and vertical limits under Ming, 40; too narrow a definition of Ming, 28
"despotism of custom": in Mill's view of China, xx
devolution: and 1984 Party rectification, 125

ing as compared to *jihu*, 278
Taoism, 41; and eunuchs, 49
Taoism and Buddhism: Chenghua emperor as protector of, 43
Taoist priests: numbers of, 41
tax collection: role of gentry and merchants in late Qing, 72
taxation and labour: under Han, 256
taxation, direct annual: early appearance in China, 51; in Europe dates from 16th century, 51
taxes: as percentage of GNP, 74
Teng Wensheng 騰文生, 192
Tenth Plenum (September 1962): Mao issues call "Never forget the class struggle", 131
textile factories: as agency for state control over other sectors of economy under Qing, 283; dependence on state apparatus, 281; part of state machine, though linked to imperial household, 289
textile-producing families (*jihu*), 270
The Communist Manifesto, 144
theory of the exclusive importance of productive forces (*wei shengchanli lun*), 179
Third Plenum of December 1978, 116
Three and Five Antis: of 1950s, 129, 135
three dukes (*san gong*), 9
Three Storehouses (*sanku*), 54
threefold articulation of power in China compared with division of powers in West, 5
thrift and consumption: relation between in Han thought, 247
throne: as sole fount of power, 47
tian lü 田律, 214, 215
tian sefu 田嗇夫, 221
tianguan 田官, 252
Tianjin customs house: headed by customs intendant subordinate to provincial treasurer of Zhili, 57
Tianmen, 329
Tianqi 天啓 emperor, 27
Tianshun 天順 period, 30, 34, 38; Guard in, 40
tianzu 田卒 : term for servicemen sent to newly established fields in Central Asia

under Han, 252
tiaozhi 條旨, 32
Tibetans, 81
titles and dignities, as means of shaping society, xxix
tizhi 體制 : reform of, 123
tongyi lingdao, fenji fuze 統一領導,分級負責, 95
tongzhengsi 通政司, 32
Tongzhou: public granaries, 54
topological conditions, influence on state structure, xvii
totalitarian régimes: Russia, Germany, Italy, Spain, Japan, etc., 160
totalitarian suppression: comparison of Guard with modern organs of, 48
totalitarianism: in Mao's China, 83, 161; outmoded in China, 168
trade: Qin law on, 229-231
traditional China: hierarchy in, 160
traditional elements, in contemporary China, xv
traditional personal rule: persistence at apex of Party hierarchy, 202
"transmitted service patent" (*chuan feng* 傳奉), 41
treasury keeper (*kudashi*), 57
triangular basis of power under Ming, 49
tributary states, 291
tribute trade, 40
tuchu geren 突出個人, 179
Twelfth Party Congress, 121, 175
types (*ge*), 18, 21

Ulpian, 4
ultra-leftists: links to Mao, 151
unification: call to combine with local expediency, 93
unified leadership and divided responsibilities (*tongyi lingdao, fenji fuze*): introduced in March 1951, 95.
unified leadership: central problem in 1943, 87
unified Party leadership, 113
uniting of hearts (*yixin*), 78
universal suffrage: Mao's call for in 1940, 92
vermilion ink, 32